Krishna Bista, *Executive Editor*
Morgan State University, USA

Chris R. Glass, *Editor-In-Chief*
Old Dominion University, USA

Vol. **11** No **2** May **2021**

JOURNAL OF INTERNATIONAL STUDENTS

A Quarterly Publication on International Education

Access this journal online at http://ojed.org/jis

This journal is a STAR Scholars Network publication.

Print ISSN 2162-3104
Online ISSN 2166-3750

Disclaimer
Facts and opinions published in *Journal of International Students* (JIS) express solely the opinions of the respective authors. Authors are responsible for their citing of sources and the accuracy of their references and bibliographies. The editors cannot be held responsible for any lacks or possible violations of third parties' rights.

Special Issues

Special Issue | English
Internationalization for an Uncertain Future: Emerging Conversations in Critical Internationalization Studies (2021)
Special Issue Co-Editors:
Sharon Stein, University of British Columbia, Canada
Dale M. McCartney, University of the Fraser Valley, Canada

Special Issue | English
Reflection and Reflective Thinking (2020)
Special Issue Co-Editors:
Georgina Barton, University of Southern Queensland, Australia
Mary Ryan, Macquarie University, Australia

Special Issue | *Bahasa Indonesia*
International Students and COVID-19 (2020)
Special Issue Co-Editors:
Handoyo Puji Widodo, King Abdulaziz University, Saudi Arabia
Sandi Ferdiansyah, Institut Agama Islam Negeri, Indonesia and
Lara Fridani, Universitas Negeri Jakarta, Indonesia

Special Issue | *Chinese*
International Students in China (2020)
Special Issue Co-Editors:
Mei Tian and Genshu Lu
Xi'an Jiaotong University, China

Special Issue | English
Fostering Successful Integration and Engagement Between Domestic and International Students (2018)
Special Issue Co-Editors:
CindyAnn Rose-Redwood and Reuben Rose-Redwood
University of Victoria, Canada

Special Issue | English
Role of Student Affairs in International Student Transition and Success (2017)
Special Issue Co-Editors:
Christina W Yao, University of Nebraska-Lincoln, US
Chrystal A. George Mwangi, University of Massachusetts Amherst, US

Special Issue | English
International Student Success (2016)
Special Issue Editor: *Rahul Choudaha, DrEducation, US*

Routledge Studies in Global Student Mobility Series

This Routledge Series offers a scholarly forum for original and innovative research to understand the issues and challenges as well as share the best practices related to international student mobility in K-12 and beyond, education abroad, and exchange programs globally that creates a professional network of researchers and practitioners. Submit your proposal via emails.

Series Editors
Dr. Chris R. Glass & Dr. Krishna Bista,
For questions and submission, email at crglass@odu.edu

Published Titles

Inequalities in Study Abroad and Student Mobility

The Experiences of International Faculty in Institutions of Higher Education

International Students in Community Colleges

Critical Perspectives on Equity and Social Mobility in Study Abroad

Online Teaching, Learning and Virtual Experiences in Global Higher Education

International Student Support and Engagement

Impact of COVID-19 on Global Student Mobility and Higher Education

Cross-Cultural Narratives

Stories and Experiences of International Students

Edited by Ravichandran Ammigan (2021)

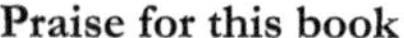

Praise for this book

Through rich and engaging stories, *Cross-Cultural Narratives* offers important personal accounts of the challenges and triumphs of international students navigating diverse and foreign academic and cultural landscapes. This inspiring and thought-provoking collection adds to other noble qualitative documentation of the international student experience.

Anthony L. Pinder, EdD
Associate Vice President for Academic Affairs – Internationalization & Global Engagement
Emerson College, USA

***

This is a great resource for researchers, university staff, and students to (re)-situate themselves in the day-to-day reality of international students at U.S. universities. In our data driven world abounding with echo chambers, it is critical that we as humans continue to nurture and attend to diverse individual narratives of challenge, success, failure, humor, learning, shock, community, belonging, and resiliency. Let us listen to the next generation as they share the ties that bind us across differences.

Nelson Brunsting, PhD
Director, RAISE Center
Research Associate Professor, International Studies
Wake Forest University, USA

***

This edited collection of stories offers insight into the concrete details of US life that international students find confounding: that bread is soft and sweet, that everyone asks, "How are you?" but no one wants to know the answer, that fellow students don't know the metric system, and that people are startled if you kiss them on the cheek in greeting. All of these examples, in the students' own voices, will be valuable to practitioners and faculty who want to understand how life on and off campus appears from multiple perspectives.

Martha C. Merrill, PhD
Associate Professor, Higher Education
Kent State University, USA

ISSN: 2162-3104 Print/ ISSN: 2166-3750 Online

http://ojed.org/jis

Editorial Team

Recent Publications

CRITICAL PERSPECTIVES ON EQUITY AND SOCIAL MOBILITY IN STUDY ABROAD

INTERROGATING ISSUES OF UNEQUAL ACCESS AND OUTCOMES

Edited by
Chris Glass and Peggy Gesing

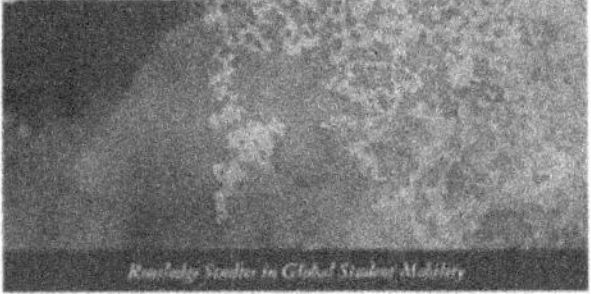

INEQUALITIES IN STUDY ABROAD AND STUDENT MOBILITY

NAVIGATING CHALLENGES AND FUTURE DIRECTIONS

Edited by
Suzan Kommers and Krishna Bista

THE EXPERIENCES OF INTERNATIONAL FACULTY IN INSTITUTIONS OF HIGHER EDUCATION

ENHANCING RECRUITMENT, RETENTION, AND INTEGRATION OF INTERNATIONAL TALENT

Edited by
Chris Glass, Krishna Bista and Xi Lin

JOURNAL OF UNDERREPRESENTED AND MINORITY PROGRESS

OJED.ORG / JUMP

JOURNAL OF INTERDISCIPLINARY STUDIES IN EDUCATION

JOURNAL OF INTERNATIONAL STUDENTS

2021 VOL. 11, NO. 1

DELINKING, RELINKING, AND LINKING WRITING AND RHETORICS

Marohang Limbu (Yakthung)

STARSCHOLARS

Indexing

ISSN: 2162-3104 Print/ ISSN: 2166-3750 Online
Journal of International Students
http://ojed.org/jis

All articles published in the *Journal of International Students* are indexed and listed in major databases and sources:

SUBJECT: EDUCATION – HIGHER DEWEY # 378

CEDROM SNI
- Eureka.cc, 01/01/2017-
- Europresse.com, 01/01/2017-

Directory of Open Access Journals
- Directory of Open Access Journals, 2011-

EBSCOhost
- Education Source, 03/01/2012-

Gale
- Academic OneFile, 09/01/2011-
- Contemporary Women's Issues, 09/01/2011-
- Educator's Reference Complete, 09/01/2011-
- Expanded Academic ASAP, 09/01/2011-
- InfoTrac Custom, 09/01/2011-

Multiple Vendors
- Freely Accessible Social Science Journals, 2011-

ProQuest
- Education Collection, 10/01/2011-
- Education Database, 10/01/2011-
- Education Database (Alumni Edition), 10/01/2011-
- ProQuest Central, 10/01/2011-
- ProQuest Central - UK Customers, 10/01/2011-
- ProQuest Central (Alumni Edition), 10/01/2011-
- ProQuest Central (Corporate), 10/01/2011-
- ProQuest Central (US Academic Subscription), 10/01/2011-
- ProQuest Central China, 10/01/2011-
- ProQuest Central Essentials, 10/01/2011-
- ProQuest Central Korea, 10/01/2011-
- ProQuest Central Student, 10/01/2011-
- ProQuest Research Library, 10/01/2011-
- ProQuest Research Library (Corporate), 10/01/2011-
- ProQuest Social Sciences Premium Collection, 10/01/2011-
- ProQuest Social Sciences Premium Collection - UK Customers, 10/01/2011-
- Research Library (Alumni Edition), 10/01/2011-
- Research Library China, 10/01/2011-
- Research Library Prep, 10/01/2011-
- Social Science Premium Collection, 10/01/2011-

Clarivate Analytics
- Web of Science
- Emering Sciences Citation Index
- Higher Education Abstracts

Source: Ulrichsweb Global Serials Directory

You may access the print and/or digital copies of the *Journal of International Students* from 586 libraries worldwide (as of Nov 8, 2020).

The Journal of International Students (Print ISSN 2162-3104 & Online ISSN 2166-3750) is a member of the STAR Scholars Network Open Journals in Education (OJED), a OJS 3 platform for *high-quality, peer-reviewed* academic journals in education.

JIS is a Gold Open Access journal and indexed in major academic databases to maximize article discoverability and citation. JIS follows best practices on publication ethics outlined in the COPE Code of Conduct. Editors work to ensure timely decisions after initial submission, as well as prompt publication online if a manuscript is accepted for publication.

Upon publication articles are immediately and freely available to the public. The final version of articles can immediately be posted to an institutional repository or to the author's own website as long as the article includes a link back to the original article posted on OJED.

None of the OJED journals charge fees to individual authors thanks to the generous support of our institutional sponsors.

For further information

Editorial Office
Journal of International Students
URL: http://ojed.org/jis
E-mail: contact@jistudents.org

ISSN: 2162-3104 Print/ ISSN: 2166-3750 Online
2021 Volume 11, Number 2
© *Journal of International Students*
http://ojed.org/jis

CONTENTS

Editorial

Articles

Research in Brief

Study Abroad Reflections

Book Reviews

JOURNAL OF INTERNATIONAL STUDENTS
2020 VOL. 10, NO. S1

JOURNAL OF INTERNATIONAL STUDENTS
2020 VOL. 10, NO. S3

JOURNAL OF INTERNATIONAL STUDENTS
2020 VOL. 10, NO. 4

JOURNAL OF INTERNATIONAL STUDENTS
Special Issue: Reflection and Reflective Thinking
2020 VOL. 10, NO. S2
Access this journal online at ojed.org/jis

To order online, visit
www.ojed.org/jis
Paperback and e-books
available.
available at
amazon
Google Play
App Store

JOURNAL OF INTERNATIONAL STUDENTS
2021 VOL. 11, NO. 1

Editorial

© *Journal of International Students*
Volume 11, Issue 2 (2021), pp. i-vii
ISSN: 2162-3104 (Print), 2166-3750 (Online)
doi: 10.32674/jis.v11i1.3731
ojed.org/jis

Why Deteriorating Relations, Xenophobia, and Safety Concerns Will Deter Chinese International Student Mobility to the United States

Ryan M. Allen
Chapman University, USA

Ying Ye
Shanghai Normal University, China

ABSTRACT

Collaborations between American and Chinese universities have been critical to global knowledge production. Chinese students accounted for over a third of all international students in the United States prior to COVID-19, but the pandemic paused most global mobility in 2020. We argue that this international mobility to the United States will not fully recover if larger stressors are left unaddressed. First, relations between the United States and China have deteriorated in recent years, especially under the Trump administration, with growing suspicion against Chinese researchers and scholars. Second, viral acts of violence and anti-Asian incidents have painted the United States as unsafe for Chinese students. Finally, given the mismanaged response to the pandemic, it may take years before trust returns from abroad. While the Biden administration has promised to curb some of these issues, the perceptions of the United States may have been permanently altered, especially as China has improved its domestic higher education sector in recent years.

Keywords: Chinese students, COVID-19, student mobility, xenophobia

---

INTRODUCTION

China is the largest sender of international students to the United States, accounting for over 372,000 students in the academic year before COVID-19 hit (Institute of International Education, 2020). This means that roughly one out of every three international students studying on American campuses came from China, contributing over $15 billion to the U.S. economy every year (Malden & Stephens, 2020). Lee and Haupt (2019) showed that collaborative research by American and Chinese scientists has dramatically risen in recent decades, while Evans et al. (2020) argued that joint research efforts will need to be amped up to stave off the next global pandemic. Due to the level of engagement, the relationship between China and the United States is the most consequential for the American higher education sector. But the relationship has been threatened in recent years due to a variety of reasons, and not only because of the pause in global mobility related to COVID-19.

One weekend defined a culmination of these larger issues in the relationship. On the weekend after January 9, 2021, Americans, still locked in quarantine for almost a year, were reeling from the shocking footage of rioting and insurrection at the nation's capitol building. The images also shocked people in China, but attention that weekend was centered on Yiran Fan, a Chinese international student murdered in Chicago during a random rampage in the city. Together these events highlighted the poor management of the COVID-19 crisis, disgraceful imagery of riots, and tangible threats of gun violence—reinforcing the idea that the United States is dangerous, unpredictable, and unwelcoming—not exactly an ideal location to study for international students.

The election of Donald Trump was particularly damaging to international higher education in the United States, with the Muslim ban, increased vetting of student visas, and general antiforeigner rhetoric. Rose-Redwood and Rose-Redwood (2017) said that the "travel ban had the effect of undermining this core mission of higher education" (p. iii). While many hoped that the Biden administration could reset the sector, the lingering effects stemming from Trump and other controversies cannot be easily mended, particularly with China. In this commentary, we argue that international student engagement will not fully recover from the pause in mobility due to the pandemic if these larger stressors are left unaddressed.

U.S.–China Relations

Trump campaigned on taking a harder stance against China and enacted a series of targeted policies against the nation, such as tariffs on certain goods. At one point, Trump even considered banning Chinese students from coming to American universities, but eventually decided against the measure (Sevastopulo & Mitchell, 2018). However, the administration did add restrictions to some graduate students and canceled visas for roughly 1,000 students and researchers with reported connections to the military (Mervis, 2018). These reactions were part of growing distrust toward Chinese scientists and researchers, with loud accusations of spying. Even before Trump, Confucius Institutes had been continually targeted by American policymakers as a kind of catch-all boogeyman for espionage. Headlines have been made about researchers being arrested for hiding their inclusion with China's Thousand Talents Plan when receiving federal government grants. In some cases, though, missing from the conversation was that the researchers also did not disclose programs with other countries like South Korea or Japan (U.S. Department of Justice, 2021).

Exacerbated by the Trump administration's rhetoric, the sentiments only worsened with the global outbreak of COVID-19. When the pandemic began, Trump blamed China for failing to contain the virus early on, insisting on calling it the "Chinese virus" and demanding that the Chinese government "pay a big price" for letting it happen (as quoted by Walsh, 2020). Devlin et al. (2020) reported that during the height of the pandemic, Americans' unfavorable views of China reached record levels. Tangibly throughout the lockdown, anger and suspicion boiled over with a spike in racist and xenophobic attacks against Chinese people or other Asians mistaken for Chinese, which were only fueled by bombastic rhetoric from the Trump administration and other U.S. officials. In this environment, Chinese students have faced increased scrutiny at U.S. airports, been labeled as technology thieves, and harassed due to national origin.

Safety

Safety has been a concern for international students in the United States (Nicholls, 2018). Uncertainties and distance breeds anxieties, and the ubiquity of guns and high-profile shootings have undoubtedly shaped students' and parents' perceptions of security in American schools. But cameras and smartphones have inundated feeds with images and news of violence like never before, bolstering fears that have been prevalent in the past. Now, protesters and even rioters routinely livestream or post to social media, which is viewed across the world, sometimes losing important contextual information. For instance, the summer protests of 2020 were bookended by the riots at the Capitol, sending the signal that the United States is not only dangerous but also unstable. Even if these incidents were isolated or focused, the viral nature of the imagery puts them in the palm of every parent with a child studying abroad.

These threats are exacerbated for Chinese students due to the anti-Chinese sentiments rising in recent years on and around campuses (Ma, 2020). While apparently random, the death of Yiren Fan at the University of Chicago only made these images all too real for prospective international students. Furthermore, there have been other hate crimes against Asian Americans stemming from misplaced xenophobia connected to China. These events and others like it, such as the Atlanta spa shooting, have made violence against Asians a salient issue. It is easy to understand how Chinese parents or students would ask: What if that was me? What if my son got caught in a riot? How can I know my daughter will be safe? Even if American campuses are generally safe, there is a sense that the entire United States is dangerous. Students and parents feel their safety could be at risk at any time. Under such circumstances, we wonder how many Chinese parents would agree to send their children to study under such conditions.

Handling of COVID-19

The mismanagement of COVID-19 in the United States has led to a staggering number of deaths and an elongated pandemic. The world has noticed. People in China have watched the reckless, inept approach that American leaders have taken in dealing with the virus and could only compare to the coordinated, serious efforts by their own government. The clips of antimask protests or public freak-outs against basic precautions were not isolated to the internet in the United States; they have been shared and mocked on WeChat and other social media. In contrast, China took the most stringent prevention and control measures to prevent the spread of the epidemic. Residents were required to wear masks in public places, lockdowns were enforced, and contract tracing/testing was implemented nationally. Wuhan, Hubei province in China, where the epidemic situation was the most severe, returned to some normalcy after a few months of lockdown. People there were allowed to leave the city if they held a green health code, meaning no contact with any infected or suspected COVID-19 cases. It is because of such an aggressive response that hundreds of thousands of people in China were prevented from contracting the virus. Even with the vaccine rollout underway, the comparative death tolls in the United States have been staggering.

MOVING FORWARD

Given the importance of this relationship, American universities must work to gain back the trust of Chinese students, and much of this work must go beyond singular institutions. The rollout of the vaccine is a major test for the United States in the eyes of the world. Many stakeholders are hoping for a return to some normalcy by the Fall 2021 semester, unpausing the global mobility freeze. Given the last year, though, there are still those who will remain skeptical, and it may take years before that trust returns from abroad. If society does open back up, some of the unrest may subside. Likewise, the Biden administration has already shown a more subdued approach to the presidency, which should be felt by other people around the world. While some incidents will always occur, the shocking and unprecedented scenes from the last year could make way for calmer imagery.

Similarly, Biden has already released a Presidential Memorandum order condemning the anti-Asian sentiments that plagued most of 2020 and beyond ("Condemning and Combating Racism," 2021). While he hasn't promised to reverse all of Trump's policies, the bombastic and unpredictable approach to foreign policy from the previous president has been halted by Biden. However, there are still many officials hawkish on China, such as Republican Senator Tom Cotton, who recently proposed a new ban on Chinese students in certain STEM areas, more intense visa vetting, and the severance of ties with Chinese universities nationally (Cotton, 2021). Even Biden's nominee for CIA director, William J. Burns, suggested that universities should cut ties with Confucius

Institutes in his Senate hearing (CBS News, 2021). This kind of mistrust from the highest levels trickles down to students and individuals.

Unfortunately, some efforts might be too late, as the image of the United States in China has likely been permanently altered. Chinese students are already taking seriously other locales around the world with friendlier policies, perceived safer environments, and better handling of COVID-19. Furthermore, China's own domestic sector has rapidly improved in terms of international standing in recent years (Allen, 2017). While capacity issues have been a problem, the central government has recently mandated more seats for students in master's programs in Chinese universities (Wang, 2021). Likewise, policymakers have also made efforts to improve various parts of the sector, such as the Teacher Professional Development Center in Shanghai Normal University, a program targeted at improving the quality of private higher education in Shanghai.

Educators did have similar concerns after the attacks on 9/11 precipitated drops in foreign students, but the worries proved to be misplaced and the sector rebounded to record gains only a few years later. However, much of those gains were made from increased Chinese student intake. If the sector hopes to maintain and thrive after COVID-19, the larger relationship between the United States and China must be mended. Stories like Yiran Fan or other viral acts of violence or xenophobia, along with a bombastic foreign policy, will only continue the descent. American higher education certainly did not cause these issues, but the sector will face the brunt of their consequences.

REFERENCES

Allen, R. M. (2017). A comparison of China's "Ivy League" to other peer groupings through global university rankings. *Journal of Studies in International Education*, *21*(5), 395–411.

CBS News. (2021, February 24). *CIA director nominee William Burns questioned at Senate confirmation hearing* [Video]. Youtube. https://www.youtube.com/watch?t=4568&v=smHNSwt9B0M&feature=youtu.be

Condemning and combating racism, xenophobia, and intolerance against Asian Americans and Pacific Islanders in the United States, Presidential Memorandum, No. 2021-02073, 86 FR 7485. (2021, January 26). https://www.federalregister.gov/documents/2021/01/29/2021-02073/condemning-and-combating-racism-xenophobia-and-intolerance-against-asian-americans-and-pacific

Cotton, T. (2021). *Beat China: Targeted decoupling and the economic long war*. Office of Senator Tom Cotton. https://www.cotton.senate.gov/imo/media/doc/210216_1700_China%20Report_FINAL.pdf?utm_campaign=latitude%28s%29&utm_medium=email&utm_source=Revue%20newsletter

Devlin, K., Silver, L., & Huang, C. (2020, April 21). U.S. views of China increasingly negative amid Coronavirus outbreak. *Pew Research Center*.

https://www.pewresearch.org/global/2020/04/21/u-s-views-of-china-increasingly-negative-amid-coronavirus-outbreak/.

Evans, T. S., Shi, Z., Boots, M., Liu, W., Olival, K. J., Xiao, X., Vandewoude, S., Brown, H., Chen, J.-L., Civitell, D. J., Escobar, L., Grohn, Y., Li, H., Lips, K., Liu, Q., Lu, J., Martinez-Lopez, B., Shi, J., Shi, X., … Getz, W. M. (2020). Synergistic China–US ecological research is essential for global emerging infectious disease preparedness. *EcoHealth*, *17*(1), 160–173.

Institute of International Education. (2020). *Open Doors fast facts 2020.* https://opendoorsdata.org/fast_facts/fast-facts-2020/

Lee, J. J., & Haupt, J. P. (2019). Winners and losers in US-China scientific research collaborations. *Higher Education*, *80,* 57–74.

Ma, Y. (2020). *Ambitious and anxious: How Chinese college students succeed and struggle in American higher education.* Columbia University Press.

Malden, K., & Stephens, S. (2020). *Cascading economic impacts of the COVID-19 outbreak in China* [Staff Research Report]. US-China Economic and Security Review Commission. https://www.uscc.gov/sites/default/files/2020-04/Cascading_Economic_Impacts_of_the_Novel_Coronavirus_April_21_2020.pdf

Mervis, J. (2018, June 11). More restrictive US policy on Chinese graduate student visas raises alarm. *Science*. doi:10.1126/science.aau4407

Nicholls, S. (2018). Influences on international student choice of study destination: Evidence from the United States. *Journal of International Students*, *8*(2), 597–622.

Rose-Redwood, C., & Rose-Redwood, R. (2017). Rethinking the politics of the international student experience in the age of Trump. *Journal of International Students*, *7*(3), i–ix.

Sevastopulo, D., & Mitchell, T. (2018). US considered ban on student visas for Chinese nationals. *Financial Times*. https://www.ft.com/content/fc413158-c5f1-11e8-82bf-ab93d0a9b321

U.S. Department of Justice (2021). *Senior NASA scientist pleads guilty to making false statements related to Chinese Thousand Talents Program participation and professorship.* U.S. Attorney's Office, Southern District of New York. https://www.justice.gov/usao-sdny/pr/senior-nasa-scientist-pleads-guilty-making-false-statements-related-chinese-thousand

Walsh, J. (2020, October 8). Trump is demanding China pay 'big price' for Covid-19. *Forbes*. https://www.forbes.com/sites/joewalsh/2020/10/08/trump-is-demanding-china-pay-big-price-for-covid-19/?sh=5c6fc77c41c8

Wang, V. (2021, January 18). China's college graduates can't find jobs. The solution: Grad school. *The New York Times*. https://www.nytimes.com/2021/01/18/business/china-graduate-school-white-collar.html

---

RYAN M. ALLEN, PhD, is an assistant professor at Chapman University's Donna Ford Attallah College of Educational Studies. He primarily works with the college's doctoral program partnered with Shanghai Normal University. His research focuses on internationalizations of higher education, EdTech, academic publishing, and the East Asian region. He serves on the executive board of the Study Abroad and International Student SIG within the Comparative and International Education Society, where he shares his passion for supporting global mobility and promoting study abroad. Email: ryallen@chapman.edu

YING YE, EdD, is a faculty in the School of Education of Shanghai Normal University, mainly responsible for the international programs. She received her doctoral degree from East Normal University in China, majoring in Education Leadership. She has also been exploring how international collaboration and communication can be established between universities from different countries in terms of both research and practice. Email: yeying@shnu.edu.cn

Peer-Reviewed Article

© *Journal of International Students*
Volume 11, Issue 2 (2021), pp. 278-298
ISSN: 2162-3104 (Print), 2166-3750 (Online)
doi: 10.32674/jis.v11i2.1726
ojed.org/jis

The First Year of Acculturation: A Longitudinal Study on Acculturative Stress and Adjustment Among First-Year International College Students

Katie K. Koo
Texas A&M University-Commerce, USA

Ian Baker
Michigan State University, USA

Jiyoon Yoon
University of Texas at Arlington, USA

ABSTRACT

We analyzed 192 first-year international college students in the Mid-Atlantic region to examine the change in international students' acculturative stress, adjustment, and collegiate experiences during their first year of enrollment in U.S. higher education. We found that male students, students from low socioeconomic status backgrounds, and students majoring in the humanities showed higher rates of acculturative stress and lower rates of satisfaction with college experiences compared with their counterparts. International students reported decreased acculturative stress and homesickness and increased English proficiency, social connectedness, and satisfaction with college experiences during the last week of the first year compared to the first week of their first semester. Satisfaction with college experiences, English proficiency, social connectedness, and self-esteem were significant predictors of acculturative stress. Lastly, acculturative stress at the beginning of the first year and satisfaction with college experiences at the end of the first year affected each other reciprocally over 1 year, according to our longitudinal investigation. Implications for research and practice are discussed.

Keywords: acculturative stress, adjustment difficulties, English proficiency, first-year college students, homesickness, international students

INTRODUCTION

International students contribute to the United States in many ways, such as growing the economy and helping the United States lead in innovation (NAFSA, 2019). In addition, international students, particularly those in graduate schools, bring a wide range of skills and knowledge, thus enriching the intellectual capital of U.S. universities and the U.S. workforce (Zhang, 2016). Further, the individual resources of international students promote the internationalization of higher education and enrich diverse campus climates (Ward et al., 2015).

International students, however, face many challenges while pursuing their degrees at U.S. higher education institutions. Living and studying in a foreign country can lead to experiences of acculturative stress (i.e., stress from life changes through the acculturation process) and adjustment problems (Berry, 2006). Research has found that international students encounter difficulties with language barriers, finances, adjustments to a new educational system, social customs and norms, and homesickness (Gold, 2016; Ma, 2020; Mukminin, 2019; Tang et al., 2018; Telbis et al., 2014; Xing & Bolden, 2019). These challenges can impact their mental well-being (Forbes-Mewett & Sawyer, 2016; Koo, Kim, et al., 2021). Researchers estimate that 15%–20% of international students are at risk of experiencing mental health problems due to acculturative stress and acculturation-related problems (Zhang & Goodson, 2011). In addition, while researchers have studied first-year college students' adjustment-related difficulties with mental health concerns (Boyraz et al., 2017), social development (Means & Pyne, 2017), and academic adjustment (Lattuca & Stark, 2009), first-year experiences among international students have received little attention.

Many studies have been conducted on international students' acculturative stress and adjustment in the United States (Luo et al., 2019; Sullivan & Kashubeck-West, 2015; Telbis et al., 2014; Xiong & Zhou, 2018). However, researchers have not focused on predictors of acculturative stress but on acculturative stress itself. Additionally, although there is a growing body of research on international students, there is a paucity of longitudinal studies. With the exception of a few longitudinal designs, (e.g., Cemalcilar & Falbo, 2008), research on international students' adjustment has used cross-sectional designs to assess their developmental processes (e.g., Luo et al., 2019; Koo, Nyunt, et al., 2021). Such designs do not enable researchers to explore change over time. There are also few studies empirically exploring relationships among diverse factors (e.g., relationships among English proficiency, length of stay, social connectedness, and self-esteem, etc.) and acculturative stress.

Understanding stressors as predictors of acculturative stress will provide in-depth knowledge about international students' adjustment. In addition, given the fact that the first-year transition presents various challenges and adjustment difficulties (Means & Pyne, 2017), studying first-year international college students and factors associated with acculturative stress will provide useful insight.

Therefore, the purpose of the study is to examine changes in first-year international college students' acculturative stress and collegiate experiences from the beginning of their first semester to the end of their first year in college. Four research questions guided this study:

1. How does the rate of acculturative stress among first-year international students vary based on students' gender, major, and socioeconomic status (SES)?
2. How do acculturative stress and collegiate experiences change over 1 year among first-year international students?
3. What are the predictors of acculturative stress among first-year international college students, and how do these change during their first year?
4. How does adjustment impact students' acculturative stress, and how does acculturative stress impact students' adjustment reciprocally over one year?

LITERATURE REVIEW

Acculturation and Acculturative Stress Among International Students During the First Year in College

The growing literature on college student mobility and the international dimensions of American higher education includes few studies of international students in the United States during this critical first year. Much of the literature addresses persistence and retention (Bowman & Holmes, 2017; Cintina & Malia Kana'iapuni, 2019; Sansone & Tucker Segura, 2020), adjustment (Espinoza, 2018; York & Fernandez, 2018), and first-year experiences (Boyraz et al., 2017; Tukibayeva & Gonyea, 2014). Little addresses the experiences of international students who face additional challenges beyond those experienced by most college students (Yan & Sendall, 2016).

The limited research examining international student experiences tends to problematize the first year as one of stress and challenge. One finding is that while colleges tend to aggressively recruit international students, these students often do not feel integrated into American campuses and frequently feel that university functions do not operate harmoniously to support their success (Briggs & Ammigan, 2017). Structured support systems that help international students adjust to the first year seldom exist. Further, little research explores international students' first year of college and its impact on acculturative stress.

Acculturation and Acculturative Stress During the First Year of College

Acculturation entails "the transferring of culture from one group of people to another group in response to contact with one another" (Amason et al., 1999, p. 312). Originally conceptualized as a process by which new immigrants become incorporated into the dominant culture (Padilla & Perez, 2003), in the 21st century, the unidimensional nature of acculturation has been reduced, with institutions viewing international students as sources of both revenue and diverse cultural exposure rather than as individuals to be assimilated (Chankseliani, 2018).

Acculturative stress is a particular type of stress resulting from the process of acculturation (Berry et al., 1987). It refers to mildly pathological and disruptive behaviors and experiences commonly generated during acculturation. Symptoms may include depression, anxiety, physical complaints, anger, identity confusion, substance abuse, and family conflict (Berry & Kim, 1988; Sandhu & Asrabadi, 1994). Berry (2006) argued that the degree to which an individual feels able to cope with the stress introduced via the acculturation process influences the degree of acculturative stress experienced. International students with adequate resources and strategies to overcome acculturative stress tend to experience it less strongly than those lacking adequate coping mechanisms or utilizing maladaptive coping strategies (Berry, 2006).

Factors Associated With Acculturative Stress Among International Students

Race/ethnicity, geographical region, marital status, sex/gender, age, English proficiency, length of residency in the United States, social connectedness, self-esteem, and academic adjustment have been investigated in studies regarding acculturation and adjustment difficulties among international students (Hirai et al., 2015; Lopez & Bui, 2014; Luo et al., 2019; Telbis et al., 2014). Consistent contributing factors include perceived English proficiency (Luo et al., 2019), social connectedness (Sullivan & Kashubeck-West, 2015), self-esteem (Lopez & Bui, 2014), and adjustment difficulties (Jackson et al., 2013). Demographic predictor variables have produced inconsistent results (Poyrazli et al., 2001).

International students with better social connectedness show less adjustment strain, better adjustment to the host culture, and better academic performance (Luo et al., 2019; Sullivan & Kashubeck-West, 2015). Social connectedness, particularly to domestic students, has also been shown to increase retention rates (Trice, 2004). International students lacking social connectedness also face academic issues and higher dropout rates (Li et al., 2010). Social connectedness, then, is important for the successful acculturation of first-year international students.

Higher self-esteem predicts academic adjustment of international students (Telbis et al., 2014), and better psychological adjustment among international students (Jackson et al., 2013). Self-esteem is a personality trait that contributes to psychological well-being, sociocultural adjustment, and health-promoting behaviors (Wei et al., 2008). Unfortunately, self-esteem often suffers among international students, which can lead to reduced physical and mental health. A lack of culturally responsive treatment approaches on many college campuses further exacerbates this problem.

International students who feel comfortable speaking English show better psychological and sociocultural adjustment (Luo et al., 2019; Ma, 2020) and lower levels of acculturative stress (Poulakis et al., 2017). Perceived English proficiency also strongly influences social connectedness and academic success, key factors in acculturative stress (Wang et al., 2018; Xing & Bolden, 2019). More frequent interactions and perceived confidence in one's English skills can lead to positive feelings of adjustment and reduced loneliness (Poulakis et al., 2017). Additionally, research has found that perceived English proficiency facilitates more successful interpersonal relationships with English-speaking students (Mukminin, 2019). High English proficiency also affects international students' academic accomplishment (Li et al., 2010), encourages them to speak in class (Yeh & Inose, 2003), and produces better psychological adjustment (Poyrazli, 2003). One challenge international students must also navigate is pressure to utilize English in all aspects of daily life, which can increase stress (J. Lee, 2017; Shahjahan & Kezar, 2013; Suspitsyna & Shalka, 2019). Models of mutual engagement between international students and domestic peers could alleviate some of these concerns, but conceptualizations of English based on mutual reciprocity have been limited in research and practice (Thomas et al., 2018).

Academic stress related to adjusting to a different educational environment is one of the largest sources of acculturative stress (Ying, 2005). Challenges with academic adjustment often result from the difference between international students' experiences of classroom life in their home countries and their experiences in the United States (Zhou & Zhang, 2014). International students may be unaccustomed to instructors asking questions in class and be particularly troubled if called upon without having raising their hands (Tang et al., 2018). While limited programming efforts to help international students adapt to American academic expectations and norms exist, few institutions have embraced such programs (Smith & Khawaja, 2011; Yan & Sendall, 2016).

THEORETICAL FRAMEWORK

We used Ward and Kennedy's (1994) psychological and sociocultural adjustment model to frame international students' acculturative stress and adjustment processes. This model is frequently employed in studies of acculturative stress and adjustment (Luo et al., 2019; Xiong & Zhou, 2018). It conceptualizes adjustment as the sum of two distinctive types—psychological and sociocultural adjustment—and investigates the relationship between acculturation attitudes and cross-cultural adjustment (Ward & Kennedy, 1994). According to Ward and Kennedy (1994), these adjustment types involve different predictors: Psychological adjustment involves personality, life changes, self-esteem, and social support, and sociocultural adjustment involves length of stay in the host country, ethnic identity, contact with individuals from the host country, and language proficiency. We explore these interrelated concepts of psychological and sociocultural adjustment among first-year international students. Based on our literature review, we conclude that both psychological and sociocultural adjustment factors are in play when international students begin studying in the United States. We selected Ward and Kennedy's (1994) model for the depth of its conceptualization of psychological and sociocultural adjustment, alignment with our research questions, and centering of the experiences of international students abroad.

METHOD

Procedure

The first wave of data was collected during the first week of the fall semester in September 2010, and the second in May 2011, via online surveys. Students were recruited during the new international student orientation, where the first author of this study gave a brief presentation about the study. An email invitation was sent at the end of the orientation day; interested students visited the online survey and participated. Twenty percent of participants had a chance to win a $25 Starbucks gift card as compensation. Data from participants who completed both the first and second wave surveys were included for analysis.

Participants

Participants included 192 international students from 12 different countries who enrolled in a degree program at a large private research university in the Mid-Atlantic region under F-1 visas. Fifty-eight percent were female, 33% were from China, 30% from India, 15% from South Korea, 8% from Saudi Arabia, 2% Turkey, and 2% from Greece. Ninety-five percent were single, and 81% spoke English as a second language. Lastly, 42% indicated that they came from a high SES family, 47% from a middle-class family, and 11% from a low SES family.

Instruments

Acculturative Stress

We used the Acculturative Stress Scale for International Students by Sandu and Asrabadi (1994) to measure acculturative stress. This scale was developed to measure culture-related stress among international students in the United States. It consists of 36 questions scored on a 5-point Likert scale. Sample questions include "I feel lost leaving my relatives behind," and "I am treated differently in social situations." Cronbach's α for the current study was .91.

Homesickness

To measure homesickness, we employed the Utrecht Homesickness Scale (UHS) developed by Stroebe and colleagues (2002). The UHS consists of 20 items under five subscales scored on a 5-point Likert scale: missing family, missing friends, feeling lonely, having difficulty adjusting, and ruminating about home. Sample questions include "Do you miss your family?" and "Do you miss home?" Cronbach's α for the current study was .90.

Adjustment Difficulties

We used the adjustment difficulties subscale of the UHS (Stroebe et al., 2002) to measure adjustment difficulties. This includes four items scored on a 5-point Likert-type scale. A sample question is "I feel uncomfortable in a new situation." For the current investigation, Cronbach's α was .87.

Self-Esteem

We employed the Unconditional Self-Regard Scale by Betz and colleagues (1995) to measure self-esteem. This scale was developed to capture individuals' perceived self-esteem. The scale is a 28-item measure scored on a 5-point Likert scale. Sample items are "I really value myself," and "Whether other people criticize me or praise me makes no difference to the way I feel about myself." For the current investigation, Cronbach's α was .91.

Social Connectedness

We applied the Social Connectedness Scale by R. Lee and Robbins (1995) to measure social connectedness. It includes eight items scored on a 6-point Likert-type scale. A sample item is "I catch myself losing all sense of connectedness with society." For the current investigation, Cronbach's α was .92.

Satisfaction with College

To measure international students' satisfaction with overall college experiences, we utilized 27 items on the Satisfaction with Overall College Experiences section from the College Student Survey administered by the Higher Education Research Institute (Astin, 1993). All responses are scored on a 6-point Likert-type scale. A sample question is "I am satisfied with overall experiences in college." For the current investigation, Cronbach's α was .92.

English Proficiency

We used four questions about perceived level of English mastery in listening, speaking, reading, and writing skills to measure English proficiency.

Demographic Information

A brief questionnaire asked for demographic information regarding nationality, age, gender, marital status, education, major, ethnicity, SES, and length of stay in the United States.

Data Analysis

To explore participants' overall characteristics, we performed descriptive statistics. For within-group comparisons of answers to the first research question, we performed cross-tabulations. We employed a paired *t* test to investigate changes in students' experiences over two semesters to answer the second research question. Upon correlation analysis to explore relationships among variables, we performed hierarchical multiple regression to examine predictors of acculturative stress to answer the third research question. Lastly, we performed an autoregressive cross-lagged (ARCL) panel model approach (Curran, 2000) to explore causal and reciprocal impacts between acculturative stress and satisfaction with college experiences in two semester intervals to answer the last research question. We used SPSS 23.0 and Mplus 6.12 for data analysis.

RESULTS

Descriptive Statistics

As displayed in Table 1, male students, students with low SES backgrounds, and students majoring in the humanities reported higher rates of acculturative stress compared to their female peers, mid-high SES students, and STEM and social science counterparts. For satisfaction with overall college experiences, female students, mid-high SES students, and social science majors were more likely to be satisfied. Female students, mid-high SES students, and social science majors' grade point averages (GPAs) were slightly higher than those of their counterparts.

Change Over Time: Beginning Versus End of the First Year

For longitudinal comparison of acculturative stress and college experiences between the first week of the first semester (Time 1) and the last week of the second semester (Time 2), we utilized paired *t* tests (see Table 2). International students reported lower levels of acculturative stress, higher rates of social connectedness, lower rates of homesickness, lower levels of adjustment difficulties, and higher rates of English proficiency at the end of the first year than at the beginning. These factors were statistically significant at the $p < .001$ and $p < .01$ level. Self-esteem and satisfaction with overall college experiences increased after two semesters, but these differences were not statistically significant.

Table 1: Distribution of Acculturative Stress, Satisfaction with College Experiences, and GPA at the end of the First Year by Gender, SES, and Major

	Gender		SES			Major	
	M (n = 84)	F (n = 108)	Low (n = 17)	Mid-high (n = 182)	High-upper (n = 8)	SS (n = 40)	STEM (n = 142)
Acculturative stress							
Low	6.4	15.2	3.3	9.6	1.3	2.5	1.7
Middle	64.1	53.5	58.0	56.8	54.6	50.5	57.4
High	29.5	26.3	36.5	33.4	51.1	47.0	41.9
Satisfaction							
Low	5.7	2.2	16.8	13.3	28.6	20.4	20.6
Middle	36.9	37.4	51.8	60.7	52.9	38.8	46.6
High	57.3	60.4	33.4	25.7	28.6	40.8	31.4
GPA							
Low	12.2	10.9	10.7	2.3	12.5	6.9	13.9
Middle	60.3	64.4	59.5	67.0	55.4	64.1	61.1
High	24.6	27.7	21.6	28.3	22.1	27.5	24.3

Note. N = 192. SES = socioeconomic status; SS = social sciences; STEM = science, technology, engineering, and math; GPA = grade point average.

Table 2: Means, Standard Deviations, and Results of the *t*-Test Comparisons Between Time 1 and Time 2

Variable	Time 1 M	Time 1 SD	Time 2 M	Time 2 SD	t value
Acculturative stress	2.58	0.58	2.25	0.60	−3.022***
Satisfaction overall	3.31	0.65	3.34	0.61	0.49
Self-esteem	3.23	0.69	3.28	0.68	0.85
Social connectedness	3.32	0.64	3.69	0.63	1.23***
Homesickness	3.52	0.74	3.21	0.80	−1.72**
Adjustment difficulties	2.86	0.93	2.56	1.03	−0.58*
English proficiency	2.95	1.00	3.12	1.03	0.64**

Note. N = 192. *$p < .05$, **$p < .01$, ***$p < .001$

Predictors of Acculturative Stress over the First Year

Table 3 shows the R^2 change for the regressions performed at Time 1 and Time 2. The amount of variance explained by the independent variables was similar between groups, with 47% explained for Time 1 and 45% for Time 2. We entered variables into the regression model in seven blocks according to Ward and

Kennedy's (1994) model. We entered students' background and demographic information first, followed by satisfaction with overall college experiences in Block 2, self-esteem (Block 3), social connectedness (Block 4), homesickness (Block 5), adjustment difficulties (Block 6), and English proficiency (Block 7). The dependent variable was students' self-reported acculturative stress.

Table 3 also illustrates predictors of acculturative stress in the regression model at the beginning of the first semester and the end of the second semester. Gender, self-esteem, social connectedness, and English proficiency were significant predictors of acculturative stress among first-year international students at both Time 1 and Time 2. Adjustment difficulties and homesickness were significant predictors of acculturative stress only at Time 1. First-year international students with higher self-esteem, higher levels of English proficiency, and higher levels of social connectedness were less likely to experience acculturative stress. These factors were significant at the $p < .001$ and $p < .05$ levels.

Table 3: Predictive Model for Acculturative Stress for Time 1 and Time 2.

	Time 1			Time 2		
Block	R^2	β at entry	Final β	R^2	β at entry	Final β
1. Characteristics	.05			.09		
Age		.026	.02		.025	.05
GPA		−.045	−.03		−.088	−.07
SES		−.04	−.03		−.049	.001
Gender		.15***	.06*		.275***	.116*
Parents' ed		−.007	−.005		−.053	−.040
2. Satisfaction	.22	−.023	−.030	.23	−.087	−.002
3. Self-esteem	.42	−.275***	−.139***	.44	−.112***	−.113***
4. Social	.45	−.174***	−.139***	.45	−.107*	−.077*
5. Homesickness	.46	.068**	.051**	.46	.111	.03
6. Adjustment	.46	.074*	.052*	.47	.067	.018
7. English	.47	−.113***	−.113***	.48	−.096*	−.096*

Note. GPA = grade point average. *$p < .05$, **$p < .01$, ***$p < .001$

ARCL

As observed in Table 4, the estimation of the ARCL model indicated an acceptable fit to the observed data among the variables of gender, SES, stress, and adjustment to overall college experiences. As shown in Table 4 from the ARCL analysis, the two semesters' lagged effect of acculturative stress on satisfaction with overall college experiences was not statistically significant (β = −.013, $p >$ .05). The two semesters' lagged effect of adjustment to overall college experiences was statistically significant (β = −.104, $p < .05$). At baseline, gender was positively related to acculturative stress (β = .606, $p < .05$) and adjustment to overall college experiences (β = .121, $p <.05$). SES was negatively related to stress

($\beta = -.071$, $p < .05$) and positively associated with adjustment to college experiences ($\beta = .435$, $p < .05$).

Table 4: Predictors of Acculturative Stress for Time 1 and Time 2

Predictors	Outcome	β	*SE*
Gender	T1-Stress	.606	.028**
	T1-Adjustment	.121	.022**
SES	T1-Stress	−.071	.035**
	T1-Adjustment	.435	.032**
Time 1 Acculturative stress	T2-Stress	.471	.008**
	T2-Adjustment	−.013	.006
Time1 Adjustment to college	T2-Stress	−.104	.010**
	T2-Adjustment	.681	.005**

Note. β = standardized coefficient; *SE* = standard error of the estimate; SES = socioeconomic status. $^{**}p < .01$; $^{*}p < .05$

DISCUSSION

This study examined first-year international students' acculturative stress, adjustment, and associated factors using a longitudinal design exploring changes in these factors over a year. Overall, male students, students from low SES backgrounds, and students in humanities majors appeared to be more stressed by acculturation, while female students, students with mid-high SES backgrounds, and students in social science majors were more likely to be satisfied with their overall college experiences. Findings suggest that there was a significant decrease in acculturative stress and adjustment difficulties between the first week of the first semester and the end of the first academic year. It appears that there was a significant increase in social connectedness and English proficiency in one academic year. In other words, international students reported less acculturative stress and fewer adjustment difficulties and an increased sense of social connectedness and improvements in English proficiency within one academic year.

Additionally, we examined relationships among acculturative stress and associated factors. We found that acculturative stress was positively associated with adjustment difficulties and negatively associated with social connectedness and English proficiency. This finding is supported by previous research (Sullivan & Kashubeck-West, 2015; Zhang & Jung, 2017). Moreover, adjustment difficulties were negatively associated with social connectedness and English proficiency. The findings suggest that international students with more social connectedness have fewer adjustment difficulties and report less acculturative stress. In addition, those with more English proficiency report more social connectedness, fewer adjustment difficulties, and less acculturative stress. Overall, social connectedness, English proficiency, and adjustment difficulties are significant indicators of acculturative stress among international students, and these factors and outcomes change over one academic year. Findings suggest that

English proficiency plays a significant role in reducing acculturative stress and adjustment difficulties and increasing social connectedness.

Within-group comparisons show that male students, students from low SES backgrounds, and students in the humanities showed higher levels of acculturative stress. Although our findings are not consistent with a previous study by Zhang and Jung (2017) that reported no significant differences in acculturative stress by gender and major, we inferred that female students are more adaptive to new environments, which may cause them to feel less stressed by acculturation. Gender comparison of acculturative stress is an underdeveloped area of study; more investigations are needed. We also inferred that international students studying humanities are more likely to feel stressed than their counterparts in STEM because the humanities require advanced cultural and social knowledge and more advanced language skills compared with other disciplines (Edmunson, 2013; Lewis, 2017). Subgroup analysis of international students' adjustment and acculturation by major may be informative.

Regarding the causal directions of acculturative stress and adjustment to overall college experiences, the findings point to detrimental effects of acculturative stress on levels of adjustment. Acculturative stress and adjustment to overall college experiences during the first week of the first semester predicted international students' level of acculturative stress during the final week of their first year. Therefore, the reciprocal and causal relationships between these two factors was confirmed. The findings partially support the adjustment model (Ward & Kennedy, 1993) in that social connectedness was related to psychological adjustment. In addition, perceived English proficiency was significantly related to sociocultural adjustment, which supports Ward and Kennedy's (1994) adjustment model. With respect to bivariate relationships between associated factors and acculturative stress, international students who were confident in English and socially active reported fewer adjustment difficulties and less acculturative stress, which is consistent with findings using multinational international student samples (Yeh & Inose, 2003). Regarding the best model for acculturative stress, perceived English skills and social connectedness were significant contributing factors. These findings are consistent with previous studies (Yeh & Inose, 2003) in which both perceived English skills and social connectedness were found to be significant predictors of acculturative stress.

Answering our fourth research question with ARCL analysis, our findings confirmed that international students' acculturative stress at the beginning of the first year is related to their satisfaction with their overall college experience at the end of that year. With the ARCL method, reciprocal and causal directions between acculturative stress and satisfaction with college experiences within two semesters of the first year were explained. Such findings strengthen recommendations to enhance orientation and support programs for international students in the first few weeks at U.S. institutions. The significant association between the first week's acculturative stress and the final week's satisfaction with college also provides the insight that creating a positive campus climate during the first semester is crucial to reduce first-year international students' acculturative stress. In a recent study by Yoon and Martin (2017), sharing culture and languages with native English-speaking peers built a learning environment where all students, including international students, improved their confidence and better understood other cultures, thus developing a positive campus climate. It is assumed that other associated factors also impact the relationship between international students' acculturative stress and adjustment. Further investigation of associated factors is needed.

Limitations

This study has limitations. One is that the data were collected during the 2010–2011 academic year. Changes to U.S. and international higher education over the past 8 years could mean that the study results no longer hold true. However, we see this as unlikely. The primary changes to U.S. higher education for international students revolve around the 2016 election of Donald Trump and the accompanying increase in visa scrutiny (Chen et al., 2019; Hefner-Babb & Khoshlessan, 2018). Practical challenges (such as securing legal immigration status) have impacted international student recruitment since the post-9/11 period (Johnson, 2018), a trend that has continued since 2016 (Chen et al., 2019; Hefner-Babb & Khoshlessan, 2018). While increasing legal barriers have a serious impact on international higher education, they do not relate directly to our dependent or independent variables; in our review of the literature, we found no evidence that post-2016 visa policy changes impact acculturative stress, self-esteem, English proficiency, social connectedness, or homesickness. Research on the acculturative experiences of international students also seems not to have changed very much in the last decade (reflecting approximately 6 years prior to and 4 years after the election of Donald Trump). This suggests that using data from 2010–2011 does not obscure factors related to acculturative stress caused by or associated with changes in U.S. visa policy following the 2016 election. The dataset employed in our study is, to our knowledge, the only longitudinal data set that examines acculturative stress among international students during the first year of college. We contend that the value of such data far outweighs the possibility that the findings may differ if the study were conducted today.

Research Recommendations

The findings suggest several research directions. It is important to continue examining relationships between various contributing factors and acculturative stress so that academic advisors, staff, faculty, and student affairs professionals understand how to best support international students.

This research studied international students from different countries as one group; comparing experiences of students from different countries is a useful future research direction. Students from different countries and cultural backgrounds may have different experiences of acculturation and adjustment. Therefore, subgroup analysis and comparisons will provide additional insight. We recommend two approaches to address these questions. Most studies in this area have utilized cross-sectional research designs. Further longitudinal studies are necessary because it is important to detect changes over time in this population and its subgroups. We also suggest that further research on the relationships between variables is merited. Similar to prior studies, our research does not show whether the relationships among the variables explored are reciprocal or causal (Koo, 2021a). More work is needed to understand how these variables interact with and influence one another.

Based on the finding about the relationship between English proficiency and acculturative stress, in-depth analysis of the impact of English proficiency and the benefits of language training programs would help advisors and student affairs professionals better understand international students and make appropriate referrals. While our study addressed the relationship between English proficiency and acculturative stress, it did not examine the impact of specific language-related interventions. This is a prime area for further research, especially as more college campuses invest in language programming.

Lastly, we recommend further exploratory qualitative study to capture students' genuine and vivid experiences of acculturative stress and adjustment difficulties so that in-depth life stories behind factors found from this study can be presented.

Practical Implications

This study's results offer significant insights for practitioners seeking to help international students. Our research demonstrates that those who are socially connected exhibit lower levels of acculturative stress. We recommend that student affairs practitioners design intentional social experiences that foster relationships among international students, their domestic peers, and staff and faculty. While many institutions already engage in such practices, we suggest that they could be expanded. We also recommend that student affairs practitioners become acquainted with clubs, organizations, and groups on campus that may be of interest to international students. Such organizations need not be focused on international student issues. Rather, the idea is to provide access to organizations, groups, clubs, sports teams, etc. that offer a chance to meet domestic students and develop interpersonal relationships with them.

A key factor influencing international students' ability to develop meaningful interpersonal relationships with domestic students and succeed academically is English proficiency. While all international students studying in the United States must demonstrate considerable English proficiency, levels of comfort using English and degrees of proficiency vary. We recommend that institutions invest in courses with a focus on the applied use of English. Student affairs practitioners should develop programming that offers international students informal opportunities to practice their English in small groups. The second author of this article has previously facilitated small conversation circles with groups of international students. These meet for an hour per week, and the focus is on the use of English in day-to-day life. The facilitator (ideally a native English speaker) serves as a guide, helping students feel comfortable speaking in an informal social setting. Other institutions have recently begun to invest in similar programming, which we see as a positive development in the field of student affairs.

Concerns about the impacts of mental health on the acculturative stress and adjustment of international students should not be ignored. Unfortunately, while mental health concerns are common among students on U.S. college campuses, often campus mental health treatment centers are rooted in Western thinking and practice, to the exclusion of international students (Choy & Alon, 2019; Koo & Nyunt, 2020). We recommend that university counseling centers consider the "systemic and cultural context in which a student presents" (Choy & Alon, 2019, p. 62). A multicultural perspective on mental health counseling could help address challenges that arise when international students seek treatment (Koo & Nyunt, 2020).

We recommend that university counseling centers make explicit their ethical and legal obligation not to disclose to students' parents or family members the details of their mental health treatment. While this is the standard of practice in mental health treatment, international students may not be aware that they can seek treatment without their families finding out, especially if exposure to a campus counseling center is their first exposure to the American healthcare system. Removing this barrier would offer an opportunity to seek treatment without fear of consequences from family members.

It is of note that for most of our variables, international students reported lower levels of acculturative stress at the end of the first year compared to the beginning. This may suggest that institutions are already engaged in practices that reduce acculturative stress. Alternatively, it may suggest that acculturative stress tends to naturally lessen in intensity with time. Our recommendations for practice bridge this gap by suggesting that while many international students display substantial resilience in navigating acculturative stress, the process of adjustment could be made easier with an increase in targeted institutional interventions.

Higher education institutions need to be supportive of international students' cultures and their native languages. To address acculturative stress, faculty must connect with students culturally and linguistically to make their learning meaningful and transformative (Koo, 2021b). Higher education institutions need to provide spaces where international students can share and celebrate their cultures and languages with their peers. Thus, institutions need to emphasize the importance of cultural and linguistic diversity on campus.

CONCLUSION

The study contributes to the body of research on first-year international college students' collegiate experiences, acculturative stress, and predictors of acculturative stress. Given that international students experience unique challenges and stressors that impact the acculturation process (Koo, Kim, et al., 2021), the findings provide insights to help scholars, faculty, and staff who work with international students provide culturally sensitive guidance.

In addition, this study reports on stressors associated with international students' acculturative stress, examined via longitudinal analysis. Analysis of causal and reciprocal relationships among adjustment issues and acculturative stress is still underdeveloped; thus, the reciprocal and causal relationship found between adjustment and acculturative stress among first-year international college students contributes to this body of literature.

Interpretation of the results should take into consideration specific teaching tools or educational interventions that have contributed to changes in international students during their first year in college. This study suggests educational mechanisms that colleges should adopt so that international students can enjoy smooth academic progress and a comfortable life on campus. Faculty should utilize educational intervention programs, like culturally responsive instruction (Koo & Nyunt, 2020), to reduce international students' acculturative stress. We hope that this study will assist educators, administrators, policy makers, and researchers in better meeting the needs of international students.

REFERENCES

Astin, A. W. (1993). *What matters in college?* Jossey-Bass.

Amason, P., Allen, M. W., & Holmes, S. A. (1999). Social support and acculturative stress in the multicultural workplace. *Journal of Applied Communication Research*, *27*(4), 310–334.

Berry, J. W. (2006). Stress perspectives on acculturation. In D. L. Sam & J. W. Berry (Eds.), *The Cambridge handbook of acculturation psychology* (pp. 43–57). Cambridge University Press.

Berry, J. W., & Kim, U. (1988). Acculturation and mental health. In P. R. Dasen, J. W. Berry, & N. Sartorius (Eds.), *Health and cross-cultural psychology* (pp. 207–236). SAGE.

Berry, J. W., Kim, U., Minde, T., & Mok, D. (1987). Comparative studies of acculturative stress. *International Migration Review*, *21*(3), 491–511.

Betz, N., Wohlgemuth, E., Serling, D., Harshbarger, J., & Klein, K. (1995). Evaluation of a measure of self-esteem based on the concept of unconditional self-regard. *Journal of Counseling and Development,* 74(1), 76–83. https://doi.org/10.1002/j.1556-6676.1995.tb01826.x

Bowman, N. A., & Holmes, J. M. (2017). A quasi-experimental analysis of fraternity or sorority membership and college student success. *Journal of College Student Development*, *58*(7), 1018–1034.

Boyraz, G., Horne, S. G., & Granda, R. (2017). Depressive symptomatology and academic achievement among first-year college students: The role of effort regulation. *Journal of College Student Development*, *58*(8), 1218–1236.

Briggs, P., & Ammigan, R. (2017). A collaborative programming and outreach model for international student support offices. *Journal of International Students*, *7*(4), 1080–1095.

Chankseliani, M. (2018). Four rationales of HE internationalization: Perspectives of U.K. universities on attracting students from former Soviet countries. *Journal of Studies in International Education*, *22*(1), 53–70.

Chen, Y. A., Li, R., & Hagedorn, L. S. (2019). Undergraduate international student enrollment forecasting model: An application of time series analysis.

Journal of International Students, *9*(1), 242–261. https://doi.org/10.32674/jis.v9i1.266

Cemalcilar, Z., & Falbo, T. (2008). A Longitudinal Study of the Adaptation of International Students in the United States. *Journal of Cross-Cultural Psychology*, *39*(6), 799–804. https://doi.org/10.1177/0022022108323787

Choy, Y., & Alon, Z. (2019). The comprehensive mental health treatment of Chinese international students: A case report. *Journal of College Student Psychotherapy*, *33*(1), 47–66.

Cintina, I., & Malia Kana'iapuni, S. (2019). Finishing strong: GPA and timely college graduation outcomes among native Hawaiian STEM majors. *The Review of Higher Education*, *42*(4), 1459–1487.

Curran, P. J. (2000). A latent curve framework for the study of developmental trajectories in adolescent substance abuse. In J. S. Rose, L. Chassin, C. C. Presson, & S. J. Sherman (Eds.), *Multivariate applications in substance use research* (pp. 1–4). Erlbaum.

Edmundson, M. (2013). Why major in humanities? Not just for a good job—for a good life. *Yale Global Online.*

Espinoza, B. D. (2018). Reconciliatory socialization: Conceptualizing the experiences of Evangelical Christian doctoral students in secular higher education. *International Journal of Christianity & Education*, *22*(3), 233–251.

Forbes-Mewett, H., & Sawyer, A. M. (2016). International students and mental health. *Journal of International Students*, *6*(3), 661–677.

Gold, S. J. (2016). International students in the United States. *Society*, *53*(5), 523–530.

Hefner-Babb, T. S., & Khoshlessan, R. (2018). Iranian student experience pursuing admission to universities in the United States. *Journal of International Students*, *8*(4), 1926–1940. https://doi.org/10.5281/zenodo.1482777

Hirai, R., Frazier, P., & Syed, M. (2015). Psychological and sociocultural adjustment of first-year international students: Trajectories and predictors. *Journal of Counseling Psychology*, *62*(3), 438–452.

Jackson, M., Ray, S., & Bybell, D. (2013). International students in the U.S.: Social and psychological adjustment. *Journal of International Students*, *3*(1), 17–28.

Johnson, K. A. C. (2018). 9/11 and international student visa issuance. *Journal of Studies in International Education2*, *22*(5), 393–413.

Koo, K. (2021a). Am I welcome here?: Campus climate and psychological well-being among racially minoritized students. *Journal of Student Affairs Research and Practice*. 58 (2), 196-213. https://doi.org/10.1080/19496591.2020.1853557

Koo, K. (2021b). Distressed in a foreign country: Mental health and well-being among international students in the United States during COVID-19. In K. Bista & R. Chan (Eds.), *Routledge studies in global student mobility series-impact of COVID-19 on global student mobility and higher education.* Routledge

Koo, K., Kim, Y., & Lee, J., & Nyunt, G. (2021). It's my fault? A qualitative study on Korean international graduate students' psychological well-being and experiences. *Journal of International Students, 11(4).* https://doi.org/10.32674/jis.v11i4

Koo, K., & Nyunt, G. (2020). Culturally sensitive assessment of mental health for international students. *New Directions for Student Services*, *2020*(169), 43–52. https://doi.org/10.1002/ss.20343

Koo, K., Nyunt, G., & Wang, B. (2021). Who spends too much time online?: Associated factors of Internet addiction among international college students in the United States. *Journal of International Students*, *11*(1), 122–143. https://doi.org/10.32674/jis.v11i1.2063

Lattuca, L. R., & Stark, J. S. (2009). *Shaping the college curriculum: Academic plans in context* (2nd ed.). Jossey-Bass.

Lee, J. J. (2017). Neo-nationalism in higher education: Case of South Africa. *Studies in Higher Education*, *42*(5), 869–886.

Lee, R., & Robbins, S. B. (1995). Measuring belongingness: The social connectedness and the social assurances scales. *Journal of Counseling Psychology*, *42*(2), 232–241.

Lewis, C. S. (2017). Crisis rhetoric, stigma play: The contested status of humanities majors on an elite university campus. *Symbolic Interaction, 40*(3), 378–395. doi:10.1002/symb.288

Li, G., Chen, W., & Duanmu, J.-L. (2010). Determinants of international students' academic performance. *Journal of Studies in International Education*, *14*(4), 389–405.

Lopez, I. Y., & Bui, N. H. (2014). Acculturation and linguistic factors on international students' self-esteem and language confidence. *Journal of International Students*, *4*(4), 314–329.

Luo, Z., Wu, S., Fang, X., & Brunsting, N. C. (2019). International students' perceived language competence, domestic student support, and psychological well-being at a U.S. university. *Journal of International Students*, *9*(4), 954–971. https://doi.org/10.32674/jis.v0i0.605

Ma, J. (2020). Supporting practices to break Chinese international students' language barriers: The first step to facilitate their social adjustment. *Journal of International Students*, *10*(1), 84–105. https://doi.org/10.32674/jis.v10i1.773

Means, D. R., & Pyne, K. B. (2017). Finding my way: Perceptions of institutional support and belonging in low-income, first-generation, first-year college students. *Journal of College Student Development*, *58*(6), 907–924.

Mukminin, A. (2019). Acculturative experiences among Indonesian graduate students in Dutch higher education. *Journal of International Students*, *9*(2), 488–510. https://doi.org/10.32674/jis.v0i0.265

NAFSA. (2019). *International students contribute to our economy and American innovation.*https://www.nafsa.org/policy-and-advocacy/policy-resources/international-students-contribute-our-economy-and-american-innovation

Padilla, A. M., & Perez, W. (2003). Acculturation, social identity, and social cognition: A new perspective. *Hispanic Journal of Behavioral Sciences, 25*(1), 35–55.

Poulakis, M., Dike, C. A., & Massa, A. C. (2017). Acculturative stress and adjustment experiences of Greek international students. *Journal of International Students, 7*(2), 204–228.

Poyrazli, S. (2003). Ethnic identity and psychosocial adjustment among international students. *Psychological Reports, 92*(2), 512–514.

Poyrazli, S., Arbona, C., Bullington, R., & Pisecco, S. (2001). Adjustment issues of Turkish college students studying in the U.S. *College Student Journal, 35*(1), 52–62.

Sandhu, D. S., & Asrabadi, B. R. (1994). Development of an acculturative stress scale for international students: Preliminary findings. *Psychological Reports, 75*(1), 435–448.

Sansone, V. A., & Tucker Segura, J. S. (2020). Exploring factors contributing to college success among student veteran transfers at a four-year university. *The Review of Higher Education, 43*(3), 887–915.

Shahjahan, R. A., & Kezar, A. J. (2013). Beyond the "national container": Addressing methodological nationalism in higher education research. *Educational Researcher, 42*(1), 20–29.

Smith, R. A., & Khawaja, N. G. (2011). A review of the acculturation experiences of international students. *International Journal of Intercultural Relations, 35*(6), 699–713.

Stroebe, M., Van Vliet, T., Hewstone, M., & Willis, H. (2002). Homesickness among students in two cultures: Antecedents and consequences. *British Journal of Psychology, 93*, 147–168.

Sullivan, C., & Kashubeck-West, S. (2015). The interplay of international students' acculturative stress, social support, and acculturation modes. *Journal of International Students, 5*(1), 1–11.

Suspitsyna, T., & Shalka, T. R. (2019). The Chinese international student as a (post)colonial other: An analysis of cultural representations of a US media discourse. *The Review of Higher Education, 42*, 287–308.

Tang, X., Collier, D. A., & Witt, A. (2018). Qualitative study on Chinese students' perception of U.S. university life. *Journal of International Students, 8*(1), 151–178.

Telbis, N. M., Helgeson, L., & Kingsbury, C. (2014). International students' confidence and academic success. *Journal of International Students, 4*(4), 330–341.

Thomas, V. F., Ssendikaddiwa, J. M., Mroz, M., Lockyer, K., Kosarzova, K., & Hanna, C. (2018). Leveraging common ground: Improving international and domestic students' interaction through mutual engagement. *Journal of International Students, 8*(3), 1386–1397. https://doi.org/10.5281/zenodo.1254599

Trice, A. G. (2004). Mixing it up: International graduate students' social interactions with American students. *Journal of College Student Development, 45*(6), 671–687.

Tukibayeva, M., & Gonyea, R. M. (2014). High-impact practices and the first-year student. *New Directions for Institutional Research, 2013*(160), 19–35.

Wang, C. H., Harrison, J., Cardullo, V., & Lin, X. (2018). Exploring the relationship among international students' English self-efficacy, using English to learn self-efficacy, and academic self-efficacy. *Journal of International Students, 8*(1), 233–250. https://doi.org/10.5281/zenodo.1134299

Ward, C., & Kennedy, A. (1993). Psychological and socio-cultural adjustment during cross-cultural transitions: A comparison of secondary students overseas and at home. *International Journal of Psychology, 28*(2), 129–147. doi:10.1080/00207599308247181

Ward, C., & Kennedy, A. (1994). Acculturation strategies, psychological adjustment, and sociocultural competence during cross-cultural transitions. *International Journal of Intercultural Relations, 18*(3), 329–343. doi:10.1016/0147-1767(94)90036-1

Ward, T., Jacobs, J., & Thompson, R. (2015). The number of international students. *College and University, 91*(1), 3.

Wei, M., Ku, T., Russell, D.W., Mallinckrodt, B., Liao, K.Y. (2008) Moderating effects of three coping strategies and self-esteem on perceived discrimination and depressive symptoms: A minority stress model for Asian international students. *Journal of Counseling Psychology, 55*(4), 451–462. http://doi:10.1037/a0012511. PMID: 22017552.

Xing, D. C., & Bolden, B. (2019). Exploring oral English learning motivation in Chinese international students with low oral English proficiency. *Journal of International Students, 9*(3), 834–855. https://doi.org/10.32674/jis.v9i3.749

Xiong, Y., & Zhou, Y. (2018). Understanding east Asian graduate students' socio-cultural and psychological adjustment in a U.S. Midwestern university. *Journal of International Students, 8*(2), 769–794. https://doi.org/10.5281/zenodo.1250379

Yan, Z., & Sendall, P. (2016). First year experience: How we can better assist first-year international students in higher education. *Journal of International Students, 6*(1), 35–51.

Yeh, C. J., & Inose, M. (2003). International students' reported English fluency, social support satisfaction, and social connectedness as predictors of acculturative stress. *Counselling Psychology Quarterly, 16*(1), 15–28.

Ying, Y. W. (2005). Variation in acculturative stressors over time: A study of Taiwanese students in the United States. *International Journal of Intercultural Relations, 29*(1), 59–71.

York, T. T., & Fernandez, F. (2018). The positive effects of service-learning on transfer students' sense of belonging: A multi-institutional analysis. *Journal of College Student Development, 59*(5), 579–597.

Yoon, J., & Martin, L. (2017). Infusing culturally responsive science curriculum into early childhood teacher preparation. *Research in Science Education, 49,* 697–710. doi:10.1007/s11165-017-9647-x.

Zhang, J., & Goodson, P. (2011). Predictors of international students' psychosocial adjustment to life in the United States: A systematic review. *International Journal of Intercultural Relations*, *35*(2), 139–162.

Zhang, Y. L. (2016). International students in transition: Voices of Chinese doctoral students in a US research university. *Journal of International Students*, *6*(1), 175–194.

Zhang, Y., & Jung, E. (2017). Multi-dimensionality of acculturative stress among Chinese international atudents: What lies behind their struggles? *International Research and Review, 7*(1),23-43.

Zhou, G., & Zhang, Z. (2014). A study of the first year international students at a Canadian university: Challenges and experiences with social integration. *Canadian and International Education*, *43*(2), Article 7.

KATIE K. KOO, PhD, is an assistant professor of higher education at Texas A&M University-Commerce. Her research focuses on underrepresented students' collegiate experiences, mental health issues, and adjustment, including international students' psychological well-being. Email: katie.koo@tamuc.edu

IAN BAKER, MA, is a PhD student in higher education at Michigan State University. Ian is also working as a learning and assessment coordinator of LAS Hub Program at the University of Michigan. Ian is interested in international students' experiences and advising. Email: bakerian@msu.edu

JIYOON YOON, PhD, is an associate professor of science education at the University of Texas at Arlington. She is interested in acculturation and culturally sensitive practice for international students. She has also established and directed international programs to exchange teaching methods and culture between the Korea and the United States. Email: jiyoon@uta.edu

Peer-Reviewed Article

© *Journal of International Students*
Volume 11, Issue 2 (2021), pp. 299-321
ISSN: 2162-3104 (Print), 2166-3750 (Online)
doi: 10.32674/jis.v11i2.2038
ojed.org/jis

The Differential Impact of Learning Experiences on International Student Satisfaction and Institutional Recommendation

Ravichandran Ammigan
University of Delaware, USA

John L. Dennis
University of Perugia, Italy

Elspeth Jones
Leeds Beckett University, UK

ABSTRACT

This research uses i-graduate's International Student Barometer to investigate whether overall satisfaction and institutional recommendation are influenced by student nationality and destination country, while controlling for the covariates of learning experiences. The result of our analysis is the identification of a conceptual framework for the differences between evaluations (reflecting satisfaction with an experience) and behavioral intentions (willingness to recommend that experience to others), and this important frame has consequences for how institutions recruit and retain international students. These results indicate that student nationality, destination country, and learning experience differentially influence both overall satisfaction and institutional recommendation. The study finds that student nationality and destination country significantly influenced both satisfaction and recommendation. While learning experience "teaching" variables ("program organization" and "quality of lectures") mattered most for overall satisfaction, "study" variables ("English language support" and "employability skills") were mainly associated with institutional recommendation. Practical implications for international educators and marketers are discussed, along with pointers for future research.

Keywords: international students, learning experience, learning recommendation, satisfaction surveys, student recruitment

INTRODUCTION

The enrollment of international students is a key target at national and institutional levels for economic, political, cultural, and academic reasons (de Wit, 2016; Roberts & Dunworth, 2012). Although they may be considered "transient visitors," international students form an integral part of their university's fabric (Montgomery, 2010) and, with a purposeful approach to integration and pedagogy (Leask, 2015), can facilitate the global and intercultural competence of domestic students, faculty, and staff (Irina et al., 2017). However, for these and other benefits to be realized, international student recruitment must be an increasing priority. To be successful in this endeavor, institutions must be strategic in incorporating international student perspectives, including what they value, how these values influence satisfaction, and how likely international students are to recommend the institution based on their experiences.

In this article, we explore whether learning experience variables, nationality, and destination country differentially influence students' satisfaction with their overall experience and willingness to recommend their institution to others, using data from the International Student Barometer (ISB; i-graduate, n.d.).

Before presenting the results, we define terms, then discuss international student learning experiences and the relationship between these and student satisfaction. Reflecting on the difference between recommendation and satisfaction then leads to consideration of the connection between institutional recommendation and student learning experiences.

LITERATURE REVIEW

Definitions of Key Terms

For international students, we use the Organisation for Economic Co-operation and Development's (2015) definition, which states, "International students are those who received their prior education in another country and are not residents of their current country of study."

For the present study, we use data from the ISB, which is said to be the world's leading benchmarking tool of international student satisfaction in higher education (Garrett, 2014). Based on the ISB instrument, and for this article, we define learning experiences as those which students experience within academic settings at their respective institutions, including the teaching, studies, services, and facilities used in their educational environment. Additionally, student satisfaction is defined as "a short-term attitude resulting from an evaluation of a student's educational experience" (Elliott & Healy, 2001, p. 2). We define institutional recommendation as students' willingness to recommend their current institution to prospective applicants, based on their experience at that institution.

Conceptual Framework

The difference between evaluations and behavioral intentions forms the framework for this article and acts as the basis for understanding how student learning experiences differentially influence satisfaction and recommendation. The literature on consumer behavior is thus a key starting point.

In a seminal paper, Cronin et al. (2000) studied the relationship between the core constructs of consumer evaluations (quality, value, satisfaction) and consumer behavioral intentions (e.g., recommendation). Their research demonstrated that quality (the relationship between expectations and performance) and value (the relationship between what was received and what was given) lead to satisfaction (whether something met or exceeded expectations). Together these three factors of quality, value, and satisfaction influence behavioral intentions—that is, a conscious plan to perform a specific behavior. Satisfaction, for this model, describes whether a consumer believes that a service evokes positive feelings (Rust & Oliver, 1994), while recommendation describes when consumers will say positive things about a service, and recommend that service (Babakus et al., 1987). Essentially, factors influencing satisfaction can differ from those that influence recommendation (Gajjar, 2013).

In research on the connection between institutional recommendation and satisfaction, Mavondo et al. (2004) suggested that satisfied students are more likely to engage in word-of-mouth recommendation to potential or future students. Similar results were found by Padlee and Reimers (2015). Yet, within the broader research area of customer satisfaction, studies demonstrate that not all satisfied customers recommend what they have purchased (Gounaris et al., 2010; Lobo et al., 2007). Importantly, this means that people can be satisfied with a product but still not be willing to recommend it. Recommendations, as behavioral intentions, are often crucially important when making purchase decisions (Hennig-Thurau et al., 2004; Zhu & Zhang, 2010). As such, they are pivotal for word-of-mouth recommendations in higher education (Arndt, 1967; Westbrook, 1987) and so, in terms of international student recruitment in particular, the distinction merits further consideration.

Cubillo et al. (2006) studied different factors influencing the decision-making processes when international students choose a destination country or an institution. They found five variables determining institutional choice: (a) work (postgraduation career prospects, opportunities to work while at the institution, recognition by future employers, and enhanced language skills); (b) institution (ranking, campus atmosphere, research opportunities, experience and expertise of faculty, quality of education, academic resources, and international contacts); (c) program of study (tuition costs, variety, and quality of courses); (d) host country (cost of living, visa procedures, social-life prospects); and (e) local setting (safety and security, social facilities, and the local environment).

As institutions of higher education face increasing competition to attract international students, factors influencing purchase decisions grow in importance, and understanding the difference between student evaluations and behavioral intentions is crucial. The former are possibly short-term and reflect satisfaction, quality, and value, while behavioral intentions reflect (amongst other things) willingness to recommend an institution.

Within the conceptual framework distinguishing satisfaction and recommendation, the goal of the present study is to investigate which international student learning experiences predict overall satisfaction and whether these differ from those that predict institutional recommendation, and as a function of student nationality or destination country.

International Student Learning Experiences

While research on conceptual models of student satisfaction has demonstrated relationships between quality, value, satisfaction, loyalty, and word-of-mouth recommendation (Alves & Raposo, 2007; Douglas et al., 2008; Padlee & Reimers, 2015), those models have largely not been applied to international students—despite growth in their numbers on university campuses (Institute of International Education, 2020). Additionally, the limited available literature on student satisfaction and learning focuses largely on domestic students (García-Aracil, 2009; Karemera et al., 2003; Umbach & Porter, 2002). Using the ISB allows examination of what influences satisfaction and institutional recommendation, and to do this both on a large scale and in a global context. Typically, 60,000–85,000 international students in over 30 countries complete the ISB each year. We were given access to an anonymized version of the resulting large-scale dataset. It is important to note that, although the ISB shares with participating institutions their own "results benchmarked against competitor groups, national and international indices" (i-graduate, n.d.), for confidentiality reasons, no individual institution is identified to others, nor named in the dataset made available for the current study.

Improving the experience for all students (including international students) is an important strategic priority at many higher education institutions (Baranova et al., 2011; Shah & Richardson, 2016). Coping with a new academic environment can be challenging for all students, and even more so for international students as they adapt to a new culture, and often to a language that is not their first (Andrade, 2006; Bista & Foster, 2016; Perrucci & Hu, 1995).

A range of factors exert a direct influence on the experience of international students in their academic, living, and social settings, and Jones (2017) grouped these into four categories or contexts: personal, familial, institutional, and national. Elsharnouby (2015), meanwhile, argued that student experiences are "commonly acknowledged" to be either at the core (centering around academic experiences) or supplementary levels, such as the physical environment, library facilities, educational technology, university layout, social environment, and campus climate.

Satisfaction and Student Learning Experiences

In the first comparative study to use ISB data, Ammigan and Jones (2018) investigated over 45,000 undergraduate, degree-seeking international students at

96 institutions in Australia, the United Kingdom, and the United States. Of the four dimensions of university experience studied (arrival, living, learning, and support services), learning was found to influence overall satisfaction the most. In an extension of the previous research, Ammigan (2019) found that overall student satisfaction predicted institutional recommendation and that learning experience was the most significant of the four dimensions for international students' willingness to recommend their institution to prospective applicants. These two studies provide a strong base for closely examining how different aspects of the learning environment influence satisfaction and recommendation. No prior research has used ISB data to determine this differential influence.

In earlier studies, Wiers-Jenssen et al. (2002) and Sahin (2014) found the quality of teaching, among other factors, to be an important determinant of student satisfaction. The relationship between student satisfaction and educational offerings at higher education institutions was also examined by Butt and Rehman (2010), who found that teacher expertise, quality of courses offered, learning environment, and classroom facilities all enhanced satisfaction. Asare-Nuamah (2017) concluded that library services, teacher contact, class size, course content, reading materials, and general administrative services were key to enhancing student experiences.

While these studies support different aspects as being influential in the student experience, the current research is unique in its large sample size, using data from the ISB, and its focus on the differential influence of various dimensions of the student learning experience on satisfaction and institutional recommendation.

METHOD

This study examines whether overall satisfaction and institutional recommendation are influenced by student nationality and destination country while controlling for learning experience variables for international students in 10 participating countries around the world. It was declared exempt from the requirements of human subject protection by the relevant institutional review board since nonidentifiable, pre-existing data was used for analysis.

Instrument

The ISB is administered by i-graduate, a United Kingdom–based company. It seeks to track and compare the decision-making, expectations, perceptions, intentions, and satisfaction of international students from application to graduation (i-graduate, n.d.). Since its inception in 2005, the ISB has gathered feedback from over 3 million students in more than 1,400 institutions across 33 countries (i-graduate, n.d.). The questionnaire measures international students' satisfaction in the arrival, learning, living, and support services dimensions of their experience by asking them to evaluate how satisfied they are with multiple aspects within each of these dimensions (i-graduate, n.d.). Two summary questions capture how international students evaluate their overall experience—

that is, satisfaction ("Overall, how satisfied are you with all aspects at [university name]") and institutional recommendation ("Based on your impressions at this stage of the year, would you recommend your university to other students thinking of applying here?"). The full questionnaire, consisting of 256 closed- and open-ended questions, has been refined through 18 cycles and, according to Brett (2013), is considered the industry gold standard for assessing the international student experience.

Variables

Independent Variables: Student Nationality and Destination Country

The two categorical independent variables—student nationality and destination country—were at 10 levels (or countries) each. Categorical variables consist of separate, indivisible, and distinct groups that take on values that are names or labels (Gravetter & Wallnau, 2013, p. 20). For student nationality (see Tables A1 and A2), the 10 most frequent home country nationalities in the ISB data were included: China, Malaysia, Germany, the United States, India, Singapore, Hong Kong, France, South Korea, and Italy. These students were hosted in one of 10 destination countries: Australia, Canada, Germany, Hong Kong, Ireland, Malaysia, Netherlands, Sweden, United Kingdom, and the United States (see Tables A1 and A3).

Dependent Variables: Overall Satisfaction and Institutional Recommendation

The two continuous dependent variables (see Table A1)—overall satisfaction and institutional recommendation—were both set to Likert scales, with the former being a 4-point scale, where 1 = *very dissatisfied*, 2 = *dissatisfied*, 3 = *satisfied*, and 4 = *very satisfied,* and the latter being a 5-point scale, where 1 = *actively discourage*, 2 = *discourage*, 3 = *neither encourage or discourage*, 4 = *encourage*, and 5 = *actively encourage*. Continuous variables are numeric variables that have an infinite number of possible values that fall between any two observed values (Gravetter & Wallnau, 2013).

Covariate Variables: Learning Experience Variables

A covariate is a continuous variable that is expected to change, vary, or correlate with the outcome variable of a study (Salkind, 2010). The 22 continuous covariate learning experience variables were grouped into three categories (see Table A1): teaching-related (11 in total); studies-related (six in total); and facilities-related (five in total). One variable, "satisfaction with laboratories," was removed from the analysis, as it had over 44% missing values (see Data Analysis for further discussion of this issue).

Participants

Our sample included 32,015 international students from the 10 most frequent home country nationalities in the ISB data. These students were hosted in one of 10 countries and had completed the online ISB questionnaire via email between September and December 2016. To ensure confidentiality, deidentified responses, without institutional identifiers, were made available to the researchers by i-graduate.

Table A2 indicates the distribution of 32,015 international students from the 10 most frequent home country nationalities. Table A3 indicates the distribution of institutions for the 10 most frequent destination countries. Table A4 indicates the demographic makeup of students who participated in this study.

Data Analysis

Testing for Outliers, Homoscedasticity, and Normality

Data analysis was planned in successive steps. The analysis focused on the 10 most frequent home country nationalities as this allowed us to retain most of our learning variables (see discussion below on missing values). This choice reduced the sample from 66,272 to 32,015. Before and after the next data analysis step, we used the generalized extreme studentized deviate test to detect outliers (Rosner, 1983), Bartlett's test for homoscedasticity (Snedecor & Cochran, 1989), and Shapiro-Wilk's test for normality (Shapiro & Wilk, 1965), with none being significant.

Dealing with Missing Values

The 23 learning variables as well as the overall institutional recommendation question were optional questions and, on average, items in our dataset had 18.35% missing values. Therefore, a missing values analysis was performed, and we found satisfaction with laboratories to have over 44% missing values. It was therefore removed from future analysis, reducing the number of learning variables to 22. Little's missing completely at random test (1988) was significant, $X^2(58{,}870, N = 32{,}015) = 74{,}717.39, p < .001$. To accommodate for nonrandom missing values, we performed an approximate Bayesian bootstrap hot-deck nearest neighbor imputation method (Andridge & Little, 2010; Demirtas et al., 2007). In this technique, missing values are replaced with observed values that reflect similar response characteristics. We completed subsequent analysis using imputed data derived from this method.

Our Model: Analysis of Covariance

The goal of this research was to determine whether overall satisfaction and institutional recommendation were differentially impacted by international students' home and destination countries and by learning experience variables. As the learning experiences are predicted to co-vary with overall satisfaction, we chose to run a stepwise analysis of covariance (ANCOVA) model as it offers both simplicity (i.e., as few regressors as possible) and fit (i.e., as many regressors as needed). With this model, variables are included in the model if they meet two significant levels, one for adding (set at .05) and one for removing (set at .10).

RESULTS

Overall Satisfaction and Student Nationality

A one-way stepwise ANCOVA model was conducted to determine the effect of student nationality on overall satisfaction while controlling for learning experience variables. The ANCOVA was significant, $F(23, 31{,}991) = 340.90$, $p < .0001$. In terms of learning experience covariates, 13 of 22 were found to significantly influence overall satisfaction with program organization doing so the most, followed by quality of lectures and English language support. Grading criteria was found to be negatively associated with overall satisfaction, meaning that as satisfaction with grading criteria increased, overall satisfaction decreased (see Table 1). The adjusted R^2 for the goodness of fit indicates that about 20% of the variance in overall satisfaction is explained by our independent and covariate variables. Among the explanatory variables, based on the Type III sum of squares, student nationality was the most influential.

Table 1: ANCOVA Results of Overall Satisfaction as a Function of Student Nationality and Learning Experience Covariates

Source	*df*	*SS*	*MS*	*F*	*Pr > F*
Student nationality	9.00	184.73	20.53	64.06	0.000
Program organization	1.00	77.02	77.02	240.38	0.000
Quality of lectures	1.00	39.84	39.84	124.33	0.000
English language support	1.00	35.57	35.57	111.02	0.000
Expertise of faculty	1.00	20.27	20.27	63.25	0.000
Academic and program content	1.00	18.76	18.76	58.56	0.000
Physical library	1.00	17.15	17.15	53.53	0.000
Learning support	1.00	14.88	14.88	46.44	0.000
Employability skills	1.00	11.13	11.13	34.74	0.000
Quality of classrooms	1.00	9.28	9.28	28.96	0.000
Multicultural study environment	1.00	5.76	5.76	17.97	0.000
Teaching ability of faculty	1.00	5.21	5.21	16.25	0.000
Work experience during studies	1.00	3.60	3.60	11.25	0.001
Assessment of coursework	1.00	3.44	3.44	10.73	0.001
Grading criteria	1.00	1.61	1.61	5.00	0.025

Note. df = degrees of freedom; *SS* = sum of squares; *MS* = mean squares; *F* = *F* ratio; *Pr* > *F* = *p* value for *F* statistic.

Students holding nationalities from six different countries, all in Asia, had a significant influence on overall satisfaction (see Figure 1 for mean overall satisfaction by student nationality).

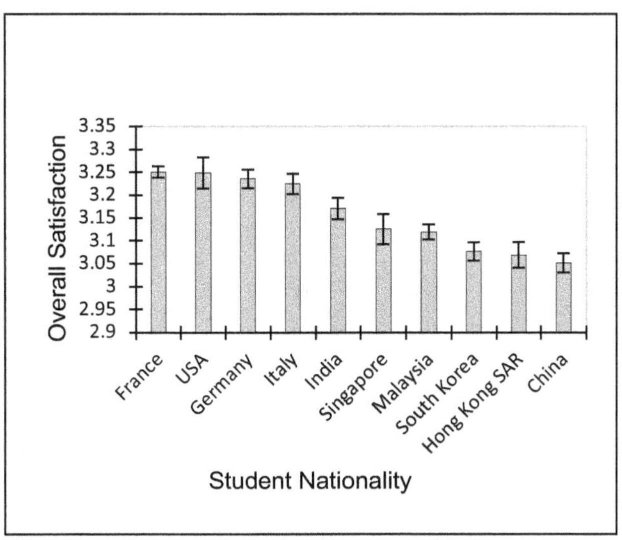

Figure 1: Student Nationality and Overall Satisfaction

Overall Satisfaction and Destination Country

A one-way stepwise ANCOVA model was conducted to determine the effect of destination country on overall satisfaction while controlling for learning experience variables. The ANCOVA was significant, $F(23, 31{,}991) = 308.47$, $p < .0001$. In terms of learning experience covariates, 15 of 22 were found to significantly influence overall satisfaction with program organization doing so the most, followed by English language support and quality of lectures. Grading criteria was found to be negatively associated with overall satisfaction, meaning that as satisfaction with grading criteria increased, overall satisfaction decreased (see Table 2). The adjusted R^2 for the goodness of fit indicates that about 19% of the variance in overall satisfaction is explained by our independent and covariate variables. Among the explanatory variables, based on the Type III sum of squares, program organization was the most influential.

Students enrolled in universities in four of the 10 countries—Ireland, Sweden, United Kingdom, and the Netherlands—significantly influenced overall satisfaction (see Figure 2 for mean overall satisfaction by destination country).

Table 2: ANCOVA Results of Overall Satisfaction as a Function of Destination Country and Learning Experience Covariates

Source	*df*	*SS*	*MS*	*F*	*Pr > F*
Program organization	1.00	74.63	74.61	230.35	0.000
Destination country	9.00	67.16	7.46	23.03	0.000
English language support	1.00	43.28	43.28	133.58	0.000
Quality of lectures	1.00	37.21	37.21	114.85	0.000
Expertise of faculty	1.00	28.76	28.76	88.77	0.000
Academic and program content	1.00	17.32	17.32	53.46	0.000
Physical library	1.00	17.08	17.08	52.72	0.000
Learning support	1.00	14.36	14.36	44.33	0.000
Multicultural study environment	1.00	12.31	12.31	38.01	0.000
Quality of classrooms	1.00	12.10	12.10	37.34	0.000
Employability skills	1.00	10.52	10.52	32.46	0.000
Grading criteria	1.00	4.44	4.44	13.69	0.000
Teaching ability of faculty	1.00	3.01	3.01	9.30	0.002
Assessment of coursework	1.00	2.02	2.02	6.23	0.013
English of academic staff	1.00	1.55	1.55	4.79	0.029
Work experience during studies	1.00	1.38	1.38	4.27	0.039

Note. df = degrees of freedom; *SS* = sum of squares; *MS* = mean squares; *F* = *F* ratio; *Pr* > *F* = *p* value for *F* statistic.

Institutional Recommendation and Student Nationality

A one-way stepwise ANCOVA model was conducted to determine the effect of student nationality on institutional recommendation while controlling for learning experience variables. The ANCOVA was significant, $F(24, 31{,}990) = 311.22$, $p < .0001$. In terms of learning experience covariates, 15 of 22 were found to significantly influence overall satisfaction with English language support doing so the most, followed by employability skills and multicultural study environment. Performance feedback and multicultural study environment were found to be negatively associated with institutional recommendation, meaning that as satisfaction with these variables increased, institutional recommendation decreased (see Table 3). The adjusted R^2 for the goodness of fit indicates that about 19% of the variance in overall satisfaction is explained by our independent and covariate variables. Among the explanatory variables, based on the Type III sum of squares, student nationality is the most influential.

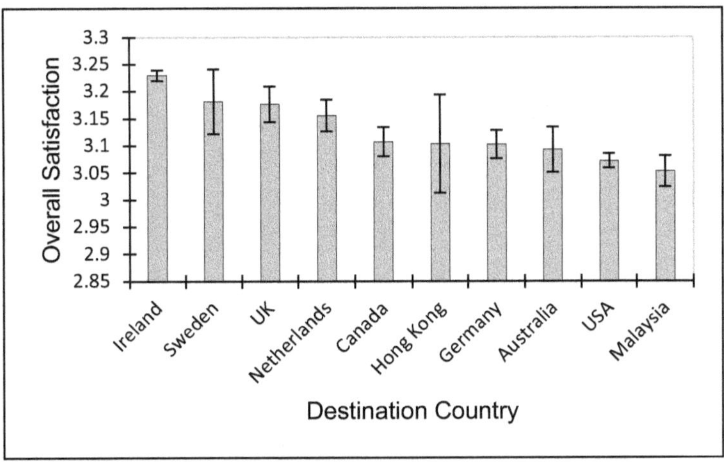

Figure 2: Destination Country and Overall Satisfaction

Table 3: ANCOVA Results of Institutional Recommendation as a Function of Student Nationality and Learning Experience Covariates

Source	*DF*	*SS*	*MS*	*F*	*Pr* > *F*
Student nationality	9.00	410.37	45.60	80.26	0.000
English language support	1.00	193.24	193.24	340.14	0.000
Employability skills	1.00	106.70	106.70	187.82	0.000
Multicultural study environment	1.00	100.90	100.90	177.61	0.000
Academic and program content	1.00	72.59	72.59	127.77	0.000
Program organization	1.00	52.47	52.47	92.37	0.000
Quality of lectures	1.00	35.95	35.95	63.28	0.000
Learning support	1.00	20.97	20.97	36.91	0.000
Expertise of faculty	1.00	20.83	20.83	36.66	0.000
Virtual learning	1.00	16.64	16.64	29.29	0.000
Physical library	1.00	14.72	14.72	25.91	0.000
Assessment of coursework	1.00	11.11	11.11	19.55	0.000
Classroom technology	1.00	9.19	9.19	16.18	0.000
Quality of classrooms	1.00	8.54	8.54	15.04	0.000
Performance feedback	1.00	8.10	8.10	14.26	0.000
Teaching ability of faculty	1.00	6.88	6.88	12.12	0.001

Note. *DF* = degrees of freedom; *SS* = sum of squares; *MS* = mean squares; *F* = *F* ratio; *Pr* > *F* = *p* value for *F* statistic.

Students holding nationalities from six different countries, all in Asia, had a significant influence on institutional recommendation (see Figure 3 for mean recommendation responses by student nationality).

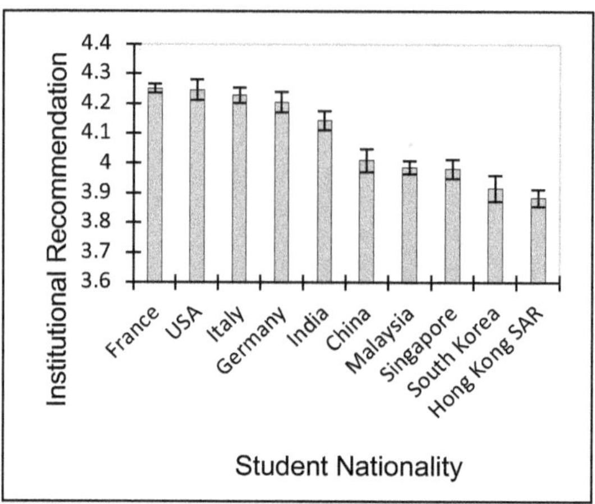

Figure 3: Student Nationality and Institutional Recommendation

Institutional Recommendation and Destination Country

A one-way stepwise ANCOVA model was conducted to determine the effect of destination country on institutional recommendation while controlling for learning experience variables. The ANCOVA was significant, $F(24, 31{,}990) = 294.58, p < .0001$. In terms of learning experience covariates, 15 of 22 were found to significantly influence overall satisfaction with English language support doing so the most, followed by employability skills and multicultural study environment. Performance feedback and multicultural study environment were found to be negatively associated with institutional recommendation, meaning that as satisfaction with these variables increased, institutional recommendation decreased (see Table 4). The adjusted R^2 for the goodness of fit indicates that about 18% of the variance in overall satisfaction is explained by our independent and covariate variables. Among the explanatory variables, based on the Type III sum of squares, institution country is the most influential.

Students enrolled in universities in all of the ten countries, excluding Malaysia, Australia, and the United States, significantly influenced institutional recommendation (see Figure 4 for mean recommendation responses by destination country).

Table 4: ANCOVA Results of Institutional Recommendation as a Function of Destination Country and Learning Experience Covariates

Source	*df*	*SS*	*MS*	*F*	*Pr > F*
Institution country	9.00	224.53	24.95	43.47	0.000
English language support	1.00	221.06	221.06	385.19	0.000
Employability skills	1.00	95.85	95.85	167.00	0.000
Multicultural study environment	1.00	77.78	77.78	135.53	0.000
Academic and program content	1.00	70.00	69.99	121.95	0.000
Program organization	1.00	52.78	52.78	91.96	0.000
Quality of lectures	1.00	32.40	32.40	56.46	0.000
Expertise of faculty	1.00	29.10	29.10	50.71	0.000
Learning support	1.00	23.71	23.71	41.32	0.000
Physical library	1.00	15.79	15.79	27.50	0.000
Quality of classrooms	1.00	15.34	15.34	26.74	0.000
Performance feedback	1.00	13.43	13.43	23.41	0.000
Virtual learning	1.00	12.58	12.58	21.91	0.000
Classroom technology	1.00	10.77	10.76	18.75	0.000
Assessment of coursework	1.00	8.19	8.18	14.26	0.000
Teaching ability of faculty	1.00	5.93	5.93	10.32	0.001

Note. df = degrees of freedom; *SS* = sum of squares; *MS* = mean squares; *F* = *F* ratio; *Pr > F* = *p* value for *F* statistic.

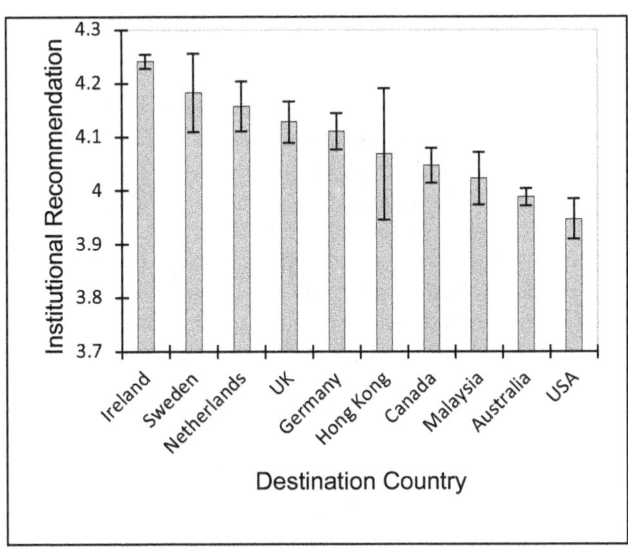

Figure 4: Destination Country and Institutional Recommendation

DISCUSSION

The framing concept for this article is that satisfaction with an experience does not necessarily result in a willingness to recommend it. Findings with our international student sample confirm this and, moreover, that different learning experience variables influence satisfaction and recommendation. Results also show variation by student nationality and destination country. The following discussion explains the findings in more detail.

Overall Satisfaction

When considering overall satisfaction with their institution, international students value teaching-related variables the most of learning experience variables (see Table 2). Indeed, eight of the 14 learning variables influencing overall satisfaction were in this category. Since students spend a good amount of their time in classes while at the university, the influence of teaching-related variables on overall satisfaction is perhaps unsurprising. These findings add detail to previous research (Ammigan & Jones, 2018; Butt & Rehman, 2010; Elsharnouby, 2015; Sahin, 2014; Wiers-Jenssen et al., 2002), which indicated various aspects of teaching as important determinants of student satisfaction.

In terms of student nationality, it was interesting that students from the Asian countries in our sample gave relatively lower satisfaction ratings than others. This echoes previous research in healthcare, which found lower levels of satisfaction among Asian respondents and those of Asian descent, reportedly due to different response tendencies or cultural norms rather than differences in experience (Brédart et al., 2007; Hung et al., 2016; Saha & Hickam, 2003).

Recommendation

For institutional recommendation, learning experience variables described as studies are what international students value the most (see Table 6), particularly English language support and employability skills. The significant predictive power of employability skills on institutional recommendation is consistent with Cubillo et al.'s (2006) findings that career prospects and opportunities to work during a program of study were significant factors in influencing international student decision-making during university selection. It is important to note that English language skills represent a key factor in communication, one of the most important elements of employability, and so these two variables are closely linked.

Two facilities variables, virtual learning and classroom technology, significantly influenced institutional recommendation but failed to influence overall satisfaction. This is in line with our conceptual framework and echoes findings that factors influencing satisfaction can differ from those influencing recommendation (Gajjar, 2013; Ghorbanzade et al., 2019).

Satisfaction Compared with Recommendation

It is worth reflecting on the finding that a multicultural study environment positively predicts overall satisfaction but negatively predicts recommendation. Previous research (Arkoudis et al., 2013; Williams & Johnson, 2011; Yu et al., 2016) has indicated that cross-cultural perspectives and intercultural friendships are highly rewarding experiences for international students, although making friends with local students may be difficult (Hendrickson et al., 2011; Montgomery & McDowell, 2009; Rienties & Nolan, 2014). While students might appreciate the resources, engagement opportunities, and other efforts institutions put in place to ensure a diverse and multicultural setting on campus, it can still be stressful adjusting to new academic, social, and cultural environments (Bastien et al., 2018; Mesidor & Sly, 2016). Cultural differences can present challenges and, reflecting upon these experiences, students might be less inclined to recommend them to others.

Teaching variables predicted overall satisfaction more than studies or facilities variables, but this was not the case for recommendation, where learning variables classed as studies predicted willingness to recommend the institution. Once more, this important difference is in line with our conceptual framework, endorsing research by Cronin et al. (2000) that recommendations are fundamentally different from satisfaction judgments. Student recommendations are influenced by evaluations of quality and value as well as satisfaction. The fact that employability skills influenced institutional recommendation almost twice as much as overall satisfaction, could mean future employment considerations are regarded as important indicators of value (Cronin et al., 2000).

Another possible explanation for the predictive power of employability on satisfaction and recommendation lies in healthcare research. Tung and Chang (2009) demonstrated that the interpersonal skills of healthcare providers are important for overall satisfaction, but to go beyond this to recommendation, it is technical skills that are key. Employability skills might thus be regarded as equivalent to those technical skills, which institutions must provide to go beyond student satisfaction to institutional recommendation.

Implications

The global market for attracting and retaining talented international students has become increasingly competitive. But the unprecedented challenges brought by the COVID-19 pandemic mean the future of international exchange and student mobility is at stake, with substantial disruptions caused by campus closures, travel restrictions, remote learning due to health and safety concerns, and suspensions in visa issuance. It is unlikely that universities will resume their complete schedule of face-to-face classes in the near future and, thus, significant declines in international student numbers are expected. This will undoubtedly intensify the competition in student recruitment, once institutions resume their academic operations and students can travel safely again. It is therefore even more critical that universities remain focused on their marketing and admissions goals and, at the same time, strategically incorporate student perspectives at all levels of their operations so that innovative learning practices and adequate support services are implemented to enhance students' curricular and co-curricular experiences.

This study's findings—that different learning experiences influence satisfaction and recommendation—offer some pointers to support these recruitment goals. Specifically, the learning environment is crucial for international student satisfaction, whereas longer term issues related to communication skills and future employment are critical in their willingness to recommend. Employment-related successes, such as job placement rates, average salaries, and work-related experiences during studies should, therefore, be an increasing focus of institutional policy, and highlighted to prospective students.

The study also has important implications for how universities recruit, train, and retain faculty who can deliver high-quality, content-rich courses. Courses and curricula suitable for a diverse student population are of increasing importance, and there must be a focus on learning and teaching across cultures in delivering and assessing them (Carroll, 2015; Leask, 2015; Leask & Carroll, 2013). Furthermore, institutional leaders, human resource professionals, educational developers, and those involved in student recruitment efforts, must understand that teaching variables, like "program organization" and "quality of lectures" are fundamentally important for both satisfaction and recommendation. Policy, strategy, and practice should reflect this, with intentional showcasing of the institution's academic strengths when working with prospective students. These may include students' on-program experiences, achievements, and personal stories focusing on the teaching variables that significantly influence satisfaction.

The overwhelming importance of the learning and teaching environment is a vital finding for student retention strategies, requiring a constant drive to assess and improve quality. Previous research by Ammigan and Jones (2018) demonstrated that of the four ISB categories of arrival, living, learning, and support services, learning variables were paramount for student satisfaction, and the present study confirms this. Intentional showcasing of teaching quality, expertise of lecturers, academic content, and course organization will also be valuable for student recruitment.

Finally, from a support services standpoint, institutions should consider placing greater emphasis on those programs and services that help enhance the learning experiences and future employment of international students.

Limitations and Future Research

Every research project has its limitations and while using the ISB results produced a large, global dataset, it is nevertheless a self-report questionnaire. As with all such questionnaires, social desirability bias and positivity bias could have influenced responses (Fisher, 1993; King & Bruner, 2000). In a more qualitative study, techniques such as movement pattern analysis could be used to complement self-reporting (Connors et al., 2016).

The ISB focuses primarily on degree-seeking, on-campus international undergraduate students, so generalizing the findings beyond this group is another limitation. Generalizability is limited further by the fact that approximately 65% of those included in the study were at either Australian or United Kingdom institutions.

Perceptions of value should also be mentioned as a limitation and an area for future research. Spencer-Oatey and Dauber (2019) noted that many questionnaires measure international student satisfaction on Likert scales, arguing that these are problematic since students could be highly satisfied with an experience and yet not value it. Spencer-Oatey and Dauber (2019) overcame this by asking students to evaluate the importance of an experience indicator before evaluating the experience itself, resulting in an intersection between the two. Consideration of Kano et al.'s (1984) importance–satisfaction model, developed to measure customer expectations, might also be worthwhile in future research on student satisfaction, and how institutions could in turn adjust services and resources to enhance the international student experience.

Another limitation is that, in general, fewer people respond to questions regarding recommendations than about their overall satisfaction (Cheng et al., 2003). This study showed the same effect, with around 8% of respondents who had completed all the satisfaction questions failing to answer the single question about institutional recommendation.

CONCLUSION

Using a large dataset from the ISB, this article offers insight into the difference between student evaluations, reflecting satisfaction, and behavioral intentions, representing international students' willingness to recommend an institution. It identifies the different variables influencing each and supports the argument that the learning environment is crucially important for satisfaction, whereas longer term, employment-related issues are fundamentally important for recommendation. The study offers targeted strategic advice for institutional policy and practice, and for enhancing recruitment and retention of international students, while suggesting pointers for further research in this important area.

Note

Appendices for this article can be found on the JIS website at https://www.ojed.org/index.php/jis

REFERENCES

Alves, H., & Raposo, M. (2007). Conceptual model of student satisfaction in higher education. *Total Quality Management and Business Excellence*, *18*(5), 571–588. https://doi.org/10.1080/14783360601074315

Ammigan, R. (2019). Institutional satisfaction and recommendation: What really matters to international students? *Journal of International Students*, *9*(1), 253–272. https://doi.org/10.32674/jis.v9i1.260

Ammigan, R., & Jones, E. (2018). Improving the student experience: Learning from a comparative study of international student satisfaction. *Journal of Studies in International Education*, *22*(4), 283–301. https://doi.org/10.1177/1028315318773137

Andrade, M. S. (2006). International students in English-speaking universities: Adjustment factors. *Journal of Research in International Education*, *5*(2), 131–154. https://doi.org/10.1177/1475240906065589

Andridge, R. R., & Little, R. J. A. (2010, April). A review of hot deck imputation for survey non-response. *International Statistical Review*, *78*, 40–64. https://doi.org/10.1111/j.1751-5823.2010.00103.x

Arkoudis, S., Watty, K., Baik, C., Yu, X., Borland, H., Chang, S., Lang, I., Lang, J., & Pearce, A. (2013). Finding common ground: Enhancing interaction between domestic and international students in higher education. *Teaching in Higher Education*, *18*(3), 222–235. https://doi.org/10.1080/13562517.2012.719156

Arndt, J. (1967). Role of product-related conversations in the diffusion of a new product. *Journal of Marketing Research*, *4*(3), 291–295. https://doi.org/10.2307/3149462

Asare-Nuamah, P. (2017). International students' satisfaction: Assessing the determinants of satisfaction. *Higher Education for the Future*, *4*(1), 44–59. https://doi.org/10.1177/2347631116681213

Babakus, E., Ferguson, C. E., & Joreskog, K. G. (1987). The sensitivity of confirmatory maximum likelihood factor analysis to violations of measurement scale and distributional assumptions. *Journal of Marketing Research*, *24*(2), 222–228. https://doi.org/10.2307/3151512

Baranova, P., Morrison, S., & Mutton, J. (2011). Enhancing the student experience through service design: The University of Derby approach. *Perspectives: Policy and Practice in Higher Education, 15*(4), 122–128. https://doi.org/10.1080/13603108.2011.599883

Bastien, G., Seifen-Adkins, T., & Johnson, L. R. (2018). Striving for success: Academic adjustment of international students in the U.S. *Journal of International Students*, *8*(2), 1198–1219. https://doi.org/10.5281/zenodo.1250421

Bista, K., & Foster, C. (2016). *Exploring the social and academic experiences of international students in higher education institutions*. IGI Global.

Brédart, A., Coens, C., Aaronson, N., Chie, W. C., Efficace, F., Conroy, T., Blazeby, J. M., Hammerlid, E., Costantini, M., Joly, F., Schraub, S., Sezer, O., Arraras, J. I., Rodary, C., Constantini, A., Mehlitz, M., Razavi, D., & Bottomley, A. (2007). Determinants of patient satisfaction in oncology settings from European and Asian countries: Preliminary results based on the EORTC IN-PATSAT32 questionnaire. *European Journal of Cancer*, *43*(2), 323–330. https://doi.org/10.1016/j.ejca.2006.10.016

Brett, K. J. (2013). *Making the most of your International Student Barometer data : A guide to good practice.* https://www.i-graduate.org/assets/2012-Making-the-Most-of-ISB-Data.pdf

Butt, B. Z., & Rehman, K. U. (2010). A study examining the students satisfaction in higher education. *Procedia - Social and Behavioral Sciences, 2*, 5446–5450. https://doi.org/10.1016/j.sbspro.2010.03.888

Carroll, J. (2015). *Tools for teaching in an educationally mobile world.* Routledge.

Cheng, S. H., Yang, M. C., & Chiang, T. L. (2003). Patient satisfaction with and recommendation of a hospital: Effects of interpersonal and technical aspects of hospital care. *International Journal for Quality in Health Care, 15*(4), 345–355. https://doi.org/10.1093/intqhc/mzg045

Connors, B. L., Rende, R., & Colton, T. J. (2016). Beyond self-report: Emerging methods for capturing individual differences in decision-making process. *Frontiers in Psychology, 7*. https://doi.org/10.3389/fpsyg.2016.00312

Cronin, J. J., Brady, M. K., & Hult, G. T. M. (2000). Assessing the effects of quality, value, and customer satisfaction on consumer behavioral intentions in service environments. *Journal of Retailing, 76*(2), 193–218. https://doi.org/10.1016/S0022-4359(00)00028-2

Cubillo, J. M., Sánchez, J., & Cerviño, J. (2006). International students' decision-making process. *International Journal of Educational Management, 20*(2), 101–115. https://doi.org/10.1108/09513540610646091

de Wit, H. (2016). Foreward. In K. Bista & C. Foster (Eds.), *Exploring the social and academic experiences of international students in higher education institutions.* IGI Global.

Demirtas, H., Arguelles, L. M., Chung, H., & Hedeker, D. (2007). On the performance of bias-reduction techniques for variance estimation in approximate Bayesian bootstrap imputation. *Computational Statistics and Data Analysis, 51*(8), 4064–4068. https://doi.org/10.1016/j.csda.2006.12.047

Douglas, J., McClelland, R., & Davies, J. (2008). The development of a conceptual model of student satisfaction with their experience in higher education. *Quality Assurance in Education, 16*(1), 19–35. https://doi.org/10.1108/09684880810848396

Elliott, K. M., & Healy, M. A. (2001). Key factors influencing student satisfaction related to recruitment and retention. *Journal of Marketing for Higher Education, 10*(4), 1–11. https://doi.org/10.1300/J050v10n04_01

Elsharnouby, T. H. (2015). Student co-creation behavior in higher education: The role of satisfaction with the university experience. *Journal of Marketing for Higher Education, 25*(2), 238–262. https://doi.org/10.1080/08841241.2015.1059919

Fisher, R. J. (1993). Social desirability bias and the validity of indirect questioning. *Journal of Consumer Research, 20*(2), 303–315. https://doi.org/10.1086/209351

Gajjar, N. B. (2013). Factors affecting consumer behavior. *International Journal of Research in Humanities, 1*(2), 10–15.

García-Aracil, A. (2009). European graduates' level of satisfaction with higher education. *Higher Education*, *57*(1), 1–21. https://doi.org/10.1007/s10734-008-9121-9

Garrett, R. (2014). Explaining international student satisfaction: Insights from the International Student Barometer. Retrieved August 15, 2016, from https://www.i-graduate.org/assets/2014-Explaining-Satisfaction.pdf

Ghorbanzade, D., Mehrani, H., & Rahehagh, A. (2019). The effect of experience quality on behavioral intentions of domestic tourists in visiting water parks. *Cogent Business and Management*, *6*(1). https://doi.org/10.1080/23311975.2019.1580843

Gounaris, S., Dimitriadis, S., & Stathakopoulos, V. (2010). An examination of the effects of service quality and satisfaction on customers' behavioral intentions in e-shopping. *Journal of Services Marketing*, *24*(2), 142–156. https://doi.org/10.1108/08876041011031118

Gravetter, F. J., & Wallnau, L. B. (2013). *Statistics for the behavioral sciences. Statistics for the behavioral sciences* (9th ed.). Wadsworth.

Hendrickson, B., Rosen, D., & Aune, R. K. (2011). An analysis of friendship networks, social connectedness, homesickness, and satisfaction levels of international students. *International Journal of Intercultural Relations*, *35*(3), 281–295. https://doi.org/10.1016/J.IJINTREL.2010.08.001

Hennig-Thurau, T., Gwinner, K. P., Walsh, G., & Gremler, D. D. (2004). Electronic word-of-mouth via consumer-opinion platforms: What motivates consumers to articulate themselves on the Internet? *Journal of Interactive Marketing*, *18*(1), 38–52. https://doi.org/10.1002/dir.10073

Hung, L. W., Gillespie, K., Liang, S., Schwartz, R., Chung, S., & Halley, M. C. (2016). Understanding Asian patients' lower satisfaction with health care. *Journal of Patient-Centered Research and Reviews*, *3*(3), 179–180. https://doi.org/10.17294/2330-0698.1302

i-graduate. (n.d.). *International Student Barometer*. Retrieved March 5, 2019, from https://www.i-graduate.org/services/international-student-barometer/

Institute of International Education. (2020). *Open Doors Report*. Retrieved February 13, 2020, from https://www.iie.org/Research-and-Insights/Open-Doors/Data/International-Students/Enrollment

Irina, S., Gregg, T., & Martha, M. (2017). Fostering global competence through internationalization at American research universities. *Research & Occasional Paper Series*. https://publications.hse.ru/en/preprints/211232094

Jones, E. (2017). Problematising and reimagining the notion of 'international student experience.' *Studies in Higher Education*, *42*(5), 933–943. https://doi.org/10.1080/03075079.2017.1293880

Kano, N., Seraku, N., Takahashi, F., & Tsuji, S. (1984). Attractive quality and must-be quality. *Journal of the Japanese Society for Quality Control*, *14*(2), 39–48.

Karemera, D., Reuben, L., & Sillah, M. (2003). The effects of academic environment and background characteristics on student satisfaction and performance: The case of South Carolina State University's School of Business. *College Student Journal*, *37*(2), 298–309.

King, M. F., & Bruner, G. C. (2000). Social desirability bias: A neglected aspect of validity testing. *Psychology and Marketing*, *17*(2), 79–103.

Leask, B. (2015). *Internationalizing the curriculum*. Routledge.

Leask, B., & Carroll, J. (2013). *Learning and teaching across cultures. Good practice principles and quick guides*. International Education Association of Australia. https://www.ieaa.org.au/documents/item/397

Little, R. J. A. (1988). A test of missing completely at random for multivariate data with missing values. *Journal of the American Statistical Association*, *83*(404), 1198–1202. https://doi.org/10.1080/01621459.1988.10478722

Lobo, A., Maritz, A., & Mehta, S. (2007). Enhancing Singapore travel agencies' customer loyalty: An empirical investigation of customers' behavioural intentions and zones of tolerance. *International Journal of Tourism Research*, *9*(6), 485–495. https://doi.org/10.1002/jtr.619

Mavondo, F. T., Tsarenko, Y., & Gabbott, M. (2004). International and local student satisfaction: Resources and capabilities perspective. *Journal of Marketing for Higher Education*, *14*(1), 41–60. https://doi.org/10.1300/J050v14n01_03

Mesidor, J. K., & Sly, K. F. (2016). Factors that contribute to the adjustment of international students. *Journal of International Students*, *6*(1), 262–282.

Montgomery, C. (2010). *Understanding the international student experience*. Macmillan International Higher Education.

Montgomery, C., & McDowell, L. (2009). Social networks and the international student experience. *Journal of Studies in International Education*, *13*(4), 455–466. https://doi.org/10.1177/1028315308321994

Organisation for Economic Co-operation and Development. (2015). *Education indicators in focus*. http://www.oecd-ilibrary.org/education/education-at-a-glance-2015_eag-2015-en;jsessionid=5ifbrtjg0urmg.x-oecd-live-02

Padlee, S. F., & Reimers, V. (2015). International student satisfaction with, and behavioural intentions towards, universities in Victoria. *Journal of Marketing for Higher Education*, *25*(1), 70–84. https://doi.org/10.1080/08841241.2015.1042098

Perrucci, R., & Hu, H. (1995). Satisfaction with social and educational experiences among international graduate students. *Research in Higher Education, 36,* 491–508. https://doi.org/10.1007/BF02207908

Rienties, B., & Nolan, E.-M. (2014). Understanding friendship and learning networks of international and host students using longitudinal Social Network Analysis. *International Journal of Intercultural Relations*, *41*, 165–180. https://doi.org/10.1016/j.ijintrel.2013.12.003

Roberts, P., & Dunworth, K. (2012). Staff and student perceptions of support services for international students in higher education: A case study. *Journal of Higher Education Policy and Management*, *34*(5), 517–528.

Rosner, B. (1983). Percentage points for a generalized ESD many-outlier procedure. *Technometrics*, *25*(2), 165–172. https://doi.org/10.1080/00401706.1983.10487848

Rust, R. T., & Oliver, R. L. (1994). Service quality: Insights and managerial implications from the frontier. In R. T. Rust & R. L. Oliver (Eds.), *Service quality: New directions in theory and practice* (pp. 1–20). SAGE.

Saha, S., & Hickam, D. H. (2003). Explaining low ratings of patient satisfaction among Asian-Americans. *American Journal of Medical Quality*, *18*(6), 256–264. https://doi.org/10.1177/106286060301800606

Sahin, O. (2014). An investigation of student satisfaction factors. *Journal of Research in Business and Management*, *2*(6), 8–12.

Salkind, N. J. (2010). *Encyclopedia of research design*. SAGE. doi:10.4135/9781412961288

Shah, M., & Richardson, J. T. E. (2016). Is the enhancement of student experience a strategic priority in Australian universities? *Higher Education Research and Development*, *35*(2), 352–364. https://doi.org/10.1080/07294360.2015.1087385

Shapiro, S. S., & Wilk, M. B. (1965). An analysis of variance test for normality (complete samples). *Biometrika*, *52*(3–4), 591–611. https://doi.org/10.2307/2333709

Snedecor, G., & Cochran, W. (1989). Statistical methods. In *Statistical methods* (8th ed.). Iowa State University Press.

Spencer-Oatey, H., & Dauber, D. (2019). Internationalisation and student diversity: how far are the opportunity benefits being perceived and exploited? *Higher Education*, *78*(6), 1035–1058. https://doi.org/10.1007/s10734-019-00386-4

Tung, Y.-C., & Chang, G.-M. (2009). Patient satisfaction with and recommendation of a primary care provider: Associations of perceived quality and patient education. *International Journal for Quality in Health Care*, *21*(3), 206–213. https://doi.org/10.1093/intqhc/mzp006

Umbach, P. D., & Porter, S. R. (2002). How do academic departments impact student satisfaction? Understanding the contextual effects of departments. *Research in Higher Education*, *43*(2), 209–234. https://doi.org/10.1023/A:1014471708162

Westbrook, R. A. (1987). Product/consumption-based affective responses and postpurchase processes. *Journal of Marketing Research*, *24*(3), 258–270. https://doi.org/10.2307/3151636

Wiers-Jenssen, J., Stensaker, B., & Grøgaard, J. B. (2002). Student satisfaction: Towards an empirical deconstruction of the concept. *Quality in Higher Education*, *8*(2), 183–195. https://doi.org/10.1080/1353832022000004377

Williams, C. T., & Johnson, L. R. (2011). Why can't we be friends? Multicultural attitudes and friendships with international students. *International Journal of Intercultural Relations*, *35*(1), 41–48. https://doi.org/10.1016/j.ijintrel.2010.11.001

Yu, X., Isensee, E., & Kappler, B. (2016). Using data wisely to improve international student satisfaction: Insights gained from International Student Barometer. In K. Bista & C. Foster (Eds.), *Exploring the social and academic experiences of international students in higher education institutions* (pp. 212–232). IGI Global.

Zhu, F., & Zhang, X. (Michael). (2010). Impact of online consumer reviews on sales: The moderating role of product and consumer characteristics. *Journal of Marketing*, *76*(2), 133–148. https://doi.org/10.1509/jmkg.74.2.133

RAVICHANDRAN AMMIGAN, PhD, is Associate Deputy Provost for International Programs and Assistant Professor of Education at the University of Delaware. His primary research focuses on the international student experience at institutions of higher education globally. Email: rammigan@udel.edu

JOHN L. DENNIS, PhD, is an affiliated professor with the Centre for Higher Education Internationalisation, Università Cattolica del Sacro Cuore, an adjunct professor at the University of Perugia, and a visiting professor at John Cabot University. As a behavioral scientist, he does research on how people intentionally influence their lives and behavior. Email: john.dennis@unipg.it

ELSPETH JONES is emerita professor of the Internationalisation of Higher Education, Leeds Beckett University UK, and honorary visiting fellow and member of the Scientific Committee, Centre for Higher Education Internationalisation (CHEI), Università Cattolica del Sacro Cuore, Milan. She has published widely and is editor of the book series, *Internationalization in Higher Education* (Routledge). Email: ej@elspethjones.com

Peer-Reviewed Article

© *Journal of International Students*
Volume 11, Issue 2 (2021), pp. 322-340
ISSN: 2162-3104 (Print), 2166-3750 (Online)
doi: 10.32674/jis.v11i2.1640
ojed.org/jis

"Come Join Us and Lose Your Accent!" Accent Modification Courses as Hierarchization of International Students

Johanna Ennser-Kananen
Mia Halonen
Taina Saarinen
University of Jyväskylä, Finland

ABSTRACT

In this article, we examine the hierarchization of international students by bringing together perspectives of linguistic legitimacy and language ideologies. Our data stems from 26 accent reduction or accent modification course descriptions and websites from U.S. universities. Based on their analysis, we discuss the sociopolitical implications of the phenomenon of these courses for international students and the ways in which language-based, particularly accent-based, arguments are used to create or reinforce different categories of students. We argue that while international students are presented as having different kinds of "comprehensibility problems" that accent modification and reduction courses are claimed to remedy, the seemingly linguistic arguments that are used for marketing do not hold. Rather, what is presented as an accent issue actually seems to be an ideological one, drawing on the students' ethnic or geographical origins, and thereby racializing the question of language proficiency.

Keywords: accent, international study, language ideology, student hierarchization

> This course is designed for high-level non-native speakers of English who want to modify their accent and increase their confidence in a variety of speaking situations. —*College A*

In order to study internationally, students generally need to have command of the language(s) of their hosting institutions. In English-speaking countries, language skills are often measured by standardized tests such as the Test of English as a Foreign Language (TOEFL) or International English Language Testing System (IELTS), which are used to measure certain aspects of the linguistic performance of nonnative English-speakers.[1] The notion of "high-level" skills in the extract above from a U.S.-based college refers to such test scores. The tests have, however, been problematized for ethicality, validity, washback effects, and cultural bias (e.g., McNamara & Roever, 2006), and even high-level nonnative English-speaking international students are commonly offered so-called accent reduction (AR) or accent modification (AM) courses in order to ease their problems in adjusting to their studies and the community. The above extract from College A highlights the paradox we want to analyze and discuss in this article: While international students have demonstrated high-level skills in English, they are still presented as needing to modify their accent.

AM or AR courses are a phenomenon familiar in professional, medical, and educational sectors (see for instance, Blommaert, 2009; Ramjattan, 2019), as foreign accents are believed to interfere with the success of international professionals and students. Although these courses claim to boost students' study and labor market success, there is evidence that they reinscribe racial inequalities (Ramjattan, 2019). While there is research on professional and business AM/AR courses (Blommaert, 2009; Ramjattan, 2019), no work exists that investigates such courses in the context of international study. This article fills this gap by analyzing AM/AR courses from the perspective of language ideologies and their repercussions for the hierarchization of international students. Ideologies of accent allow us a window into social power dynamics and ethnic hierarchizations that are implicated in the discourses on the websites that constitute our data. With this, we address de Wit's (2020) concern in the 10th Anniversary Series essay of the *Journal of International Students*, as he called for a more ethical and qualitative approach in order to understand new dimensions of international study.

LITERATURE REVIEW

According to recent estimates, approximately one in four international students (1.1. million) study in the United States (Zong & Batalova, 2018). We follow the general definition by the Organization for Economic Co-operation and Development (OECD, 2013) of international students as those having crossed borders for the purpose of study, who are not residents of their country of study, or who have received their secondary education in another country. From 2016–2017, China was the top country of origin of these students, making up 33% of the total, followed by India (17%), South Korea (5%), and Saudi Arabia (5%;

---

[1] Although "nonnative speaker" is a highly problematic concept, we use it here in order to speak back to data and prior literature on the topic.

Zong & Batalova, 2018). In all, at least two-thirds of international students in the United States came from Asia, another 7% from the Middle East, and 4% from Latin America (Statista, 2019). Our literature review focuses on language issues of international study and the role AM/AR may have in addressing them.

The Paradox of High Language Skills and AM Courses

The problems international students face in the United States are commonly summarized as "adapting to a new culture, English language problems, financial problems and lack of understanding from the broader university community" (Sherry et al., 2010, p. 33). This has led to recommendations for pedagogical development of the staff in receiving institutions (Wolf & Phung, 2019). However, Lee and Rice (2007) have pointed out that not all problems international students face can and should be understood as matters of individual adjustment. Rather, based on a case study of one large U.S. university, they suggested that neo-racism (i.e., discrimination based on proxies for race such as culture and national origin) was a key problem international students experienced, surfacing as feelings of discomfort, direct and indirect confrontations, and verbal abuse. While students from Europe, Canada, and New Zealand reported nothing of the kind, Middle Eastern, Latin American, and Asian students experienced "considerable discrimination" (Lee & Rice, 2007, p. 393), pointing to racism as the underlying problem. Language, particularly accent, is were bias often surfaces. For instance, Yeo et al. (2019) observed that Asian American students reported being racialized based on their perceived English proficiency, prompting them to speak "exaggeratedly [...] well-formed English" to signal belonging to the group of domestic students (p. 52).

Interestingly, a discrepancy exists between perceived and tested language skills. For instance, Xu (1991) found that while standardized TOEFL test scores did not predict students' perceived academic difficulty significantly, self-rated proficiency in English was the most significant predictor. Thus, even though language tests are required for entry, previous research does not support a straightforward link between test results and academic success. We want to examine this apparent discrepancy a bit closer.

Language arguments are rarely about language alone. Similarly, accent is not only a linguistic but also a sociocultural phenomenon that has been the focus of a lot of research in recent years (e.g., Lippi-Green, 2012; Moyer, 2013). Accent does not refer to so-called intelligibility ('understandability') of the speech, that is, formal language proficiency. Instead, it refers to features that do not affect meaning in a way that vocabulary, prepositions, or idiomatic expressions do. Accent refers to the listeners' perception of how closely the pronunciation approaches a so-called phonetic norm of a native speaker (Flege, 1988). Even though native speech accents also vary, foreign accent is perceptually so fundamental that humans are able to detect one from very early age on, even in a single word played backwards or in a language one does not know (Kinzler, 2008; Major, 2007). The experience of immediate recognition of hearing others speak one's own first language with a foreign accent is familiar, relatable, and intuitive.

This does not, however, make foreign accented speech unintelligible. On the contrary, it has been shown that native-speaking listeners are easily and rapidly able to adapt to different foreign accents when exposed to them; comprehensibility is not only collaborative but also learnable (Bradlow & Bent, 2008). However, what foreign accented speech might affect is the listeners' willingness to understand, that is, *comprehensibility*. Comprehensibility is a mediation concept between understanding speech (intelligibility) and stance toward a speaker. It refers to the perceived ease or difficulty of understanding a speaker and is thus per definition always a two-way street. In other words, comprehension does not hinge solely on the speaker; rather, all the participants are responsible for the communicative process (Munro & Derwing, 1999; Trofimovich & Isaacs, 2012).

Research (e.g., Major et al., 2005) documents clearly that some accents are perceived as more legitimate in particular contexts than others and that these perceptions are not ideologically innocent. For instance, a study by Wang et al. (2018) on communication between international and local students in the United States showed that local students viewed international students with mild accents as more intelligent and educated than those with stronger accents, thus illustrating that perceived accentedness is neither socially nor ideologically neutral.

A focus on accents oftentimes serves as a basis for stereotyping and hierarchizing students and categorizing speakers as groups assumed to share a general geographical origin (e.g., *Asia*) and a particular accent (e.g., *Asian accent*). Focus on language thus becomes indexical of country of origin or ethnicity. As Blommaert (2009) noted in his analysis of web-based AM courses, AM is "not about learning American English, but learning to sound like an American" (pp. 245–246).

Linguistic Legitimacy and the Mismatch Between Comprehensibility and Accent

As high proficiency in English, as documented by standardized tests, is a prerequisite for being accepted to study at U.S. institutions, the students who are targeted by AM/AR courses already are proficient in English. How can speakers have high proficiency and "incomprehensible" accents at the same time? At the point at which the listener thinks they hear a so-called *wrong* pronunciation, they have already understood. In more academic terms, paradoxically, comprehensibility precedes the claimed necessity of AR/AM courses.

In order to understand the role that accents play in the experiences of international students, we outline how language practices are socially perceived, that is, what is considered a legitimate linguistic practice in a given context.

The concept of linguistic legitimacy can be traced back to Bourdieu (1977) who defined a "legitimate language" as

> … uttered by a legitimate speaker, i.e. by the appropriate person … ; uttered in a legitimate situation, i.e. on the appropriate market … and addressed to legitimate receivers; … [i.e.] formulated in the legitimate

> phonological and syntactic forms (what linguists call grammaticalness), except when transgressing these norms is part of the legitimate definition of the legitimate producer. (p. 650, emphasis removed)

Building on the Bourdieuian foundations, Norton (2000) examined and theorized the limited "right to speak" of adult English learners in Canada, whose high investment in language learning did not always transfer to being perceived as legitimate speakers. Relatedly, Ennser-Kananen's (2018) work with multilingual German foreign language learners in the United States underlined the fluid nature of linguistic legitimacy, defined as "discursively constructed acceptance or validation for their language use" (p. 18). When AM/AR courses advertise an expected improvement of comprehension, what may on the surface be described as a problem of speech is in fact an issue related to its speakers, who are for various reasons positioned as *illegitimate communicators*.

AM courses operate on the assumption that some accents are more legitimate than others and substantiate this by describing nonnative accents as interfering with their speakers' comprehensibility and ultimately their social integration and professional credibility. However, (in)comprehensibility is never ideologically neutral, but a complex relationship between linguistic and ethnoracial category-making (Rosa, 2019).

Despite comprehensibility being a two-way street, in practice it is usually shouldered by those who are considered foreign to a particular context. For instance, while international students have been shown to be concerned about understanding local accents (Marginson et al., 2010), the AM/AR courses in our data encouraged students to lose their accent rather than the teachers to adjust theirs in order to be more comprehensible. How are such misinterpretations of comprehensibility used as an efficient market bait for AM/AR courses?

First, as argued above, even though accents rarely affect intelligibility, they are usually immediately recognized. Therefore, accents do also provide an easy link to the assumed (ethnic, national, linguistic) background of the speaker. As Creese and Kambere (2002) argued, perceptions of accents are racializing as they are "embodied markers of immigration" (p. 10).

Second, accent tends to convey a certain sociopolitical innocence that allows the concept to be used apparently unproblematically. According to Nguyen (1993), as labor market discrimination in the United States based on sex, race, color, national origin, and religion became regulated by the Civil Rights Act of 1964, accent has become a common ground for discrimination of nonnative English-speakers. The notion of comprehensibility, including non-accentedness, has thus taken the place of a racist gatekeeper in labor and education markets by constructing accents as ideologically neutral rather than as intrinsically tied to the speakers and their origins.

METHOD

Research Design

Our research design is descriptive, explorative, and phenomenon-based. Our different expertise (linguistic legitimacy, language ideologies, higher education internationalization) were critical for the design, as our collaborative engagement provided a certain amount of researcher triangulation when identifying themes and conducting the analysis. As researchers, we position ourselves within a critical paradigm. We thus subscribe to a research-based understanding of higher education as socially stratified and language use as functional, culturally shaped, and communicatively situated. In keeping with a critical approach to language in education, we want to make inconsistencies, inaccuracies, inequalities, and hidden agendas in real-world data visible.

Research Questions

Given the scarcity of literature that discusses AM courses from a higher education policy and language ideological perspective, our exploratory and analytical efforts aimed at understanding the role of language, the constructed legitimacy of languages and accents, and the process of student hierarchization in course descriptions of AM/AR courses at U.S. higher education institutions.

The following research questions motivated our study:

1. What does the promotion of AM/AR courses tell us about the role of languages (and by proxy their speakers) in the internationalization of U.S. higher education? What view of language is promoted in the course descriptions?
2. What accents or varieties are described as valued and legitimate and how is this done? In which way do these descriptions intersect with other social factors, particularly race and ethnicity?
3. What hierarchizations of international students are constructed through the ways in which some accents are presented? Who is the imagined target audience?

Through this, we invite a discussion around the sociopolitical implications of the phenomenon in international student mobility, and show that AM/AR courses are not primarily about language skills but use (intentionally or not) the notion of *language* ideologically to construct hierarchies based on nationality and ethnicity.

Data

Data for this study consists of texts from 26 websites of U.S.-based higher education institutions that, at the time of data collection, in the Spring 2018 semester, offered AM/AR courses. While the commercial market (often directed at professionals in fields such as business, education, or medicine) is another significant context for such courses (Ramjattan, 2019), this study focuses on higher education. The selection of data from college websites was a result of a Google search for strings "accent reduction course" and "accent modification course."

The websites for the courses we analyzed are located at departments of speech pathology, communication and communication disorders, and health, or were situated within continuing education and professional development departments. We focused on the course descriptions on these websites that had the twofold purpose of advertising the courses and informing readers about their content, goals, materials, design, costs, and prerequisites. Because of our interest in a systemic phenomenon rather than the individual institutions, we anonymized our data.

Data Analysis

As a first step, we conducted a qualitative content analysis (Mayring, 2000) of our data with a combination of inductive and deductive strategies. Inductively, we identified themes that emerged in the course of multiple in-depth readings across different data sources. Our deductive strategies included scanning for data that related to concepts from our literature resources, such as comprehensibility or legitimacy. Both strategies were combined to identify key themes in the texts.

As a next step, we selected shorter excerpts and phrases from our data for a closer critical discourse analysis (Fairclough, 2003) to understand their discursive, sociopolitical, and historical layers of meaning more deeply. For instance, we took a closer look at names for presented varieties of English, such as "Standard American English" to unpack their meaning and implications. We paid special attention to medical terms ("diagnosis," "therapy") and how they were used to describe accents. To understand hierarchization, we focused on direct and indirect hierarchizations of the target group students as others (i.e., "foreign," "nonnative," etc).

Last, we put our identified themes into connection, usually by mapping them visually on a whiteboard, with the goal of understanding them in relation to each other and to bigger societal discourses. This process produced answers to our research questions.

RESULTS

Our analyses produced responses to the research questions that we organized into three themes: images of language and accent, homogenization, and hierarchization of targeted (imagined) speakers.

Images of Language and Accent: Language as Building Blocks and Accent as Pathology

Language and language skills are presented as one major source of problems that international students identify as standing in the way of their academic success and of integrating in the higher education community. However, rather than addressing language(s) as a whole, these websites focus on one component of it, accent. In response to our first research question, we examined the understanding of language that undergirds the content of the course websites.

Accents and Language as Building Blocks

A recurring pattern that was prominent on numerous websites was the notion of accent, language, and the learning process as consisting of independent or isolated pieces that are to be acquired in a particular consecutive order. Similar to a set of building blocks, language acquisition or AM is presented happening as a process of putting together individual parts (e.g., vowels, consonants, stress, intonation, etc.) until a particular desired construction is completed. This also applies to language itself, which seems to be viewed as separated from accent, so that the accent block can be simply added onto the previous language blocks that the participants have acquired earlier. For instance, course websites may state the following:

> Topics covered include a quick, basic, and useful introduction to where and how speech sounds are produced; individual sounds of American English in isolation, with close attention to typically problematic consonants and vowels; difficult combinations of sounds; word stress; intonation; and pronunciation differences between formal and casual speech. —*College B*

This extract illustrates the notion of accent as made up of individual sounds that can be learned and taught (quickly and) "in isolation." Other bricks of accent include "combinations of sounds," "word stress," and "intonation." The description of some of these linguistic building blocks as "typically problematic" or "difficult" raises questions about the implied target audience, which is constructed in opposition to users of "American English" (see also next subsection on homogenization). It further invites problematizations of what constitutes "difficult" language or accent features in this context and for whom. A similar targeted variety of English is referred to in the next extract, which also provides examples for "particular sounds" and "melodies" that the respective course addresses:

> ACT involves direct instruction and models for articulation (the way sounds are produced) and prosody (the melody of speech) in Mainstream American English (MAE). It provides opportunities to practice learned skills in a variety of communication settings and situations (e.g., presentations, interviews, ordering food), as well as direct feedback on performance from the

> instructors. The content includes customized instruction of articulation and prosody in MAE to fit an individual's specific needs. The particular sounds (e.g., "th" sound as in "the" and melodies of speech (e.g., stressing/emphasizing the second syllable in "deVElop" instead of the first syllable "DEvelop") that are targeted in training depend on those identified during the evaluation. —*College C*

This extract offers improved pronunciation of particular sounds and correct syllable stress as examples of the course content, all with the goal of complying with "Mainstream American English," a variety that, by any linguistic measures, is purely imaginary and a folk-linguistic belief at best (Niedzielski & Preston, 1999; see also next subsection on homogenization). In addition to reinforcing the notion of accent as a set of building blocks, this extract also distinguishes between "learning" and "practicing," thus introducing another level of Lego-like structures where practice is added on top of learned skills. The notion of a set of building blocks is thereby extended to the process of AM (or, more generally speaking, language learning) itself. In addition to the notion of block building being applied to the three levels of accent, language, and learning, our data analysis also revealed an implied order of this process.

> The class will follow the order of the textbook, emphasizing stress, intonation, rhythm, linking and reductions, as well as vowels and consonants. We will also focus on fluency with exercises designed to encourage the free flow of communication. The course will be a mix of listening to the CDs that come with the book, focused practice, and other fun exercises. —*College A*

As this extract suggests, class and textbook follow a particular order, which implies that the process of modifying one's accent is viewed as consecutive, adding or joining together building blocks. Among the later ones seems to be the block of "fluency," which is also noteworthy for its potential to "encourage the free flow of communication."

In all, a common theme in our data was the understanding of languages, accent, and the AM/learning process as acts of adding isolated building blocks onto earlier constructions in a particular order. This runs counter to current understandings of language as a dynamic, social, and multimodal tool of meaning making and of language learning as a complex and multidirectional process of using and combining a variety of multimodal resources to acquire and negotiate ways of communicating, being in, and making sense of the world (Lantolf & Poehner, 2014; The New London Group, 1996). All of these are skills that both international as well as local students need during their studies and lives.

Pathologization of Accent

Another theme that characterized the websites' discourses on language was the pathologization of accent. Although several websites assure their readers that having an accent is nothing outside of the ordinary, even an important part of one's cultural identity, and a reason for pride, such statements were often overshadowed by a strikingly forthright discourse of accent pathologization.

> The N. N. Speech and Hearing Clinic offers diagnostic and therapy services for Accent Modification (also called Accent Reduction). These elective clinical services are designed to assist individuals in changing their accents/dialects to Standard American English. … this "elective" therapy focuses on the individual needs of the client, with the objectives selected after an evaluation of linguistic skills. —*College D*

As this extract states, the courses introduced on the respective website are offered by a speech and hearing clinic, which situates accents (here understood as any speech other than so-called Standard American English) in the realm of pathological abnormalities that need to be attended to. Against this backdrop, it is not surprising that common medical procedures such as diagnostic and therapy services are offered to prospective client(s). The following extract from the website of the American Speech-Language-Hearing Association was linked from College D's website: "Insurance companies will not pay for services to change your accent. This is because an accent is not a speech or language disorder. You will need to speak with your SLP about how you can pay for services."

The mention of insurance in this extract roots AM courses firmly in the pathological realm. The statement "accent is not a speech or language disorder" appears almost ironic, as it seems to apply merely to payment options yet not to the legitimacy of the targeted participants' accents. One consequence of accent being pathologized in ways described above is the impossibility of a natural or independent recovery. In other words, the implication of a "condition" as complicated as accent seems to be that it can only be treated under the supervision and guidance of a professional. The following extracts speak to this point: "The international speaker of English can greatly improve pronunciation with the assistance of this professional speech-language pathologist" (College F).

The pathologization of accent thus goes hand in hand with the need for a professionally trained expert (speech-language pathologist) who can remedy the course participants' deviation from what is described as Standard American English pronunciation. In connection to this elevation of a professional expert, some promises the websites make struck us as noteworthy—for example, the ones stated on the American Speech-Language-Hearing Association website that is behind a link on the website of College E, which invites participants who seek to "… modify their speech pronunciation, sentence intonation, learn the subtleties and implied meanings in English, improve comprehension of English and cultural pragmatics" (College E).

Whether international students (as well as domestic ones) may or may not need the help of a speech pathologist is not the issue here. The placement of some of the courses within a setting of speech pathologies, and the consequent construction of accents in need of remedies and cures, nonetheless implies accents as a pathology. This plays toward a unidirectional construction of comprehensibility hinging on the speaker, and the solution being an intervention with them.

Homogenization: International Students and Imagined Native Speaker Communities

Having discussed the construction of accent as a linguistic problem, we now shift toward what is offered as the solution in AM/AR programs, namely the language varieties that are promoted in the courses.

The notion of "English spoken in the United States" not only refers to English being used within the U.S. context, but also denotes a particular variety in the hierarchization of World Englishes. We acknowledge that not all international students are nonnative speakers of English, but may come from English-speaking countries. However, the English proficiency of these students is also complicated by the fact that different varieties of English have been hierarchized into inner and outer circles. While English is the official language of about 60 countries in the world, it enjoys a different and sociohistorically unique status in the United States, United Kingdom, Anglophone Canada, Australia, New Zealand, and Ireland, which is reflected in Kachru's (1992) term "inner circle" for these countries. Other native Englishes spoken, for example, in India, Pakistan, Singapore, and Nigeria are considered to be "outer circle" (e.g., Kachru, 1992). Although these hierarchies within English are subject to negotiation in any given context, differences in status and prestige are often reproduced and perpetuated in higher education (Saarinen & Nikula, 2013). The course descriptions offered a variety of target accents to be learned:

- English/English pronunciation
- North/American English
- Standard American English / Standard American English accent (SAE)
- Mainstream American English (MAE)
- General American English (GAE)
- The American English
- New standard American patterns

The varieties North/American English and English in most language learning contexts might be taken as neutral and commonsensical. However, Standard American English and Standard American English accent are inventions having no basis in research. With regard to the English spoken in the area of North America, linguistically speaking there is no such thing as a standard variety (Labov, 2012), as native speakers' speech always varies idiomatically, regionally, and situationally. In other words, by linguistic standards, American English is a myth. Also the variety described as the new standard American patterns implies and promotes a particular standard, even though the word "pattern" slightly softens the underlying claim of a stable variety.

Given the fact that from a linguistic standpoint there is no such thing as a unified standard variety of American English, AM/AR courses advertising exactly that become highly problematic. In the case of AM/AR courses, these speakers are as imagined as the variety itself. Who is this imagined homogenous community of imagined native speakers speaking the imagined ideal standard variety that is promoted? A common means of portraying such an ideal is the language ideological process of erasure (Irvine & Gal, 2000) of language internal variation of English(es) and of language in general, also known as homogenization. In the course promotions, this is achieved through three means.

First, the imagined standard is constructed by acronymizing and capitalizing the descriptive words that usually remain rather vague, like General American English (GAE) and Mainstream American English (MAE). From a discourse analytical standpoint, this could be described as a claim of legitimacy (Ennser-Kananen, 2018; Van Leeuwen, 2008), with the invented names mimicking commonly accepted acronyms such as AmE for American English to obtain authority by association. Such invented terms and abbreviations refer to English spoken in Northern America as one homogeneous unit, which is further highlighted by the use of the definite article in the variety name "the American accent."

The second means of homogenization does quite the opposite of naming a variety of assumed standards; it simply does not acknowledge any kind of situational, contextual, regional, or idiosyncratic variation. The imagined standard is described as being spoken to an imagined homogeneous group of passive recipients, who have difficulties comprehending the speech of nonnative speakers. Applying Anderson's (1991) concept of an imagined community, such an imagined native speaker community is discursively constructed as uniform and homogenous on the basis of assumed commonalities, in this case, assumed similar ways of speaking.

Third, a quite common means of homogenization is to chop language up into disconnected building blocks (see above subsection on accent and language as building blocks), which is usually tied to the implication that some features of language are thought of and presented as more prominent and legitimate than others, and that changing them would change the perception of the whole variety. Such a view conceives of language as an indexical field (Eckert, 2008), in which one block can index a whole variety. In our case, the pronunciation of particular linguistic features becomes representative of a homogenous (yet nonexistent) variety of American English.

Through these means, an ideal language and speaker community is created, which seems to serve the promotion of AM/AR courses rather than address an actual linguistic issue.

Hierarchization: International Students as "Others"

In our final analysis section, we look into how students are categorized with ways that emerge from behind the descriptions of assumed language skills and desired accent. The course participants and their accents are described in ways that mark them as others. Their otherness may be implicit, based on language criteria such as nonnativeness, or it may be explicit, based on being "foreign" or "international."

Implicit Otherness: "Nonnatives" as Opposed to "Natives"

The most salient description in our data for potential participants was their so-called nonnativeness. In many second language classrooms, nativeness was and sometimes still is seen as a goal of language learning: A native speaker is considered authentic, has acquired the language from birth on, and is in possession of the so-called correct knowledge of the language (Paikeday, 1985). Such models have been criticized and largely abandoned by language education scholars (e.g., Rampton, 1990), although they pervasively continue to exist in many language learning contexts. In addition to being an obstacle to learning, the ideal of nativeness is ideologically loaded, linking language to constructions of a national and cultural identity, and to a particular (nation) state (McCambridge & Saarinen, 2015).

The extract below is an example of a course description in which nonnative speakers are addressed as the target group and othered as lacking the knowledge of "subtleties and implied meanings in English"—in other words, the knowledge of native speakers' language. The construction of otherness and nonbelonging is not a (purely) linguistic one. As the nonnative speakers are described as others vis-a-vis native speakers of an imagined variety of General American English (see subsection on homogenization above), they become positioned as outside of, or even in opposition to, a group that is understood to share the status of *being American*. In other words, through the equation of accent and geographical region, linguistic othering becomes an exclusion based on nationality and cultural background, or more simply put, based on a pragmatic knowledge of what is deemed to be American and non-American. "Accent modification is an 'elective' service designed for nonnative speakers of English who want to modify their speech pronunciation, sentence intonation, learn the subtleties and implied meanings in English, improve comprehension of English and cultural pragmatics" (College E).

In the next extract, native speakers are implicitly treated as the model, while the focus is on the homogeneously constructed group of nonnative speakers. Defining speakers through their nonnativeness is not only a deficit-based approach that erases a large amount of variation and difference; it also uses language as a tool to mark nonnative speakers as "the others" (Tajfel & Turner, 1979) who need to conform to an implied, self-evident norm. As the need is formulated as something the nonnative speakers *want*, it is crucial to remember that our data are market-oriented suggestions from course websites rather than the target groups' self-reported needs (see also Riuttanen, 2019). Implicitness thus strengthens the weight of native-speaker status as a given, self-evident criteria that appears to need no further discussion, offering ideologically charged information as common ground (Bertucelli, 2006).

Not surprisingly, in several course descriptions, nonnative and native speakers of English are referred to explicitly side by side, with native speakers being represented as the natural counterpart of the non-native speakers. The following extracts are typical examples of this juxtaposition: "… designed for mid to high level nonnative speakers of English speaking with native English speakers" (College A) and "... to help non-native speakers feel more at home and confident in their communications with native speakers" (College G).

Apart from the hierarchy that is repeatedly established between native and nonnative speakers, native speakers are subject to a process of homogenization, as they are represented as a monolithic community of model language users (see above). Representing native speakers as linguistic models and nonnative speakers as linguistically deficient draws on and reproduces an outdated but still common hierarchy, which emphasizes and perpetuates the otherness of nonnative speakers. An added peculiarity is that the need for AM/AR seems to apply only to communication between native and nonnative speakers, as communication among nonnative speakers is not mentioned. Despite constituting the larger group of English users, nonnative speakers are measured against elusive native-speaker standards, which sets them up for failure in multiple ways.

Explicit Otherness Based on "Foreignness" or Ethnicity

While most of the target group descriptions are based on an implied otherness, some courses explicitly define *international* or *foreign* students as their target group. The next extract explicitly mentions international professionals in the name of the course and continues to describe the course goal by talking about "communication barriers" and the somewhat glorified "unique cultural identity" of the students. "Each course is tailored to a specific aspect of Accent Reduction (vowel sounds, consonant sounds, intonation and speaking skills) to minimize your communication barriers while maintaining your unique cultural identity" (College H).

The excerpt describes English learners as possessing unique cultural identity, a description that can be read as exoticizing. Additionally, the legitimacy of cultural identity is presented as something that has its limits. While it is presented as worth maintaining, accent is also presented as needing to be minimized for the sake of comprehensibility. If the nonnative speaker could indeed not produce English sounds or had no speaking skills, it would surely be a problem. In that case, the problem would lie in general proficiency, in *knowing* English. However, the courses we focus on in this article are marketed for high-level English speakers with test-proven proficiency. The course descriptions, in turn, refer to accents, which do not affect intelligibility but might affect native speaker's willingness to comprehend (see literature review above). Thus, College H specifically continues to place the problem at the nonnative speakers' side, rather than viewing comprehension as bidirectional.

The next excerpt combines the description of foreign as the target group with the implication that the students feel an intrinsic need to take the course: "... designed for foreign-born students, faculty, and staff who feel their ability to communicate effectively and their employment options are limited by intelligibility issues" (College I).

The construct "foreign born" is an apparent attempt to avoid mentioning language. However, it explicates what the majority of courses only imply: It is the foreignness of the students that is seen as the key problem. While we have seen the representation of these others or so-called foreigners as a monolithic group, what becomes clear in this extract is the problem of "foreignness." While, on the surface, AM/AR courses aim to solve language-related problems, neither international nor foreign are linguistic categories.

CONCLUSION

In this article, we have analyzed texts from 26 university websites that promote AR/AM courses. We asked what view of language and accent they promote, what mechanisms of language ideologies are at work, and how the target audience of these courses is perceived.

While international students are presented as having different kinds of *comprehensibility problems*, the seemingly linguistic arguments that the courses are marketed with are not valid. We recognize that the desire to reduce a so-called foreign accent is urgent to many speakers, and the modification of an accent may even produce an experience of empowerment and success. Our goal here is not to dismiss these experiences. However, what is identified as a language issue in the context of these courses is actually an ideological one, drawing on the students' ethnic or geographical origins and consequently racializing the question of language skills. This not merely erases recent foundational work in the field of applied linguistics (e.g., Creese & Kambere, 2002; Rosa, 2019), but is especially problematic for the target audience of AM/AR courses—international students—who are set up for failure through such an approach.

The idealized native-like speech promoted in the courses but only imagined in reality is a misleading premise that ignores the vast variation among varieties of Englishes as well as individual variation stemming from regional, socioeconomical, and other differences. The homogenized view on language promotes a deficit perspective on nonnative speakers, who will perpetually lag behind an obscure norm. This approach disregards the complex, and often contradictory, reality of learning trajectories, multilingual and multimodal meaning making and communication, and the role of social (status, power, gender, class, race, ability, etc.) and societal (globalization, neoliberalism, technologization, etc.) factors, all of which constantly permeate and shape language use, as well as the role of language users. Combined with requirements to take high-stakes standardized tests (which are an equity issue per se) and a perpetuation of harmful native-speakerist ideologies, this creates the perfect storm of failure for international students, who are led to believe that their experienced failure in becoming a full member of the academic community is a personal rather than a systemic one.

Discourses of pathologization reinforce this setup as they position international students as deficient in a process of AM, to which only speech specialists hold the key. Creating such a relationship of dependency robs students of their agency and negates their skills and experiences. Pathologizing accent isolates questions of comprehensibility even more from social and societal processes and simultaneously makes the issues not just individual but intrinsic to the students.

The targeted audience, international students, are not the only ones who are depicted in simplistic ways in our data. The imagined goals of AM/AR are fictional representations, simplifying diversity and variation in ways that go against current research. Additionally, variation is also erased from languages and accents within the community of native speakers, problematically positioned as role models. By constructing imaginary languages, variations, and acronyms, the native speaker community is presented as one monolithic unit that is the source and owner of one monolithic accent.

The homogenization of language and speakers as native and nonnative is an ideal condition for juxtaposition and othering. With the (fictional) groups described as clear cut and uniform, hierarchies of *us* and *them* are easy to establish and reproduce with the help of discursive strategies that create opposition and othering. Within this power game, we also found some evidence of attempts to carve out spaces for the building and expressing of cultural identities. However, given their effort to restrict *cultural uniqueness* to particular (unidentified) times and spaces (presumably outside of accent) and their tendency to exoticize and essentialize cultural identities, they can only be described as limited and limiting.

If the linguistic arguments for AM/AR courses do not hold, what then, is behind this effort to advertise these courses? Our analysis indicated that not all students were imagined or addressed in the same way. While native speakers of American English were presented as accent-free, socially and academically successful students, potential participants for the courses were depicted as deficient and struggling in their academic lives. While the talk of students as nonnative, international, and foreign is void of any explicit mention of race or ethnicity, the majority of international students in the United States are from racialized groups (Statista, 2019), meaning that AR or modification may, in the end, become an exercise in reducing or modifying non-White race and ethnicity. International students face problems that are diverse and related to a variety of socioeconomic factors (Lee & Rice, 2007; Sherry et al., 2010); a focus on so-called accent oversimplifies and misrepresents their experiences.

The motivations behind these courses are beyond the scope of our study. However, if higher education contexts promote such discourses, intentionally or not, native speakers may learn very quickly that it is not their responsibility to establish successful communication with international students. The message to international students is, in turn, that there is almost no limit to the expense and effort they have to invest in order to fit in. While none of this may be the intention of higher education policy makers, it is nonetheless a likely consequence. If such courses are to be organized, we suggest their focus should not be on accent but, more broadly, on successful communication in linguistically and culturally diverse academic contexts. In order to actively challenge native speakerism, racism, and other means of hierarchization that permeate predominantly White institutions, it is critical for such courses to call in all participants of an academic community, particularly those who consider their communication skills to be standard, unproblematic, or neutral. The issue to be tackled here is not the accents but the systemic othering that AM/AR courses reproduce.

REFERENCES

Anderson, B. (1991). *Imagined communities: Reflections on the origin and spread of nationalism* (2nd ed.). Verso.

Bertucelli, M. (2006). Implicitness. In *Handbook of pragmatics online*. John Benjamins.

Blommaert, J. (2009). A market of accents. *Language Policy*, *8*(3), 243–259.

Bourdieu, P. (1977). The economics of linguistic exchanges. *Social Science Information*, *16*(6), 645–658.

Bradlow, A., & Bent, T. (2008). Perceptual adaptation to non-native speech. *Cognition*, *6*(2), 707–729.

Creese, G., & Kambere, E. N. (2002). *What colour is your English?* (Working paper No. 02-20). Vancouver Centre of Excellence.

de Wit, H. (2020). Internationalization of higher education. *Journal of International Students*, *10*(1), i–iv.

Eckert, P. (2008). Variation and the indexical field. *Journal of Sociolinguistics, 12*(4), 453–476.

Ennser-Kananen, J. (2018). "That German stuff": Negotiating linguistic legitimacy in a foreign language classroom. *Journal of Language and Education*, *4*(1), 18–30. https://doi.org/10.17323/2411-7390-2018-4-1-18-30

Fairclough, N. (2003). *Analysing discourse: Textual analysis for social research*. Routledge.

Flege, J. E. (1988). The production and perception of foreign language speech sounds. In H. Winitz (Ed.), *Human communication and its disorders* (pp. 224–401). Ablex.

Irvine, J. T., & Gal, S. (2000). Language ideology and linguistic differentiation. In P. Kroskrity (Ed.), *Regimes of language* (pp. 35–83). School of American Research Press.

Kachru, B. B. (1992). Models for non-native Englishes. In B. B. Kachru (Ed.), *The other tongue: English across cultures* (2nd ed., pp. 48–74). University of Illinois Press.

Kinzler, K. (2008). *The native language of social cognition: Developmental origins of social preferences based on language* [Unpublished doctoral dissertation]. Harvard University.

Labov, W. (2012). *Dialect diversity in America: The politics of language change*. University of Virginia Press.

Lantolf, J. P., & Poehner, M. E. (2014). *Sociocultural theory and the pedagogical imperative in L2 education: Vygotskian praxis and the research/practice divide.* Routledge.

Lee, J. J., & Rice, C. (2007). Welcome to America? International student perceptions of discrimination. *Higher Education, 53*(3), 381–409.

Lippi-Green, R. (2012). *English with an accent: Language, ideology, and discrimination in the United States* (2nd ed.). Routledge.

Major, R. C. (2007). Identifying a foreign accent in an unfamiliar language. *Studies in Second Language Acquisition*, *29*(4), 539–556.

Major, R., Fitzmaurice, S., Bunta, F., & Balasubramanian, C. (2005). The effects of nonnative accents on listening comprehension: Implications for ESL assessment. *TESOL Quarterly, 36*(2), 173–190.

Marginson, S., Nyland, C., Sawir, E., & Forbes-Mewett, H. (2010). *International student security.* Cambridge University Press.

Mayring, P. (2000). Qualitative content analysis. *Forum Qualitative Sozialforschung / Forum: Qualitative Social Research, 1*(2), Article 20. http://nbn-resolving.de/urn:nbn:de:0114-fqs0002204

McCambridge, L., & Saarinen, T. (2015). "I know that the natives must suffer every now and then": Native / non-native indexing language ideologies in Finnish higher education. In S. Dimova, A. K. Hultgren, & C. Jensen (Eds.), *English-medium instruction in European higher education.* (pp. 291–316). Mouton de Gruyter.

McNamara, T., & Roever, C. (2006). *Language testing: The social dimension. A supplement to Language Learning 56.* Blackwell Publishing.

Moyer, A. (2013). *Foreign accent: The phenomenon of non-native speech.* Cambridge University Press.

Munro, M. J., & Derwing, T. M. (1999). Foreign accent, comprehensibility, and intelligibility in the speech of second language learners. *Language Learning, 49*(1), 285–310.

The New London Group. (1996). A pedagogy of multiliteracies: Designing social futures. *Harvard Educational Review, 66*(1), 60–93.

Nguyen, B. (1993). Accent discrimination and the test of spoken English: A call for an objective assessment of the comprehensibility of nonnative speakers. *California Law Review, 81*(5), 1325–1361.

Niedzielski, N. A., & Preston, D. R. (1999). *Folk linguistics.* Mouton de Gruyter.

Norton, B. (2000). *Identity and language learning: Gender, ethnicity and educational change.* Pearson Education.

Organisation for Economic Cooperation and Development. (2013). *Education indicators in focus 2013/5* (July). https://www.oecd.org/education/skills-beyond-school/EDIF%202013--N%C2%B014%20(eng)-Final.pdf

Paikeday, T. (1985). *The native speaker is dead!* Paikeday Publishing.

Ramjattan, V. A. (2019). Racializing the problem of and solution to foreign accent in business. *Applied Linguistics Review.* https://doi.org/10.1515/applirev-2019-0058

Rampton, M. B. H. (1990). Displacing the "native speaker": Expertise, affiliation, and inheritance. *ELT Journal, 44*(2), 97–101.

Riuttanen, S. (2019). *"Neutralize your native accent": The ideological representation of accents on accent reduction websites* [Master's thesis]. University of Jyväskylä.

Rosa, J. (2019). *Looking like a language, sounding like a race: Raciolinguistic ideologies and the learning of Latinidad.* Oxford University Press.

Saarinen, T., & Nikula, T. (2013). Implicit policy, invisible language: Policies and practices of international degree programmes in Finnish higher education. In A. Doiz, D. Lasagabaster, & J. M. Sierra (Eds.), *English-medium instruction at universities: Global challenges* (pp. 131–150). Multilingual Matters.

Sherry, M., Thomas, P., & Chui, W. H. (2010). International students: A vulnerable student population. *Higher Education*, *60*(1), 33–46.

Statista. (2019). *Number of international students studying in the United States in 2017/18, by country of origin.* https://www.statista.com/statistics/233880/international-students-in-the-us-by-country-of-origin/

Tajfel, H., & Turner, J. (1979). An integrative theory of intergroup conflict. In W. Austin & S. Worschel (Eds.), *The social psychology of intergroup relations* (pp. 33–47). Brooks/Cole.

Trofimovich, P. & Isaacs, T. (2012). Disentangling accent from comprehensibility. *Bilingualism: Language and Cognition*, *15*(4), 905–916.

Van Leeuwen, T. (2008). *Discourse and practice: New tools for critical discourse analysis.* Oxford University Press.

Wang, I.-C., Ahn, J. N., Kim, H. J., & Lin-Siegler, X. (2018). Why do international students avoid communicating with Americans? *Journal of International Students*, *7*(3), 555–582.

Wolf, D. M., & Phung, L. (2019). Studying in the United States: Language learning challenges, strategies and support services. *Journal of International Students*, *9*(1), 211–224.

Xu, M. (1991). The impact of English-language proficiency on international graduate students' perceived academic difficulty. *Research in Higher Education*, *32*(5), 557–570.

Yeo, H. T., Mendenhall, R., Harwood, S. A., & Huntt, M. B. (2019). Asian international student and Asian American student: Mistaken identity and racial microaggression. *Journal of International Students*, *9*(1), 44–70.

Zong, J., & Batalova, J. (2018). *International students in the United States.* Retrieved May 9, 2018, from https://www.migrationpolicy.org/article/international-students-united-states

JOHANNA ENNSER-KANANEN, PhD, is an Academy of Finland research fellow at the Department of Language and Communication Studies, University of Jyväskylä. Her current work focuses on linguistically and culturally sustaining education for migrant teachers and anti-oppressive (language) pedagogies for migrant students, particularly those with refugee experience. Email: johanna.f.ennser-kananen@jyu.fi

MIA HALONEN, PhD, is a senior researcher at the Centre for Applied Language Studies, University of Jyväskylä. Her recent areas of research include sociophonetics and historical sociolinguistics as well as language attitudes and stereotyping related to language ideologies and policies. Email: mia.m.halonen@jyu.fi

TAINA SAARINEN, PhD, is a research professor at the Finnish Institute for Educational Research, University of Jyväskylä. Her major research interests lie in the area of language ideologies and language policies in higher education. Email: taina.m.saarinen@jyu.fi

Peer-Reviewed Article

© *Journal of International Students*
Volume 11, Issue 2 (2021), pp. 341-360
ISSN: 2162-3104 (Print), 2166-3750 (Online)
doi: 10.32674/jis.v11i2.1779
ojed.org/jis

"We Begin 300 Meters Behind the Starting Line": Adaptation of Iranian Students in Hungary in the Post-Sanctions Era

Sara Hosseini-Nezhad
Eötvös Loránd University, Hungary

Saba Safdar
University of Guelph, Canada

Lan Anh Nguyen Luu
Eötvös Loránd University, Hungary

ABSTRACT

This longitudinal qualitative research investigated the psychosocial adaptation trajectory of Iranian international students in Hungary and the challenges they encountered. Semi-structured interviews were conducted between 7-month to 1-year intervals with 20 Iranian students. Inductive content analysis was utilized to analyze the interview transcripts. Three themes identified were visa and banking challenges, the impact of the currency crisis in Iran on mental health, and positive and negative changes in psychological well-being. The results revealed that almost all students' well-being improved over time, despite facing challenges related to visas, banking, and Iran's recent economic crisis.

Keywords: banking challenges, economic crisis, international student, Iran, mental health

The number of international students enrolled at Hungarian universities in the academic year of 2017–2018 was 32,309, out of which 1,878 were Iranians (Oktatási Hivatal, 2018). This study explores the trajectory of the psychosocial adaptation of Iranian students in Hungary and the challenges they faced regarding visas, banking, and the currency crisis. The currency crisis refers to the rapid depreciation of the Iranian currency (the rial) to a historic low point against the U.S. dollar in 2018, after the United States unilaterally withdrew from the Joint Comprehensive Plan of Action, commonly known as the Iran nuclear deal, and imposed sanctions against Iran in 2018.

By looking at the lists of restricted and sanctioned countries (EU Sanctions Map, 2020; Office of Foreign Assets Control, 2019), Iran, compared with the other top 10 countries with the highest number of international students in Hungary,[1] is the only one that is restricted and sanctioned by three regions/organizations namely, the United States, European Union (EU), and United Nations. A majority of the students in Hungary are from countries that either have no sanction imposed on them, or their sanctions are less restrictive compared with Iran.

This study aims to create new knowledge by focusing on students from one of the Middle Eastern countries with the highest number of students in Hungary and one that is under more restrictive regulations and sanctions. To date, no studies have longitudinally investigated the psychosocial adaptation of Iranian students in Hungary regarding the effects of sanctions against Iran on Iranian students' mental health.

Generally, research on the adaptation of international students is primarily based on a cross-sectional design, and there is a paucity of longitudinal studies (Hirai et al., 2015). Consequently, as suggested by Ward and Geeraert (2016), it is time to move beyond cross-sectional studies and focus on longitudinal studies to advance acculturation theory and research. Ward and Geeraert (2016) called attention to the importance of including the broader ecological context in the home and host cultures. Policies such as visa and banking restrictions as well as sanctions could be understood as consequential changes in the ecological context that impact international students' adaptation.

LITERATURE REVIEW

There is considerable research on international students that has mainly focused on psychological and social aspects of their experiences. However, comparatively few studies have investigated international students' experiences from political viewpoints (Rose-Redwood & Rose-Redwood, 2017). International students share common experiences, but there are specific experiences that are comparatively more challenging for Iranian students than for those from other countries, especially nations with fewer or no restrictions or sanctions imposed on them.

[1] The 10 countries with the highest number of international students in Hungary were (in descending order): Germany, Romania, China, Serbia, Iran, Slovakia, Ukraine, Turkey, Norway, and Nigeria (Oktatási Hivatal, 2018).

Previous research reported a range of challenges that Iranian international students encounter, such as finding jobs, language problems, culture shock, cultural distance (Mehdizadeh & Scott, 2005), obtaining a visa, immigration processes, and financial problems due to an unsteady economy and sanctions on Iran (Khodabandelou et al., 2015). In this study, we focused exclusively on visas, banking, and currency crisis challenges facing Iranian students in Hungary. Below we present examples of these obstacles found in the literature.

Visa and Immigration Challenges

Before the Iranian revolution in 1979, many Iranian students went abroad unhindered to continue their studies; however, during that time, Iranians could travel without a visa to many places, and the Iranian rial was strong (Ehteshami, 2017). Following the revolution, sanctions were imposed against Iran, resulting in weak diplomatic ties with the West, and restricted freedom of movement for Iranians traveling abroad (Bianchi & Stephenson, 2014).

The sanctions influenced many things, such as visa processing, which was considerably slowed down or halted altogether. Currently, the Iranian passport is globally ranked 101st (Henley & Partners, 2019), making it one of the world's weakest passports. Based on the Henley and Partners (2019) Passport Index, holders of the Iranian passport require a visa for 187 countries and can travel visa-free to 39.

Generally, international students have been found to face adaptation difficulties related to visas and immigration (Tummala-Narra & Claudius, 2013). These include strict visa policies ranging from difficulties getting an entrance visa and extending a visa, to preparing documents. One study reported that the main issues that the Iranian students faced in the Netherlands were related to getting a visa, gathering documents, such as the proof of financial support for living and studying permit, providing an income certificate and passport for accommodation, and obtaining work permits (Astinova, 2011).

Iranian students in the United States have also experienced challenges such as difficulties obtaining visas before and after entering the United States (Ditto, 2014). In Ditto's (2014) study, the process of getting a visa frustrated Iranian students the most. Similarly, in another study, Iranian students in the United States reported that the limitations imposed on the validity and length of their student visas impacted their life to the point that they could not return to Iran to visit their family for an extended time out of the fear of losing their visa (Karimzad, 2016).

Banking Challenges

Following the sanctions, many banks discriminated against their Iranian customers by either making it difficult for them to open a bank account (Eurofast Global Ltd, 2017) or abruptly freezing or closing their bank accounts in compliance with economic sanctions against Iran (Mobasher, 2018). As a result of bank closures, Iranian students abroad faced challenges regarding transferring funds from Iran (Astinova, 2011), making it difficult for many families to transfer money to their children (Hafezi, 2016). Iranian students in European countries, such as Spain, Germany, Italy, and France, reported that the banks either refused to open bank accounts for them or froze their bank accounts (Jafari, 2019). Iranian students in Scandinavia (Johansson, 2013) and Canada (Eybagi, 2013) faced similar banking challenges.

Currency (Economic) Crisis Challenges

Shortly after the revolution, during the 1979–1981 hostage crisis, the United States imposed its first sanctions against Iran (Laub, 2015). In May 2018, the United States exited the Iran nuclear deal and reinstated economic sanctions against Iran (Gearan & DeYoung, 2018). Since 2018, Iran's economic situation has been sinking into a deep recession, and the Iranian currency is on the brink of collapse (Hossein-Zadeh, 2018). As of July 2020, the rial is considered the least valued currency in the world (Internet Forex Resource, 2020).

The sanctions affected ordinary people, including Iranian students abroad (Mehrabi, 2014). Students who were financially dependent on their families had to return home because their families could not afford to pay their tuition fees (Mehrabi, 2014). The situation has become even more difficult for students since there are reports that the Iranian government has prevented students from buying dollars at a subsidized government rate ("No more cheap currency," 2018; Torbati, 2012), which is lower than the free market rate.

Iranian students in Malaysia reported being affected by the collapse of the rial, which has led to many students withdrawing from their studies and dropping out (Bani Kamal & Hossain, 2017). The decline of the Iranian currency has also impacted Iranian students in the United States. The currency crisis has made financial transactions difficult for students and for parents to transfer their children's tuition fees (Ditto, 2014). Iranian students in Scandinavia were also negatively affected by economic sanctions on Iran (Johansson, 2013). A majority of students were financially dependent on their parents, and as a result of the currency crisis, they either had less money to support themselves or had to ask their parents to send more money to pay for their expenses (Johansson, 2013). Similar currency crisis obstacles were experienced by Iranian students in Canada (Eybagi, 2013).

Aim of the Study

The current study explored the trajectory of psychosocial adaptation of Iranian students in Hungary and the challenges they faced. This study was conducted over a 7–12-month period to ensure there was at least a 6-month gap between the first and the second interviews (i.e., at least one full semester). The second interviews were conducted in the new academic year (2018–2019) as students' psychological adaptations in the host country tend to fluctuate with the new academic year (Golden, 1973; Hechanova-Alampay et al., 2002). We attempted to make sure that enough time passed between the two interviews to enable us to follow up on changes over at least one full semester.

We focused specifically on visas, banking, and currency crisis challenges. In April 2018, the Iranian currency fell to its lowest rate in 35 years against the U.S. dollar, which occurred in between the two interviews. Initially, we did not predict specific challenges; however, after reading the interviews, the main sociopolitical and economic challenges that adversely impacted students' mental health were reported to be the currency crisis, visas, and bank-related issues. Hence, the main research questions guiding this study are as follows:

> Q1: What are the main challenges that Iranian students face in Hungary that negatively impact their mental health?
>
> Q2: How do Iranian students' mental health and adaptations change over time?

METHOD

This study adopted a longitudinal design using an inductive approach to qualitative content analysis (Graneheim & Lundman, 2004). We conducted semi-structured interviews with Iranian undergraduate and graduate students in Budapest, Hungary, between October 2017 and October 2018. This study received ethical approval from the Research Ethics Committee at a Hungarian university in Budapest.

Participants

Twenty Iranian international students (13 males and seven females) participated in the first interview, of which 25% were graduates and 75% undergraduates. Their ages ranged from 18 to 36 ($M = 25.8$, $SD = 5.59$), and they were studying in English. Students' fields of study included medicine, psychology, dentistry, pharmacy, fine arts, business administration and management, international relations, and architecture.

Students were mostly recruited online from different university-exclusive community groups in Hungary and a few via snowball sampling. The benefit of the snowball sampling technique is that it "often shorten[s] the time and diminish[es] the cost required to assemble a participant group of sufficient size and diversity" (Sadler et al., 2010, p. 370). Out of the 20 Iranian students, 12 (five females and seven males) agreed to participate in the follow-up interviews. The rest did not respond or had left Hungary due to the currency crisis.

Procedures

The first interviews were carried out face to face by the first author between October 2017 and February 2018. The follow-up interviews were also conducted by the first author between September 2018 and October 2018 via an audio call. The main reason why we chose to do the face-to-face interviews for the first round was to establish rapport with the participants. The second interviews were conducted via audio call since the interviews were anticipated to take less time.

Also, rapport had already been established in the first interviews. All first-round interviews were conducted in Persian, except for three interviews conducted in English. All the follow-up interviews were conducted in Persian.

In total, we had 32 interviews: 20 for the first round and 12 for the second round. The first interviews lasted between 60 and 120 min, and the follow-up interviews were between 30 and 60 min in duration. The first author, fluent in both Persian and English, concurrently translated the Persian interviews to English and transcribed them on oTranscribe software. The three English interviews were also transcribed directly on oTranscribe. The audio-recorded interviews were all transcribed verbatim. All the interviews were transferred from oTranscribe to Microsoft Word. The longest interview transcription in the first round was 29 pages; the shortest was 16 pages. For the follow-up interviews, length ranged from six to eight pages.

Materials

Semi-structured Interview Questions

In the first interviews, we asked questions regarding participants' demographic data (e.g., age, gender, the field of study, financial status, etc.). Semi-structured interview questions addressed topics including psychological and sociocultural adaptation, academic and life hassles, changes in psychosocial adaptation, and the effect of the currency crisis in Iran on students' mental health. Some of the questions asked in the interviews included: "What are the daily hassles you have to deal with?," "How has your mental health changed since the first interview?," and "Would you have better psychological health living in Hungary or Iran?"

Data Analysis

We employed an inductive approach to content analysis to analyze the interview transcripts (Graneheim & Lundman, 2004). An inductive approach is one of the most common methods of analyzing data utilized in qualitative research, in which the authors do not have any preconceived theories or categories for data analysis (Burnard et al., 2008). During the first stage, the lead author listened to the tape, translated and transcribed the data on oTranscribe, and read over the transcripts to familiarize herself with the data while looking for recurring patterns and themes.

The interviews were considered as units of analysis, as "the most suitable unit of analysis is whole interviews" (Graneheim & Lundman, 2004, p. 106). After, we divided each interview text into meaning units. We considered our meaning units as the paragraphs or sentences from the interview transcripts that were similar with regards to the content.

We then constructed codes from these meaning units. In order to formulate codes, the first and third authors performed open coding on Atlas.ti, line by line. All the authors reviewed the initial codes for similarity in content, and we then combined them into code groups on Atlas.ti. In the Code Manager, we classified 59 distinct code groups for the first interviews and 27 code groups for the follow-up interviews. We present examples of meaning units and codes in Table 1.

Table 1: Meaning Unit to Code from Interview Transcripts

Meaning unit	Code
"The visa that immigration gives is miserably hard to get. The visa expires very soon."	Immigration visa validity and obtaining a visa challenge
"One day, you wake up, and you realize that the currency's value has decreased by half."	A substantial decrease in the value of the rial

Table 2: Themes Emerging from Interview Transcripts

Topic	Higher order category	Code group
Visa and banking challenges	Obtaining and expiry of a visa	• Problems with obtaining a visa • Frustration with visa expiration
	Bank account opening and closure issues	• Problems with opening a bank account • Bank account closure
Impact of the currency crisis in Iran on mental health	Currency crisis issues	• A decrease in the value of the rial • Financial pressure due to the currency crisis
	Currency crisis and mental health	• Currency crisis causing depression or anxiety • Currency crisis causing uncertainty
Positive and negative changes in psychological well-being	Positive mental health	• Mental health improved in Hungary • Optimism about future
	Negative mental health	• Mental health got worse in Hungary

We then combined similar or overlapping code groups into higher order categories on Atlas.ti. We further clustered similar higher order categories into potential topics. As in content analysis, we did not stop at categories but created comprehensive topics in terms of the research question by merging similar higher order categories (Erlingsson & Brysiewicz, 2017). Examples of code groups, higher order categories, and topics are presented in Table 2. Finally, we summarized and analyzed the emerged topics and findings using the relevant literature.

RESULTS

Three major interconnected themes emerged from the data. They were visa and banking challenges, impact of the currency crisis in Iran on mental health, and positive and negative changes in psychological well-being. All topics that emerged from the data analysis are presented separately below.

Visa and Banking Challenges

Challenges in obtaining and extending visas and the underlying reasons made students anxious. According to many participants, one of the reasons they faced visa challenges was their nationality, which was perceived to be discriminatory. One participant who encountered many problems applying for a visa to spend one semester studying in another country stated, "My worst experience was anxiety regarding visas … I think because I am Iranian, things will continue like this."

The anxiety caused by applying for a visa as an Iranian person seemed to persist over time. Some participants also expressed worries about extending their visas after graduation. However, participants were aware that being an Iranian was an obstacle, which created uncertainty. One participant elaborated, "A big question mark appears after graduation, about what we should do … For us, Iranians, things are much harder because we are not EU citizens."

This new graduate student seemed ready to start doing her residency in a field of study that she liked; however, she felt discriminated against because she was aware that her EU peers could easily work after graduation, without visa complications. She noted, "We are placed in the second level. First, they give jobs to EU citizens … to us much later. Hassles about visas are in the first place."

Iranian students have to leave Hungary after graduation since they cannot easily extend their visas unless they plan to work or continue with their studies. Most international students, especially students from the EU, will return to their home country to start working after graduation since their degree is recognized in their country. However, they also have the opportunity to stay in Hungary for work or to move to other EU countries where they could find jobs. Since this opportunity is not available to Iranian students, it created a sense of inferiority among many students related to their peers from the EU.

A participant used the analogy of a "marathon" to show the hardships Iranian students go through due to economic, political, and visa problems. He commented, "Consider a marathon that everyone wants to compete. If some start from 100 meters and others start from zero, we [Iranian students] begin 300 meters behind the starting line."

The visa obstacles created anxieties and uncertainties among Iranians because they were unsure whether they would be able to extend their visas. This created even more anxiety because if they were not able to get a visa, they had to leave Hungary.

A majority of the participants did not intend to go back to Iran after graduation, because if they left the country, there would be no guarantee that they would be able to obtain a visa again; that is, there would be no way for them to return.

Considering that obtaining a visa is not guaranteed, and the visa application takes time, students were motivated to find jobs before their student visa expired so they could apply for a working visa, which is valid for a longer time than a student visa. Obtaining a working visa allows students to stay in Hungary longer and offers them enough time to apply for a visa to another country. One participant said, "If I could find a job, I would be able to solve my visa problems because I would like to stay here."

Iranian students put their best efforts into finding jobs so they would be able to extend their visas to stay abroad longer and avoid getting deported. Their adaptation would have been improved if Hungary would "give [students] visas, treat them better, and let them study, stay and work," as one student acknowledged.

Another problem that Iranian students faced was banking restrictions. Due to regulations associated with the sanctions, Iranians could not hold a bank account in almost any bank in Hungary. The discriminatory actions of many banks against Iranians (including terminating their bank account abruptly or not opening an account for them, allegedly because of their nationality) were unreasonable for students. One participant reflected, "I went to open an account, and they asked for my passport … they said, you can't open an account because you are Iranian."

Even the banks that allowed Iranians to open a bank account required more strict paperwork for countries under sanctions. The fact that the banking processes took longer only because of their nationality disappointed many students. One female participant noted,

> When I went to open a bank account, they told me to go home and get my passport. Although it only took my friend ten minutes to get her bank card … They said, "You should get permission because you're Iranian."

Besides the problem of opening a bank account, students reported problems with bank account closures. Because the banks had to comply with regulations, providing financial services to Iranians was halted. Many banks started to close the bank accounts of Iranians abroad. One participant expressed his anxiety regarding closures of bank accounts: "Anxieties exist for Iranians abroad … I received a letter from a bank … They are planning to close all Iranians' accounts." This participant spoke about the anxieties that Iranians have to go through because if their bank accounts get closed, they have no idea where to keep their money.

Banking obstacles are not common challenges among international students; they seem isolated to students whose countries are under sanction. One participant perceived that banking obstacles were "specific to Iranians ... that Iranians are struggling with."

Impact of Currency Crisis in Iran on Mental Health

During the second round of interviews, students reported that the sudden and steep decline in the value of the Iranian currency adversely influenced their mental health. One participant stated, "One day, you wake up, and you realize that the currency's value has decreased by half ... This makes people depressed ... These things make me sad."

The devaluation of the currency affected her so much that she preferred "not to check the news" and "the price of Euro." She was glad that she did not have to live in Iran to directly witness the crisis: "If I were in Iran, my depression would have been worse."

A majority of the participants were from the upper-middle class, and during the first interview, they did not report financial hassles. However, in the second interview, almost all of them reported financial difficulties. Many participants' families had to sell their belongings or find a second job, and could not afford to pay for their children's tuition fees. One participant claimed, "When I buy something, the price is three times higher. I had two cars: one of them is gone ... I am not mentally healthy because the value of the euro keeps going up [relative to the rial]."

This high-upper class participant was also affected by the currency crisis, as she had to sell one of her cars when planned to open a business, and she was asked by her father to go back to Iran.

A majority of the participants were financially dependent on their parents, and after the economic crisis, they were motivated to find jobs and to work harder to earn more money to compensate for their monetary losses. The currency crisis made them anxious about their future. One participant noted, "I get stressed that in addition to my studies ... I have to start working."

The preceding demonstrates that the currency crisis prevented this student from focusing on both the academic and career aspects of her life. She acknowledged that if she had a job, she could "at least pay for [her] weekly expenses."

Additionally, participants' families were unable to transfer money to their children, because the money exchange services stopped transfers until the currency rate stabilized. This issue led to some participants looking for jobs as it was not possible to transfer money from Iran. The currency crisis seemed to be one of the main reasons for students' psychological problems, as it directly affected other issues, such as financial security, the need for employment, and obtaining a visa.

Positive and Negative Changes in Psychological Well-Being

During the second round of interviews, most participants reported that they felt better than they had at the time of the first interview. However, a few reported being more anxious and depressed. A number of participants stated that they were satisfied to be in Hungary and that their anxiety had decreased. One female participant reported, "My mental well-being has changed because I have never lived independently … This independence has made me grow … I am still happy [to be in Hungary]."

Independent living was a challenge for many participants at the beginning. However, it became a great asset for them after living in Hungary as they believed they learned to complete life chores independently, such as cooking, cleaning, managing life expenses, and so on. Participants seemed to be happy to live their own way as one student acknowledged that "independence will never develop when the family is present."

Other factors associated with better mental health among participants were economic opportunities and educational attainments in Hungary. Many participants believed that because the economic situation was unstable in Iran, and their future was unknown. One participant remarked, "I feel better in Hungary … In Iran, your future is unknown, and an unknown future gives you a bad feeling."

Furthermore, participants emphasized the importance of the social and political freedom that they experienced in Hungary, which improved their mental health. One participant, when asked whether he felt mentally better in Hungary or in Iran, replied, "Definitely here [in Hungary] … There are some low-level freedoms that you have here, but you don't in Iran … I don't want to live in Iran now with the current situation." Similar to most participants, he also desired higher order freedoms such as freedom of speech and gender equality that existed to a greater extent in Hungary than in Iran. However, even simple freedoms in clothing were perceived as essential and helped him "compensate for [his] bad days."

Overall, a majority of participants felt more content over time. They valued more independence along with better sociopolitical and economic opportunities abroad than they would have had living in Iran. Previous research (Hosseini-Nezhad et al., 2019) also found that Iranian students in Hungary embraced the independence and freedom they had in Hungary.

A few participants in the second interview reported that their mental health had declined over time, mainly due to the economic crisis. One female participant said she was depressed, and that her mental health got worse as "the Euro is getting expensive."

Despite various challenges, participants stayed hopeful. Their positive attitude as a way of coping with their challenges was evident in their statements that they were "optimistic about future," they tried "not to think about the economic crisis," and felt that "future will change." Participants were aware that they had no choice but to stay positive, as they would not be able to stay focused on their goals otherwise.

It is expected that students' anxieties will persist as the Iranian currency's value continues to tumble, given that the United States imposed strong sanctions on Iran and that the Iranian government cut subsidies and increased the prices of goods. This is evident from one student's remark: "The subsidies cut down ... every day the price of meat, cheese, and milk is increasing."

DISCUSSION

This study explored the adaptation trajectory as well as the challenges of Iranian students in Hungary. Each of the themes that emerged will be investigated by referring to relevant literature.

Visa and Banking Challenges

Iranian students in Hungary experienced issues with visas and with opening and closing bank accounts due to sanctions. The visa challenges faced by Iranian students in Hungary were not without precedent; several studies have reported visa and immigration challenges among Iranian (Hefner-Babb & Khoshlessan, 2018) and Chinese (Yan, 2017) international students in the United States, and other international students in South Africa (Lee et al., 2017). Considering that most international students in Hungary are from countries with no or less restrictive sanctions compared with Iran and that the Iranian passport is one of the weakest globally, Iranians probably struggle with visa and immigration processes more than most international students.

Another challenge some Iranian students experienced in Hungary due to sanctions was discriminatory banking restrictions and policies. Iranians reported problems opening a bank account, and some existing bank accounts were closed abruptly. As a result, they had to withdraw their cash from the bank and either keep it at home, or transfer it to another bank. The banks that allowed Iranians to open an account required them to go through extra hurdles of passport and security checks. Banking obstacles in response to the sanctions have been previously reported among Iranian students in the United States (National Iranian American Council, 2020), Canada (Mobasher, 2018), and elsewhere.

The banking and visa challenges created a sense of inferiority and perceptions of discrimination among Iranians. When they compared themselves to other international students, they realized that peers from the EU did not experience obstacles similar to theirs in obtaining visas, finding jobs, and opening bank accounts. People perceive a situation as discriminatory and experience identity threat once they realize that they are being categorized and negatively treated based on their group membership (Branscombe et al., 1999), as was reported by the Iranian students in our study.

Iranians might have experienced relative deprivation, which is defined as "a judgment that one or one's in-group is disadvantaged compared to a relevant referent, and that this judgment invokes feelings of anger, resentment, and entitlement" (Smith & Pettigrew, 2015, p. 2). The feeling of being relatively deprived is salient to how Iranian students felt when they compared themselves to EU students.

Our findings highlight the significance of considering visa and banking challenges that have created mental health problems among Iranian students abroad and indicate that international students' challenges extend far beyond micro level aspects, and macro level policies require allocation of more attention.

Impact of Currency Crisis in Iran on Mental Health

Our study represents one of the few studies that provides an understanding of the impact of the currency crisis on Iranian students' mental health, with the broader intention to inform about the adverse consequences of economic sanctions on students' adaptation and mental health abroad. This study contributes to literature as it has analyzed a critical phenomenon that deserves closer attention.

A majority of the Iranian students moved to Hungary with their parents' financial support and with at least half the price of the current value of the Iranian currency. Following the economic crisis, Iranian students' financial situation has become so dire that it has caused anxiety and depression among them. Students were in a rush to find jobs, and many decided to return home. International students in China (Shi, 2016), Venezuela (Valverde & Hemlock, 2015), and South Korea (McNeill, 2009) have reported facing currency crisis challenges akin to Iranian students' challenges in Hungary.

Similar to the visa and banking challenges in the host country, the currency crisis in the sending country proved to significantly impact the adaptation of Iranian international students in our study. This finding is in line with Ward and Geeraert's (2016) model that posits the significance of ecological context in both the host and home countries.

Notwithstanding all the challenges Iranian students face, they have remained strong. However, these challenges will continue to get worse for them, especially after the increased levels of the Iran-US conflict in January 2020, which followed additional U.S. sanctions against Iran (Timofeev, 2020), and the COVID-19 pandemic[2], all of which occurred after our interviews.

Positive and Negative Changes in Psychological Well-Being

A majority of participants in our study felt that their psychological health had improved, their anxieties declined over time, and they were happy to be in Hungary. Only a few participants felt mentally worse in the second interview. The findings of our study are consistent with previous studies (Hechanova-Alampay et al. 2002; Hirai et al., 2015; Ward et al., 1998), in which the adaptation of international students enhanced over time.

---

[2] The Coronavirus (COVID-19) crisis exacerbated Iran's economic crisis as it led to a further depreciation of the rial (Wallace, 2020).

Inconsistent with our findings, Cemalcilar and Falbo (2008) reported that the psychological well-being of international students in the United States significantly decreased over time. On one hand, our findings indicated that mental health of a majority of participants improved over time while on the other hand, it demonstrated a decline in the mental health of a few Iranians. Thus, Thakar's (2010) result is more compatible with our findings, as the author found significant variations in the mental health trajectories of international students from India in the United States.

Participants in the current study reported that the currency crisis had a negative impact on their well-being. It is important to note that while a majority of the students expressed their sadness and anxiety regarding the currency crisis and the psychosocial challenges they experienced; as a result, a majority remained positive overall. They believed that their mental health was better in Hungary than in Iran due to a range of factors, including more freedom, independence, sociopolitical stability, and better economic and career prospects.

Additionally, participants' negative or positive feelings could be associated with whether they made an upward comparison with out-group members or a downward comparison with their in-group members (Martinot & Redersdorff, 2006). In our study, students seemed to report more negative emotions when they made an upward comparison with the situations of other international students, especially those from EU countries. They also reported more positive emotions when they adopted a downward comparison with circumstances back home in Iran, where they would be less satisfied with the sociopolitical and economic situations relative to Hungary.

Limitations

This study has some limitations. One is the rate of participant attrition, as many students had to leave Hungary due to the currency crisis. Another limitation relates to the limitations inherent in content analysis techniques. We had the difficult task of deciding on which sets of categories and themes to focus on from those that emerged through the content analysis. Other potential themes were set aside for later consideration, and only themes related to sociopolitical and economic conditions in Iran were analyzed.

Implications and Conclusion

This study provides relevant information to various sectors (such as governments, the EU, and the United Nations) about the challenges confronting Iranian international students. Understanding these challenges by these sectors could help with policy reforms designed to improve the students' situations.

Iranian students' challenges also have negative long term implications for universities across Hungary. Over time, they will face a decline in enrollment of new international students who contribute to social, cultural, and economic growth in Hungary. Consequently, they need to continue to support international students who experience challenges, especially when they are fundamentally political (Todoran & Peterson, 2019).

This research has focused primarily on the psychosocial adaptation trajectory and challenges faced by Iranian students in Hungary. Our research indicates the negative impacts of visas, banking, and currency crisis challenges (due to sanctions on Iran) on Iranian students' mental health. These challenges have been shown to create negative feelings such as anxiety, depression, uncertainty, perceived discrimination, identity threat, and relative deprivation among the students. We hope this study contributes to policy changes and is useful for the policy sectors. If these challenges persist, students' mental health might decline, and more complex interventions may be needed to ameliorate the adverse impact.

Additionally, to better understand international students' adaptation processes, future studies are encouraged to address the broader ecological context of intercultural contacts. Ward and Geeraert (2016) acknowledged the importance of the home and host cultures' ecological contexts on the familial, institutional, and societal levels. Factors such as sanctions, visas, and banking issues operate within a broader ecological context that impacts acculturation and adaptation of international students. We argue there is an essential gap in the literature concerning this specific group since few studies have considered the broader ecological context. There is also a paucity of longitudinal studies on the negative impacts of challenges on Iranian international students' mental health as a result of sanctions on Iran.

REFERENCES

Astinova, M. (2011). *Legal, social and economic issues of international students in Saxion University* [Unpublished bachelor's thesis]. The Saxion University of Applied Science.

Bani Kamal, A. M., & Hossain, I. (2017). The Iranian diaspora in Malaysia: A socio-economic and political analysis. *Diaspora Studies, 10*(1), 116–129. https://doi.org/10.1080/09739572.2016.1239439

Bianchi, R. V., & Stephenson, M. L. (2014). *Tourism and citizenship: Rights, freedoms and responsibilities in the global order*. Routledge.

Branscombe, N. R., Ellemers, N., Spears, R., & Doosje, B. (1999). *The context and content of social identity threat.* In N. Ellemers, R. Spears, & B. Doosje (Eds.), *Social identity: Context, commitment, content* (pp. 35–58). Blackwell Science.

Burnard, P., Gill, P. W., Stewart, K. F., Treasure, E., & Chadwick, B. (2008). Analysing and presenting qualitative data. *British Dental Journal, 204*(8), 429–432. https://doi.org/10.1038/sj.bdj.2008.292

Cemalcilar, Z., & Falbo, T. (2008). A longitudinal study of the adaptation of international students in the United States. *Journal of Cross-Cultural Psychology, 39*(6), 799–804. http://doi.org/10.1177/0022022108323787

Ditto, S. (2014). *Red tape, iron nerve: The Iranian quest for U.S. education.* The Washington Institute for Near East Policy.

Ehteshami, A. (2017). *Iran stuck in transition.* Routledge.

Erlingsson, C., & Brysiewicz, P. (2017). A hands-on guide to doing content analysis. *African Journal of Emergency Medicine,* *7*(3), 93–99. https://doi.org/10.1016/j.afjem.2017.08.001

EU Sanctions Map. (2020, February 27). *Thematic restrictions.* https://www.sanctionsmap.eu/#/main

Eurofast Global Ltd. (2017, March 23). *Iran: Opening a bank account in Europe for Iranians.* Mondaq. https://www.mondaq.com/financial-services/576970/opening-a-bank-account-in-europe-for-iranians?fbclid=IwAR05QjGSiQQvr-1tDqK1XWNvmcpeoHZnO8MIYPcnyLoVIc4rD5IepM8yJIw

Eybagi, M. (2013). *Human consequences of economic sanctions: Analyzing the experiences of Iranian residents in Toronto and Halifax about the international sanctions against Iran.* [Master's thesis, Dalhousie University]. DalSpace Institutional Repository. http://hdl.handle.net/10222/35424

Gearan, A., & DeYoung, K. (2018, May 8). Trump pulls United States out of Iran nuclear deal, calling the pact 'an embarrassment'. *The Washington Post.* https://www.washingtonpost.com/politics/trump-will-announce-plans-to-pull-out-of-iran-nuclear-deal-despite-pleas-from-european-leaders/2018/05/08/4c148252-52ca-11e8-9c91-7dab596e8252_story.html

Golden, J. B. (1973). Student adjustment abroad: A psychiatrist's view. *International Educational and Cultural Exchange*, *8*(4), 28–36.

Graneheim, U. H., & Lundman, B. (2004). Qualitative content analysis in nursing research: Concepts, procedures and measures to achieve trustworthiness. *Nurse Education Today,* *24*(2), 105–112. http://doi.org/10.1016/j.nedt.2003.10.001

Hafezi, P. (2016, January 27). *Hope but also frustration for Iranians after sanctions lifted.* Reuters. https://www.reuters.com/article/us-iran-sanctions-people/hope-but-also-frustration-for-iranians-after-sanctions-lifted-idUSKCN0V527L?fbclid=IwAR0dvVL9ncRCFz-_Y4WH9Ljz8JxPoXLZmiEEloeoNtV4mHpYRdQfvfZDHfI

Hechanova-Alampay, R., Beehr, T. A., Christiansen, N. D., & Van Horn, R. K. (2002). Adjustment and strain among domestic and international student sojourners: A longitudinal study. *School Psychology International, 23*(4), 458–474. https://doi.org/10.1177/0143034302234007

Hefner-Babb, T. S., & Khoshlessan, R. (2018). Iranian student experience pursuing admission to universities in the United States. *Journal of International Students,* *8*(4), 1926–1940. http://doi.org/10.5281/zenodo.1482777

Henley & Partners. (2019). *The Henley passport index.* https://www.henleypassportindex.com/passport

Hirai, R., Frazier, P., & Syed, M. (2015). Psychological and sociocultural adjustment of first-year international students: Trajectories and predictors. *Journal of Counseling Psychology,* *62*(3), 438–452. http://doi.org/10.1037/cou0000085

Hossein-Zadeh, I. (2018, October 3). *Neoliberal economics: The plague of Iran's economy.* Counterpunch. https://www.counterpunch.org/2018/10/03/neoliberal-economics-the-plague-of-irans-economy/?fbclid=IwAR0KN_bsCyIqwOVX_hXYQmEoy3iHfUZcSWJi8BQju8KNozuGj9seir9MxCw

Hosseini-Nezhad, S., Safdar, S., & Nguyen Luu, L. A. (2019). Longing for independence, yet depending on family support: A qualitative analysis of psychosocial adaptation of Iranian international students in Hungary. *International Journal of Higher Education, 8*(4), 16–4174. https://doi.org/10.5430/ijhe.v8n4p164

Internet Forex Resource. (2020, July 7). *Top 10-the weakest world currencies in 2020.* https://fxssi.com/top-10-of-the-weakest-world-currencies-in-current-year

Jafari, S. (2019, January 13). *US sanctions hit Iranian students seeking bank accounts in Europe.* Al-Monitor: The Pulse of the Middle East. https://www.al-monitor.com/pulse/originals/2019/01/iran-students-sanctions-impact-banks-europe-us-visa.html

Johansson, C. (2013). *The sanctioned students: An empirical study of sanctions effects on Iranian students studying abroad* [Bachelor's thesis, Linnaeus University]. DiVA Portal. http://www.diva-portal.org/smash/get/diva2:605951/FULLTEXT01.pdf

Karimzad, F. (2016). Life here beyond now: Chronotopes of the ideal life among Iranian transnationals. *Journal of Sociolinguistics, 20*(5), 607–630. https://doi.org/10.1111/josl.12211

Khodabandelou, R., Karimi, L., & Ehsani, M. (2015). Challenges of international higher education students in a foreign country: A qualitative study. *Higher Education for the Future, 2*(2), 165–174. https://doi.org/10.1177/2347631115584121

Laub, Z. (2015, July 15). *International sanctions on Iran.* Council on Foreign Relations. https://www.cfr.org/backgrounder/international-sanctions-iran?fbclid=IwAR1Jf5sWcuE52ZAdtI9RomLvuQORP6Uc2cAm1fx7dAsjGn99pkj6oTdOjtI

Lee, J. J., Paulidor, K., & Mpaga, Y. A. (2017). Sliding doors: Strategic ambiguity in study visas to South Africa. *Studies in Higher Education, 43*(11), 1–14. https://doi.org/10.1080/03075079.2017.1296825

Martinot, D., & Redersdorff, S. (2006). The variable impact of upward and downward social comparisons on self-esteem: When the level of analysis matters. In S. Guimond (Ed.), *Social comparison and social psychology: Understanding cognition, intergroup relations and culture* (pp.127–150). Cambridge University Press.

McNeill, D. (2009, April 7). *South Korean students, hit hard by currency decline, opt to stay home.* Chronicle of Higher Education. https://www.chronicle.com/article/south-korean-students-hit-hard-by-currency-declines-opt-to-stay-home-47169/

Mehdizadeh., N., & Scott, G. (2005). Adjustment problems of Iranian international students in Scotland. *International Education Journal*, *6*(4), 484–493.

Mehrabi, S. (2014). International economic sanctions, university life, and global citizenship education: The case of Iran. *Cultural and Pedagogical Inquiry*, *6*(1), 43–66. https://doi.org/10.18733/C3D30T

Mobasher, M. M. (2018). *The Iranian diaspora: Challenges, negotiations, and transformations*. University of Texas Press.

National Iranian American Council. (2020, February 24). *NIAC presses treasury on discriminatory bank account closures.* https://www.niacouncil.org/press_room/niac-presses-treasury-discriminatory-bank-account-closures/?locale=en&fbclid=IwAR1NPufvPH3XJSXqyB51LHJSxR0ErtoDBnxFtjvJPvDN2d3Xv8ozV1_TNvs

No more cheap currency for Iranian students. (2018, April 8). *Financial Tribune.* https://financialtribune.com/articles/economy-business-and-markets/84286/no-more-cheap-currency-for-iranian-students?fbclid=IwAR2xV3jYX-N_QMM6VqWiOHVpn31PxZlktP9V-bpC7t7bHEArbayb6RPnAk8

Office of Foreign Assets Control. (2019). *Sanctions programs and country information.* U.S. Department of the Treasury. https://www.treasury.gov/resource-center/sanctions/Programs/Pages/Programs.aspx?fbclid=IwAR3UPiBnp7R6OGnoFByyEg10cDxiR3PqY-NKdbaKqnMyN-z0dfcKeg8GHIw

Oktatási Hivatal. (2018). *Higher educational statistics.* https://www.oktatas.hu/felsooktatas/kozerdeku_adatok/felsooktatasi_adatok_kozzetetele/felsooktatasi_statisztikak

Rose-Redwood, C., & Rose-Redwood, R. (2017). Rethinking the politics of the international student experience in the age of Trump. *Journal of International Students*, *7*(3), i–ix. https://doi.org/10.32674/jis.v7i3.201

Sadler, G. R., Lee, H.-C., Lim, R. S.-H., & Fullerton, J. (2010). Recruitment of hard-to-reach population subgroups via adaptations of the snowball sampling strategy. *Nursing and Health Sciences, 12*(3), 369–374. https://doi.org/10.1111/j.1442-2018.2010.00541.x

Shi, M. (2016, January 21). *China's overseas students are dumping yuan to hedge against tuition hikes*. Quartz. https://qz.com/590831/chinas-weak-yuan-hits-home-for-thousands-of-overseas-students/?fbclid=IwAR0tr9f_PVPOTjN-gekq0a2IV2Q3fZctr_4VxS8Lbvqkz45D8MjZZu2DrmM

Smith, H. J., & Pettigrew, T. F. (2015). Advances in relative deprivation theory and research. *Social Justice Research, 28*(1), 1–6. https://doi.org/10.1007/s11211-014-0231-5

Thakar, D.A. (2010). *Trajectories of mental health and acculturation among first year international graduate students from India* (no. 255) [Doctoral dissertation, University of Massachusetts-Amherst]. Open Access Dissertations. https://scholarworks.umass.edu/open_access_dissertations/255

Timofeev, I. (2020, January 22). *US sanctions against Iran: New escalation*. The Russian International Affairs Council. https://russiancouncil.ru/en/analytics-and-comments/analytics/us-sanctions-against-iran-new-escalation/

Todoran, C., & Peterson, C. (2019). Should they stay or should they go? How the 2017 U.S. travel ban affects international doctoral students. *Journal of Studies in International Education, 24*(4), 1–16. https://doi.org/10.1177/1028315319861344

Torbati, Y. (2012, October 17). *Iranian students feel the pain as currency collapses*. Reuters. https://www.reuters.com/article/us-iran-students/iranian-students-feel-the-pain-as-currency-collapses-idUSBRE89G10220121017?fbclid=IwAR0604mCj21vbjR0qBJ0g0dONC2wa3mqoY6sixYLVtEGBHKVC3w0vOLVCSc

Tummala-Narra, P., & Claudius, M. (2013). A qualitative examination of Muslim graduate international students' experiences in the United States. *International Perspectives in Psychology: Research, Practice, Consultation, 2*(2), 132–147. https://doi.org/10.1037/ipp0000003

Valverde, M., & Hemlock, D. (2015). *Venezuela's economy squeezes students in South Florida*. Sun Sentinel. https://www.sun-sentinel.com/business/fl-venezuelan-students-dollars-20151002-story.html

Wallace, P. (2020, February 26). *Coronavirus panic causes more woes for Iran's currency: Chart.* Bloomberg. https://www.bloomberg.com/news/articles/2020-02-26/coronavirus-panic-causes-more-woes-for-iran-s-currency-chart

Ward, C., & Geeraert, N. (2016). Advancing acculturation theory and research: The acculturation process in its ecological context. *Current Opinion in Psychology, 8*, 98–104. https://doi.org/10.1016/j.copsyc.2015.09.021

Ward, C., Okura, A., Kennedy, A., & Kojima, T. (1998). The U-curve on trial: A longitudinal study of psychological and sociocultural adjustment during cross-cultural transition. *International Journal of Intercultural Relations, 22*(3), 277–291. https://doi.org/10.1016/S0147-1767(98)00008-X

Yan, K. (2017). *Chinese international students' stressors and coping strategies in the United States*. Springer. https://doi.org/10.1007/978-981-10-3347-6

SARA HOSSEINI-NEZHAD is a PhD student in the Doctoral School of Psychology, Faculty of Education and Psychology, at Eötvös Loránd University (ELTE), in Budapest, Hungary, under the joint supervision of Dr. Lan Anh Nguyen Luu from ELTE and Dr. Saba Safdar from the University of Guelph, Ontario, Canada. Her primary research interests lie in the area of clinical, social, and cross-cultural psychology. Email: sara_hosseininezhad@yahoo.com

SABA SAFDAR is an Iranian-born Canadian-educated professor in the psychology department at the University of Guelph in Canada. She received her PhD in 2002 from York University, Toronto, Canada, and has held an academic position at the University of Guelph since 2002. She is Director of the Centre for Cross-Cultural Research at the University of Guelph. Her research focus is on acculturation and understanding the adaptation processes of newcomers, including immigrants, refugees, and international students. Professor Safdar's research has been funded by the Social Sciences and Humanities Research Council of Canada, the Canada Foundation for Innovation, and Erasmus Mundus Scholarship, amongst others. In addition to her Canadian academic position, Professor Safdar has held academic appointments in the United States, the United Kingdom, France, Spain, India, Kazakhstan, and Russia. Email: ssafdar@uoguelph.ca

LAN ANH NGUYEN LUU is a Vietnamese-born, Budapest-based intercultural/social psychologist. She is an associate professor and director of the Institute of Intercultural Psychology and Education and the Socialization and Social Processes PhD Program at the Psychology Doctoral School at the Eötvös Loránd University in Budapest, Hungary. Her main research interests are acculturation, ethnic identity, gender beliefs, and teachers' attitudes toward diversity. Email: lananh@ppk.elte.hu

Peer-Reviewed Article

© *Journal of International Students*
Volume 11, Issue 2 (2021), pp. 361-376
ISSN: 2162-3104 (Print), 2166-3750 (Online)
doi: 10.32674/jis.v11i2.2092
ojed.org/jis

Internet Addiction and Acculturative Stress Among International College Students in the United States

Jiaqi Li
Wichita State University, USA

Xun Liu
University of South Carolina, USA

ABSTRACT

While Internet use plays an increasingly important role in individuals' lives, many college students have found themselves totally unconsciously plunged into Internet addiction (IA). Guided by the acculturative stress theory, we examined the relationships between acculturative stress, gender, age, length of stay, and IA among international college students. Data were collected from 111 international undergraduate and graduate students studying in the United States. Hierarchical multiple regression analyses reported that acculturative stress and gender significantly predict IA among international college students. In this sample, neither age nor length of stay predicted IA. Our findings paint a picture of the potential influence of acculturative stress on IA. We offer suggestions for future research on Internet addiction and acculturative stress, particularly for international college students.

Keywords: acculturative stress, college counselor, international college students, Internet addiction

---

Over the past decades, Internet addiction (IA) has become a campus health issue that cannot be ignored in the United Stated and other countries in the world (Anderson, 2001; Cardak, 2013; Carlisle et al., 2016; Kandell, 2009). Estimates indicate that 71% of 18–24 year olds would qualify as being addicted to the

Internet, and prevalence rates of IA are as high as 8.2% in the general population (Gaille, 2017; Weinstein & Lejoyeux, 2010). To date, IA on college campuses is a growing concern as more and more studies are revealing (Chai et al., 2012; Ostovar et al., 2016). Research has indicated that college students with IA are likely to experience depression (Ineme et al., 2017; Ostovar et al., 2016), anxiety (Ostovar et al., 2016), loneliness (Zeliha, 2019), and poor physical health such as vision problems and weight gain or loss (Gregory, 2019). Of college students, international students appear to be more at risk of IA because their acculturation experiences entail adjustment difficulties and stress, which are related to excessive Internet use (Chai et al., 2012; Hirai et al., 2015; Ye, 2005). Research has shown that acculturative stress may contribute to IA (Jin & Berge, 2016; Ye, 2005). International students use the Internet as a means to cope with unpleasant feelings (e.g., perceived discrimination, cultural shock) during the process of acculturation (Ye, 2005). Despite the attention to IA, a limited number of studies on international students with IA have been reported. Given the prevalence and complexities of IA among international students, it is imperative to identify the factors implicated in IA so that counselors can more effectively target intervention to reduce the likelihood of IA. In the current study, we therefore examined the relationships between acculturative stress, gender, age, and length of stay among international college students in the United States. The findings from this study are intended to expand the existing literature on IA of international college students and its correlating factors.

BACKGROUND

IA was first proposed by Young (1998) and referred to as problematic Internet use, computer addiction, Internet use disorder, or excessive Internet use (Caplan, 2002; Van Rooij & Prause, 2014; Young, 1996). Conceptualizations of IA have adhered to two distinct explanations: (a) it is a broad term that covers a wide variety of behavioral and impulse-control problems (Young, 1999), and (b) "many of these excessive users are not 'Internet addicts' but just use the Internet excessively as a medium to fuel other addictions" (Griffiths, 2000, p. 416). Although IA has not been included in the spectrum of addictive disorders in the *Diagnostic and Statistical Manual of Mental Disorders, Fifth Edition* (*DSM*-5) or the *International Classification of Diseases Tenth Edition* (*ICD*-10), concern is rapidly increasing with respect to its risk factors (Choi et al., 2015; Hyun et al., 2015). For example, research has identified several risk factors that are closely related to IA of college students, including psychological well-being (e.g., stress and loneliness; Ostovar et al., 2016), social contexts (e.g., lack of family support, poor academic performance; Cheng & Hong, 2017; Jun & Choi, 2015), coping strategies (Chou et al., 2015), and personal habits (e.g., poor control of Internet use; Lam, 2014). These risk factors are often presented individually, coexist and interact with one another, and increase the likelihood of getting college students addicted to the Internet (Choi et al., 2015).

International College Students

Over the last years (2009–2010 to 2019–2020), the number of international students seeking degrees in the United States has increased substantially, from nearly 202,970 to 267,712 (Institute of International Education, 2020). The transition to college life, and to a potentially more diverse and more multicultural environment on the university campus, always brings new demands and challenges to international students (Ruberman, 2014). These demands and challenges are especially acute for racial and cultural minority international students from Asian countries (Ching et al., 2017). For example, Sherry et al. (2010) found that Asian international students often feel culturally misunderstood and socially isolated in the university community. These students appear to be more at risk of addiction during this process of cultural change (Blanco et al., 2008; Lonner et al., 2007). In an investigation of 110 Chinese international students studying in Korea, Kim et al. (2015) found that 40% of their participants were at-risk smartphone users; smartphone addiction may also have an adverse impact on physical health in the process of cross-cultural adaptation.

Acculturative Stress

The transition to the university environment often creates considerable stress in the lives of students and shapes how they perceive and respond to these kinds of life changes in the future (Besser & Zeigler-Hill, 2014). In this study, I refer to *acculturative stress* as the stress associated with adjustment to a different culture and "a response by people to life events that are rooted in intercultural contact" (Berry, 2005, p. 43). This term includes two major theoretical perspectives: (a) psychological difficulty associated with cultural contact (e.g., from African American neighborhoods to low-diversity, White-dominant neighborhoods; or from Eastern cultures to Western cultures), or how individuals handle negative, stressful experiences during their adaption to the new environment; and (b) the sources of the negative experiences (e.g., perceived discrimination, loneliness) existing in the interaction between cultures (Bachman et al., 2011; Brown & Aktas, 2011; Lazarus & Folkman, 1984). According to Berry (2005), acculturative stress is a phenomenon that may have a negative impact on the health of individuals.

Research has noted several factors associated with acculturative stress. The most salient of these factors include gender (Livingston et al., 2007), ethnic identity (Walker et al., 2008), racial identity (Thompson et al., 2000), language proficiency (Li et al., 2016), perceived discrimination (Utsey et al., 2000), homesickness (Poyrazli & Lopez, 2007), hate and rejection (Henson et al., 2013; Schmitt et al., 2003), fear (Brown & Aktas, 2011; Chao et al., 2014), social support (Ra & Trusty, 2016), and cultural shock (Lombard, 2014; Torres, 2009; Winkelman, 1994). Moreover, longitudinal studies have indicated that acculturative stress is positively associated with depression (Du et al., 2015), homesickness (Tartakovsky, 2007), and substance abuse (Lorenzo-Blanco & Unger, 2015) among international students and immigrants. Likewise, Jin and

Berge (2016) reported that an individual's levels of acculturative stress predict their levels of IA. In the investigation of 115 East Asian international students in the United States, Ye (2005) found that acculturative stress is associated with motives for Internet use. For example, fear and perceived discrimination are significant predictors of social utility motivation among international students (Ye, 2005).

Purpose of the Present Study

International college students represent a group that could be more prone to IA because they are using the Internet at high rates (Doring et al., 2015). The transition to a culturally different college life might become a major turning point that affects international college students' habit of Internet use, making them more vulnerable to IA. In addition, prior research has primarily focused on homogeneity in effect sizes of IA among college students but is limited by a lack of racially and culturally diverse samples, or without considering acculturative stress.

In this pilot study, we therefore explored the relationship between acculturative stress, gender, age, length of stay, and IA in a sample of international college students using a multiple regression model. Specially, we were interested in the associations of acculturative stress with IA. Previous studies have shown that acculturative stress has been widely linked to addictive behaviors and psychological well-being among international college students (Conn et al., 2017; Jin & Berge, 2015; Li et al., 2013). Thus, I hypothesized that acculturative stress would significantly predict IA while individual-level variables (i.e., age, gender, and length of stay) were held constant.

METHOD

Participants

A random sample of 300 international college students was invited to participate in a web-based survey that took 15–20 min to complete. These participants first reviewed the informed consent approved by the university's institutional review board. As part of the consent form, participants were informed that they could also stop participating at any time and that choosing to discontinue participating would not affect their academic performance. Of 111 responses, 93 fully completed the survey and were included in my final data analysis. Therefore, I received a 31% response rate.

Of the 93 participants, 63 (67.7%) were male, 28 (30.1%) were female, and two (2.2%) were unidentified. Ages ranged from 22 to 40 years old ($M = 28.62$, $SD = 3.69$). Regarding race/ethnicity, eight (8.6%) were Caucasian, five (5.4%) were African American, 63 (67.7%) were Asian, and 12 (12.9%) were biracial. Thirty-eight (40.9%) were undergraduate and 55 (59.1%) were master's students. Participants were from 27 countries. The top three countries were India ($n = 21$), China ($n = 9$), and Sri Lanka ($n = 6$).

Procedure

Institutional review board approval was obtained prior to beginning the study. Participants were international students pursuing baccalaureate or graduate degrees in a large Midwestern research institution in the United States. I selected participants for the current study on the basis of specific criteria: (a) current enrollment in the target university; (b) possession of a valid student visa; (c) literate in English; and (d) between the ages of 18 and 70 years. Participants were recruited through a university research laboratory. A convenience sample was used based on who voluntarily responded. The research laboratory sent a recruitment email to 300 students studying in the university. The email included a brief introduction to the study as well as an anonymous link, which took potential participants to an online survey portal in Qualtrics. After participants provided online assent, they responded to the survey questions, which consisted of the IA test, acculturative stress questionnaire, and a brief demographic questionnaire. Two reminder emails were sent at 2-week intervals to those who had not yet completed the survey. An incentive, four $25 Amazon gift cards, was offered with 1:75 odds.

Measures

Demographic Questionnaire

I developed a demographic questionnaire for this study using the tailored design method (Dillman et al., 2014). Participants were asked to self-report their racial and ethnic background, birthplace, age, gender, length of time in the United States, and educational history.

Internet Addiction Test

The Internet Addiction Test (IAT; Young, 1998) is a 20-item scale that measures the presence and severity of Internet dependency among adults. The IAT views IA as an impulse-control disorder and the term *Internet* refers to all types of online activity (Young, 1998). The 20-item questionnaire measures characteristics and behaviors associated with use of the Internet that include compulsivity, escapism, and dependency. Questions also assess problems related to addictive use in personal, occupational, and social functioning. Questions are randomized, and each statement is weighted along a Likert-scale continuum that ranges from 0 (*less extreme behavior*) to 5 (*most extreme behavior*) for each item.

Studies have found that the IAT is a reliable measure that covers the key characteristics of problematic Internet use (Boysan et al., 2017; Young, 1998). The assessment measures the extent of a respondent's involvement with the Internet and classifies the addictive behavior in terms of mild, moderate, or severe impairment. The IAT is a worldwide accepted and validated testing instrument and is the most widely used IA scale. The test has been translated into several languages including English, Chinese, French, Italian, Turkish, and Korean.

Cronbach's alpha coefficient was .93 in Noh and Kim's study (2016) and .91 in the current study, showing that the IAT is highly reliable.

Acculturative Stress Scale

Acculturative stress was assessed with the 36-item Acculturative Stress Scale for International Students (ASSIS; Sandhu & Asrabadi, 1994). Items were rated on a 5-point Likert-type scale from 1 (*strongly disagree*) to 5 (*strongly agree*), with higher scores indicating greater level of acculturative stress, such as "I feel that my people are discriminated against" or "I am treated differently because of my color." It consisted of seven subscales, including perceived discrimination (eight items), homesickness (four items), perceived hate/rejection (five items), fear (four items), stress due to change/culture shock (three items), guilt (two items), and nonspecific concerns (10 items). For this study, five nonspecific concerns were taken from the ASSIS scale. Several studies reported high internal consistency reliability of the ASSIS ranging from .87 to .93 (Bai, 2016; Constantine et al., 2004). Internal consistency reliabilities in this sample were as follows: total scale: .91; perceived discrimination, .83; homesickness, .75; perceived hate, .84; fear, .83; culture shock, .59; guilt, .66; and nonspecific concerns, .61.

Data Analysis

I conducted a preliminary analysis to determine whether a relationship existed between age, gender, length of stay, and acculturative stress. The presence of a relationship would warrant further exploration of the relationship between IA and acculturative stress. I assessed normality across study variables by examining skewness, kurtosis, and quantile-quantile plots. According to George and Mallery (2005), skewness and kurtosis for all predictor variables fell within normal ranges (−1 to +1). Therefore, I determined no transformation of the data was needed. No apparent multicollinearity issues occurred among predictor variables. Several instances of missing or discrepant data found on the demographic questionnaire were addressed by using pairwise deletion.

RESULTS

I used SPSS (Version 24) to conduct statistical analyses. I conducted multiple regression analyses to examine how the individual-level variables (age, gender, length of stay) and seven subscales of the acculturative stress (discrimination, homesickness, hate, fear, cultural shock, guilt, and nonspecific concerns) predicted IA among international college students. Table 1 summarizes the descriptive statistics of the acculturative stress and IA.

Table 1: Descriptive Statistics of Acculturative Stress and Internet Addiction

	Min	Max	*M*	*SD*
Internet addiction	22	80	37.82	12.93
Discrimination	8	35	20.95	6.38
Homesickness	4	20	10.96	3.50
Hate	5	22	10.72	4.19
Fear	4	18	8.58	3.72
Cultural Shock	3	15	7.65	2.87
Guilt	2	10	4.63	2.17
Nonspecific	5	21	13.84	4.04

To address our hypothesis, two clusters of variables were entered sequentially to complete hierarchical multiple regression analyses. First, individual-level variables (age, gender, and length of stay) were included in Model 1, explaining 42.9% of variance in IA, F (3,66) = 4.97, p = .004. Second, in Model 2, seven subscales of the acculturative stress were added into Model 1. The total variance in Model 2 was 58.6%, F (10,59) = 3.09, p = .003. The seven subscales explained an additional 15.7% of the variance in Model 2, after controlling age, gender, and length of stay.

Table 2: Generalized Linear Modeling Predicting Internet Addiction

Predictors	Model 1 (β)	Model 2 (β)
Age	−.17	−.22
Gender	.39**	.33**
Length of stay	.18	.20
Discrimination		−.07
Homesick		.03
Hate		.16
Fear		.14
Cultural shock		.34*
Guilt		.03
Nonspecific concerns		−.18
R^2	.18	.34

Note. *$p < .05$, **$p < .01$; ***$p < .001$

As can be seen in Table 2, gender is the variable significantly predicting IA in both Models 1 and 2. Male students apparently were more likely than female students to show symptoms of IA. Model 2 indicates that only cultural shock (β = .34, $p = .02$) significantly predicted IA, after controlling for the individual-level variables. Therefore, our hypothesis was supported.

DISCUSSION

The main purpose of this study was to investigate acculturative stress in relation to IA among a random sample of international college students studying in a large

Midwestern research institution in the United States. Given the acculturative stress theory provided by Berry (1977, 2005), which postulates that contextual factors impact the level of acculturative stress, this study yields a few important findings about the relationships between acculturative stress and IA in a diverse college student sample. Notably, acculturative stress was a statistically significant variable in Model 2 and may be a warning sign for international college students who might use the Internet to meet their cultural and social-emotional needs while moving from a familiar culture to one that is unfamiliar. Our findings are consistent with a large body of research suggesting that perceived discrimination, homesickness, and cultural shock are still prevalent in international students living in the United States (Chai et al., 2012; Chao et al., 2014; Henson et al., 2013; Li et al., 2013; Poyrazli & Lopez, 2007), and that acculturative stress in particular plays a significant role in contributing to mental health (Ran et al., 2016; Thompson et al., 2000; Torres et al., 2012). Thus, student service personnel and college counselors need to be concerned with psychological changes of international students who have experienced discrimination and cultural shock. Universities should deliver culturally responsive education to this population and help them deal with stress associated with race- and culture-based discrimination.

Acculturative stress, including its subscales such as cultural shock, may be considered as a predictor of IA in our study. Our finding might be regarded as an extension of previous studies in the literature regarding perceived stress that is related to addictive behaviors (Cheng & Hong, 2017; Gil et al., 2015; Sinha & Jastreoboff, 2013). The similarity of the findings may be explained by the prevalence of the sense of insecurity and the stress associated with acculturation in unfamiliar surroundings among international college students. However, although literature has indicated there might be a possible causal relationship between these psychological symptoms (i.e., stress) and IA, some scholars argue that this association needs further investigation (Ostovar et al., 2016). Our results assume that international college students become addicted to the Internet as a means of relieving their psychological distress caused by life changes. Thus, a culturally responsive counselor should begin with examining recent life experience and coping strategies of college students before addressing their addictive problems.

Another significant finding of the present study was that gender moderated the relationship between acculturative stress and IA. This finding is consistent with previous research (Khan et al., 2017; Livingston et al., 2007) and Berry's acculturative stress theory (1997, 2005), which indicate that gender is a significant moderating factor for acculturative stress (Berry, 1977, 2005; Dawson & Panchanadeswaran, 2010). Our finding is also in line with previous studies examining the effect of gender difference on problematic Internet use (Gupta et al., 2018; Ioannidis et al., 2018). In particular, male students apparently show a higher level of IA than female students when they are of a similar age. The current study highlights the need for researchers and college counselors to thoroughly weigh the gender factor in terms of international students' vulnerability to IA. Given that much research has focused on cause, diagnosis, and treatment of IA in college students, additional research is needed that incorporates a more nuanced view of these demographic factors (e.g., marital status, ethnicity/racial identity, socioeconomic status) for IA in international college student populations.

Limitations and Future Research

Although our findings contribute to the acculturative stress and IA research pertaining to international college students, several limitations must be considered. First, although expected, these small sample sizes may have resulted in statistical power being lower than desired. Future research could pool a larger sample to examine relationships between IA and acculturative stress among international college students. Second, because of the lack of prior research on acculturative stress and IA, we developed our research questions based on the available acculturation research (Chai et al., 2012; Chao et al., 2014; Henson et al., 2013; Li et al., 2013; Poyrazli & Lopez, 2007). Some other important variables (e.g., acculturation strategies, personality) potentially should have been included in our study. In addition, we tested individual-level variables (e.g., gender, age, length of stay) in the current study and future researchers could supply knowledge on acculturative stress and IA by exploring moderating factors of acculturation (e.g., social support, societal attitudes, coping strategies) as well as additional demographic factors (e.g., socioeconomic status, racial/ethnicity identity, marital status). Third, the measures used in the web-based survey were not mandatory, which may account for the incompleteness.

Implications for College Counselors

This study was innovative in examining the influence of acculturative stress on IA among international college students. Two key findings from this study were that (a) acculturative stress has a positive influence on IA; and (b) gender and cultural shock may have unique contributions to IA among international college students. With the established research linking acculturative stress and IA, some clinical implications for college counselors emerge from this study. College counselors should consider how acculturative stress might be exacerbating addictive Internet use. Previous research linking multicultural counseling competences suggests that (a) multicultural counselors should be aware of self, client, and potential barriers in the counseling process when working with international and minority students; (b) discussions with students around confidentiality should be initiated beforehand to help ward off fear or culture-related stress that may occur, particularly when working with international students; and (c) college counselors should focus on a more directive approach to counseling this population (Mau & Jepsen, 1988; Yau et al., 1992; Yakunina et al., 2013). Likewise, when dealing with international students who are addicted to the Internet, college counselors are encouraged to review contemporary literature regarding IA associated with different psychological symptoms. As the findings reported, cultural sensitivity should be used to interpret perceived discrimination, homesickness, hate, and cultural shock and empathy should be shown for students from diverse cultural backgrounds. A college counselor should pay particular attention to these issues that may lead to unintended harm on students.

CONCLUSION

Given the prevalence of IA in U.S. colleges and universities, the factors that contribute to this addictive behavior are increasingly important to understand. Using acculturative stress theory that accounts for a sociocultural transition and examining moderating factors that influence the transition can help college counselors understand needs of international students. Furthermore, the findings from this study also shift our current understanding of the relationship between acculturative stress and IA. Male students' higher acculturative stress apparently has a significant influence on IA. Hopefully, this study contributes to the growing literature on IA from a perspective of cultural transition. Findings from this study also present additional research questions that warrant further consideration in future research.

REFERENCES

Anderson, K. (2001). Internet use among college students: An exploratory study. *Journal of American College Health, 50*, 21–26. doi:10.1080/07448480109595707

Bachman, R., Randolph, A., & Brown, B. L. (2011). Predicting perceptions of fear at school and going to and from school for African American and White students: The effects of school security measures. *Youth & Society, 43*, 705–726. doi:10.1177/0044118X10366674

Bai, J. (2016). Development and validation of the Acculturative Stress Scale for Chinese college students in the United States (ASSCS). *Psychological Assessment, 28*, 443–447. doi:10.1037/pas0000198

Berry, J. W. (1977). Immigration, acculturation, and adaptation. *Applied Psychology: An International Review, 46*, 5–34. doi:10.111/j.14640597.1977.tb01087.x

Berry, J. W. (2005). Acculturation: Living successfully in two cultures. *International Journal of Intercultural Relations, 29*, 697–712. doi:10.1016/j.ijintrel.2005.07.013

Besser, A., & Zeigler-Hill, V. (2014). Positive personality features and stress among first-year university students: Implications for psychological distress, functional impairment, and self-esteem. *Self & Identity, 13*, 24–44. doi:10.1080/15298868.2012.736690.

Blanco, C., Okuda, M., Wright, C., Hasin, D. S., Grant, B. F., Liu, S.-M., & Olfson, M. (2008). Mental health of college students and their non-college-attending peers: Results from the national epidemiologic study on alcohol and related conditions. *Archives of General Psychiatry, 65*, 1429–1437. doi:10.1001/archpsyc.65.12.1429

Boysan, M., Kuss, D. J., Barut, Y., Ayköse N., Güleç, M., & Özdemir, O. (2017). Psychometric properties of the Turkish version of the Internet Addiction Test (IAT). *Addictive Behaviors, 64*, 247–252. doi:10.1016/j.addbeh.2015.09.002

Brown, L., & Aktas, G. (2011). Fear of the unknown: A pre-departure qualitative study of Turkish international students. *British Journal of Guidance & Counselling, 39*, 339–355. doi:10.1080/03069885.2011.576314

Caplan, S. E. (2002). Problematic Internet use and psychosocial well-being: Development of a theory-based cognitive-behavioral measurement instrument. *Computers in Human Behavior, 18*, 553–575. doi:10.1016/S0747-5632(02)00004-3

Cardak, M. (2013). Psychological well-being and Internet addiction among university students. *Turkish Online Journal of Educational Technology - TOJET, 12*(3), 134–141.

Carlisle, K. L., Carlisle, R. M., Polychronopoulos, G. B., Goodman-Scott, E., & Kirk-Jenkins, A. (2016). Exploring Internet addiction as a process addiction. *Journal of Mental Health Counseling, 38*, 170–182. doi:10.17744/mehc.38.2.07

Chai, P. M., Krägeloh, C. U., Shepherd, D., & Billington, R. (2012). Stress and quality of life in international and domestic university students: Cultural differences in the use of religious coping. *Mental Health, Religion & Culture, 15*, 265–277. doi:10.1080/13674676.2011.571665

Chao, R. C., Longo, J., Wang, C., Dasgupta, D., & Fear, J. (2014). Perceived racism as moderator between self-esteem/shyness and psychological distress among African Americans. *Journal of Counseling & Development, 92*, 259–269. doi:10.1002/j.1556-6676.2014.00154.x

Cheng, K. T., & Hong, F. Y. (2017). Study on relationship among university students' life stress, smart mobile phone addiction, and life satisfaction. *Journal of Adult Development, 24*, 109–118. doi:10.1007/s10804-016-9250-9

Ching, Y., Renes, S. L., McMurrow, S., Simpson, J., & Strange, A. T. (2017). Challenges facing Chinese international students studying in the United States. *Educational Research and Reviews, 12*, 473–482. doi:10.5897/err2016.3106

Choi, S. W., Kim, D. J., Choi, J. S., Ahn, H., Choi, E. J., Song, W. Y., & Youn, H. (2015). Comparison of risk and protective factors associated with smartphone addiction and Internet addiction. *Journal of Behavioral Addictions, 4*, 308–314. doi:10.1556/2006.4.2015.043

Chou, W., Ko, C., Kaufman, E. A., Crowell, S. E., Hsiao, R. C., Wang, P. W., Lin, J., & Yen, C. F. (2015). Association of stress coping strategies with Internet addiction in college students: The moderating effect of depression. *Comprehensive Psychiatry, 62*, 27–33. doi:10.1016/j.comppsych.2015.06.004

Conn, B. M., Ejesi, K., & Foster, D. W. (2017). Acculturative stress as a moderator of the effect of drinking motives on alcohol use and problems among young adults. *Addictive Behaviors, 75*, 85–94. doi:10.1016/j.addbeh.2017.06.017

Constantine, M. G., Okazaki, S., & Utsey, S. O. (2004). Self-concealment, social self-efficacy, acculturative stress, and depression in African, Asian, and Latin American international college students. *American Journal of Orthopsychiatry*, *74*, 230–241. doi:10.1037/0002-9432.74.3.230

Dawson, B. A., & Panchanadeswaran, S. (2010). Discrimination and acculturative stress among first-generation Dominicans. *Hispanic Journal of Behavioral Sciences, 32*, 216–231 doi:10.1177/0739986310364750

Dillman, D. A., Smyth, J. D., & Christian, L. M. (2014). *Internet, phone, mail, and mixed-mode surveys: The tailored design method* (4th ed.). Wiley.

Doring, N., Daneback, K., Shaughnessy, K., Grov, C., & Byers, E. S. (2015). Online sexual activity experience among college students: A four-country comparison. *Archives of Sexual Behavior, 46*, 1641–1652. doi:10.1007/s10508-015-0656-4

Du, H., Li, X., Lin, D., & Tam, C. (2015). Collectivistic orientation, acculturative stress, cultural self-efficacy, and depression: A longitudinal study among Chinese internal migrants. *Community Mental Health Journal, 51*(2), 239–248. doi:10.1007/s10597-014-9785-9

Gaille, B. (2017, May 22). *33 interesting Internet addiction statistics*. http://brandongaille.com/32-interesting-internet-addiction-statistics/

George, D., & Mallery, P. (2005). *SPSS for Windows: Step by step* (5th ed.). Pearson.

Gil, F., Chamarro, A., & Oberst, U. (2015). Addiction to online social networks: A question of "Fear of Missing Out"? *Journal of Behavioral Addictions, 4*(S1), 51. doi:10.1556/JBA.4.2015.Suppl.1

Gregory, C. (May 22, 2019). *Internet addiction disorder*. PSYCOM. https://www.psycom.net/iadcriteria.html

Griffiths, M. (2000). Internet addiction—Time to be taken seriously? *Addiction Research, 8*(5), 413–418. doi:10.3109/16066350009005587

Gupta, A., Khan, A. M., Rajoura, O. P., & Srivastava, S. (2018). Internet addiction and its mental health correlates among undergraduate college students of a university in north India. *Journal of Family Medicine and Primary Care, 7*(4), 721–727. doi:10.4103/jfmpc.jfmpc_266_17

Henson, J. M., Derlega, V. J., Pearson, M. R., Ferrer, R., & Holmes, K. (2013). African American students' responses to racial discrimination: How race-based rejection sensitivity and social constraints are related to psychological reactions. *Journal of Social & Clinical Psychology, 32*, 504–529. doi:10.1521/jscp.2013.32.5.504

Hirai, R., Frazier, P., & Syed, M. (2015). Psychological and sociocultural adjustment of first-year international students: Trajectories and predictors. *Journal of Counseling Psychology, 62*, 438–452. doi:10.1037/cou0000085

Hyun, G. J., Han, D. H., Lee, Y. S., Kang, K. D., Yoo, S. K., Chung, U., & Renshaw, P. F. (2015). Risk factors associated with online game addiction: A hierarchical model. *Computers in Human Behavior, 48*, 706–713. doi:10.1016/j.chb.2015.02.008

Ineme, M. E., Ineme, K. M., Akpabio, G. A., & Osinowo, H. O. (2017). Predictive roles of depression and demographic factors in Internet addiction: A cross-sectional study of students in a Nigerian university. *International Journal of Cyber Criminology, 11*, 10–23. doi:10.5281/zenodo.495776

Institute of International Education. (2020). *New International Student Enrollment.* https://opendoorsdata.org/data/international-students/new-international-students-enrollment/

Ioannidis, K., Treder, M. S., Chamberlain, S. R., Kiraly, F., Redden, S. A., Stein, D. J., Grant, J. E. (2018). Problematic internet use as an age-related multifaceted problem: Evidence from a two-site survey. *Addictive Behaviors, 81*, 157–166. doi:10.1016/j.addbeh.2018.02.017

Jin, S. W., & Berge, J. (2015). An emerging global concern of Internet addiction: Socio-cultural influences on immigrant families. *Global Studies Journal, 9*(1), 15–34.

Jun, S., & Choi, E. (2015). Academic stress and Internet addiction from general strain theory framework. *Computers in Human Behavior, 49*, 282–287. doi:10.1016/j.chb.2015.03.001

Kandell, J. J. (2009). Internet addiction on campus: The vulnerability of college students. *CyberPsychology & Behavior, 1*, 11–17. doi:10.1089/cpb.1998.1.11

Khan, M. A., Shabbir, F., & Rajput, T. A. (2017). Effect of gender and physical activity on Internet addiction in medical students. *Pakistan Journal of Medical Sciences, 33*, 191–94. doi:10.12669/pjms.331.11222

Kim, S., Kim, J., & Jee, Y. (2015). Relationship between smartphone addiction and physical activity in Chinese international students in Korea. *Journal of Behavioral Addiction, 4*. http://dx.doi.org/10.1556/2006.4.2015.028

Lam, L. T. (2014). Risk factors of Internet addiction and the health effect of Internet addiction on adolescents: A systematic review of longitudinal and prospective studies. *Current Psychiatry Reports, 16*(11), 508–516. doi:10.1007/s11920-014-0508-2

Lazarus, R. S., & Folkman, S. (1984). *Stress, appraisal and coping*. Springer.

Li, J., Liu, X., Wei, T., & Lan, W. (2013). Acculturation, Internet use, and psychological well-being among Chinese international students. *Journal of International Students, 3*(2), 174–192.

Li, J., Marbley, A. F., Bradley, L., & Lan, W. (2016). Attitudes toward seeking counseling services among Chinese international students: Acculturation, ethnic identity, and language proficiency. *Journal of Multicultural Counseling and Development, 44*, 65–76. doi:10.1002/jmcd.12037

Livingston, I. L., Neita, M., Riviere, L., & Livingston, S. L. (2007). Gender, acculturative stress and Caribbean immigrants' health in the United States of America—An exploratory study. *The West Indian Medical Journal, 56*, 213–222. doi:10.1590/s0043-31442007000300004

Lombard, C. A. (2014). Coping with anxiety and rebuilding identity: A psychosynthesis approach to culture shock. *Counselling Psychology Quarterly, 27*, 174–199. doi:10.1080/09515070.2013.875887

Lonner, W., Wong, P. T., & Wong, L. C. (2007). *Handbook of multicultural perspectives on stress and coping*. Springer Science & Business Media.

Lorenzo-Blanco, E., & Unger, J. U. (2015). Ethnic discrimination, acculturative stress, and family conflict as predictors of depressive symptoms and cigarette smoking among Latina/o youth: The mediating role of perceived stress. *Journal of Youth & Adolescence, 44*, 84–97. doi:10.1007/s10964-015-0339-4

Mau, W. C., & Jepsen, D. A. (1988). Attitudes toward counselors and counseling processes: A comparison of Chinese and American graduate students. *Journal of Counseling and Development, 67*, 189–192.

Noh, D., & Kim, S. (2016). Dysfunctional attitude mediates the relationship between psychopathology and Internet addiction among Korean college students: A cross-sectional observational study. *International Journal of Mental Health Nursing, 25*, 588–597. doi:10.1111/inm.12220

Ostovar, S., Allahyar, N., Aminpoor, H., Moafian, F., Nor, M. M., & Griffiths, M. D. (2016). Internet addiction and its psychosocial risks (depression, anxiety, stress and loneliness) among Iranian adolescents and young adults: A structural equation model in a cross-sectional study. *International Journal of Mental Health and Addiction, 14*, 257–267. doi:10.1007/s11469-015-9628-0

Poyrazli, S., & Lopez, M. D. (2007). An exploratory study of perceived discrimination and homesickness: A comparison of international students and American students. *Journal of Psychology, 141*, 263–280. doi:10.3200/JRLP.141.3.263-280

Ra, Y. A., & Trusty, J. (2017). Impact of social support and coping on acculturation and acculturative stress of East Asian international students. *Journal of Multicultural Counseling and Development, 45*, 276–291. doi:10.1002/jmcd.12078

Ruberman, L. I. (2014). Challenges in the transition to college: The perspective of the therapist back home. *American Journal of Psychotherapy, 68*(1), 103–115.

Sandhu, D. S., & Asrabadi, B. R. (1994). Development of an acculturative stress scale for international students: Preliminary findings. *Psychological Reports, 75*, 435–448. doi:10.2466/pr0.1994.75.1.435

Schmitt, M. T., Spears, R., & Branscombe, N. R. (2003). Constructing a minority group identity out of shared rejection: The case of international students. *European Journal of Social Psychology, 33*, 1–12. doi:10.1002/ejsp.131

Sherry, M., Thomas, P., & Chui, W. (2010). International students: A vulnerable student population. *Higher Education, 60*, 33–46. doi:10.1007/s10734-009-9284-z

Sinha, R., & Jastreboff, A. M. (2013). Stress as a common risk factor for obesity and addiction. *Biological Psychiatry, 73*, 827–835. doi:10.1016/j.biopsych.2013.01.032

Tartakovsky, E. (2007). A longitudinal study of acculturative stress and homesickness: High-school adolescents immigrating from Russia and Ukraine to Israel without parents. *Social Psychiatry & Psychiatric Epidemiology, 42*, 485–494. doi:10.1007/s00127-007-0184-1

Thompson, C. P., Anderson, L. P., & Bakeman, R. A. (2000). Effects of racial socialization and racial identity on acculturative stress in African American college students. *Cultural Diversity and Ethnic Minority Psychology, 6*, 196–210. doi:10.1037/1099-9809.6.2.196

Torres, K. (2009). 'Culture shock': Black students account for their distinctiveness at an elite college. *Ethnic & Racial Studies, 32*(5), 883–905. doi:10.1080/01419870701710914

Torres, L., Driscoll, M. W., & Voell, M. (2012). Discrimination, acculturation, acculturative stress, and Latino psychological distress: A moderated mediational model. *Cultural Diversity and Ethnic Minority Psychology, 18*, 17–25. doi:10.1037/a0026710

Utsey, S. O., Ponterotto, J. G., Reynolds, A. L., & Cancelli, A. A. (2000). Racial discrimination, coping, life satisfaction, and self-esteem among African Americans. *Journal of Counseling & Development, 78*, 72–80. doi:10.1002/j.1556-6676.2000.tb02562.x

Van Rooij, A. J., & Prause, N. (2014). A critical review of "Internet addiction" criteria with suggestions for the future. *Journal of Behavioral Addictions, 3*(4), 203–213. doi:10.1556/JBA.3.2014.4.1

Walker, R. L., Wingate, L. R., Obasi, E. M., & Joiner, T. E. (2008). An empirical investigation of acculturative stress and ethnic identity as moderators for depression and suicidal ideation in college students. *Cultural Diversity and Ethnic Minority Psychology, 14*, 75–82. doi:10.1037/1099-9809.14.1.75

Weinstein, A., & Lejoyeux, M. (2010). Internet addiction or excessive internet use. *The American Journal of Drug and Alcohol Abuse, 36*(5), 277–283. doi:10.3109/00952990.2010.491880

Winkelman, M. (1994). Cultural shock and adaptation. *Journal of Counseling & Development, 73*, 121–126. doi:10.1002/j.1556-6676.1994.tb01723.x

Yakunina, E. S., Weigold, I. K., Weigold, A., Hercegovac, S., & Elsayed, N. (2013). International students' personal and multicultural strengths: Reducing acculturative stress and promoting adjustment. *Journal of Counseling & Development, 91*(2), 216–223. doi:10.1002/j.1556-6676.2013.00088.x

Yau, T. Y., Sue, D., & Hayden, D. (1992). Counseling style preference of international students. *Journal of Counseling Psychology, 39*, 100–104. doi:10.1037/0022-0167.39.1.100

Ye, J. (2005). Acculturative stress and use of the Internet among East Asian international students in the United States. *Cyberpsychology & Behavior, 8*, 154–161. doi:10.1089/cpb.2005.8.154

Young, K. S. (1996, August). *Internet addiction: The emergence of a new clinical disorder* [Paper presentation]. 104th Annual Meeting of the American Psychological Association, Toronto, Ontario, Canada.

Young, K. S. (1998). Internet addiction: The emergence of a new clinical disorder. *CyberPsychology & Behavior, 1*(3), 237–244. doi:10.1089/cpb.1998.1.237

Young, K. S. (1999). Internet addiction: Symptoms, evaluation, and treatment. In L. Vande Creekve & T. Jackson (Eds.), *Innovations in clinical practice: A source book* (pp. 19–31). Professional Resources Press.

Zeliha, T. (2019). Internet addiction and loneliness as predictors of Internet gaming disorder in adolescents. *Educational Research and Review, 14*, 465–473. doi:10.5897/err2019.3768

JIAQI (JASON) LI, PhD, is an associate professor in the Department of Counseling, Educational Leadership, Educational and School Psychology in the College of Applied Studies at Wichita State University. He received his PhD in Counselor Education and Supervision at Texas Tech University. His research interests are broadly in the areas of career development, addictive behaviors, and mental issues of underrepresented groups in the school setting. He is a licensed professional counselor and national certified counselor in the state of Kansas. Email: Jason.li@wichita.edu

XUN LIU, PhD, is Independent Methodologist in the Consortium for Family Strengthening Research in the College of Education at University of South Carolina. Her research interests focus on quantitative research methodology, marriage and family studies, scale development and measurement. Email: xuntwoxun@gmail.com

Peer-Reviewed Article

© *Journal of International Students*
Volume 11, Issue 2 (2021), pp. 377-396
ISSN: 2162-3104 (Print), 2166-3750 (Online)
doi: 10.32674/jis.v11i2.2081
ojed.org/jis

Egyptian Students' Disinterest in Overseas Academic Mobility: A Behavioral Approach Based on the Capability-Opportunity-Motivation Model

Hélène Syed Zwick
ESLSCA University, Egypt

ABSTRACT

This study uses the capability-opportunity-motivation behavior framework as a theoretical basis and partial least squares structural equation modeling as an empirical research method to identify factors that influence the interest in studying abroad. We rely on primary microdata collected through a self-administered questionnaire among Egyptian students and apply a structural equation model to estimate the different relationships. Our analysis yielded interesting results: (a) 58% of our respondents were somehow interested in studying abroad; (b) physical capability, physical opportunity, and automatic motivation were the main predictors of interest in overseas academic mobility; and (c) a three-pillar policy program based on guidelines, communication and marketing, and regulation could be implemented to promote the interest of young Egyptians in studying abroad.

Keywords: behavioral change wheel, behavioral mobility economics, capability-opportunity-motivation behavior model, Egypt, evidence-based policy

INTRODUCTION

International student mobility (ISM) has become a crucial fragment of contemporary migration, especially within the context of rapid internationalization of higher educational systems. According to the Organisation for Economic Cooperation and Development (OECD, 2019), about 5 million students in tertiary education studied abroad, compared to 0.8 million in 1975. However, while some countries are well inserted within the ISM system like the United States, the United Kingdom, Australia, and Germany, other countries remain at its margin (Perkins & Neumayer, 2014). This is typically the case of less developed countries from Africa and South America. Unfortunately, scholars have not drawn enough attention to these countries and the inherent trends that occur (see Netz, 2015, among others).

It is precisely this gap that my study desires to emphasize and explore. This study's contribution to the literature is therefore threefold. Firstly, I argue that there is an important gap in ISM research that mostly focuses on students who have been mobile rather than on students in general who are thinking about whether or not to study abroad in the future (King & Sondhi, 2018; Syed Zwick, 2020a). Arango (2000) explained that most models on migratory processes in general fail to explain why so few people do move. This point of view is also in line with Schewel (2015, 2019) who considered this practice as an analytical and methodological mobility bias and Carling (2002) who advised to deconstruct the migration decision-making process into aspiration and ability phases. However, a small number of studies puts emphasis on would-be mobile students (Syed Zwick & Syed, 2015, for instance), but misses the opportunity to incorporate a behavioral dimension to their analysis. This leads to the second contribution of my study.

Secondly, I claim that current empirical research on ISM fails to systematically include cognitive considerations within a complete behavioral model. I agree with the analysis of Koikkalainen and Kyle (2016) who argued that more empirical research focusing on cognitive migration and on people imagining possible mobile or immobile futures is required in migration research. My study shifts from observed mobility in the present to probable mobility in the future, tht incorporating dreams, thoughts, and feelings but also implying uncertainty and risk (Czaika, 2015). This cognitive approach contributes to the necessary rethinking of economics as an interdisciplinary field, which has been highlighted by the OECD through its New Approaches to Economic Challenges initiative (OECD, 2017). The organization claims that a new narrative is needed to integrate the hopes, values, attitudes, and behaviors of people into economics, along with the facts and data that economists are more used to dealing with. Some studies have explored the influence of cognitive dimensions on the migration decision-making process of specific would-be migrants (Schewel, 2015; Syed Zwick, 2020b; Van der Velde & van Naerssen, 2015).

Thirdly, I call for evidence-based student mobility programs that address needs of students. So far, and to the best of my knowledge, there are a few studies on ISM drawing attention to situations wherein policy decisions are informed by rigorously established objective evidence. My interest in evidence-based student mobility programs reflects the recent and noteworthy revival of the debate on the relationship between research and public policy. Several contributions (Cairney, 2016; Parkhurst, 2017; Stoker & Evans, 2016) have provided new insights into an old discussion that arose in the late 1970s and early 1980s with Caplan (1979). Like Howes et al. (2018), I argue that basing student mobility programs more firmly on sound evidence is even more challenging for less developed countries, commonly characterized by weak institutions and a lack of strong incentives to conduct good programs or policies. My study aims to foster and encourage evidence-based policymaking in the field of ISM in a less developed country, Egypt.

To do so, I rely on two psychological models—Capability-Opportunity-Motivation Behavior (COM-B) and the Behavioral Change Wheel (BCW) originally designed by Michie and Prestwich (2010) and Michie et al. (2011), respectively. These models aim to design evidence-based interventions and policies that will be selected transparently and systematically (Michie, Hyder, et al., 2011a). Such models, considered supramodels as they can explain any human behavior, have been successfully applied in health psychology and in the medical field (Alexanders et al., 2014; Barker et al., 2016; Michie, Van Stralen, & West, 2011b), but never in the field of migration or academic mobility.

This study is finally guided by the following research question: What is the respective influence of capabilities, opportunities, and motivations in students' interest in overseas academic mobility? I empirically focus on Egypt and address this research question through a research design based on a self-administered survey, shaped by the COM-B and BCW models, and quantitatively estimated through a partial least squares structural equation modeling (PLS-SEM). To that end, I established three hypotheses:

H1: The higher the degree of capability, the higher the interest in academic mobility.

H2: The higher the degree of opportunity, the higher the interest in academic mobility.

H3: The higher the degree of motivation, the higher the interest in academic mobility.

LITERATURE REVIEW

UNESCO Institute of Statistics (UIS, 2019) measured the total outbound international mobile students' indicator as the number of students who crossed a national border for the purpose of education and were at that time enrolled outside their country of origin. In 2017, this number exceeded 5 million. In terms of total outbound international mobile students in 2017, the Arab region represented 10%, Asia and the Pacific (42%), and Central and Eastern Europe and Central Asia (15%). In these measures, Egypt has remained at the periphery of the ISM system. On one hand, data show a significant increase in the number of Egyptian students studying abroad since 2008 from 12,000 to 35,000 in 2017. As a result, Egypt was the fourth largest sending country of international students in the Arab world, after Saudi Arabia, Morocco, and Syria (UIS, 2019). On the other hand, Egypt is also the most populous country in the region, with almost 100 million people in 2018. Consequently, while considering the study outbound rate, which gives the number of students from a given country studying abroad, expressed as a percentage of total tertiary enrolment in that country, Egypt exhibited the lowest rate in the Arab world despite its increase from 2013 (0.83%) to 2017 (1.19%). As a comparison, Jordan's outbound rate in 2017 was 8 times higher at 8.7%, followed by Lebanon. Morocco and Saudi Arabia, despite a slight decline over time, displayed an outbound rate of 5% in 2017 (UIS, 2019).

Literature on ISM is vast and growing. Scholars have extensively explored determinants and motivations of students in mobility (Brooks & Waters, 2011; Findlay et al., 2017; King & Sondhi, 2018; among others). While mainly relying on economic and financial factors, they distinguish between three main reasons for students to decide to study abroad. The first reason refers to the capacity-building thesis (Lowell & Khadka, 2011; Rosenzweig, 2007). Students rationally decide to study abroad because they see it as a first step toward an international professional career. ISM is therefore first considered a career-enhancing investment by human capital theoreticians (Findlay et al., 2017; King & Sondhi, 2018; Nilsson & Ripmeester, 2016), and second, a highly skilled migration or brain circulation (Collins et al., 2017; Rosensweig, 2007).

The second reason refers to opportunistic behavior in a global society where mobility is life-stage consumption good (King & Sondhi, 2018). This approach goes beyond economics. It belongs to a multidimensional stream in the literature that also includes ethnographic and sociologic studies (Beck & Beck-Gernsheim, 2002; Cresswell, 2006; Soong et al., 2017; Urry, 2007; Waters, 2008). These latter studies scrutinize social norms of mobility in general based on the Bourdieusian (Bourdieu, 1986) forms of capital. They consider mobile students' international and multicultural experiences as embodied in a specific form of mobility capital (Murphy-Lejeune, 2002; Syed Zwick & Syed, 2015). Mobility is part of the culture. In their studies, Mondain and Diagne (2013) and Newell (2012) talked about an "almost obligatory rite of passage" (Mondain & Diagne, 2013, p. 512) and consumption good, respectively.

The third reason refers to the constrained-schooling thesis, which applies to origin countries. This thesis appeared in the 1970s and 1980s and found ground in the emergence of Africa and Asia as postcolonies and origin countries of mobile students (Cummings, 1984; Lee & Tan, 1984). It states that students study abroad because they lack study and training opportunities in their origin country: Fees might be too high or the tertiary-education supply might be too low, for instance. It therefore assumes that there is a negative relationship between tertiary-education supply and education outflows (see Chen, 2007, especially). Neglected for 20 years, Kritz (2016) recently brought it up to date by assessing its relevance to current student outflows.

Such literature has overfocused on motivational factors. From my point of view, the absence of conceptual framework in empirical studies has led to a neglect of other important dimensions of any decision-making processes. Yet, I found a few scholars who adopted behavioralist and cognitive psychology models to explain overseas academic mobility (Kubota, 2016; Lo, 2019). Kubota (2016), for instance, explored and critically examined social imaginary experiences in mobility but without using a well-defined theoretical framework. Lo (2019) introduced the capability approach to reframe the meaning of ISM, but the study remained at the theoretical level.

Furthermore, I have noticed that the mobility bias in migration research recently denounced by Schewel (2019) concerns studies on ISM as well. As far as I know, very few academic studies have attempted to explain student immobility and the lack of interest in overseas academic mobility in general (Breines et al., 2019; British Council, 2017; Syed Zwick & Syed, 2015). For example, the British Council has been publishing a Broadening Horizons report on a yearly basis to communicate the evolution and degree of interest of students in study abroad. Over time, the percentage of students reporting a disinterest in study abroad has varied from 80% in 2013, to 66% in 2015, and to 82% in 2017, raising concerns about the factors explaining this high structural proportion. Among the key motivators identified in the report are language training, information on funding, and evidence of positive labor market outcomes. Such a study is instructive; however, the survey does not rely on any solid theoretical framework, leading to omission of substantial dimensions critical to understanding the ISM decision-making process. In the present study, I propose a theoretically founded empirical analysis that allows us to methodically identify the three predictors that explain this process.

CONCEPTUAL FRAMEWORK

The COM-B Model

The COM-B model offers a comprehensive, parsimonious, and applicable model to all behaviors (Barker et al., 2016). It articulates three conditions or predictors, which are capability, opportunity, and motivation. These elements are considered important drivers to transit from a behavioral intent and ideation to a behavior. In other words, they deconstruct the decision-making process. Figure 1 represents the model and indicates that motivational factors ground a behavioral intention and ideation to the individual. This intention is usually defined as a person's perceived likelihood or subjective probability that they will engage in a given behavior. This intention depends on motivational factors, but is moderated also by opportunistic and capability factors. According to Michie, Stralen, and West (2011), motivational factors activate or inhibit behavior, opportunistic factors enable the behavior, while capability factors enact it.

Capability is the first predictor of the COM-B model. It is defined by Michie, Van Stralen, and West (2011) as the "individual's psychological and physical capacity to engage in the activity concerned. It includes having the necessary knowledge and skills. [...] We distinguish between physical and psychological capability" (p. 4). Psychological capability is the capacity to engage in the necessary thought processes in reference to comprehension or reasoning, while physical capability relates to skills. Individuals must possess the appropriate set of skills in the relevant area to be able to perform a given behavior. In our case, studying abroad could imply adaptability, personal care, and independence among others.

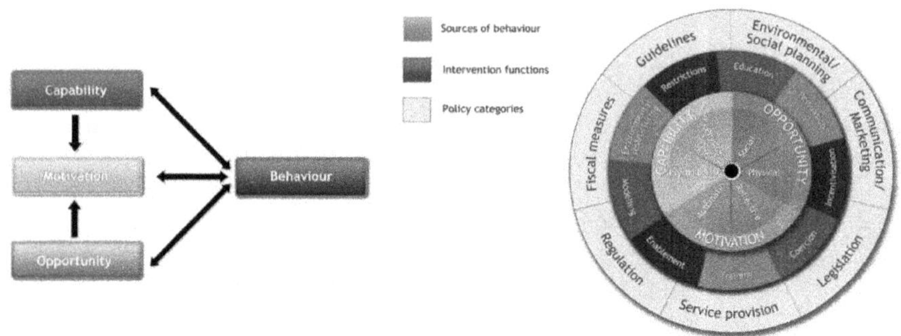

Figure 1: The COM-B Representation (Michie et al., 2011b)

Opportunity is the second predictor of the COM-B model. It is defined as the external circumstances that allow for or facilitate people to perform a behavior (Hung & Petrick, 2012). It points out the behavior under external environmental constraints (Lai et al., 2018). This definition reflects on the concept of facilitating conditions developed by Triandis (1977) in his theory of interpersonal behavior. Triandis stated that individuals may have the intention to perform a certain act; however, they may be unable to do so as the environment prevents the act from being performed. In my study, I distinguish between physical and social opportunity. While the first refers to opportunities afforded by the environment, including time, location, and resources, the latter is defined as opportunities afforded by social factors, including cultural norms. Physical opportunity occurs when there are no time, material, energy, knowledge, or geographical constraints limiting the individual's desires to be mobile and study abroad. Regarding social opportunity, cultural norms are attitudes and behaviors that are considered typical or average within a society or a group. Literature distinguishes four degrees of cultural norms: the taboo, the laws, folkway, and mores. A taboo is a topic refrained from being talked over normally and implies harsh consequences if broken, while a folkway is a taboo for which breaking the topic does not cause such severe impact. Mores denote topics that sound normal in usual circumstances in a given society, while the last degree is laws, which correspond to a set of agreed rules and regulations. Social culture is another dimension of the social factor, which is a complex set of meanings, habits, and values adopted by one or more social formations like the family or peers. Studying abroad could be seen in Egypt as a folkway and even a habit for some individuals. Finally, more generally, opportunities can be reframed into possibilities.

Finally, the third predictor of the COM-B model is motivation. This factor can directly affect the occurrence of individual behaviors, in terms of intensity but also direction (Bettman, 1979; Hung & Petrick, 2012). Following Michie, Van Stralen, and West (2011), I consider two types of motivation. Reflective motivation, on one side, involves evaluations and plans, while automatic motivation, on the other, involves emotions and impulses that arise from associative learning and/or innate dispositions. Reflective motivation could be seen as an extrinsic motivation that arises from the outside and leads to the exhibiting of a behavior to avoid a penalty or earn a reward. It may include parental expectations or expectations of other trusted role models. Similarly, automatic motivation could be seen as an intrinsic motivation that derives from intangible factors arising from within and that is personally rewarding. Intrinsic motivational factors are generally long-lasting and self-sustaining but slow to affect behaviour. On the opposite, extrinsic motivational factors usually more readily produce behavior changes and typically involve little effort, but mainly are changes in the short run. Over time, they tend to disappear. When applied to overseas mobility, extrinsic motivators relate to labor market outcomes and social identity.

It is worth noticing that there is a bidirectional relationship between these three predictors and behavior. Such relationship is represented in Figure 1 by the double-headed arrow. Also, behavior is defined as an action that is observable and measurable. This is often a response of an individual or group of individuals to an action, environment, person or stimulus. The COM-B is a starting-point to design interventions that aim to impulse a change in behavior.

The BCW Model

Designed originally by Michie, van Stralen, and West (2011), the BCW model aims to improve the systematic and transparent identification and design of effective behavior change interventions and policy areas. The authors defined these intervention functions as coordinated sets of activities designed to change specified behavior patterns. Such are measured in terms of prevalence or incidence of specific behaviors in a specified population (Figure 1).

The BCW model provides a framework of these interventions based on the three predictors. The framework defines nine intervention functions that aim to address deficits in one or more of these conditions. These functions are education, restriction, environmental restructuring, modeling, enablement, training, coercion, incentivization, and persuasion. Articulated around these nine intervention functions are seven categories of policy that could enable those interventions to occur. These are guidelines, fiscal measures, regulation, service provision, legislation, communication and marketing, and environmental and social planning.

METHOD

Operationalization of the COM-B Framework

The operationalization of the COM-B framework consisted of identifying a gap between the target behavior—increasing outward student mobility—and effective behaviors—not interested in student mobility. I sought to analyze whether the targets of the intervention, namely students, have the capability, opportunity, and motivation to perform the target behavior—studying abroad. For each of them (C, O, and M), I assigned different potential influencing factors and formulated six general assessments in line with the definitions given in the theoretical framework. The general assessments come from empirical evidence. I also used a common answer scale across the three groups of constructs based on a 5-point Likert scale (1 = *I totally disagree*; 5 = *I totally agree*).

I started with the capability predictor. Its operationalization is given in Table 1. The six general assessments are noted as C1–C6. From the operationalization, I established my first hypothesis:

> H1: The higher the degree of capability, the higher the interest in academic mobility.

With regards to opportunity, I used six general assessments from O1 to O6. Table 1 displays constructs, reflecting physical opportunity on one side (O1–O2) and social opportunity on the other (O3–O6). The second hypothesis is as follows:

> H2: The higher the degree of opportunity, the higher the interest in academic mobility.

Finally, I operationalized the motivation predictor. Both reflective and automatic motivation have three constructs (M1–M3 and M4–M6). The third hypothesis is as follows:

> H3: The higher the degree of motivation, the higher the interest in academic mobility.

Regarding the endogenous predictor, which refers to the behavior itself, I operationalized it through a single-item construct. I used self-reported degree of interest in academic mobility by using the following Likert-scaled question: Rate your interest in studying abroad from 1 (*I am not at all interested*) to 5 (*I am very interested*).

Table 1: Operationalizing the Predictors

ID	Domains	Constructs	General assessments
Capability predictor			
C1	Physical	Skills	I have the required skills to study abroad.
C2		Skills development	I believe that studying abroad would not be beyond my control.
C3		Skills development	I can handle being on my own abroad.
C4	Psychological	Procedural knowledge	I know how to plan to study abroad.

ID	Domains	Constructs	General assessments
C5		Knowledge	I have knowledge about the benefits of studying abroad.
C6		Knowledge	I have no concerns in studying abroad.
Opportunity predictor			
O1	Physical	Barriers	It is easy to plan for studying abroad.
O2		Resources	I can afford studying abroad.
O3	Social	Environmental stressors	Studying abroad is well accepted in the Egyptian society.
O4		Social pressure	My relatives and friends pressure me to study abroad.
O5		Social support	My university supports academic student mobility.
O6		Group norm	I have relatives and friends who studied abroad.
Motivation predictor			
M1	Reflective	Identity	I believe that studying abroad would positively change who I am.
M2		Social identity	I believe that studying abroad would improve the image my family and friends have about me.
M3		Optimism	I believe that studying abroad can positively affect my professional career.
M4	Automatic	Belief	Overall, I am satisfied with myself.
M5		Positive affect	When I try, I generally succeed.
M6		Interest	My interest in studying abroad has increased over time.

Note. 1 = *I totally disagree*, 2 = *I agree*; 3 = *Neither...Nor*; 4 = *I disagree*; 5 = *I totally agree*.

Data Collection

I used primary microdata collected through a self-administered questionnaire that I distributed in greater Cairo and its suburbs. I included two screening questions at the beginning of the questionnaire, after a brief introduction and consent, to limit participation to those who were actually Egyptians studying in a public or private university based in Egypt.

I designed and implemented the questionnaire in Arabic rather than in English. My choice was motivated by the willingness to avoid any self-selection bias. A questionnaire in English would have naturally selected Egyptian students with English skills and knowledge, while the national and official language in Egypt is Arabic. The sample of respondents would not have been representative of the whole student population, which could lead to bias the findings and then to spurious results. Because I am not an Arabic native, I utilized a specific method. I elaborated first the questionnaire in English. Then, a professional Egyptian translator, familiar with economic topics, translated the English version to Arabic. In order to validate the translated version, I used the back-translation method that allows for a second professional Egyptian translator to translate this second version into English. I then compared the first and second English versions. I had to adjust few sentences, before reiterating the process one more time. I found no differences between the third versions. Additionally, I launched a pilot survey with 10 student respondents in order to avoid any cultural offense. This pilot survey did not raise any issue. There were no missing data for the survey responses as the participants responded in person. On average, respondents took 6 min to answer the questionnaire.

I distributed the survey during 4 months from October 1, 2018, to February 25, 2019. The study finally relied on a primary microdataset of 484 participants who voluntarily accepted to complete the survey. In order to increase the respondent rate, I used the snowball sampling technique.

Descriptive statistics indicate that most respondents were women (62% of the total sample), aged between 18 and 25 years old ($M = 22$ years old). On average, the majority (58%) of respondents mentioned that they were somewhat interested in studying abroad (rating at least 3 out of 5).\

Structural Equation Modeling

SEM is a second generation of multivariate analysis methods that appeared in the early 1990s. Developed for analyzing complex interrelationships among both unobserved (latent) and observed variables in a model simultaneously, such models benefit from a growing interest in diverse academic fields (Hair et al., 2012). According to Ullman (2001), SEM is a combination of factor analysis and linear regression. It analyzes the direct and indirect effects of a series of moderators on the relationship between the independent and dependent variables. There are several advantages of SEM over regression that are well discussed in Bollen and Pearl (2013). Among others, SEM allows for the estimation of multiple and interrelated dependence relationships and for the representation of unobserved concepts in these relationships.

Econometrics literature offers competing SEM approaches—the co-variance-based and variance-based. In order to choose between both, I referred to the rule of thumb provided by Hair et al. (2012) and more recently by Hair et al. (2017). The authors explained that when a study has an exploratory dimension based on a small sample size, and it aims to identify key driver constructs on one side, and include formatively measured constructs in opposition to reflectively measured ones, a variance-based approach is preferable over a co-variance approach. More specifically, variance-based estimators give proxies for constructs before estimating model parameters based on these proxies. Among the variance-based approach, I selected the PLS-SEM approach, which is considered "the most fully developed and general system" (McDonald, 1996, p. 240). The estimator uses ordinary least squares (OLS) based on a nonparametric bootstrap technique to test for the significance of the coefficients.

PLS-SEM models consist of two main elements: a structural model and a measurement model. The structural model shows the associations—graphically represented by a path between the formatively measured constructs (represented by circles). The measurement model displays the associations between these constructs and the indicator variables (graphically represented by rectangles). In my case, I had exogenous constructs, which were my three predictors (capability, opportunity, and motivation) on one side, and an endogenous construct, which referred to my variable of interest, namely the interest in academic mobility. All of them were the latent variables of my proposed model. The indicator variables, which were also the observed variables (or the responses in the questionnaire), were used to represent these three exogenous variables in the statistical model. The model estimates the associations between the latent variables and explains the target constructs of interest. In other terms, the PLS-SEM approach allowed me to estimate weights between indicator variables and constructs, on one side, and latent variable scores, on the other.

Figure 2 displays my research model. The general statements presented in Table 1 were used to identify the impact of individual indicator constructs within the three predictors of the COM-B model on the degree of interest in student mobility.

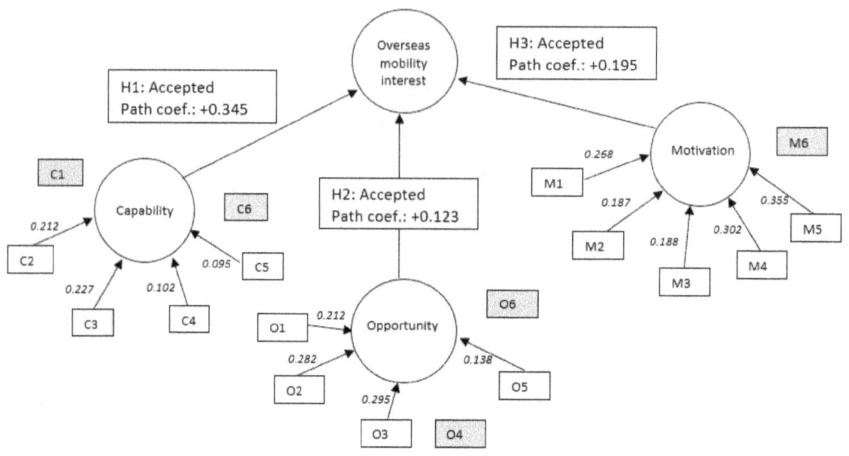

Figure 2: Proposed Research Model

RESULTS

In order to obtain a valid research model, I assessed both the measurement model and the structural model. With regard to the measurement model, I checked for collinearity through the variance inflation factors and for significance and relevance of the constructs' indicators. With regard to the structural model, I evaluated the coefficient of determinant R^2 and path coefficients.[1] Figure 2 displays the final estimated research model.

Hypothesis Testing: Focusing on the Structural Model

All path coefficients for the three predictors had a significant and positive impact on the interest in overseas academic mobility. They also had a value higher than 0.2, which interprets the COM-B predictors as meaningful (Nitzl, 2016). My three hypotheses were therefore accepted, but the path coefficient in scale differed significantly across them. While the path coefficient equaled .345 between capability and interest in studying abroad, it equaled .123 and .195 for motivation and opportunity, respectively. Additionally, I noted that size effects were different in scale and relatively low for the capability and motivation predictors (.025 and .017, respectively). Figure 2 and Table 2 display the findings of my hypotheses.

[1] Results are available upon request.

Table 2: Structural Model Results

Path	Path coefficient	*p*	Effect sizes	Decision
Capability → academic interest	.345	.000	.025	H1: Accepted
Opportunity → academic interest	.123	.000	.184	H2: Accepted
Motivation → academic interest	.195	.000	.017	H3: Accepted

Indicator Constructs Evaluation: Focusing on the Measurement Model

Table 3 shows the results of the measurement model. Out of 18, there were 13 formative indicators that had significant weights at the 10% level. Five items were found insignificant and were therefore not included in the final PLS-SEM (C1, C6, O4, O6, and M6).

Table 3: Measurement Model Results

Path calculations	Indicators	Weights	Loadings	*p* (weights)
Capability + .345	C2***	.212	.425	.000
	C3***	.227	.447	.001
	C4**	.102	.224	.065
	C5**	.094	.344	.011
Opportunity + .123	O1***	.212	.385	.001
	O2***	.282	.315	.001
	O3***	.295	.474	.001
	O5***	.138	.452	.000
Motivation + .195	M1***	.268	.385	.001
	M2**	.187	.244	.065
	M3**	.188	.258	.058
	M4***	.302	.564	.003
	M5***	.355	.284	.004

Note. Bootstrapping: 5,000 samples ($n = 484$). PLS estimation algorithm: Mode A/correlation weights. ***$p < .01$, **$p < .05$, *$p < .10$.

Starting with the indicators of the capability predictor, my results interestingly indicated that assessments C2, *I believe that studying abroad would not be beyond my control*, and C3, *I can handle being on my own abroad*, had the highest outer weights (.212 and .227), while assessment C5, *I have knowledge about the benefits of studying abroad*, was associated with the lowest one (.094). Such findings reveal the crucial role of physical capability in the degree of interest in studying abroad, despite the non-significance of assessment C1.

With regard to opportunistic factors, two assessments, construct O5, *My university supports academic student mobility*, which reflected social support, showed the lowest outer weight within this dimension with a value of .138. On the contrary, assessments O1, O2, and O3 that belonged to physical opportunity displayed the highest outer weights with .295, .282, and .212, respectively.

Finally, with regard to motivational factors, only one assessment (M6) appeared not significant, *My interest in studying abroad has increased over time.* Automatic motivation associated with assessments M4, *Overall, I am satisfied with myself,* and M5, *When I try, I generally succeed,* had the highest outer weights within the motivational dimension, with .302 and .355, respectively.

DISCUSSION

While the academic literature examining ISM has primarily focused on economic, financial, and social factors to understand study abroad decision-making processes, I have argued that the complexity of any decision-making process necessitates that, in addition to such factors, we must assess the role of psychologic factors that can drive the interest in overseas mobility using a conceptual framework well-known in psychology studies. Results confirm my argument, and the relevance of the COM-B model to explain the interest of students in overseas academic mobility in three dimensions—capability, opportunity, and motivation—is meaningful. This corroborates the fact that the study abroad decision-making process depends on a complex combination of economic, financial, social, and psychologic factors.

In the context of the predictor of capability, my first hypothesis was confirmed, and results highlighted its critical role in overseas mobility interest. Two main constructs related to skills development were crucial in this context: *I believe that studying abroad would not be beyond my control* and *I can handle being on my own abroad.* Unfortunately, I acknowledge two main weaknesses in previous literature that explain the lack of empirical evidence on these dimensions: First, there is an overrepresentation of economic, social, and financial factors in the study of determinants of ISM (Brooks & Waters, 2011; Findlay et al., 2017; King & Sondhi, 2018, especially) and a lack of psychologic factors. Second, there is a general mobility bias (Schewel, 2019) that prevents focusing on students who are not interested in studying abroad. Traveling and living abroad on your own is challenging and requires significant effort to adapt and adjust to new social and cultural environments. As highlighted by Goodwin and Nacht (1988), living abroad offers more opportunities for change than almost any other human endeavor. This transformative experience that triggers personal growth and self-awareness may be too stressful for many individuals. A positive psychology approach briefly appeared in the British Council's report (2017) and Beerkens et al. (2016).

With respect to the predictor of opportunity, my second hypothesis was validated. Social opportunities related to environmental stressors (*studying abroad is well accepted in the Egyptian society*) was the most crucial factor. As highlighted in theory and previous literature, social norms play a role in behavior and decision-making processes. In my case, overseas mobility in Egypt appears as a habit and well-accepted norm, far from being a taboo, suggesting that the approach stating that mobility is a life-stage consumption good may be relevant in the Egyptian context. Support for this can be found in Soong et al. (2017), Mondain and Diagne (2013), and Waters (2008). The second most crucial factor within opportunity is resources. Highlighted in Beerkens et al. (2016) and Souto-Otero et al. (2013), financial concerns are consistently identified as secondary factors. My findings are consistent with such trends despite the fact that Egypt is a developing country where average disposable income is lower than developed countries, where most studies took place.

Finally, with regard to my third hypothesis and the predictor of motivation, my results confirmed the crucial role of motivators in the decision-making process, as highlighted in previous empirical literature (Findlay et al., 2017; King & Sondhi, 2018; Lee & Tan, 1984; Lowell & Khadka, 2011; Nilsson & Ripmeester, 2016). However, my study goes a step further by distinguishing between intrinsic and extrinsic motivators. In this study, findings show that intrinsic motivators through belief and positive affect are primary factors. Interestingly, high levels of self-esteem and self-satisfaction were associated with academic advantages such as greater student engagement and academic self-efficacy, implying higher likelihood to be interested in overseas mobility (Ojeda et al., 2011). In this sense, such a dimension is related to cognitive dispositions highlighted within the capability predictor. On the opposite hand, extrinsic motivators seemed to play a secondary role. As explained earlier, theory states that extrinsic motivation that includes parental expectations and expectations of other trusted role models does not require extensive knowledge of individual students.

CONCLUSION

In this study, I have argued that research in ISM requires a more systematic approach that includes a cognitive dimension and that focuses on those who are not studying abroad yet. Such an approach will allow scholars to transparently and systematically identify and design effective evidence-based interventions and policies to boost students' interest in overseas studies.

Thanks to a primary dataset collected among Egyptian students, I quantified the influence of different factors associated with the COM-B framework. Findings obtained through a PLS-SEM highlighted the primordial role of physical capability, physical opportunity, and automatic motivation. The study's respondents seemed to suffer from a lack of self-confidence and independence. They did not feel comfortable with being on their own in a foreign country and having to autonomously handle their life. In order to increase the interest in overseas academic mobility, it appears therefore timely to simultaneously address these three dimensions when it comes to designing student mobility programs.

Using the BCW, I was able to formulate effective functional interventions and policy areas that would contribute to increase the interest in overseas studies. Three pillars characterize my policy program: The first pillar is based on the use of guidelines, which implies the creation of documents that present and discuss ISM's best practices. This goes hand in hand with the second pillar that consists of communication and marketing. The use of broadcast media especially could be critical to induce positive feelings or stimulate actions toward overseas mobility. Finally, the third pillar consists of regulating behavior to enable students feel more self-confident by, for instance, providing students with role-model to aspire to and by offering psychologic support and counseling to reframe opportunities into possibilities.

This study confirms that interest in overseas academic mobility is a complex behavioral issue that requires considering both traditional factors (economic, social, political) and contemporary ones (cognitive). For this reason, I would argue that scholars who integrate this dimension into their future empirical research projects in this field will find not only an original but also a valuable means of understanding the interest in overseas academic mobility.

Limitations and Future Studies

This paper has several limitations. First, my analysis does not allow for any causal interpretations as the data are cross-sectional. A longitudinal perspective would be useful to track changes over time in motivations, opportunities, and capabilities and their effect on the degree of interest in overseas mobility. Second, the sample was not representative of the whole Egyptian student population. Due to the lack of sampling frame at the national level, the generalization of results is therefore not possible. For future research, I suggest implementing a random sampling strategy on a larger scale and for comparative purposes, to replicate my approach across other countries. Third, data were collected before the COVID-19 pandemic. Given the socioeconomic and behavioral changes on the one hand and international travel restrictions on the other, mobility considerations and mobility decision-making processes have necessarily been affected. With regard to further research, I therefore recommend building a measurement model that would include these new parameters especially through the opportunity channel within the COM-B framework. Nonetheless, the present study can still be seen as a substantial contribution to a better and comprehensive understanding of the ISM decision-making process.

REFERENCES

Alexanders, K. E., Brijnath, B., & Mazza, D. (2014). Barriers and enablers to delivery of the Healthy Kids Check: An analysis informed by the theoretical domains framework and COM-B model. *Implementation Science*, *9*(1), Article 60. https://doi.org/10.1186/1748-5908-9-60

Arango, J. (2000). Explaining migration: A critical review. *International Social Science Journal*, *52*(165), 283–296.

Barker, F., Atkins, L., & de Lusignan, S. (2016). Applying the COM-B behaviour model and behaviour change wheel to develop an intervention to improve hearing-aid use in adult auditory rehabilitation. *International Journal of Audiology*, *55*(3), S90–S98. https://doi.org/10.3109/14992027.2015.1120894

Beck, U., & Beck-Gernsheim, E. (2002). *Individualization*. SAGE.

Beerkens, M., Souto-Otero, M., de Wit, H., & Huisman, J. (2016). Similar students and different countries? An analysis of the barriers and drivers for Erasmus participation in seven countries. *Journal of Studies in International Education, 20*(2), 184–204. https://doi.org/10.1177/1028315315595703

Bettman, J. R. (1979). *An information processing view or consumer choice.* Addison-Wesley.

Bollen, K. A., & Pearl, J. (2013). Eight myths about causality and structural equation modeling. In S. L. Morgan (Ed.), *Handbook of causal analysis for social research* (pp. 301–328). Springer.

Bourdieu, P. (1986). The forms of capital. In J. G. Richardson (Ed.), *Handbook for theory and research in the sociology of education* (pp. 241–258). Greenwood Press.

Breines, M. R., Raghuram, P., & Gunter, A. (2019). Infrastructures of immobility: Enabling international distance education students in Africa to not move. *Mobilities, 14*(4), 484–499. https://doi.org/10.1080/17450101.2019.1618565

British Council. (2017). *Broadening horizons 2017: Addressing the needs of a new generation.* https://www.britishcouncil.org/education/he-science/knowledge-centre/student-mobility/broadening-horizons-2017-addressing-needs-new

Brooks, R., & Waters, J. (2011). *Student mobilities, migration and the internationalization of higher education.* Palgrave Macmillan.

Cairney, P. (2016). *The politics of evidence-based policy making*. Springer.

Caplan, N. (1979). The two-communities theory and knowledge utilization. *American Behavioral Scientist, 22*, 459–470. https://doi.org/10.1177/000276427902200308

Carling, J. (2002). Migration in the age of involuntary immobility: Theoretical reflections and Cape Verdean experiences. *Journal of Ethnic and Migration Studies*, *28*(1), 5–42. https://doi.org/10.1080/13691830120103912

Chen, L. H. (2007). East-Asian students' choice of Canadian graduate schools. *International Journal of Education Advancement, 7*(4), 271–306. https://doi.org/10.1057/palgrave.ijea.2150071

Collins, F. L., Ho, K. C., Ishikawa, M., & Ma, A. H. (2017). International student mobility and after-study lives: The portability and prospects of overseas education in Asia. *Population, Space and Place, 23*, Article e2029. https://doi.org/10.1002/psp.2029

Cresswell, T. (2006). *On the move*. Routledge.

Cummings, W. K. (1984). Going overseas for higher education: The Asian experience. In E. G. Barber, P. G. Altbach, & R. G. Myers Eds.), *Bridges to knowledge: Foreign students in comparative perspective* (pp. 130–146). University of Chicago Press.

Czaika, M. (2015). Migration and economic prospects. *Journal of Ethnic and Migration Studies*, *41*(1), 58–82. https://doi.org/10.1080/1369183X.2014.924848

Findlay, A. M., King, R., & Stam, A. (2017). Producing international student migration: An exploration of the role of marketization in shaping international study opportunities. In M. van Riemsdijk & Q. Wang (Eds.), *Rethinking international skilled migration* (pp. 19–35). Routledge.

Goodwin, C. D., & Nacht, M. (1988). *Abroad and beyond: Patterns in American overseas education*. Cambridge University Press.

Hair, J. F., Hult, G. T. M., Ringle, C. M., & Sarstedt, M. (2017). *A primer on partial least squares structural equation modeling* (2nd ed.). SAGE.

Hair, J. F., Ringle, C. M., & Sarstedt, M. (2012). Partial least squares: The better approach to structural equation modeling? *Long Range Planning*, *45*(5–6), 312–319. https://doi.org/10.1016/j.lrp.2012.09.011

Howes, S., Betteridge, A., Sause, L., & Ugyel, L. (2018). Evidence-based policy making in the tropics: Are developing countries different? *Development Policy Centre Discussion Paper No. 59*. https://dx.doi.org/10.2139/ssrn.3009196

Hung, K., & Petrick, J. F. (2012). Testing the effects of congruity, travel constraints, and self-efficacy on travel intentions: An alternative decision-making model. *Tourism Management*, *33*(4), 855–867. https://doi.org/10.1016/j.tourman.2011.09.007

King, R., & Sondhi, G. (2018). International student migration: A comparison of UK and Indian students' motivations for studying abroad. *Globalisation, Societies and Education*, *16*(2), 176–191. https://doi.org/10.1080/14767724.2017.1405244

Koikkalainen, S., & Kyle, D. (2016). Imagining mobility: The prospective cognition question in migration research. *Journal of Ethnic and Migration Studies*, *42*(5), 759–776. https://doi.org/10.1080/1369183X.2015.1111133

Kritz, M. M. (2016). Why do countries differ in their rates of outbound student mobility? *Journal of Studies in International Education, 202*, 99–117. https://doi.org/10.1177/1028315315598104

Kubota, R. (2016). The social imaginary of study abroad: Complexities and contradictions. *The Language Learning Journal*, *44*(3), 347–357. https://doi.org/10.1080/09571736.2016.1198098

Lai, H. M., Hsiao, Y. L., & Hsieh, P. J. (2018). The role of motivation, ability, and opportunity in university teachers' continuance use intention for flipped teaching. *Computers and Education*, *124*, 34–50. doi:10.1016/j.compedu.2018.05.013

Lee, K. H., & Tan, J. P. (1984). The international flow of third level lesser developed country students to developed countries: Determinants and implications. *Higher Education, 13*, 687–707. https://doi.org/10.1007/BF00137020

Lo, W. Y. (2019). Beyond competition: A comparative review of conceptual approaches to international student mobility. *Globalisation, Societies and Education*, *17*(3), 261–273. https://doi.org/10.1080/14767724.2018.1525283

Lowell, B. L., & Khadka, P. (2011). Trends in foreign-student admissions to the U.S. In B. R. Chiswick (Ed.), *High-skilled immigration in a global labor market* (pp. 83–110). American Enterprise Institute.

McDonald, R. P. (1996). Path analysis with composite variables. *Multivariate Behavioral Research*, *31*(2), 239–270. https://doi.org/10.1207/s15327906mbr3102_5

Michie, S., Hyder, N., Walia, A., & West, R. (2011). Development of a taxonomy of behaviour change techniques used in individual behavioural support for smoking cessation, *Addictive Behaviours*, *36*(4), 315–319. http://dx.doi.org/10.1016/j.addbeh.2010.11.016

Michie, S., & Prestwich, A. (2010). Are interventions theory-based? Development of a theory coding scheme. *Health Psychology*, *29*(1), 1–8. https://doi.org/10.1037/a0016939

Michie, S., Van Stralen, M. M., & West, R. (2011). The behaviour change wheel: A new method for characterizing and designing behaviour change interventions. *Implementation Science*, *6*(1), Article 42. https://doi.org/10.1186/1748-5908-6-42

Mondain, N., & Diagne, A. (2013). Discerning the reality of 'those left behind' in contemporary migration processes in Sub-Saharan Africa: Some theoretical reflections in the light of data from Senegal. *Journal of Intercultural Studies, 345*, 503–516. https://doi.org/10.1080/07256868.2013.827831

Murphy-Lejeune, E. (2002). *Student mobility and narrative in Europe: The new strangers*. Routledge.

Netz, N. (2015). What deters students from studying abroad? Evidence from four European countries and its implications for higher education policy. *Higher Education Policy*, *28*(2), 151–174. https://doi.org/10.1057/hep.2013.37

Newell, S. (2012). *The modernity bluff: Crime, consumption, and citizenship in Côte d'Ivoire*. University of Chicago Press.

Nilsson, P. A., & Ripmeester, N. (2016). International student expectations: Career, opportunities and employability. *Journal of International Students, 6*(2), 614–631.

Nitzl, C. (2016). The use of partial least squares structural equation modelling (PLS-SEM) in management accounting research: Directions for future theory development. *Journal of Accounting Literature*, *39*, 19–35. https://doi.org/10.1016/j.acclit.2016.09.003

Ojeda, L., Flores, L. Y., & Navarro, R. L. (2011). Social cognitive predictors of Mexican American college students' academic and life satisfaction. *Journal of Counseling Psychology*, *58*, 61–71. https://doi.org/10.1037/a0021687

Organisation for Economic Cooperation and Development. (2017). *Debate the issues: Complexity and policy making*. OECD Insights. http://dx.doi.org/10.1787/9789264271531-en

Organisation for Economic Cooperation and Development. (2019). *Education at a glance 2019: OECD indicators*. https://doi.org/10.1787/f8d7880d-en

Parkhurst, J. (2017). *The politics* of evidence: From evidence-based policy to the good governance of evidence. Routledge.

Perkins, R., & Neumayer, E. (2014). Geographies of educational mobilities: Exploring the uneven flows of international students. *The Geographical Journal*, *180*(3), 246–259. https://doi.org/10.1111/geoj.12045

Rosenzweig, M. R. (2007). *Higher education and international migration in Asia: Brain circulation* [Paper presentation]. Regional Bank Conference on Development Economics, Beijing.

Schewel, K. (2015). *Understanding the aspiration to stay*. Oxford University International Migration Institute Working Papers No. 107.

Schewel, K. (2019). Understanding immobility: Moving beyond the mobility bias in migration studies. *International Migration Review*, *54*(2), 328–355. https://doi.org/10.1177/0197918319831952

Soong, H., Stahl, G., & Shan, H. (2017). Transnational mobility through education: a Bourdieusian insight on life as middle transnationals in Australia and Canada. *Globalisation, Societies and Education, 16*(2), 241–253. https://doi.org/10.1080/14767724.2017.1396886

Souto-Otero, M., Huisman, J., Beerkens, M., & de Wit, H. (2013). Barriers to international student mobility: Evidence from the ERASMUS program. *Educational Researcher*, *42*, 70–77.

Stoker, G., & Evans, M. (2016). *Evidence-based policy making in the social sciences: Methods that matter*. Policy Press.

Syed Zwick, H. (2020a). Le modèle de motivation–opportunité–capacité: Application à la mobilité étudiante régionale en Asie centrale [Applying the motivation-opportunity-ability model to regional student mobility in Central Asia]. *Journal of International Mobility: Moving for Education, Training and Research, 7*, 45–68.

Syed Zwick, H. (2020b). Narrative analysis of Syrians, South Sudanese and Libyans transiting in Egypt: A motivation-opportunity-ability approach. *Journal of Ethnic and Migration Studies*. https://doi.org/10.1080/1369183X.2020.1720630

Syed Zwick, H., & Syed S. A. S. (2015). Student disinterest for mobility: Microeconomic determinants. *Current Politics and Economics of Europe*, *26*(1), 93–108.

Triandis, H. C. (1977). *Interpersonal behavior*. Brooks/Cole.

UNESCO Institute for Stastistics. (2019). UNESCO Database on education. Retrieved Month 01, 2020, from http://data.uis.unesco.org/

Ullman, J. B. (2001). Structural equation modelling. In B. G. Tabachnick & L. S. Fidell (Eds,), *Using multivariate statistics* (pp. 653–771). Allyn & Bacon.

Urry, J. (2007). *Mobilities*. Polity.

Van der Velde, M., & van Naerssen, T. (2015). The threshold approach revisited. In M. Van der Velde & T. van Naerssen (Eds.), Mobility and migration choices: Thresholds to crossing borders (pp. 267–275). Ashgate.

Waters, J. (2008). *Education, migration, and cultural capital in the Chinese diaspora: Transnational students between Hong Kong and Canada*. Cambria Press.

HELENE SYED ZWICK, PhD, is executive director in the ESLSCA Research Center of Excellence (ERCE) at ESLSCA University Egypt. Her major research interests lie in the area of human mobility, return and reintegration, migrant decision-making. Email: helene.syed@eslsca.edu.eg

---

Peer-Reviewed Article

© *Journal of International Students*
Volume 11, Issue 2 (2021), pp. 397-416
ISSN: 2162-3104 (Print), 2166-3750
(Online) doi: 10.32674/jis.v11i2.1379
ojed.org/jis

Loneliness Among African International Students at Portuguese Universities

Félix Neto
University of Porto, Portugal

ABSTRACT

International students constitute an important sojourner group. This study examined the levels and predictors of loneliness among international students. The sample included 188 Angolan, 210 Cape Verdean, and 221 domestic college students who attended Portuguese institutions of higher education. The relative strengths of background and acculturation factors in loneliness, as an indicator of psychological adaptation, were explored. Results showed that international students reported greater levels of loneliness than native-born students. As expected, results showed that students who reported poorer financial situation, greater perceived discrimination, and lower home culture and host culture acculturation orientation scores reported higher loneliness. In addition, using hierarchical regression analyses, current findings suggest that the most significant predictors of loneliness for international students were financial situation, perceived discrimination, and orientation to heritage culture. Implications of these results for reducing loneliness of international students are discussed.

Keywords: acculturation orientation, international students, loneliness, migrations, perceived discrimination

Intercultural experiences have become more common as our world becomes increasingly globalized and interconnected. One measure of the growth in such experiences is the progressive and rapid increase in international student migration. The number of international students attending institutions of higher education increased worldwide from 2 million in 1999 to 5.6 million in 2018 (Organisation for Economic Cooperation and Development, 2020).

The majority of international students attend their studies in Anglophone countries, with the United States, the United Kingdom, Australia. and Canada being the top destinations. Given the prevalence of English-speaking countries as the favorite destinations of international students, it is not surprising that most research has been conducted in Anglophone cultural contexts. In fact, much less research has been pursued in other cultural contexts, in particular, in Lusophone countries (wherein Portuguese is the official language; i.e., Portugal, Angola, Brazil, Cape Verde, East-Timor, Guinea-Bissau, Mozambique, and São Tome and Principe; França et al., 2018; Neto & Wilks, 2017; Wilks & Neto, 2016).

International students face a plethora of challenges from migration, such as dealing with social interaction with host nationals, cultural understanding and participation, language fluency, lack of familiarity with the academic system, depression, and loneliness (Brunsting et al., 2018; Safdar & Berno, 2016; Shadowen et al., 2019; Smith & Khawaga, 2011; Zhang & Goodson, 2011). The current study examined the levels and the factors related to loneliness of international students enrolled in Portuguese Universities. More specifically, the study focused on international students residing in Portugal from two African countries: Angola and Cape Verde. Understanding the needs of these students can assist host institutions in providing adequate services for these individuals.

BACKGROUND

Acculturation and Adaptation

The exploration of acculturation and its outcome, adaptation, has produced extensive cross-cultural research (Sam & Berry, 2016; Ward et al., 2001). Acculturation is defined as the process of cultural and psychological changes that occur following intercultural contact (Berry, 1997; Graves, 1967; Redfield et al., 1936). This process of change concerns sojourners. In the field of acculturation, sojourners are defined as "people who travel internationally to achieve a particular goal or objective with the expectation that they will return to their country of origin after the purpose of their travel has been achieved" (Safdar & Berno, 2016, p. 173). International students constitute one of the largest and most significant sojourner groups. Most international students not only focus on their academic objectives in a host society, but also expect to expand their views by means of cross-cultural experiences.

Concerning the adaptation of newcomers, acculturation researchers make a distinction between sociocultural adaptation and psychological adaptation (Ward et al., 2001). Sociocultural adaptation refers to the acquisition of culturally adequate skills in order to operate effectively in a particular cultural context and is interpreted within the social learning paradigm. It is measured by "the amount of difficulties experienced in the management of everyday social situation in the host culture" (Ward & Kennedy, 1996, p. 291). On the other hand, psychological adaptation can be interpreted within a stress and coping model. It refers to "how comfortable and happy a person feels with respect to being in the new culture or feeling anxious and out of place" (Demes & Geeraert, 2014, p. 91). Psychological adaptation is assessed through measuring well-being or psychological distress. Hence, loneliness has been utilized as an indicator of psychological adaptation (Neto et al., 2017).

Various changes may occur during acculturation. Living and studying abroad may involve the loss of social ties, separation from family, and a new friendship network in the host country (Imai & Imai, 2019; Mesidor & Sly, 2016; Patron, 2014; Wilks & Neto, 2016). These modifications may have an impact on the loneliness experienced by international students.

Loneliness

Loneliness is a universal phenomenon, as evidenced by investigation within a variety of cultural contexts, such as Australians (Leung, 2001), British (Victor & Yang, 2012), Cape Verdeans (Neto & Barros, 2000b), Chinese (D. Liu et al., 2014; Zhong, 2018), and Turks (Kapikiran, 2013). In a study of 25 European nations, the prevalence of loneliness ranged from 3.2% in Denmark to 34% in Ukraine (Yang & Victor, 2011). Anyone can feel lonely in any culture. Most of the definitions of loneliness outline perceived deficits in relationships. For instance, Ascher and Paquette (2003) defined loneliness as "the cognitive awareness of a deficiency in one's social and personal relationships, and ensuring affective reactions of sadness, emptiness, or longing" (p. 75). In this line, loneliness is a negative emotion that is linked to negative experiences in one's cultural context. Loneliness is a subjective (rather than an objective) experience of isolation.

The recognition of factors that are related to loneliness is significant for a variety of motives, such as links with low physical activity (Hawkley et al., 2009), poor academic competence and performance (Sletta et al., 1996), unmet intimacy needs (Cacioppo & Hawley, 2005), sleep disturbance and increased hypertension (Cacioppo et al., 2002), and mental health problems. For instance, a relationship between loneliness, depressive symptomatology, anxiety, and suicidal ideation has been evidenced (Dell et al., 2019; Mahon et al., 2006). Research shows that loneliness yields not only an enhanced risk of morbidity but also of mortality later in life (Hawkley & Cacioppo, 2010). Indeed, loneliness was found to be linked to a 26% greater likelihood of mortality, with an even greater likelihood for those below the age of 65 (Holt-Lunstad et al., 2015). Concerning personality, loneliness consistently was positively associated with neuroticism and negatively associated with extraversion (Vanhalst et al., 2012). Following this line, it is not surprising that loneliness might be characterized by high negative affect.

Relocation/significant separation is one of the salient factors explaining the causes of loneliness (Rokach & Neto, 2005). Loneliness is a significant factor in international students' adjustment to a receiving society (Oei & Notowidjojo, 1990; Rajapaksa & Dundes, 2002; Smith & Khawaja, 2011). Sawir et al. (2008) interviewed 200 international students in Australia and 65% reported that they had experienced loneliness and/or isolation in the sojourn society. Chataway and Berry (1989) found that loneliness was one of the most serious problems experienced by international students in Canada.

International Students in Portugal

Recently, Portugal has attracted an increasing number of international students. In the 2000–2001 academic year the proportion of international students attending Portuguese institutions of higher education was 3%. In 2016–2017 there were 41,997 international students enrolled in higher education in Portugal, representing 11.6% of the higher education student enrollment (Direcção Geral de Estatística de Educação e Ciência, 2016). In that academic year, Portuguese higher education received students of 179 different nationalities. Half of the international students were from Lusophone countries (50.3%), and close to a third (34.5%) from the European Union. Historically, Angolan and Cape Verdean international students have been the two largest communities; however, Brazilian international students have recently become the largest community. In the 2016–2017 academic year, the most international students were from Brazil (28.9%), followed by Angola (8.6%), Spain (8.2%), Cape Verde (6.4%), Italy (6.1%), and Germany (3.9%). Therefore, Angolan and Cape Verdean international students were the second and fourth most numerous, respectively, with 6,321 persons.

Angolan and Cape Verdean international student migration to Portugal began in the colonial era, and it has continued to be a popular destination for students from these two countries. Between 2000 and 2014 around half of Angolan international students and three quarters of Cape Verdean international students attended Portuguese institutions of higher education (França et al., 2018).

Motivations to study abroad represent nuclear factors influencing students' acculturation outcomes (Kitsantas, 2004). A variety of factors motivate African international students to study in Portugal: a common language, family members and friends already residing in the country, international agreements, standards of living, quality of teaching, and potentially more work opportunities (Mourato, 2011). A great majority of African international students plan their stay abroad as transitory (António, 2013).

The current study differs from the study of Wilks and Neto (2016) by using a quantitative methodology, and from the study of Neto and Wilks (2017) by collecting a different sample of Cape Verdean students and by including a new sample of Angolan students. Therefore, the present study examines together the levels and predictors of loneliness among the two most numerous communities of African international students in Portugal.

The Present Study

Loneliness, as a psychosocial complex phenomenon, is predicted by the interaction of personal and situational factors (Weiss, 1973). Therefore, in this investigation a set of background and acculturation variables often referred to in the culture shock field will be considered (Sam & Berry, 2016; Ward et al., 2001). More specifically, the present study has three general objectives.

The first objective is to analyze whether there are differences in the levels of loneliness between native students and African international students. In the current study, an international student is defined as an individual following "degree mobility" abroad for an entire degree program (either undergraduate or postgraduate). This is opposed to short-term international students who go abroad on a "credit mobility" scheme (Mikulás & Jitka, 2019).

International student migration provides an opportunity to understand loneliness. In line with Ponizovsky and Ritsner (2004), "Newly immigrated persons find themselves in a drastically different network of social relationships and experience multiple stressors, including losses" (p. 408). Nevertheless, quantitative research on this topic of loneliness among migrants is scarce (Neto, 2016), and previous results of research comparing the levels of loneliness between immigrant samples and nonimmigrant samples are mixed.

Some research has not evidenced differences in loneliness between migrants and native-born people. For instance, Portuguese youths residing in France and Portuguese youths without migratory experience did not show significant differences in the levels of loneliness (Neto, 1999). Similar findings were evidenced among Portuguese migrants residing in Switzerland (Neto & Barros, 2000a), and among Angolan, Cape Verdean and Indian youth migrants living in Portugal (Neto, 2002). Youth from returned migrant families to Portugal also reported lower loneliness than domestic youths (Neto, 2016).

Previous investigations have reported that international students show more adaptation difficulties than native students (Kilinc & Granello, 2003; M. Liu, 2009; Poyrazli et al., 2010). Chinese students in Australia had higher loneliness levels than Anglo-Australian students (Leung, 2001). International students in the United States felt lonelier than domestic counterparts (Rajapaksa & Dundes, 2002). A qualitative study reported that Cape Verdean students faced difficulties in adapting to Portuguese society (Wilks & Neto 2016). Emotional problems related to loneliness and homesickness, feelings of not belonging to the received community, and disorientation were some factors indicated as being stressful for these students. A quantitative study carried out in Portugal revealed that Cape Verdean students reported greater loneliness than native students (Neto & Wilks, 2017).

Therefore, grounded on the above literature showing higher loneliness among international students than among domestic students (Leung, 2001; Neto & Wilks, 2017; Rajapaksa & Dundes, 2002), I proposed the following hypothesis:

> H1: African international students will report higher levels of loneliness than domestic students.

My second objective is to scrutinize the relationship between background factors and loneliness. Background variables, such as gender, age, and duration of stay are deemed to be key factors in understanding the acculturation process (Sam & Berry, 2016). However, relationships between these factors and loneliness are mixed (Neto, 2016; Ward et al., 2001). It is possible that these inconsistent results are connected with weak effects. In a study examining the predictors of loneliness among adolescents from returned migrant families, gender, age, and length of residence were not associated with loneliness (Neto, 2016).

International students experience some lifestyle acculturative stress, such as financial problems. (Smith & Khawaha, 2011; Titrek et al., 2016). Financial problems were a cause of much distress reported by Cape Verdean students (Wilks & Neto, 2016). Background variables such as financial situation may impact loneliness. Socioeconomic status has not been a major concern in the loneliness literature (Holt-Lunstad et al., 2015). There is some research that reports a relationship between loneliness and financial status, with lower levels of loneliness linked to higher income (Chen et al., 2014; Savikko et al., 2005). Therefore, grounded on the above literature, I proposed the following hypothesis:

> H2: The financial situation of the African international students will predict loneliness; more specifically, international students with poorer financial situations will report higher loneliness.

My third objective is to analyze the relationship between loneliness and acculturation factors. Perceived discrimination and acculturation orientations are key constructs in the acculturation field (Berry, 2017; Ward et al., 2001). Perceived discrimination concerns the perception of being unfairly treated because of prejudice and ethnocentrism, and is a potentially serious acculturative stressor (Jasinskaja-Lahati et al., 2003; Mewes et al., 2015; Schmitt et al., 2014; Smith & Khawaja, 2011). Previous research supports a significant relationship between perceived discrimination, psychological distress, and adaptation. For instance, a meta-analysis examining over 100 studies of ethnic or racial discrimination against Latina/os in the United States reported that mental health indicators such as acculturative stress were mostly strongly related to discrimination (Lee & Ahn, 2011). Prelow et al. (2006) showed that perceived racial discrimination was linked to lower perceptions of social support, higher depression, and lower satisfaction with life among African American college students. International students from Africa often report significant perceived discrimination in comparison with native students (Smith & Khawaja, 2011). Perceived discrimination has been significantly associated with loneliness among migrants (D. Liu et al., 2014; Neto, 2002; Neto & Costa, 2015). As a result of experiencing discriminatory events, international students may be at risk for loneliness in the acculturation process in the host society. Therefore, grounded on the above literature, I tested the following hypothesis:

> H3: Greater perceived discrimination will predict greater levels of loneliness among international students.

In the framework of acculturation orientations advanced by Berry (1997), sojourners face two main issues: the desire to maintain their heritage culture, and the desire to adhere to the host culture. These two acculturation orientations, heritage culture and mainstream culture orientations, can be evaluated independently (Demes & Geeraert, 2014; Neto et al., 2005). There is empirical evidence pointing to a negative association between heritage orientation and psychological adaptation, and a positive relationship between mainstream orientation and psychological adaptation (Demes & Geeraert, 2014). Therefore, grounded on the above literature, I tested the following hypothesis:

H4: Greater levels of orientation to heritage culture and lower levels of orientation to mainstream culture will predict higher levels of loneliness among international students.

METHOD

Participants

A total of 398 African international students participated in this study (47% from Angola, and 53% from Cape Verde). Forty-five percent were men and 55% women. Their age ranged from 18 to 42 years ($M = 25.88$; $SD = 5.33$). No students were of Portuguese nationality and all were born in Angola or Cape Verde. The average age at arrival was 18.68 years ($SD = 4.44$), and the average length of sojourn in the host country was 7.24 years ($SD = 4.38$). Regarding their financial situation, 44% indicated themselves in a very good situation, 28% in a good situation, 19% in a fair situation, and 9% in a poor situation.

In order to compare levels of loneliness between IS and native-born students, 221 Portuguese students (119 women and 102 men; average age = 21.33 years, $SD = 3.32$) were surveyed in the same institutions of higher education where the international students were enrolled. The proportion of males to females among international students and native-born students did not differ significantly, $\chi^2(1, 619) = 0.05$, $p = .87$. The average age of international students and domestic students presented significant differences, $F(1, 617) = 133.11$, $p < .001$. Hence, age will be used as a covariate.

Materials

In addition to background information (age, gender, country of birth, nationality, and length of sojourn), the survey comprised the following instruments.

Self-Rated Financial Status

A single item was used to assess overall financial status. Participants were asked, "Globally, how would you rate your financial situation?" Responses ranged from 1 (*very good*) to 4 (*poor*). Answers were recoded such that greater numbers denoted better financial status.

Perceived Discrimination

Assessing perceived discrimination was comprised of five statements (Berry et al., 2006; Neto, 2006) assessing the direct experience of discrimination (e.g., "I don't feel accepted by the Portuguese."). Response ranged from 1 (*strongly disagree*) to 5 (*strongly agree*). In the present study, Cronbach's alpha was .89.

Acculturation Orientation

Acculturation orientation was assessed by means of the Brief Acculturation Orientation Scale (Demes & Geeraert 2014). It includes four statements for assessing acculturation towards the home country (e.g., "It is important for me to have Cape Verdean friends"), and also four items for assessing acculturation toward the host country (e.g., "It is important for me to have Portuguese friends"). Response choices ranged from 1 (*strongly disagree*) to 7 (*strongly agree*). The scores of these scales confirmed their reliability and validity among international students (Demes & Geeraert 2014; Neto & Wilks, 2017). In our sample, Cronbach's alpha was .72 for host orientation and .83 for the home orientation.

Loneliness

The brief Portuguese version of the Revised University of California–Los Angeles Loneliness Scale (Russell et al., 1980) was used (Neto, 1992, 2001, 2014). This scale comprises six items (ULS-6; e.g., "People are around me but not with me"). Response choices ranged from 1 (*never*) to 4 (*often*). Greater scores denote more loneliness. In the present sample, Cronbach's alpha was .77.

Although international students completed all these materials, domestic students completed only the loneliness scale, as well as background information.

Procedure

One research assistant recruited students in three institutions of higher education in Porto, Coimbra, and Lisbon. About a third of the participants were obtained at each site. The sample was of convenience, recruit through snowball sampling utilizing personal contacts and community groups. Drawing a convenience sample is suitable in cross-cultural investigation, namely when the researcher does not have access to an accurate list of the entire population, as was the case at the time of the study (Lonner & Berry, 1986). This kind of sample presents advantages and disadvantages as pointed out by Lonner and Berry (1986, p. 87): "Their accessibility makes them very cost-effective, in terms of both money and time; however, all such samples depart to an unknown degree from true representativeness." Potential respondents were called upon to contribute to a study on student adjustment. They then responded to a paper-and-pencil questionnaire in a quiet location in the presence of the research assistant. A Portuguese version of the survey was used (the official language of Angola and Cape Verde). The respondents' rate was about 90%.

Regarding ethical considerations, the research was performed in agreement with the legal and ethical norms of the country. Students were acquainted with the aims of the investigation and they provided informed consent. All respondents were notified that the participation was voluntary and that responses were anonymous. Participants were free to withdraw from the investigation at any time without consequence. The average length of time needed to complete the survey was approximately 20 minutes.

Data Analysis

Five types of analyses were conducted: descriptive, internal consistency, analysis of variance, correlations, and regression analyses. First, I computed the descriptive statistics of the scales to verify the respondents' standing on acculturation measures to get an overall picture of variables in their acculturation. Second, I computed the internal consistency of all scales by means of Cronbach's alpha coefficient to ensure higher internal reliability. Next, I used an analysis of variance to examine group differences, and, in particular, to test the first hypothesis. Then, I performed a Pearson product-moment correlational analysis to analyze the relationship between the research measures. Cohen (1988) provided guidelines for determining the magnitude of correlations, where those between .10 and .29 are considered small, between .30 and .49 are moderate, between .50 and .69 are large, and between .70 and .90 very large. Finally, hierarchical regression analysis was performed to analyze the relative strength of variables in predicting loneliness, allowing us to test the second, third, and fourth hypotheses. I conducted all analyses using IBM SPSS statistical software (version 25.0). In all analyses performed, significance level was set at .05.

RESULTS

Descriptive statistics of the measures utilized in the current study are presented in Table 1. In order to test the first hypothesis, univariate analysis of co-variance (ANCOVA; with age covaried) for loneliness as a dependent variable across mobility was performed. The ANCOVA of loneliness revealed that the effect of mobility was significant, $F(1, 618) = 269.23, p < .001, \eta^2 = .30$. Findings suggest that international students (M = 2.52; SD = 0.55) displayed greater levels of loneliness than the native students (M = 1.66; SD = 0.57). Hence, the prediction that international students would report higher levels of loneliness than native students (H1) was supported.

Table 1: Intercorrelations of Predictors and Criterion Variables Among International Students, Descriptive Statistics, and Cronbach Alpha

	Variables										
	1	2	3	4	5	6	7	8	M	SD	α
1 Gender	—										
2 Age	−0.17**	—							25.88	5.33	
3 Financial situation	−0.03	−0.03	—						3.06	0.99	
4 Length of stay	−0.10	0.60***	−0.27***	—					7.24	4.38	
5 Host culture	0.02	−0.05	0.38***	−0.17**	—				3.77	1.09	.72
6 Home culture	−0.01	−0.12*	0.56***	−0.28***	0.56***	—			3.87	1.15	.83
7 Perceived discrimination	0.09	0.12*	−0.29***	0.18**	−0.34***	−0.36	—		3.37	0.85	.89
8 Loneliness	0.09	0.01	−0.46***	0.16**	−0.35***	−0.48***	0.52***	—	2.52	0.55	.77

To analyze the unique contribution of independent measures to loneliness, a hierarchical multiple regression analysis was performed. Before carrying out hierarchical multiple regression analysis, the assumptions of this statistical analysis were examined. First, the assumption of singularity was met among the independent measures. An examination of the correlation matrix showed that the measures were not very largely correlated according to Cohen's (1988) guidelines (Table 1). The internal consistency of the different measures were adequate, with Cronbach's alpha ranging from .72 to .89.

Next, the analyses show that the assumptions of normality were also verified (see Table 2). The collinearity statistics (i.e., tolerance and variance inflation factor) were all within adequate limits, suggesting that the assumption of multicollinearity was deemed to have been met (Field, 2000). Furthermore, the Durbin-Watson values evidenced no autocorrelation in the regression models.

Table 2: Summary of Hierarchical Regression Analysis for Variables Predicting Loneliness Among International Students

Models	β	*p*	Tolerance	VIF	*R*	R^2	ΔR^2	Durbin-Watson
First model					.43[a]	.18	.18	1.85
Gender	.03	.49	.97	1.03				
Age	−.06	.30	.62	1.61				
Financial status	−.41	<.001	.91	1.10				
Length of stay	.07	.23	.59	1.69				
Second model					.63[a]	.39	.38	
Gender	−.02	.65	.95	1.05				
Age	−.10	.06	.62	1.61				
Financial status	−.17	.001	.66	1.52				
Length of stay	.02	.78	.58	1.71				
Host culture	−.01	.92	.66	1.51				
Home culture	−.24	<.001	.53	1.88				
Perceived discrimination	.39	<.001	.82	1.23				

Note. VIF = variance inflation factor.

A two-step hierarchical multiple regression was performed with loneliness as the dependent measure. In the first step, the background variables were entered, followed by the acculturation variables. The measures were entered in this order as it seemed plausible, based on the International Comparative Study of Ethnocultural Youth project (Berry et al., 2006), which confirms that indicators of psychological adaptation, in this case, loneliness, are impacted by acculturation factors. "Psychological adaptation can be seen as the final outcome in the model, containing or reflecting the psychological consequences of the acculturation experiences that were measured" (Berry et al., 2006, p. 157).

My findings evidenced that background variables presented a significant predictive effect on loneliness, $F(4, 374) = 21.03$; $p < .001$; these measures explained 18% of the variation in loneliness. However, only financial status appeared as a significant predictor of loneliness ($\beta = -.41$, $p < .001$). A poorer financial situation predicted greater loneliness. Gender, age, and duration of residence did not appear as significant predictors. Introducing the acculturation measures to the regression model accounted for 39% of variation in loneliness, $F(7, 371) = 34.46$; $p < .001$. The model did significantly predict loneliness. Financial status remained significant in the model ($\beta = -.17$, $p < .001$), and perceived discrimination ($\beta = .39$, $p < .001$) and orientation to home culture ($\beta = -.24$, $p < .001$) revealed a predictive effect on loneliness. However, orientation to host culture did not emerge as a significant predictor. Specifically, higher perceived discrimination and lower orientation to heritage culture predicted higher loneliness.

DISCUSSION

The purpose of this study was to examine the levels and predictors of loneliness among international students from Angola and Cape Verde. The findings support the first hypothesis, which stated that the African international students would display greater levels of loneliness than native students. This result is consonant with past studies that showed higher loneliness levels among international students than among national students (Leung, 2001; Neto & Wilks, 2017; Rajapaksa & Dundes, 2002). Current findings call our attention to the high risk of loneliness for the African international students. As I have outlined earlier, the research of past studies comparing the levels of loneliness between migrant samples and domestic samples is mixed. In some research, a significant difference was not found between migrants and nationals, or even less loneliness among migrants than nonmigrant people. Furthermore, previous research showed that the levels of loneliness between college students from Cape Verde and Portugal did not differ significantly (Neto & Barros, 2000b).

Results suggest the gender, age, and length of residence did not contribute to the regression model. These findings are in accordance with past research, which showed also that these three background variables were largely unrelated to loneliness (Neto, 2016). However, financial status emerged as a significant background predictor of loneliness.

The current study emphasizes the importance of financial status to loneliness. Its potential influence on health is not frequently considered (Hamilton et al., 2009). The findings of the current research indicate that financial status is significantly related to loneliness. Specifically, international students with poorer financial situations reported higher loneliness, thereby supporting our second hypothesis. One possible explanation for this result is that low financial status might prevent people from socially interacting with others. Another potential pathway is suggested by Ayalon (2019): "Poorer financial status might be a risk factor for social isolation and poorer health and mental health, which in return result in higher levels of loneliness" (p. 918). Indeed, past investigation showed that higher emotional distress and lower health was linked to financial hardship (Hamilton et al., 2009; Richardson et al., 2017; Roberts et al., 1999). Fröjd et al. (2006) also showed that perceived financial difficulties were associated with maladjustment outcomes, such as depression.

While studying in a host country provides international students with chances to grow psychosocially, they often face discrimination from host nationals.

International students who reported greater feelings and experiences of perceived discrimination reported greater levels of loneliness. This finding also supports Hypothesis 3 (H3). Indeed, perceived discrimination is a major acculturative stressor linked to loneliness (Neto, 2016). Current findings are in agreement with research showing that perceived discrimination is related to poor psychological well-being and depression (Mewes et al., 2015; Pascoe & Richman, 2009; Smith & Khawaja, 2011; Zhang & Goodson, 2011).

In line with Arends-Toth and van de Vijver (2006), and with Demes and Geeraert (2014), I measured home and host orientation independently. The findings of this study did not support my fourth hypothesis. Orientation toward home country negatively predicted loneliness. This finding is not in accordance with past investigation reporting that home acculturation orientation is relevant for experiencing negative feelings during acculturation (Demes & Geeraert, 2014). My findings are consonant with those pointing out the benefits of maintaining the one's own cultural heritage, such as lower depression (Ward & Kennedy, 1994), better psychological well-being (Brisset et al., 2010; Neto et al., 2005), and career adaptability (Guan et al., 2018).

On the other hand, I found that orientation toward the host country, meaning having a preference for embracing the host culture, did not significantly predict loneliness. While regression analysis did not confirm the fourth hypothesis for host orientation, bivariate correlations showed that orientation to mainstream culture and loneliness were negatively and significantly correlated. This implies that the effect of host orientation interacts with other acculturation variables, such as perceived discrimination and home orientation.

Limitations

As is usual, there were some limitations in this study. First, the participants were not chosen at random; hence, the generalizability of the results is limited. Moreover, the sample consisted of students whose official language in their countries was the same as the receiving society. The sameness in official languages may ease the psychological adaptation of international students. International students with poor language competency of the sojourn country may have several problems, such as greater difficulty understanding lectures and interaction with students from the sojourn society (Pedersen, 1991; Shadowen et al., 2019). Additionally, a cross-cultural perspective of loneliness among international students studying in other countries could be conducted in future.

Second, I have not considered whether the levels of tertiary education have an impact on loneliness. Third, only one assessment of financial status was collected. Further investigation may address this limitation by utilizing alternative measures, such as the index of financial stress (Siahpush & Carlin, 2006) and the scale of financial concern (Jessop et al., 2005). Finally, the results are based on cross-sectional data, which means that no inferences of causal relationships should be drawn. In spite of these limitations, the present research pointed out specific implications in order to help with a better adaptation of international students.

Implications

The results of this study have significant implications for institutions of higher education and mental health providers. Current findings suggest that the Angolan and Cape Verdean international students studying in Portugal may need further support services, as they tend to feel lonelier than native students do. Some international students are at greater risk for developing loneliness than others. There is evidence that loneliness can be prevented or relieved by interventions, such as those addressing maladaptive social cognition (Cacioppo et al., 2015; Masi et al., 2011). Hence, loneliness can be modified, and interventions targeting it could improve wellbeing of international students. In particular, counseling may help international students in coping with loneliness. Previous investigation has shown that there are several coping strategies to deal with loneliness and to moderate the consequences of this debilitating experience (Rokach & Neto, 2000). Establishing social support networks is a valuable strategy that international students can use in the receiving society. It is relevant for psychological and academic adaptation (Patron, 2014). Sawir et al. (2008) advocated the establishment of more educational engagements and social connections between national and international students, based on sharing and mutual respect.

My findings showed that greater levels of perceived discrimination predicted greater levels of loneliness. To address the issue of discrimination perceived by international students, higher education institutions should first make every endeavor to inhibit discrimination within the academic settings. Another possible way to decrease perceived discrimination would be to create peer-to-peer programs in which international students would be paired with a native colleague from the sojourn country. Several activities could be implanted in those programs, such as informal discussions, exchange of information about the norms in the university, or collaborative learning activities. Furthermore, these results call attention to the relevance of intervention programs specifically designed to provide support to international students in reducing the amount of discrimination experienced or for learning how to deal with it. A recent study demonstrated that international students' degree of self-disclosure did alleviate the detrimental impact of the perceived discrimination on loneliness (Imai & Imai, 2019).

My results revealed that greater levels of orientation toward home culture rather than the abandonment of orientation toward home culture is desirable for acculturating international students. The positive effect of orientation toward home country suggests that international students should get involved in social interactions with in-group members.

In addition, results show that greater financial difficulties issues predict higher loneliness. The immigration status of international students may often make it difficult for them to find work. Higher education institutions may help international students in solving some of these financial problems. For example, they can create job opportunities for students within the university context. Work provides a sense of usefulness and purpose for international students (Mesidor & Sly, 2016).

REFERENCES

António, M. (2013). Os estudantes angolanos do ensino superior em Lisboa: Uma perspectiva antropológica sobre as suas motivações e bem-estar subjectivo. *Análise Social*, *208*, XLVIII (3°), 660-682.

Arends-Toth, J., & Van de Vijver, F. J. R. (2006). Issues in the conceptualization and assessment of acculturation. In M. H. Bornstein & L. R. Cote (Eds.), *Acculturation and parent-child relationships: Measurement and development* (pp. 33–62). Erlbaum.

Ascher, S. R., & Paquette, J. A. (2003). Loneliness and peer relations in childhood. *Currents Directions in Psychological Science*, *12*, 75–78. http://dx.doi.org/10.1111/1467-8721.01233

Ayalon, L. (2019). Subjective social status as a predictor of loneliness: The moderating effect of the type of long-term care setting. *Research on Aging*, *41*, 915–935. http://dx.doi.org/10.1177/0164027519871674

Berry, J. W. (1997). Immigration, acculturation and adaptation. *Applied Psychology: An International Review*, *46*, 5–68. http://dx.doi.org/10.1111/j.1464-0597.1997.tb01087.x

Berry, J. W. (2017). *Mutual intercultural relations*. Cambridge University Press. http://dx.doi.org/10.1017/9781316875032

Berry, J. W. Phinney, J. S, Sam, D. L., & Vedder, P. (Eds.) (2006). *Immigrant youth in cultural transition: Acculturation, identity and adaptation across national contexts*. Lawrence Erlbaum.

Brisset, C., Safdar, S., Lewis, J. R., & Sabatier, C. (2010). Psychological and sociocultural adaptation of university students in France: The case of Vietnamese international students. *International Journal of Intercultural Relations*, *34*, 413–426. http://dx.doi.org/10.1016/j.ijintrel.2010.02.009

Brunsting, N. C., Zachry, C., & Takeuchi, R. (2018). Predictors of undergraduate international student psychosocial adjustment to US universities: A systematic review from 2009–2018. *International Journal of Intercultural Relations*, *66*, 22–33. http://dx.doi.org/10.1016/j.ijintrel.2018.06.002

Cacioppo, S., Grippo, A. J., London, S., Goosens, L., & Cacioppo, J. T. (2015). Loneliness: Clinical import and interventions. *Perspectives on Psychological Science*, *10*, 238–249. http://dx.doi.org/10.1177/1745691615570616

Cacioppo, J. T., & Hawley, L. C. (2005). People thinking about people: The vicious cycle of being a social outcast in one's own mind. In K. D. Williams, J. P. Forgas, & W. von Hippel (Eds.), *The social outcast: Ostracism, social exclusion, rejections, and bullying* (pp. 91–108). Psychology Press.

Cacioppo, J. T., Hawkley, L. C., Crawford, L. E., Ernst, J. M., Burleson, M. H., Kowalewski, R. B., Malarkey, W. B., Van Cauter, E., & Berntson, G. G. (2002). Loneliness and health: Potential mechanisms. *Psychosomatic Medicine*, *64*, 40–417. http://dx.doi.org/10.1097/00006842-200205000-00005

Chataway, C. J., & Berry, J. W. (1989). Acculturation experiences, appraisal, coping, and adaptation: A comparison of Hong Kong Chinese, French, and

English students in Canada. *Canadian Journal of Behavioural Science, 21*, 295–309. http://dx.doi.org/10.1037/h0079820

Chen, Y., Hicks, A., & While, A. (2014). Loneliness and social support of older people in China: A systematic literature review. *Health and Social Care in the Community, 22*, 113–123. http://dx.doi.org/10.1111/hsc.12051

Cohen, J. (1988). *Statistical power analysis for the behavioral sciences* (2nd ed.). Lawrence Erlbaum. http://dx.doi.org/10.4324/9780203771587

Dell, N. A., Pelham, M., & Murphy, A. M. (2019). Loneliness and depressive symptoms in middle aged and older adults experiencing serious mental illness. *Psychiatric Rehabilitation Journal, 42*, 113–120. http://dx.doi.org/10.1037/prj0000347

Demes, K. A., & Geeraert, N. (2014). Measures matter: Scales for adaptation, cultural distance, and acculturation revisited. *Journal of Cross-Cultural Psychology, 45*, 91–109. http://dx.doi.org/10.1177/0022022113487590

Direcção Geral de Estatística de Educação e Ciência. (2016). Ministério para a Ciência, Educação e Ensino Superior [Ministry for Science, Education and Higher Education].

Field, A. (2000). *Discovering statistics: Using SPSS for Windows.* Sage Publications.

França, T., Alves, E., & Padilla, B. (2018). Portuguese policies fostering intentional student mobility: A colonial legacy or a new strategy? *Globalisation, Societies and Education, 16*, 325–338.

Fröjd, S., Marttunen, M., Pelkonen, M., Pahlen, B., & Kaltiala-Heino, R. (2006). Perceived financial difficulties and maladjustment outcomes in adolescence. *European Journal of Public Health, 16*, 542–548. http://dx.doi.org/10.1093/eurpub/ckl012

Graves, T. (1967). Psychological acculturation in a tri-ethnic community. *South-Western Journal of Anthropology, 23*, 337–350. http://dx.doi.org/10.1086/soutjanth.23.4.3629450

Guan, Y., Liu, S., Guo, M. J., Li, M., Wu, M., Chen, S. X., Xu, S. L., & Tian, L. (2018). Acculturation orientation's and Chinese student sojourners' career adaptability: The roles of career exploration and cultural distance. *Journal of Vocational Behavior, 104*, 228–239.

Hamilton, H., Noh, S., & Adlaf, E. (2009). Perceived financial status, health, and maladjustment in adolescence. *Social Science & Medicine, 68*, 1527–1534. http://dx.doi.org/10.1016/j.socscimed.2009.01.037

Hawkley, L. C., & Cacioppo, J. T. (2010). Loneliness matters: A theoretical and empirical review of consequences and mechanisms. *Annals of Behavioral Medicine, 40*, 218–227.

Hawkley, L. C., Thisted, R. A., & Cacioppo, J. T. (2009). Loneliness predicts reduced physical activity: Cross-sectional & longitudinal analysis. *Health Psychology, 28*, 354–363.

Holt-Lunstad, J., Smith, T., Baker, M., Harris, T., & Stephenson, D. (2015). Loneliness and social isolation as risk factors for mortality: A meta-analytic review. *Perspectives on Psychological Science, 10*, 227–237. http://dx.doi.org/10.1177/1745691614568352

Imai, T., & Imai, A. (2019). Cross-ethnic self-disclosure buffering negative impacts on prejudice on international students' psychological and social well-being. *Journal of International Students, 9,* 66–83. http://dx.doi.org/10.32674/jis.v9i1.279

Jasinskaja-Lahati, I., Liebkind, K., Horenczyk, G., & Schmitz, P. (2003). The interactive nature of acculturation: Perceived discrimination, acculturation attitudes and stress among young ethnic repatriates in Finland, Israel and Germany. *International Journal of Intercultural Relations, 27,* 79–90.

Jessop, D., Herberts, C., & Solomon, L. (2005). The impact of financial circumstances on student health. *British Journal of Health Psychology, 10,* 421–439. http://dx.doi.org/10.1348/135910705X25480

Kapikiran, S. (2013). Loneliness and life satisfaction in Turkish early adolescents: The mediating role of self-esteem and social support. *Social Indicators Research, 111,* 617–632. http://dx.doi.org/10.1007/s11205-012-0024-x

Kilinc, A., & Granello, P. F. (2003). Overall life satisfaction and help-seeking attitudes of Turkish college students in the United States: Implications for college counselors. *Journal of College Counseling, 6,* 56–68. http://dx.doi.org/10.1002/j.2161-1882.2003.tb00227.x

Kitsantas, A. (2004). Study abroad: The role of college students' goals on the development of cross-cultural skills and global understanding. *College Student Journal, 38,* 441–452.

Lee, D. L., & Ahn, S. (2011). Discrimination against Latina/os: A meta-analysis of individual-level resources and outcomes. *The Counseling Psychologist, 40,* 28–65. http://dx.doi.org/10.1177/0011000011403326

Leung, C. (2001). The psychological adaptation of overseas and migrant students in Australia. *International Journal of Psychology, 36,* 251–259. http://dx.doi.org/10.1080/00207590143000018

Liu, D., Yu, X., Wang, Y., Zhang, H., & Ren, G. (2014). The impact of perception of discrimination and sense of belonging on the loneliness of the children of Chinese migrant workers: A structural equation modeling analysis. *International Journal of Mental Health Systems, 8,* 49–61. http://dx.doi.org/10.1186/1752-4458-8-52

Liu, M. (2009). Addressing the mental health problems of Chinese international college students in United States. *Advances in Social Work, 10,* 69–86. http://dx.doi.org/10.18060/164

Lonner, W. J., & Berry, J. W. (1986). Sampling and surveying. In W. J. Lonner & J. W. Berry (Eds.), *Field methods in cross-cultural research* (pp. 85–110). SAGE.

Mahon, N. E., Yarcheski, A., Yarcheski, T. J., Cannella, B. L., & Hanks, M. M. (2006). A meta-analytic study of predictors for loneliness during adolescence. *Nursing Research, 55,* 308–315. http://dx.doi.org/10.1097/00006199-200609000-00003

Masi, C. M., Chen, H. Y, Hawkley, L. C., & Cacioppo, J. T. (2011). A meta-analysis of interventions to reduce loneliness. *Personality and Social Psychology Review, 15,* 219–266. http://dx.doi.org/10.1177/1088868310377394

Mesidor, J. K., & Sly, K. F. (2016). Factors that contribute to the adjustment of international students. *Journal of International Students*, *6*, 262–282.

Mewes, R., Asbrock, F., & Laskaw, J. (2015). Perceived discrimination and impaired mental health in Turkish immigrants and their descendants in Germany. *Comprehensive Psychiatry*, *62*, 42–50.

Mikulás, J., & Jitka, S. (2019). Statistical analysis of study abroad experiences of international students in five major host countries in Europe. *Journal of International Students*, *9*, 1–18.

Mourato, I. (2011). *A política de cooperação portuguesa com os PALOPs: Contributos do ensino superior politécnico* [Unpublished doctoral dissertation]. Universidade Lusófona, Lisbon.

Neto, F. (1992). Loneliness among Portuguese adolescents. *Social Behavior and Personality: An International Journal*, *20*(1), 15–22. http://dx.doi.org/10.2224/sbp.1992.20.1.15

Neto, F. (1999). Loneliness among second generation migrants. In J.-C. Lasry, J. Adair, & K. Dion (Eds.), *Latest contributions to cross-cultural psychology* (pp. 104–117). Swets & Zeitlinger.

Neto, F. (2001). A short-form measure of loneliness among second-generation migrants. *Psychological Reports*, *88*, 201–202. http://dx.doi.org/10.2466/pr0.2001.88.1.201

Neto, F. (2002). Loneliness and acculturation among adolescents from immigrant families in Portugal. *Journal of Applied Social Psychology*, *32*, 630–647.

Neto, F. (2006). Psycho-social predictors of perceived discrimination among adolescents of immigrant background: A Portuguese study. *Journal of Ethnic and Migration Studies*, *32*, 89–109. http://dx.doi.org/10.1080/13691830500335507

Neto, F. (2014). Psychometric analysis of the short-form UCLA Loneliness Scale (ULS-6) in older adults. *European Journal of Ageing*, *11*, 313–319. http://dx.doi.org/10.1007/s10433-014-0312-1

Neto, F. (2016). Predictors of loneliness among Portuguese youths from returned migrant families. *Social Indicators Research*, *126*, 425–441. http://dx.doi.org/10.1007/s11205-015-0895-8

Neto, F., & Barros, J. (2000a). Predictors of loneliness among adolescents from Portuguese immigrant families in Switzerland. *Social Behavior and Personality: An International Journal*, *28*, 193–206. http://dx.doi.org/10.2224/sbp.2000.28.2.193

Neto, F., & Barros, J. (2000b). Psychosocial concomitants of loneliness among students of Cape Verde and Portugal. *The Journal of Psychology*, *134*, 503–514. http://dx.doi.org/10.1080/00223980009598232

Neto, F., Barros, J., & Schmitz, P. (2005). Acculturation attitudes and adaptation among Portuguese immigrants in Germany: Integration or separation. *Psychology and Developing Societies*, *17*, 19–32. http://dx.doi.org/10.1177/097133360501700102

Neto, F., & Costa, M. P. (2015). Predictors of loneliness among Ukrainian immigrants living in Portugal. In D. L. Rhodes (Ed.), *Loneliness:*

Psychosocial risk factors, prevalence and impacts on physical and emotional health (pp. 171–190). Nova Science.

Neto, J., Oliveira, E. N., & Neto, F. (2017). Acculturation, adaptation, and loneliness among Brazilian migrants living in Portugal. In I. Muenstermann (Ed.), *People's movements in the 21st century: Risks, challenges and benefits* (pp. 169–185). Intech. http://dx.doi.org/10.5772/65693

Neto, F., & Wilks, D. (2017). Predictors of psychological adaptation of Cape Verdean students in Portugal. *Journal of College Student Development*, *58*, 1087–1100. http://dx.doi.org/10.1353/csd.2017.0085

Oei, T. P., & Notowidjojo, F. (1990). Depression and loneliness in overseas students. *The International Journal of Social Psychiatry*, *36*, 121–130. http://dx.doi.org/10.1177/002076409003600205

Organisation for Economic Cooperation and Development. (2020). *Education at a glance 2020: OECD indicators*. http://dx.doi.org/10.1787/eag-2018-en

Pascoe, E. A., & Richman, L. S. (2009). Perceived discrimination and health: A meta-analytic review. *Psychological Bulletin*, *135*, 531–554. http://dx.doi.org/10.1037/a0016059

Patron, M. (2014). Loss and loneliness among international students. *Psychology Journal*, *11*, 24–43.

Pedersen, P. B. (1991). Counseling international students. *The Counseling Psychologist*, *19*, 10–58.

Ponizovski, A., & Ritsner, M. (2004). Patterns of loneliness in an immigrant population. *Comprehensive Psychiatry*, *45*, 408–414. http://dx.doi.org/10.1016/j.comppsych.2004.03.011

Poyrazli, S., Thukrad, R. K., & Duru, E. (2010). International students' race-ethnicity, personality, and acculturative stress. *Journal of Psychology and Counseling*, *2*, 25–32.

Prelow, H. M., Mosher, C. E., & Bowman, M. A. (2006). Perceived racial discrimination, social support and psychological adjustment among African American college students. *Journal of Black Psychology*, *32*, 442–454. http://dx.doi.org/10.1177/0095798406292677

Rajapaksa, S., & Dundes, L. (2002). It's a long way home: International student adjustment to living in the United States. *Journal of College Student Retention: Research, Theory & Practice,* *4*, 15–28. http://dx.doi.org/10.2190/5HCY-U2Q9-KVGL-8M3K

Redfield, R., Linton, R., & Herskovits, M. (1936). Memorandum on the study of acculturation. *American Anthropologist*, *38*, 1149–1152. http://dx.doi.org/10.1525/aa.1936.38.1.02a00330

Richardson, T., Elliot, P., Roberts, R., & Jansen, M. (2017). A longitudinal study of financial difficulties and mental health in a National sample of British undergraduate students. *Community Mental Health Journal*, *53*, 344–352. http://dx.doi.org/10.1007/s10597-016-0052-0

Roberts, R., Golding, J., Towell, T., & Weinreb, I. (1999). The effects of economic circumstances on British students' mental and physical health. *Journal of American College Heath*, *48*, 103–109. http://dx.doi.org/10.1080/07448489909595681

Rokach, A., & Neto, F. (2000). Coping with loneliness in adolescence: A cross-culturally study. *Social Behavior and Personality: An International Journal, 28*, 329–342. http://dx.doi.org/10.2224/sbp.2000.28.4.329

Rokach, A., & Neto, F. (2005). Age, culture, and the antecedents of loneliness. *Social Behavior and Personality: An International Journal, 33*, 477–494. http://dx.doi.org/10.2224/sbp.2005.33.5.477

Russell, D., Peplau, L., & Cutrona, C. (1980). The revised UCLA Loneliness Scale: Concurrent and discriminate validity evidence. *Journal of Personality and Social Psychology, 39*, 472–480. http://dx.doi.org/10.1037/0022-3514.39.3.472

Safdar, S., & Berno, T. (2016). Sojourners. In D. L. Sam & J. W. Berry (Eds.), *The Cambridge handbook of acculturation psychology* (2nd ed.; pp. 181–197). Cambridge University Press. http://dx.doi.org/10.1017/CBO9781316219218.012

Sam, D. L., & Berry, J. W. (2016). *The Cambridge handbook of acculturation psychology* (2nd ed.). Cambridge University Press. http://dx.doi.org/10.1017/CBO9781316219218

Savikko, N., Routsalo, P., Tilvis, R. S., Strandberg, T. E., & Pitkäla, K. H. (2005). Predictors and subjective causes of loneliness in an aged population. *Archives of Gerontology and Geriatrics, 41*, 223–233. http://dx.doi.org/10.1016/j.archger.2005.03.002

Sawir, E., Marginson, S., Deumert, A., Nyland, C., & Ramia, G. (2008). Loneliness and international students: An Australian study. *Journal of Studies in International Education, 12*, 148–180. http://dx.doi.org/10.1177/1028315307299699

Schmitt, M. T., Brancombe, N. R., Postmes, T., & Garcia, A. (2014). The consequences of perceived discrimination for psychological well-being: A meta-analysis. *Psychological Bulletin, 140*, 921–948.

Shadowen, N. L., Williamson, A., Guerra, N. G., Ammigan, R., & Drexler, M. L. (2019). Prevalence and correlates of depressive symptoms among international students: Implications for university support offices. *Journal of International Students, 9*, 129–148. http://dx.doi.org/10.32674/jis.v9i1.277

Siahpush, M., & Carlin, J. B. (2006). Financial stress, smoking cessation and relapse: Results from a prospective study of an Australian national sample. *Addiction, 101*, 121–127. http://dx.doi.org/10.1111/j.1360-0443.2005.01292.x

Sletta, O., Valas, H., Skaalvick, E., & Sobstad, F. (1996). Peer relations, loneliness, and self-perceptions in school-aged children. *British Journal of Educational Psychology, 66*, 431–445. http://dx.doi.org/10.1111/j.2044-8279.1996.tb01210.x

Smith, R., & Khawaja, N. (2011). A review of the acculturation experiences of international students. *International Journal of Intercultural Relations, 35*, 699–713. http://dx.doi.org/10.1016/j.ijintrel.2011.08.004

Titrek, O., Erkiliç, A, Süre, E., Güvenç, M., & Pek, N. T. (2016). The socio-cultural, financial and education problems of international postgraduate students in Turkey. *Universal Journal of Educational Research*, *4*, 160–166. http://dx.doi.org/10.13189/ujer.2016.041320

Vanhalst, J., Klimstra, T. A., Luyckx, K., Scholte, R. H., Engels, R. C., & Goossens, L. (2012). The interplay of loneliness and depressive symptoms across adolescence: Exploring the role of personality traits. *Journal of Youth and Adolescence*, *41*, 776–787. http://dx.doi.org/10.1007/s10964-011-9726-7

Victor, C., & Yang, K. (2012). The prevalence of loneliness among adults: A case study of the United Kingdom. *The Journal of Psychology*, *146*, 85–104. http://dx.doi.org/10.1080/00223980.2011.613875

Ward, C., Bochner, S., & Furnham, A. (2001). *The psychology of culture shock* (2nd ed.) Routledge. http://dx.doi.org/10.4324/9780203992258

Ward, C., & Kennedy, A. (1994). Acculturation strategies, psychological adjustment, and sociocultural competence during cross-cultural transitions. *International Journal of Intercultural Relations*, *18*, 329–343. http://dx.doi.org/10.1016/0147-1767(94)90036-1

Ward, C., & Kennedy, A. (1996). Crossing cultures: The relationship between psychological and socio-cultural dimensions of cross-cultural adjustment. In J. Pandey, D. Sinha, & D. Bhawuk (Eds.), *Asian contributions to cross-cultural psychology* (pp. 289–306). SAGE.

Weiss, R. S. (Ed.) (1973). *Loneliness: The experience of emotional and social isolation*. MIT Press.

Wilks, D. C., & Neto, F. (2016). Exploring the adaptation experiences of Cape Verdean students in Portugal. *International Journal of Educational Research*, *76*, 66–75. http://dx.doi.org/10.1016/j.ijer.2016.01.002

Yang, K., & Victor, C. (2011). Age and loneliness in 25 European nations. *Aging and Society*, 31, 1368–1388. http://dx.doi.org/10.1017/S0144686X1000139X

Zhang, J., & Goodson, P. (2011). Predictors of international students' psychosocial adjustment to life in the United States. *International Journal of Intercultural Relations*, *35*, 139–162.

Zhong, B., Liu, X., Chen, W., Chiu, H., & Conwell, Y. (2018). Loneliness in Chinse older adults in primary care: Prevalence and correlates. *Psychogeriatrics*, *18*, 334–342.

FELIX NETO, PhD, is a Full Professor Emeritus of Psychology in the Department of Psychology at the University of Porto, Portugal. His research interests include social psychology and cross-cultural psychology (especially, migration, mental health, love, loneliness, and forgiveness). Email: fneto@fpce.up.pt

Peer-Reviewed Article

© *Journal of International Students*
Volume 11, Issue 2 (2021), pp. 417-435
ISSN: 2162-3104 (Print), 2166-3750 (Online)
doi: 10.32674/jis.v11i2.1755
ojed.org/jis

Advising Experiences of First-Year International Doctoral Students

Nina Marijanović
Jungmin Lee
Thomas W. Teague, Jr.
University of Kentucky, USA

Sheryl F. Means
University of New Mexico, USA

ABSTRACT

The purpose of this qualitative study was to understand how international doctoral students were matched with their faculty advisors and how their advising experiences and satisfaction were shaped by their academic discipline. We applied the lens of developmental advising to situate the advising experiences of our sample because of the framework's emphasis on holistic support and student development. We conducted individual semistructured interviews with 21 international doctoral students attending a large research-intensive university in the Southeast. Most participants were assigned to an interim advisor, but the data revealed concerning differences in the type of advising experiences and support based on academic discipline. This study contributes to the body of literature by exploring advisor–advisee matching among international doctoral students and by further analyzing how disciplinary cultures shape perceptions of satisfaction with advising.

Keywords: advising experiences, advisor–advisee matching, doctoral students, faculty advisors, international students

---

The United States hosts a large share of international students, and it is among the top three global destinations for higher education studies (Zong & Batalova,

2018). While plentiful literature documents the types of experiences that hinder or encourage social and academic success and retention among this population, including difficulty in accessing campus support resources, campus and peer social networks, dedicated spaces for international students, and practicum and internship opportunities (Arthur, 2017; Chen et al., 2019; Heng, 2016), few studies specifically focus on international graduate students' experience with advisors (e.g., Ng et al., 2018; Zhao et al., 2007). To fill the gap, we sought to understand the advising experiences of first-year international doctoral students attending a large research-intensive university in the Southeast.

We sought to understand how international doctoral students were matched with their faculty advisors, what types of advising experiences they had, how these interactions differed by their academic discipline, and their level of satisfaction with their advising experience. We focused on advising experiences because faculty advisors are a cornerstone of students' social support networks, particularly for international doctoral students, who are often isolated from their primary support networks at home, and effective faculty advising can alleviate some of the transitional challenges faced by these students (Jeong et al., 2019). However, advising at the graduate level lacks standardization, and the diversity of advising styles leads to unequal doctoral advising experiences.

To assess the diversity of doctoral advising experiences, we applied the lens of developmental advising, which re-envisions the advising relationship as a shared give-and-take between the student and the advisor, rather than the advisor solely determining what the student needs. This advising model best captures the strengths and deficiencies experienced by our sample of international doctoral students. Our results can inform practitioners, particularly graduate faculty advisors and directors of graduate studies who are responsible for establishing and maintaining a healthy advising culture. Our results can also educate the wider international graduate student population on the importance of advising and how regular engagement with their advisor can increase academic, professional, and personal success.

CONCEPTUAL FRAMEWORK

Effective faculty advisors can increase academic self-concept and sense of belonging, particularly among international doctoral students who often enter graduate education without an established support system and with limited educational experiences with a North American style of higher education (Curtin et al., 2013; Omar et al., 2016). In this study, a graduate advisor refers to "a single faculty member the graduate student would consider in the primary, formal role of academic advisor, dissertation chair, or research supervisor" (Rice et al., 2009, p. 1). Furthermore, an international graduate student is "a student who moves to another country (the host country) for the purpose of pursuing tertiary or higher education (e.g., college or university)" (Shapiro et al., 2014, p. 2).

We chose the developmental advising model to situate the advising experiences of our sample because this model does not view the advisee as a passive participant in the advising relationship. While the advisor facilitates growth in the student's "rational processes, environmental and interpersonal interactions, behavioral awareness, problem-solving, decision-making, and evaluation skills," both parties experience different degrees of learning and growth because the relationship is meant to be reciprocal (Crookston, 1972, p. 5). Developmental advising is associated with increased retention, academic performance, satisfaction with degree selection, and overall advising experience, especially among women and minority students (Harris, 2018).

Developmental advising is more frequently applied and studied at the undergraduate level (McWilliams & Beam, 2013). Nonetheless, graduate advisors should consider updating their advising approach considering graduate students' general dissatisfaction with advising (Kong et al., 2013; Wang & Lorenz, 2018). High attrition rates among graduate students, including international graduate students, further erodes the attractiveness of graduate study and leads to lower institutional reputation and decreased funding. Implementing aspects of developmental advising at the graduate level could be one way to combat this issue.

LITERATURE REVIEW

A faculty advisor is an important agent of socialization for doctoral students, and daily interactions can significantly shape students' experiences and outcomes. A strong relationship with a faculty advisor can lead to timelier degree completion, more collaborative work with advisors, increased sense of belonging, and decreased stress and attrition (Hunter & Devine, 2016; Litalien & Guay, 2015). The faculty advisor can have many identities (Jeong et al., 2019; Zhao et al., 2007), but these identities are adopted from the faculty advisor's own experiences with advising, which are strongly influenced by their academic discipline and practices therein rather than formal training (Boyce et al., 2019; Knox et al., 2013). Insufficiency of formal training may explain why advisors often report being underprepared for the procedural and emotional factors that accompany advising (O'Meara et al., 2013). However, it is not just faculty advisors who are underprepared. Students also receive little training on how to engage with their faculty advisor, with many indicating mismatched expectations and lack of support as primary reasons for their dissatisfaction with advising (Wang & Lorenz, 2018).

Mismatching and miscommunication may arise from the process by which students are matched with their advisor. In many doctoral programs, the responsibility of securing a faculty advisor and establishing an advising relationship is placed on the student rather than on the faculty advisor. This process assumes that all students have a shared understanding about the advising role and expectations therein; however, we know that that is not the case (Omar et al., 2016). Additionally, the timing of the match is important to consider as there are disciplinary differences in *when* students match with their advisor, with students in humanities and social science fields often matching with a permanent advisor later in their doctoral program, in comparison with students in biological and physical sciences fields who often match during the admission process (Zhao et al., 2007).

Disciplinary Differences

Few studies have examined how disciplinary differences influence the advising relationship and doctoral experience. Lovitts (2001) looked at advising differences between doctoral students in natural sciences and those in social sciences and humanities. She noted that doctoral students in social sciences and humanities did not receive the same type of academic and social support as their counterparts in the natural sciences. Golde (2005) noted that advising experiences were markedly different between students pursuing degrees in science disciplines and those in humanities fields: The former had a much more close-knitted advising experience and departmental support than the latter.

Faculty in physical and biological sciences often work in tandem with their advisees in a laboratory, which doubles as a central site of socialization (Jeong et al., 2019). Furthermore, in science and science-related fields, the student and the advisor often match during the admission process, giving them more time to build their relationship (Zhao et al., 2007). This relationship is further nurtured by the culture embedded within laboratory and research groups, which emphasize cooperation, a group-centered mindset, and regular faculty contact. Conversely, students in social science and humanities fields tend to pursue more solitary activities. These fields often assign students to an interim advisor, expecting that within two to three semesters a student will establish a relationship with a permanent advisor. While these students may enjoy more individual attention, it is not until they pass their qualifying exams that they work in much closer proximity with their permanent advisor. Therefore, the length of time available to build a relationship is severely curtailed for students in these disciplines (Barnes et al., 2010).

Selection Criteria

There are several factors that international graduate students consider when they select their advisor: advisor's reputation as a mentor and a researcher, their available funding, research area, personality, time-to-degree reputation, career prospects, career stage, and gender (Janer, 2017; Joy et al., 2015). Academic discipline also plays a role in how much weight is given to the characteristics mentioned above. In Zhao et al. (2007), doctoral students in science fields were less concerned with intellectual compatibility with their advisor and more concerned with pragmatic elements (i.e., access to funding and laboratory resources) than humanities students.

A prospective advisor's demographics are also important considerations for both domestic and international doctoral students. Ellis (2001) found that female and racial minority graduate students were more likely to consider a faculty advisor's race and gender over their research-related reputation. Labon (2013) posited that the importance of these selection criteria stemmed from the general lack of representation of minority faculty of color and female faculty across various academic disciplines. This lack of representation deprives students of connecting with faculty with whom they share an important attribute and who may be better positioned to understand student concerns and to extend support (Burt et al., 2018). Najjar (2015) supported Labon's conjecture by reporting that international doctoral students who selected an international advisor were more satisfied with their advisor and doctoral program.

Differences in Advising Experiences for International Students

Takashiro (2017) noted that international doctoral students tend to value their relationship with advisors even more than domestic students and express a greater preference for advisors who are involved in their lives. However, they are less likely to experience and develop such relationships. Roksa et al. (2018) found that most international doctoral students in their sample reported a rather formal advising relationship with their faculty advisor than a more personalized and caring relationship (Dericks et al., 2019). This is unfortunate since international students are less likely to be aware of and to have access to campus resources, and an involved faculty advisor could alleviate some of the distress that occurs as part of the doctoral experience (Roberts et al., 2018).

The extent and depth of the advising relationship is also complicated by race and racism within higher education. In relation to advising, international doctoral students have reported instances of racism, stereotyping, and hostility (Glass et al., 2015). However, the ability for many of these students to change advisors may not always be possible, especially among those who often rely on institutional funding to support their education and whose funding is tied to a specific faculty advisor's research project. International doctoral students who have continued in such toxic relationships have reported increases in stress, anxiety, disengagement, and depression (Kim, 2011; Rice et al., 2016).

METHOD

Participants

Twenty-one first-year international doctoral students attending a large research-intensive Southeastern university participated in this study, hailing from the following regions: Asia, Oceania, Africa, Latin and South America, and Europe. The sample consisted of 10 female and 11 male participants, most of whom were in their mid-to-late 20s; the average age was 27 years old. A slight majority of participants had previous educational experiences in the United States before starting their doctoral program, either as study abroad participants or as degree-seeking undergraduates. However, all but three students had stayed less than 5 years in the United States at the time of interview. Their academic disciplines were grouped into one of the following categories: humanities, social science, STEM, business, and education. While we asked participants to specify their native country during the interview process, we present only a regional identifier in Table 1 to protect their anonymity.

Table 1. Descriptive Statistics of the Sample

Characteristics	*n*	%
Gender		
Female	10	48%
Male	11	52%
Region of origin		
Asia & Oceania	13	62%
Africa	2	10%
Latin & South America	3	14%
Europe	3	14%
Major discipline	5	
Humanities	1	24%
Social Science	1	5%
STEM	11	52%
Business & Education	4	19%
Age		
20–25	7	33%
26–30	11	52%
31–35	2	10%
36+	1	5%
Previous educational experiences in the US		
Yes	12	57%
No	9	43%

Research Team

The research team was composed of four researchers: one Asian female faculty member, one non-Latino White female graduate student, one non-Latino White male graduate student, and one Black female postdoctoral student. The latter acted as the project's auditor and did not participate in all team meetings in order to offer an impartial opinion during the audit process. However, she was instrumental in guiding the remaining three researchers in consensual qualitative research (CQR) data collection and analysis (Hill et al., 1997). All team members had lengthy experiences in different international contexts and were purposefully recruited because of these experiences and perspectives that they could bring to the study. Before developing the interview protocol, all team members shared their personal biases and expectations that could skew data analysis, and continually revisited them throughout the research project to ensure data integrity.

Interview Protocol

This study is a subset of a larger qualitative study focused on understanding first-year international doctoral student experiences. Questions exploring advising experiences were created by the research team and developed by consulting the literature, engaging in informal conversation with international graduate students, and participating in ongoing discussion among the research team. The final interview protocol consisted of six questions (e.g., "Can you share with us what you consider to be the most important qualities for a faculty advisor?") and appropriate probing questions (e.g., "Describe how you do or don't feel supported by your advisor."). Participants completed a short demographic questionnaire prior to scheduling their interview, which collected data on their academic discipline, country of origin, and previous educational experiences in the United States. Other demographic and descriptive information were obtained during the course of the interview (e.g., type of faculty advisor, institutional funding, and partner/dependent status).

Data Collection

After securing Institutional Review Board approval, eligible participants were recruited via email sent via the International Scholar and Student Services office on the study campus and word of mouth. Data collection lasted from late-January to May 2018. All interviews were audio-recorded and transcribed by the interviewer who conducted the interview; average interview time was approximately 60 min. Data authenticity was ensured by allowing participants the option of reviewing their interview transcript to confirm that their words and meaning were accurately represented; if discrepancies arose, the original interviewer worked with the participant to revise the transcript.

Data Analysis

We utilized CQR methodology created by Hill et al. (1997) to guide our data analysis. Given our small sample size, CQR was most appropriate because it allows researchers to conduct in-depth analyses on a smaller number of cases and attain a deeper understanding of the experience. Following Hill's (2012) CQR standards, all analysis decisions were made by group consensus to ensure that no singular perspective skewed the analysis. After concluding the transcription, team members spent about 3 weeks independently analyzing the transcripts and creating prospective themes within Microsoft Word.

Then, the team reconvened and reviewed each member's list of themes, pointing out overlap and discrepancies in the data. Based on these conversations, a single domain list was created, and the team returned to their transcripts and coded anew based on the domain list. To produce coding stability, one research team member verified all coding for accuracy and collaborated exclusively with the independent auditor to review and correct any errors in the coding scheme and/or coding on each transcript. Following this stage, the research team engaged in cross-analysis (Hill, 2012) to jointly identify shared themes across the participants, which were then grouped into thematic domains. The domains were validated by another round of coding and checks by each team member. The auditor completed a final review and the feedback was addressed by the team members and integrated into the final analysis.

RESULTS

Data analysis produced the following four domains: (a) advisor–advisee matching; (b) frequency and method of meetings with an advisor; (c) content of advising conversations; and (d) satisfaction with advising. Identified domains were further broken down into categories that were assigned a frequency label of general, typical, or rare to capture the occurrence of the theme among the participants (Hill, 2012). Table 2 provides a summary of domains, categories, and frequencies.

Table 2: Summary of Domains, Categories, and Frequencies

Domain	Frequency	*n*
Advisor–advisee matching		
Pre-enrollment	Rare	2
Interim assignment	General	17
Postmatriculation	Rare	3
Frequency & style of interaction		
Group meetings	Rare	2
Individual meetings	General	17
Infrequent meetings	Typical	10
Content of advising conversations		
Procedural elements	General	19
Personal & career topics	Rare	4
Satisfaction with advising		
Positive	General	18
Negative	Rare	2
Neutral	Typical	12

Note. $N = 21$. General = At least 17 respondents shared the same category; typical = 10–16 respondents shared the same category; rare = fewer than nine respondents shared the same category.

Advisor–Advisee Matching

This domain refers to the method of advisor matching the participant experienced in their program. Among our participants, we found three types of matching styles: (a) faculty advisor selected by the student before enrolling, (b) interim faculty advisor assigned by the department, and (c) a student currently in the process of seeking out a permanent advisor. Two participants who selected their faculty advisor had previous interactions with them at a conference or a field research site before applying to the university.

Most participants, regardless of academic discipline, were assigned to an interim advisor, typically the Director of Graduate Studies (DGS) for the program. Given that all participants were first-year students, this is not unusual. However, these participants reported being unsure of how to approach the DGS and how to begin seeking a permanent advisor. And while participants assigned to an interim advisor generally reported a favorable relationship 1 year into their assignment, many were ready to find their permanent advisor. A male participant from Africa studying computer science framed it thusly, "I don't know this person now, but I need to get to know them and maybe this will become a real partnership." However, several participants with an interim advisor also indicated not being sure if the DGS advisor *could* become a permanent advisor and engaged with them sparingly as a result.

The last category encompasses participants who were in the process of seeking out a permanent advisor (moving away from their interim advisor), and all three participants were from STEM fields. These participants indicated that their study programs generally gave them two to three semesters to find a permanent advisor. They reported feeling stressed having to "speed date" faculty members in the length of time provided, especially as many of them were not yet sure of their research agenda and graduate school goals. Participants shared different tactics to interview prospective advisors. For example, a female participant from Asia studying biomedical sciences stated:

> I have visited every professor in my department at least once so far. I have a list of questions I bring. If I've had class with them, I go back and review old class material, so that I can start a conversation based on that and then, maybe, the conversation won't be so bad.

Although others in this category were not as organized, they did have their own tactics to screen for possible advisors; for example, a male participant from Asia noticed that several faculty members from his department frequented the campus gym. He used that opportunity to befriend them and even learned how to play squash adding, "I had no clue what this sport is. But, I like to be active and they were there to teach me, so I did it." He emailed his interviewer a few weeks later and informed her that one of the squash-playing faculty members was now his permanent advisor.

Meeting Frequency and Interaction Style Based on Academic Discipline

This domain is defined by the frequency and method of advisor–advisee meetings, which we found varied based on academic discipline. Humanities and social science participants reported infrequent meetings with their faculty advisor, greater emphasis on scheduling a formal time for those meetings, and a greater frequency of conducting such meetings via email, in comparison to STEM participants. A Central European female participant studying in the social sciences added, "It's a bit hard to arrange these meetings because I wasn't quite sure who my advisor was. I mean, it's the DGS, but, for how long? It's hard to get on his schedule to talk about what comes next." The student's annoyance with scheduling was shared by several other humanities participants who also added that they felt "unimportant" in comparison with their older peers in the program whom they perceived as enjoying more direct and frequent advisor attention. Additionally, these participants also reported fewer informal gatherings amongst themselves at the departmental level indicating a more aloof atmosphere.

By way of comparison, participants majoring in STEM or in biomedical sciences reported a greater frequency of group meetings because these fields put greater emphasis on teamwork as part of laboratory work and their study curriculum (Zhao et al., 2007). For example, a male STEM participant from Southeast Asia stated, "…we have a group meeting every Monday and then there is a subgroup meeting. The subgroup meeting is an important one. We have to meet twice at least every month." Participants in this group also perceived that their advisors were available for individual consultation even though they did not always utilize the opportunity. They also reported greater occurrences of social hours built into laboratory time so that various faculty and students could mingle and engage in informal individual advising. A female participant from Southeast Asia studying biomedical sciences shared the following:

> Our department has Cookie Hours every day from four to five, and we just go into our lobby and have cookies and coffee or tea. I like that I can look forward to this every day and it's easier to meet other people and to get to know faculty and ask questions.

Because STEM and biomedical science fields tend to be more collaborative in their work in contrast to humanities and social science fields, it is natural that these departments relied on social hours and group meeting formats to create a culture of support.

Content of Advising Conversations Based on Matching Style

This domain is defined by the types of conversations and topics participants engaged in with their faculty advisor and how these conversations differed based on their matching style. Perhaps unsurprisingly, most of our participants reported engaging in formal conversations about program requirements, timelines, and procedural matters, which are reminiscent of prescriptive advising. Since most of them were assigned to an interim advisor, there was also a general unawareness of how to engage with their advisor. A male participant from northern Africa studying in a STEM field explained, "I'm not sure what I can talk about with him. So, we just talk about classes. I don't know if he wants to know more about me." Other participants felt similarly, citing that they "didn't want to bother" the faculty advisor with their stories. When asked if their faculty advisor or department ever explained their advising philosophy and the types of conversations they could engage in, many indicated that they did not recall these topics. Providing such information and encouragement may be helpful to international students who come from cultures that emphasize hierarchy and deference to authority and who may see engagement in informal conversation without proper approval as impertinence.

Among participants who selected their faculty advisor prior to commencing their programs, we found that they engaged in more holistic conversations that also included disclosure of personal and career information, which aligns with developmental advising principles. A female social sciences participant from Central Asia described the conversations with her advisor like this:

> I had a lot of trouble getting the paperwork approved to come to the United States. I also had a baby right before I arrived and so I knew no one here, and [my] husband was delayed in getting approval for several months, so I had no one. I had to ask my advisor for help. I could not have done it otherwise. And you know, my advisor was great. She was flexible with me, she let me leave class early sometimes to get my baby. She always asked me how I was doing and if I needed help.

Participants who shared an important attribute with their advisor (i.e., country of origin or gender) also reported engaging in more personal conversations, supporting Labon's (2013) conclusion. A female business participant from Southeastern Europe remarked, "I really wanted her to be my advisor because we're from the same country and that worked out. I really rely on her, on everything, and let's say I try not to overload her, but I really rely on her." The fact that the participant shared the same language, gender, and country of origin as her advisor could have increased her confidence in her chosen field of study, and she may have also felt more valued and heard because they shared the same language.

Overall, very few participants engaged in career-oriented conversations with their advisors. Among those who did, they tended to be within STEM and biomedical science fields. The applied nature of their curriculum and the higher frequency of interactions with faculty, both formal and informal, may create a natural pocket for career-oriented conversations to occur. A female participant from Oceania studying biomedical sciences stated, "I see my laboratory faculty every day. Of course, we'd talk about career prospects after school. I need their sponsorship and endorsement to get into a postdoc, or when I begin my own lab." While some participants in humanities and social sciences could articulate their career goals during the interview process, many indicated that they did not discuss these goals with their advisor due to the infrequency of their advising meetings and perceived lack of support.

Satisfaction with Advising

This domain refers to the participants' satisfaction with their advising relationship: positive, negative, or neutral. Most participants expressed positive feelings and thoughts toward their faculty advisor and advising relationship, using descriptors like knowledgeable, warm, friendly, and caring. This is a notable finding since the majority of our participants were still being advised by an assigned interim advisor rather than by one they had preselected, which is contrary to the literature. For example, a female participant from Central Europe studying in the humanities field shared, "He's like my grandfather and he's very personable. I can ask him anything and he'll always give me an answer. If he sees me on campus, he will be the first to say hello." Many cited the novelty of being on a new campus and having new experiences as enough to outweigh some negative aspects like being homesick, adjusting to new cuisine, and having to make new friends.

Even participants who had infrequent conversations with their advisors reported finding their way around their department and campus by relying on new or existing social networks, asking departmental administrative assistants, and searching the internet. They indicated feeling more in control and that they had become resourceful. A female participant from Central Europe studying social sciences added, "I'll email anyone that I can think of. People will reply, even if I shouldn't be emailing them, and they will point me in the right direction." While we applaud this type of resourcefulness as a marker of self-sufficiency, it is also a warning sign that students do not have readily accessible faculty who may be a more accurate fount of knowledge in comparison with informal friendship networks and the internet.

Participants who indicated negative feelings about their advisor usually remarked that they felt that their advisor did not have time for them and that their attempts to create a relationship were not encouraged. A female participant from South America studying in the humanities field added that she felt like her advisor considered her a "nuisance" because he rarely replied to her emails or offered his time to meet individually with her. She indicated finding greater support from the departmental administrative assistant. Similarly, a female participant from Asia studying in the social sciences recalled how repeated in-class slights by her advisor made her doubt her ability to be successful in her program. She explained that her advisor often called her research topic "meaningless" adding that "I feel he's trying to push me to think deeper, but the way he pushes me, it's really discouraging me… because his attitude to other White students is not the same as his attitude to me." Both participants felt that their educational experience and professional goals were jeopardized because their advisors did not offer help, leaving them unsure about if they should continue their studies at this study site.

Participants in the neutral category did not have clearly defined positive or negative opinion toward their advising relationship. Rather, they seemed content with the transactional nature of their advising relationship and were fine with having their advisor be a more distant figure in their lives. A male participant from Southeast Asia studying in a STEM discipline stated, "I know she's there and I can ask her what I need, but I don't see a need and so I don't." Others similarly remarked that they wished to keep a clear demarcation between school and personal lives, choosing not to engage with peers and faculty at the same frequency as others. Perhaps these students did not wish to share their deeper feelings with the interviewers, were still processing their first year, or did not have a deeper emotional connection to their graduate programs. But, these types of students may be more at risk of leaving because they are not being well-integrated in their programs.

DISCUSSION

Overall, participants in STEM and biomedical science fields reported more frequent group interactions with their faculty advisor due to the curricular configuration that relies heavily on laboratory and group work, bringing them in more routine contact with one another. These participants were also likelier to engage in career-oriented conversations with their faculty advisor, which signals a more holistic approach to graduate student development. The relative short duration of these graduate programs and their direct connections to industry may create a more natural opening for these types of conversations. Our findings controvert those of Noy and Ray (2012) who suggested that students in physical and biological sciences receive *less* attention and support than students in humanities and social science fields. It could be due to the recent emphasis that STEM fields have placed on improving their retention by modifying their culture and student support systems (Eshani et al., 2017).

Participants in the humanities and social science fields reported infrequent interactions, a harder time getting in touch with their faculty advisor, and a greater emphasis on formal meetings compared with participants in STEM fields. These students tended to have conversations with their faculty advisors about procedural requirements. While eager to engage with their advisors, many felt that they were overlooked in favor of older peers who were further along in the program.

Implications and Recommendations

Our findings suggest that baseline expectations for faculty advising need to be created and sufficiently articulated to both students and faculty advisors. Some U.S. schools have already invested in innovative ways to support and engage their doctoral students. For example, University of Pittsburgh has issued guidance to all graduate departments on what are considered elements of good academic advising (University of Pittsburgh, n.d.). Such guidance includes specific responsibilities of faculty and academic units, including providing accurate and written information regarding program requirements as well as after-graduation employment opportunities and checking students' progress and performance on a regular basis. Student responsibilities are also stipulated, like alerting advisors to uncertainty about program requirements or progress. We also suggest the use of an advising syllabus as utilized by various colleges at George Washington University to clearly communicate advising expectations to both faculty and doctoral students (George Washington University, n.d.). Lastly, we recommend institutions provide resources and workshops for faculty who teach, advise, and work with international students. For instance, Carnegie Mellon University provides online handbooks that share best practices for faculty and advisors working with international students (Eberly Center for Teaching Excellence, & Intercultural Communication Center, n.d.). These resources would help faculty become knowledgeable of different cultures and more understanding of international students.

We also recommend weaving advising opportunities into formal orientations, program curricula, and department social events. While our participants indicated attending orientations offered by their department, college, and the university's international center, many of these orientations were simply social in nature rather than substantive in content pertinent for first-year doctoral students. To alleviate the deficiency of such orientations, we recommend mandating a seminar class for all first-year graduate students and requiring them to conduct interviews with all department faculty members as a course assignment, which can be a great way to orient students to the department and to meet with faculty members. Creating an informal space (e.g., snack hours, a kitchen with coffee and a microwave, etc.) that brings faculty and students into routine contact is another recommendation, which seemed to work well for students in our sample.

Examined through the lens of developmental advising, many faculty advisors in this study engaged in routine and prescriptive advising that is far more transactional in nature rather than developing a deeper and holistic relationship with their advisees. Due to the interim assignment of most faculty advisors, it is not unusual that they would be more focused on the immediate needs of the participants rather than investing time in developing a long-term relationship. However, even though their advising obligation may be short term, interim advisors can play an important role in orienting their advisees to departmental expectations and culture. We suggest that interim faculty advisors reach out to advisees, set up regular meetings, and check up on them during major academic calendar milestones to ensure they understand appropriate departmental policies and timelines and to build more meaningful and genuine relationships with them. This way, when students are permanently matched to a faculty advisor, they enter into that new relationship prepared with more information and confidence to articulate their personal and academic goals.

For future research, we call for more empirical studies that examine advising experiences of international graduate students, and how advising influences their success in graduate school. Our study focused on their matching process and advising experiences in their first year, but it would be interesting to explore how the relationship between advisor and advisee develops and how it influences outcomes at the dissertation and job market stages. We also encourage researchers to examine faculty perspectives on graduate advising—in particular their experiences and expectations for advising international graduate students—so that we can have a better understanding of what faculty know about advising, their experiences with advising this population, and where they need assistance in improving their advising.

From a practical standpoint, faculty advisors and DGSs should consider conducting yearly advising evaluations to identify areas for improvement and success. Graduate students could also complete these evaluations anonymously so that both perspectives can be considered. This would signal to faculty and students that advising is taken seriously by the department. Additionally, departments should consider ways to reward advising excellence by publicly recognizing outstanding faculty advisors or by weighing advising excellence more in tenure and promotion decisions. After all, effective advising positively contributes to student success and to faculty development (Ruud et al., 2018). Lastly, to ensure that students get sufficient attention from their advisors and have good advising experiences, departments should consider limiting the number of students a faculty member may advise at any given time (e.g., Noble, 2000), or the type of faculty who could serve as advisor, like Stanford University (Flaherty, 2018).

Limitations

There are several limitations to this study, with the primary one being our small sample size given the total international graduate student enrollment at the study site. Additionally, this study is situated at a large research university in the Southeast. Therefore, students' advising and overall first-year experiences may differ based on geographic region, selectivity, or institutional size, which limits generalizability of the study's results to the *entire* international doctoral student population in the United States. Lastly, this study only interviewed students and lacks faculty advisors' perspectives and experiences. Future studies can incorporate both student and faculty narratives and delve deeper into how these two groups understand the nature and purpose of the advising relationship.

CONCLUSION

International doctoral students encounter plenty of challenges at the start of their academic journey in the United States. Effective advising can help these students successfully adjust to the transition and achieve their goals in graduate school. In this study, we described how international doctoral students' advising experiences varied across academic disciplines and advisor–advisee pairing methods. We suggested a few example practices that could clarify advising expectations and increase contact between advisors and advisees, both of which could improve the overall advising experience. International students are critical assets to U.S. campuses both intellectually and culturally. Ensuring their success can benefit both international and domestic students, as well as faculty. We hope that this research provides a way to help international students adjust to and succeed in graduate school in the United States.

REFERENCES

Arthur, N. (2017). Supporting international students through strengthening their social resources. *Studies in Higher Education, 42*(5), 887–894. https://doi.org/10.1080/03075079.2017.1293876

Barnes, B. J., Williams, E. A., & Archer, S. A. (2010). Characteristics that matter most: Doctoral students' perceptions of positive and negative advisor attributes. *NACADA Journal, 30*(1), 34–46. https://doi.org/10.12930/0271-9517-30.1.34

Boyce, B. A., Napper-Owen, G., Lund, J. L., & Almarode, D. (2019). Doctoral students' perspectives on their advisors. *Quest, 71*(3), 321–332. https://doi.org/10.1080/00336297.2019.1618076

Burt, B. A., Williams, K. L., & Smith, W. A. (2018). Into the storm: Ecological and sociological impediments to Black males' persistence in engineering graduate programs. *American Education Research Journal, 55*(5), 965–1006. https://doi.org/10.3102/0002831218763587

Chen, B., Tabassum, H., & Saeed, M. A. (2019). International Muslim students: Challenges and practical suggestions to accommodate their needs on campus. *Journal of International Students, 9*(4), 933–953. https://doi.org/10.32674/jis.v9i3.753

Crookston, B. B. (1972). A developmental view of academic advising as teaching. *Journal of College Student Personnel, 13*(1), 12–17.

Curtin, N., Stewart, A. J., & Ostrove, J. M. (2013). Fostering academic self-concept: Advisor support and sense of belonging among international and domestic graduate students. *American Educational Research Journal, 50*(1), 108–137. https://doi.org/10.3102/0002831212446662

Dericks, G., Thompson, E., Roberts, M., & Phua, F. (2019). Determinants of PhD student satisfaction: The roles of supervisor, department, and peer qualities. *Assessment & Evaluation in Higher Education, 44*(7), 1053–1068. https://doi.org/10.1080/02602938.2019.1570484

Eberly Center for Teaching Excellence, & Intercultural Communication Center. (n.d.). *Recognizing and addressing cultural variations in the classroom.* Carnegie Mellon University. https://doi.org/https://www.cmu.edu/teaching/resources/PublicationsArchives/InternalReports/culturalvariations.pdf

Ellis, E. M. (2001). The impact of race and gender on graduate school socialization, satisfaction with doctoral student, and commitment to degree completion. *The Western Journal of Black Studies, 25,* 30–45.

Eshani, G. L., Skaza, H., Marti, E., Schrader, P. G., & Orgill, M. (2017). Perceptions of student recruitment and retention in STEM fields. *European Journal of STEM Education, 2*(1), 1–11. https://doi.org/10.20897/esteme.201702

Flaherty, C. (2018, April 16). *Graduate advising matters.* Inside Higher Education. https://www.insidehighered.com/news/2018/04/16/stanford-seeks-improve-graduate-student-advising

George Washington University. (n.d.) A*dvising syllabus for graduate students.* Elliot School of International Affairs. https://elliott.gwu.edu/sites/g/files/zaxdzs2141/f/downloads/acad/advising/forms/Advising%20Syllabus%20for%20Graduate%20Students_Sp18.pdf

Glass, C. R., Kociolek, E., Wongtrirat, R., Lynch, R. J., & Cong, S. (2015). Uneven experiences: The impact of student-faculty interactions on international students' sense of belonging. *Journal of International Students, 5*(4), 353–367.

Golde, C. M. (2005). The role of the department and discipline in doctoral student attrition: Lessons from four departments. *The Journal of Higher Education, 76*(6), 669–700. https://doi.org/10.1080/00221546.2005.11772304

Harris, T. A. (2018). Prescriptive vs. developmental: Academic advising at a historically black university in South Carolina. *NACADA Journal*, *38*(1), 36–46. https://doi.org/10.12930/NACADA-15-010

Heng, T. T. (2016). Different is not deficient: Contradicting stereotypes of Chinese international students in US higher education. *Studies in Higher Education, 43*(1), 22–36. https://doi.org/10.1080/03075079.2016.1152466

Hill, C. E. (2012). *Consensual qualitative research: Practical resource for investigating social science phenomena.* American Psychological Association.

Hill, C. E., Thompson, B. J., & Williams, E. N. (1997). A guide to conducting consensual qualitative research. *The Counseling Psychologist, 25*(4), 207–217. https://doi.org/10.1177/0011000097254001

Hunter, K. H., & Devine, K. (2016). Doctoral students' emotional exhaustion and intentions to leave academia. *International Journal of Doctoral Studies, 11,* 35–61. http://ijds.org/Volume11/IJDSv11p035-061Hunter2198.pdf

Janer, S. J. (2017). Graduate students' satisfaction on the thesis advising practices. *Asia Pacific Journal of Multidisciplinary Research, 5*(1)*,* 23–30.

Jeong, S., Blaney, J. M., & Feldon, D. F. (2019). Identifying faculty and peer interaction patterns of first-year biology doctoral students: A latent class analysis. *CBE – Life Sciences Education, 18*(4), 1–13. https://doi.org/10.1187/cbe.19-05-0089

Joy, S., Liang, X., Bilimoria, D., & Perry, S. (2015). Doctoral advisor-advisee pairing in STEM fields: Selection criteria and impact of faculty, student and departmental factors. *International Journal of Doctoral Studies, 10,* 343–363. http://ijds.org/Volume10/IJDSv10p343-363Joy0711.pdf

Kim, J. (2011). The birth of academic subalterns: How do foreign students embody the global hegemony of American universities? *Journal of Studies in International Education, 16,* 455–476. https://doi.org/10.1177/1028315311407510

Knox, S., Sokol, J. T., Inman, A. G., Schlosser, L. Z., Nilsson, J., & Wang, Y.W. (2013). International advisees' perspectives on the advising relationship in counseling psychology doctoral programs. *International Perspectives in Psychology: Research, Practice, Consultation*, *2*(1), 45–61. https://doi.org/10.1037/ipp0000001

Kong, X., Chakraverty, D., Jeffe, D. B., Andriole, D. A., Wathington, H. D., & Tai, R. H. (2013). How do interaction experiences influence doctoral students academic pursuits in biomedical research? *Bulletin of Science, Technology & Society, 33*(3–4), 76–84. https://doi.org/10.1177/0270467613516754

Labon, T. N. (2013). *The effects of race and gender on the satisfaction levels of entering and advanced level doctoral students* [Doctoral dissertation, University of Southern Mississippi]. https://aquila.usm.edu/dissertations/432

Litalien, D., & Guay, F. (2015). Dropout intentions in PhD studies: A comprehensive model based on interpersonal relationships and motivational resources. *Contemporary Educational Psychology, 41,* 218–231. https://doi.org/10.1016/j.cedpsych.2015.03.004

Lovitts, B. E. (2001). *Leaving the ivory tower: The causes and consequences of departure from doctoral study*. Rowman and Littlefield.

McWilliams, A. E., & Beam, L. R. (2013). Advising, counseling, coaching, and mentoring: Models of developmental relationships in higher education. *Scholarship on Academic Advising, 15*, 7–16. https://doi.org/10.26209/MJ1561280

Najjar, K. (2015). *International doctoral students, their advising relationships and adaptation experiences: A qualitative study* [Doctoral dissertation, University of Nebraska-Lincoln]. https://digitalcommons.unl.edu/cehsedaddiss/255

Ng, K., Lau, J., & Crisp, G. (2018). Advising and mentoring in counselor education. In J. E. Atieno-Okech & D. J. Rubel (Eds.), *Counselor education in the 21st Century: Issues and experiences* (pp. 53–72). American Counseling Association.

Noble, J. H. (2000). Cherchez l'argent: A contribution to the debate about class size, student-faculty ratios, and use of adjunct faculty. *Journal of Social Work Education, 36*(1), 89–102. https://doi.org/10.1080/10437797.2000.10778992

Noy, S., & Ray, R. (2012). Graduate students' perceptions of their advisers: Is there systematic disadvantage in mentorships? *The Journal of Higher Education, 83*(6), 876–914. https://doi.org/10.1080/00221546.2012.11777273

Omar, F., Mahone, J. P., Ngobia, J., & FitzSimons, J. (2016). Building rapport between international graduate students and their faculty advisors: Cross-cultural mentoring relationships at the University of Guelph. *The Canadian Journal for the Scholarship of Teaching and Learning, 7*(2), 1–17. http://dx.doi.org/10.5206/cjsotl-rcacea.2016.2.8

O'Meara, K., Knudsen, K., & Jones, J. (2013). The role of emotional competencies in faculty-doctoral student relationships. *Review of Higher Education: Journal of the Association for the Study of Higher Education, 36*(3), 315–347. https://doi.org/10.1353/rhe.2013.0021

Rice, K. G., Choi, C. C., Zhang, Y., Villegas, J., Ye, H. J., Anderson, D., Nesic, A., & Bigler, M. (2009). International student perspectives on graduate advising relationships. *Journal of Counseling Psychology, 56*(3), 376–391. https://doi.org/10.1037/a0015905

Rice, K. G., Suh, H., Yang, X., Choe, E., & Davis, D. E. (2016). The advising alliance for international and domestic graduate students: Measurement invariance and implications for academic stress. *Journal of Counseling Psychology*, *63*(3), 331–342. http://dx.doi.org/10.1037/cou0000141

Roberts, P. A., Dunworth, K., & Boldy, D. (2018). Towards a reframing of student support: A case study approach. *Higher Education, 75*(3), 19–33. https://doi.org/10.1006/s10734-017-0127-z

Roksa, J., Feldon, D. F., & Maher, M. (2018). First-generation students in pursuit of the PhD: Comparing socialization experiences and outcomes to continuing-generation peers. *The Journal of Higher Education, 89*(5), 728–752. https://doi.org/10.1080/00221546.2018.1435134

Ruud, C. M., Saclarides, E. S., George-Jackson, C. E., & Lubienski, S. T. (2018). Tipping points: Doctoral students and consideration of departure. *Journal of College Student Retention: Research, Theory & Practice, 20*(3), 286–307. https://doi.org/10.1177/1521025116666082

Shapiro, S., Farrelly, R., & Tomaš, Z. (2014). *Fostering international student success in higher education*. TASOL Press.

Takashiro, N. (2017). Asian international graduate students' extrinsic motivation to pursue degrees. *Psychological Thought, 10*(1), 178–189. http://dx.doi.org/10.5964/psyct.v10i1.199

University of Pittsburgh. (n.d.). *Elements of good academic advising.* https://www.provost.pitt.edu/students/graduate-studies/elements-good-academic-advising

Wang, R., & Lorenz, A. B. (2018). International student engagement: An exploration of student and faculty perceptions. *Journal of International Students, 8*(2), 1002–1033. https://doi.org/10.5281/zenodo.1250402

Zhao, C., Golde, C. M., & McKormick, A. C. (2007). More than a signature: How advisor choice and advisor behaviour affect doctoral student satisfaction. *Journal of Further and Higher Education, 31*(3), 263–281. https://doi.org/10.1080/03098770701424983

Zong, J., & Batalova, J. (2018). *International students in the United States.* Migration Policy Institute. https://www.migrationpolicy.org/article/international-students-united-states

NINA MARIJANOVIĆ is a doctoral candidate in the Educational Policy Studies and Evaluation Department at the University of Kentucky. Her major research interests lie in the area of faculty socialization, training, and retention, with special focus on higher education institutions and policy in the Western Balkans. Email: nina.marijanovic@uky.edu

JUNGMIN LEE is an Assistant Professor in the Educational Policy Studies and Evaluation Department at the University of Kentucky. Her major research interests lie in the area of higher education policy that promotes college access and success. Email: jungmin.lee@uky.edu

THOMAS W. TEAGUE, JR. is a doctoral candidate in the Educational Policy Studies and Evaluation Department at the University of Kentucky. His major research interests lie in the area of global student mobility, spatiality, and organizational issues impacting international student support. Email: thomas.teague@uky.edu

SHERYL F. MEANS is a postdoctoral fellow in Africana Studies at University of New Mexico. Her major interests lie in the area of Afro-Latin America, racial identity formation, and comparative education studies. Email: sfmeans@unm.edu

Peer-Reviewed Article

© *Journal of International Students*
Volume 11, Issue 2 (2021), pp. 436-458
ISSN: 2162-3104 (Print), 2166-3750 (Online)
doi: 10.32674/jis.v11i2.2215
ojed.org/jis

Reconceptualizing Student Engagement: Investigating the Validity of CCSSE Benchmarks as Indicators of International Student Engagement

Dina Ghazzawi
Lyle McKinney
Catherine Horn
University of Houston, USA

Andrea Backsheider Burridge
Houston Community College, USA

Vincent Carales
University of Houston, USA

ABSTRACT

International students in the United States have been increasingly attracted to community colleges as a starting point to higher education. Recently, their enrollment has been dropping. Research highlights the importance of student engagement to international students. However, few studies investigate their engagement experiences in community colleges. This study investigated the validity of the Community College Survey of Student Engagement (CCSSE) benchmarks as proxies for international student engagement in community colleges. The original CCSSE benchmarks were a poor fit for international students. Resulting constructs and underlying items differed significantly from the original benchmarks and demonstrated poor reliability. Findings highlight the inapplicability of CCSSE benchmarks in representing international student engagement. Recommendations include adding culturally relevant variables to the CCSSE structure more applicable to international student populations, and accompanying the survey with qualitative input for in-depth knowledge of international student experiences.

Keywords: community colleges, engagement, international students, student success

In recent years, community colleges have witnessed an influx of international students (Lau et al., 2019; Zhang, 2017). During the 2018–2019 academic year, there were 86,351 international students studying at U.S. community colleges, representing 8.3% of total international enrollment in the United States (Institute for International Education, 2019). Essentially, community colleges fulfill a vital mission in providing open-access education to students from a multitude of cultures, educational backgrounds, and ethnicities (Cohen et al., 2014). Their affordability, emphasis on English language skill building, and diverse campus climates make community colleges an attractive educational environment for international students (Evelyn, 2005; Glass & Westmont, 2013; Montgomery & McDowell, 2009).

Community colleges offer international students a second chance to pursue a postsecondary education that they would not have otherwise had access to since many of them cannot afford tuition in a 4-year institution, and many did not graduate from high school or were not accepted to university in their home countries due to more stringent admission criteria (Anayah & Kuk, 2015). The community college is a viable option to gain a postsecondary education as it offers a pathway to a 4-year institution (Hagedorn & Lee, 2005; Zhang, 2017). Studies have shown that most international students at community colleges intend to transfer to 4-year institutions (Bevis & Lucas, 2007; Bohman, 2010; Hagedorn & Lee, 2005), demonstrating the importance of community colleges as stepping stones for international students' bachelor's degree attainment (Bohman, 2010).

Given that community colleges have been serving the needs of international students for over two decades, the continuous influx of these students into community colleges justifies a deeper understanding of the characteristics of this unique subpopulation to enable community college leaders and educators to ensure that they are meeting the needs of all students (Garcia et al., 2019). For this reason, this study examines whether current student engagement tools are accurate and applicable indicators of engagement for the international student population across U.S community colleges.

LITERATURE REVIEW

International Students in U.S. Higher Education

International students undergo challenges that affect their engagement with different aspects of their educational experiences in the United States. One of the most frequently mentioned challenges faced by international students in the United States is the language barrier (Chen, 1999; Furnham & Alibhai, 1985; Gallagher, 2013; Smith & Khawaja, 2011; Wu et al., 2015). According to Chen

(1999), second language anxiety can negatively impact international students both academically and socially, affecting their ability to write assignments, communicate with peers and faculty, and understand lectures. In social contexts, social language anxiety impedes international students' ability to interact and befriend domestic students (Montgomery & McDowell, 2009). Also, international students often have difficulties adapting to Western Styles of teaching, particularly students coming from collectivist cultures who are accustomed to more stringent teaching methods (Edgeworth & Eiseman, 2007; Misra et al., 2003).

Aside from academic stressors, international students also suffer from sociocultural stressors due to being away from their home country (Sherry et al., 2010). Homesickness, culture shock, and isolation are just a few of the challenges these students face upon arriving at their new educational destination (Korobova & Starobin, 2015; Smith & Khawaja, 2011). Due to cultural disparities, international students may feel overwhelmed by differences in cultural norms and religious values and beliefs, as well as social activities conducted in the new environment (Banjong, 2015; Furnham & Alibhai, 1985).

Collective findings from the literature have shown that international students experience higher levels of discrimination than domestic students, causing them to gravitate more toward forming friendships with other international students they can identify with (Poyrazli & Lopez, 2007; Schmitt et al., 2003). Research also highlights the significant role of faculty in alleviating the difficulties of acclimatization and adjustment among international students. Literature on student–faculty interactions of international students emphasizes the importance of faculty in creating inclusive classroom environments for international students and exhibiting emotional cues that signal inclusion or exclusion among international students (Glass et al., 2015; Urban & Palmer, 2015). Studies have also highlighted the significant role of student–faculty interactions in providing international students with additional academic and social support to succeed through college (Glass & Westmont, 2014; Lau et al., 2019). Studies have also found that domestic students express disinterest in forming friendships with international students, which could further alienate international students from the mainstream campus culture, although these relationships could be extremely beneficial in increasing international student engagement and overall sense of adjustment (Korobova & Starobin, 2015).

Moreover, environmental stressors including financial issues and visa restrictions can place a great deal of strain on international students throughout their academic journey (Bohman, 2014). Most international students studying at U.S. universities and community colleges hold F-1 or M-1 visas, which are temporary student visas valid for the length of the educational period (Institute of International Education, 2018). Visa requirements include enrolling full time, and work eligibility is restricted to on-campus employment for the first academic year. As a result of these restrictions, international students feel enhanced pressure to maintain their full-time enrollment status while struggling to find suitable employment that could provide some financial support, particularly because international students are ineligible for any kind of federal financial aid (Hagedorn

& Lee, 2005), the majority of international students rely on personal or family income to support them through college (Institute of International Education, 2018). Collectively, the above research findings concerning the challenges faced by international students in the United States, in addition to the recent influx of international students to U.S. community colleges, further justifies the need to gain a better grasp of their experiences in community colleges.

Purpose of the Study

Given the unique characteristics of international students enrolled in community colleges and the gap in the literature surrounding their experiences in this setting, this study examines whether the Community College Survey of Student Engagement (CCSSE) benchmarks and the items measuring each construct are empirically valid indicators of international student engagement. The overarching goal of this study is to develop a reconceptualized model of student engagement specific to international students in community colleges. In particular, the study addresses the following research questions:

1. What are the sociodemographic, precollege, and academic characteristics of international students studying at U.S. community colleges?
2. To what extent are the five CCSSE benchmarks of effective educational practices valid constructs of international student engagement in the community college context?

This study adds to the scant body of literature surrounding international student experiences in community colleges by reevaluating items in engagement constructs that may apply differently to international students as compared with their domestic peers. Findings can provide community colleges with a reconceptualized model that reveals items reflective of underlying engagement constructs specific to characteristics of international students. Community college leaders can use these findings to reassess their curricular and co-curricular components in ways that better support international students' academic success.

Assessing Student Engagement

Research demonstrates the importance of student engagement in achieving successful learning outcomes in college (Astin, 1993; Chickering & Gamson, 1987; Tinto, 1994). Student engagement has been defined as the quality of interactions with faculty and peers (Pascarella & Terenzini, 2005), involvement in active and collaborative learning (Chickering & Gamson, 1987), and the time spent using college resources (Pascarella & Terenzini, 2005). Recently, the increased demand on institutions to demonstrate effective engagement practices has led to the use of assessment instruments, namely the National Survey of Student Engagement (NSSE) and the Community College Survey of Student Engagement (CCSSE), to measure the frequency of educational practices that positively predict academic outcomes (CCSSE, 2005; Kuh, 2009; McClenney,

Marti, & Adkins, 2006). Both instruments measure how institutions are promoting student engagement across five key areas of effective educational practices, and these practices are hypothesized to measure institutional effectiveness (McClenney & Marti, 2012).

Tailored to community colleges, the CCSSE collects data from students regarding their engagement in five key benchmarks of effective educational practices. Despite the vast extent to which the CCSSE has been used for higher education development and assessment, some scholars have questioned the construct validity of the CCSSE benchmarks, particularly for students from different cultural backgrounds (Angell, 2009; Mandarino & Mattern, 2010; Nora et al., 2011). Given that international students at community colleges come from a variety of cultural backgrounds and experiences, their engagement constructs and underlying items may differ from their domestic peers. These differences could uncover meaningful information about the support services and engagement components central to international student success.

The CCSSE theorizes five key benchmarks of student engagement that are positively related to student outcomes, which include (a) active and collaborative learning, (b) student effort, (c) academic challenge, (d) student–faculty interaction, and (e) support for learners (McClenney, 2006). Several studies have demonstrated the validity of both NSSE and CCSSE benchmarks as a proxy for positive student outcomes in higher education (e.g., Carini et al., 2006; McClenney, 2007; McClenney et al., 2012; Price & Tovar, 2014). While findings of these studies broadly confirmed the reliability of engagement benchmarks, some scholars have questioned these results (e.g., Angell, 2009; Campbell & Cabrera, 2011; Mandarino & Mattern, 2010; Nora et al., 2011). Angell (2009) examined the construct validity of the CCSSE benchmarks using survey responses from a sample of 450 students. Results showed differences in the items that were loaded onto each benchmark, reflecting major differences in the way various engagement constructs are defined and characterized differently by international students, as compared with their domestic peers. Mandarino and Mattern (2010) also tested the validity of CCSSE benchmarks using confirmatory factor analysis, and found that the student effort benchmark had lower reliability compared to data reported by CCSSE ($\alpha = .38$).

Lastly, Nora et al. (2011) employed data reduction techniques using CCSSE data from a sample of 393 students, which produced latent constructs that were significantly different from CCSSE benchmarks. To begin with, the factor analysis produced two separate constructs for active and collaborative learning, conflicting with CCSSE's findings that they present one benchmark. Second, items originally under the CCSSE benchmark of student–faculty interaction did not group into a single construct but rather loaded onto other constructs including collaborative learning and faculty interactions. Items included under the academic challenge and support for learners' benchmarks also contained significant differences compared to the CCSSE benchmarks. In addition, like findings by Angell (2009), the student effort benchmark demonstrated a lack of reliability (Nora et al., 2011). These results provide further support regarding the differences in the way international students engage with the different facets of their educational experience, and give reason to further explore a more adept method of defining engagement constructs specific to international student populations.

CONCEPTUAL FRAMEWORK

Due to the lack of theoretical frameworks that specifically focus on international student populations, the conceptual framework chosen for this study is the international student engagement (ISE) model, which was drawn from multiple perspectives and theories on international student experiences, including Astin's (1993) model and Harris and Wood's (2016) socioecological outcomes model. Literature on the challenges of international students in the United States highlights the effect of cultural barriers, stereotypes, and language difficulties on the academic success and social integration of students (Banjong, 2015; Furnham & Alibhai, 1985; Smith & Khawaja, 2011; Zhang, 2017).

Model Constructs

The ISE model is presented in Figure 1. The ISE model is divided into seven key constructs, categorized into input factors, socioecological domains, and outputs. The first two constructs of the model include background and societal factors and describe background factors that have an influence on the academic success and cultural adjustment of students (Gallagher, 2013; Smith & Khawaja, 2011).

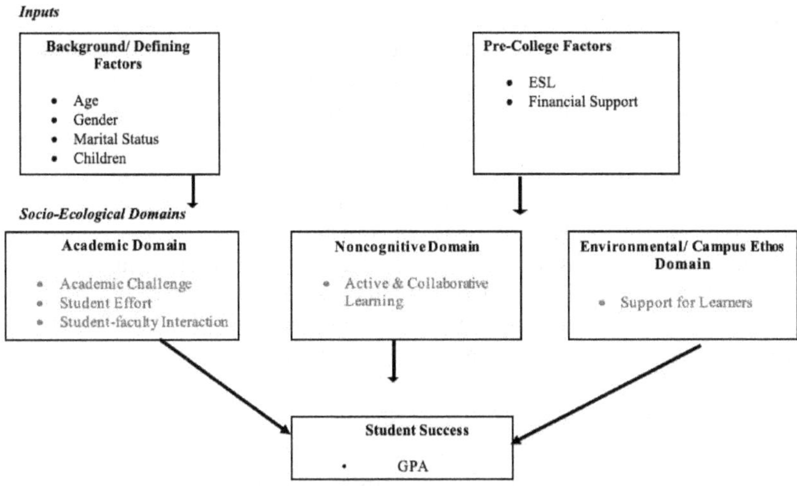

Figure 1: The International Student Engagement Model Depicting Factors Influencing the Grade Point Average and Sense of Belonging of International Students in the United States

The second construct of the model, societal factors, encompasses sociocultural forces that attract students to community colleges. For international students, sociocultural forces represent the precollege factors, including English language proficiency and financial support, that attract them toward community colleges as a starting point to U.S. higher education. Also, international students enrolled at community colleges come from a variety of different academic levels, all of which could have a significant effect on their academic achievement through college (Anayah & Kuk, 2015). For this reason, it was important to include their highest academic credential earned in this construct.

Socioecological Domains

The four socioecological domains of the ISE model represent the interactions between sociological and environmental factors that influence the academic success of international students. These domains consist of the noncognitive domain, the academic domain, the environmental domain, and the campus ethos domain (Harris & Wood, 2016). Using supporting literature and empirical findings from the CCSSE data source employed by this study, the CCSSE benchmarks of effective educational practice for international students were used to represent the socioecological domains of the SEO model. The noncognitive domain contains social variables reflecting students' emotional responses and interactions with the different contexts in a community college (Harris & Wood, 2016). This domain is represented by the active and collaborative learning benchmark, reflecting important facets of the engagement experience such as student–faculty interactions and cross-cultural interactions between domestic and international students that positively impact the engagement and belonging of international students (Garcia et al., 2018). The academic domain consists of variables associated to students' academic experiences and success in community colleges (Hagedorn et al., 2001).

The academic challenge benchmark characterizes the degree of mental challenge required by students in their coursework (CCSSE, 2016). The student effort benchmark describes time on task variables describing the amount of work students put into their academics (CCSSE, 2016). Studies on international student engagement found that students dedicate more effort than domestic students on noninteractive academic engagement, such as studying and working on class assignments, (García et al., 2016; García et al., 2018).

The environmental domain reflects external student commitments that may deter students from focusing their time and effort on academic pursuits (Harris & Wood, 2016; Horn & Nevil, 2006). These commitments include family responsibilities and financial stressors that impede the academic progress of students (Wood & Williams, 2013). Finally, the campus ethos domain represents institutional programs and internal supportive agents that shape the academic experience of students in the community college (Dowd & Bensimon 2013; Harris & Wood, 2016). Both the environment and campus ethos domain were captured in the support for learners' benchmark of the CCSSE.

METHOD

Data Source and Sample

The data used for this study was obtained from the CCSSE, an assessment tool used by community colleges since 2001 to identify institutional practices that encourage student engagement (McClenney et al., 2006). The CCSSE's survey instrument, the Community College Student Report (CCSR), is administered each spring to students in classrooms of participating community colleges (CCSSE, 2012). Eligibility of courses was assessed on whether students were in credit courses and had regularly scheduled meeting times where the survey could be administered (CCSSE, 2019). The CCSR contains 38 items asking students questions related to their engagement behaviors across the five key benchmarks of effective educational practices. Table 1 lists all 38 CCSSE items and response scales.

Table 1: Description of CCSSE Benchmarks and Item Response Scales

Benchmark	Description of items and response scales
Active and collaborative learning	• Contained seven survey items. • A 4-point response scale (*Never*, *Sometimes*, *Often*, *Very Often*) measured the frequency of the following college activities: o Made a class presentation o Asked questions or participated in class discussions o Worked with students on a project in class o Discussed ideas from class readings with others outside of class o Participated in a community-based project as part of coursework o Tutored other students
Academic challenge	• Contained 10 survey items. • A four-item response scale (*Very little*, *Some*, *Quite a Bit*, *Very Much*) measured the extent to which students did the following four activities: o Analyzed basic ideas of an element of theory o Synthesized and organized ideas in new ways o Made judgements about the soundness of information o Applied information to perform a new skill • A five-item response scale (*None*, *1–4*, *5–10*, *11–20*, *More then 20*) was used to measure the following two items: o Number of written papers or reports o Number of assigned readings, textbooks, or manuals

	• A seven-item continuous response scale (1 = *extremely easy*, 7 = *extremely challenging*) was used to measure item: o The extent to which exams have challenged students to do their best work
Student effort	• Contained eight survey items. • A four-item response scale (*Never*, *Sometimes*, *Often*, *Very Often*), measured the frequency of the following six activities: o Prepared two or more drafts of a paper before submission o Worked on a paper that required integrating ideas from various sources o Came to class without completing readings or assignments o Used peer or other tutoring o Used skills lab (writing, math, etc.) o Used computer lab • A five-item scale (*None*, *1–4*, *5–10*, *11–20*, *More than 20*) measured the following activity: o Number of books read on your own (not assigned) • A six-item scale (*None*, *1–5*, *6–10*, *11–20*, *21–30*, *More than 30*) measured the following activity: o Number of hours spent preparing for class in a 7-day week

The dataset contains a 25% a random sample of a 3-year cohort of students, beginning in Spring 2013 and ending in Summer 2015. The full sample (N = 107,429) includes data from 694 community colleges located in 47 states. Courses that did not count for institutional credit were administered to high school or incarcerated populations, as well as online courses, were excluded from the sample. International students represented 6.1% of the sample (n = 6,739). For this study, only international students enrolled in credit courses with a grade point average were included in the study. This reduced the sample to n = 6,015 students.

Variables

Guided by the tenants of the ISE model, we categorized the independent variables included in this analysis into input characteristics (including sociodemographic and precollege characteristics) and socioecological domains.

Data Analysis

To answer the research questions, we used both descriptive and inferential statistics. For the first research question, we used descriptive statistics including frequencies and percentages to indicate the proportional distributions of international students according to sociodemographic and precollege characteristics. We then used χ^2 tests to examine whether proportional differences exist between these characteristics, allowing us to highlight significant differences in predictor variables among international students.

Table 2: List of Variables and Coding Scheme

Variables	Coding scheme
Predictors: Background characteristics	
Gender	0 = male, 1 = female
Age	0 = <20; 1 = 20–29; 2 = 30–29; 3 = 40–50; 4 = >50
Married	0 = yes; 1 = no
Children	0 = yes; 1 = no
Predictors: Pre-college characteristics	
Enrollment status	0 = part time; 1 = full time
Developmental English (ESL)	0 = not required; 1 = required
Predictor: Socioecological domains	
Active and collaborative learning	Continuous (scale) raw benchmark score
Academic challenge	Continuous (scale) raw benchmark score
Student effort	Continuous (scale) raw benchmark score
Support for learners	Continuous (scale) raw benchmark score
Student–faculty interaction	Continuous (scale) raw benchmark score

For the second research question, to determine the validity of the CCSSE benchmarks and their applicability to international students at community colleges, we conducted quantitative data reduction procedures on all 38 survey items. First, we used a confirmatory factor analysis to assess the model fit of the five CCSSE structure. Subsequently, we conducted an exploratory factor analysis on all 38 CCSSE items and compared the results of these factors to the original five CCSSE benchmarks. As part of the analysis, we conducted an examination of eigenvalues, factor loadings, cross loadings, and percentage of variance explained. Statistically significant items were then given labels that matched the underlying construct depicted. The scales produced we then subjected to a reliability test, and we examined Cronbach's alpha coefficients for each scale to determine the reliability of each construct.

To calculate the raw benchmark scores of the constructs established through the factor analysis, we employed the CCSSE (2014) procedures for benchmark calculations. Table 2 displays the descriptive statistics of the newly established scales. Finally, we employed a confirmatory factor analysis on the newly established constructs in order to compare their model fit indices with the original CCSSE structure.

RESULTS

Descriptive Characteristics of International Students at U.S. Community Colleges

Descriptive findings revealed several noteworthy results regarding international student populations at U.S. community colleges. Females comprised 54% of the sample, while males comprised 46%. The majority of international students (73.6%) enrolled full time, and 26.4% enrolled part time. Of those students enrolled part time, a significantly higher proportion were females ($p < .005$). Most students in the sample were single (79.6%) and had no children (76.4%); however, results of the chi-square tests revealed that a significantly higher proportion of female students in the sample were married and had children compared with male students ($p < .005$). In terms of age, a larger number of international students were in the younger age groups, with 57.4% of students in the 20–29 age group and 24.7% of students in the below 20 age group.

In terms of precollege characteristics, over half (57.4%) of international students in the sample required remediation in English (English as a second language) courses. Three categorical variables measured the source of financial support for students, including grants/scholarships, personal income, or family income. A higher proportion of students listed parental income as a major source of financial support (39.3%), as compared to other sources.

Validity of CCSSE Engagement Constructs

To assess the validity of CCSSE engagement constructs, we conducted a confirmatory factor analysis on the original five CCSSE benchmarks to assess how representative these engagement constructs are for the international student sample. Fit indexes for the original CCSSE structure showed a statistically significant chi-square test with a value of 7273.181, $p < .005$. The NFI (Normed-Fit Index) (.729), IFI (Incremental Fit Index) (.747), CFI (Comparative Fit Index) (0.747), TLI (Tucker Lewis Index) (.728), and SRMR (Standard Root Mean Square Residual) (.061) collectively indicated the model was a poor fit for the data.

Then, we performed an exploratory factor analysis of all 38 CCSSE survey items to analyze the five-factor structure of the CCSSE benchmarks. As this study's goal was to analyze the validity of the original CCSSE benchmarks and their applicability to international student populations, we used the five-factor framework used by CCSSE in the exploratory factor analysis. Prior to running the analysis, the data were screened by assessing descriptive statistics on each survey item to ensure no univariate or multivariate assumptions were violated. The five-factor structure produced by the data reduction process revealed noticeable differences between the original CCSSE benchmarks and the underlying items within each construct for international students. Differences in items associated with each factor are summarized in Table 3.

Table 3: Comparison of CCSSE Benchmarks with Analysis Results

CCSSE benchmark	Scale for international students
Academic challenge	
• Frequency of working harder than expected to meet teachers' expectations	• Academic challenge
• Amount of course emphasis on analyzing basic elements of a theory	• Academic challenge
• Amount of course emphasis on synthesizing new ideas or organizing ideas from various information sources	• Academic challenge
• Amount of course emphasis on making judgments about the value of soundness of information, arguments of methods	• Academic challenge
• Amount of course emphasis on applying theories and concepts to practical problems	• Academic challenge
• Amount of course emphasis on using information learned to perform a new skill	• Academic challenge
• Number of assigned textbooks, manuals, books, or book-length packs of course reading	• Student effort
• Number of written papers of reports	• Did not load onto any factor
• Rate the extent to which your examinations have challenged you to do your best work	• Student–faculty interaction
• Amount of emphasis by college to encourage you to spend significant amounts of time studying	• Academic challenge
Active and collaborative learning	
• Frequency of asking questions of contributing to class discussions	• Active and collaborative learning
• Frequency of making class presentations	• Active and collaborative learning
• Frequency of working with other students	• Active and collaborative

CCSSE benchmark	Scale for international students
on projects during class	learning
• Frequency of working with other classmates outside of class to prepare class assignments	• Active and collaborative learning
• Frequency of tutoring other students (paid or voluntary)	• Active and collaborative learning
• Frequency of participating in a community-based project as part of a regular course	• Did not load onto any factor
• Frequency of discussing ideas from readings with others outside of class	• Active and collaborative learning
Student effort	
• Frequency of preparing two or more drafts of a paper or assignment before turning it in	• Student effort
• Frequency of working on a paper that required integrating ideas or information from various sources	• Did not load onto any factor
• Frequency of coming to class without completing readings or assignments	• Did not load onto any factor
• Number of books read on your own not assigned	• Student effort
• Hours spent a week preparing for class	• Did not load onto any factor
• Frequency of use: Peer or other tutoring	• Support for learners
• Frequency of use: Skills lab	• Support for learners
• Frequency of use: Computer lab	• Support for learners
Student–faculty interaction	
• Frequency of using email to communicate with an instructor	• Academic challenge
• Frequency of discussing grades of assignments with an instructor	• Active and collaborative learning
• Frequency of talking about career plans with an instructor or advisor	• Active and collaborative learning
• Frequency of discussing ideas from your readings or classes with instructors outside of class	• Active and collaborative learning
• Frequency of receiving prompt feedback from instructors on your performance	• Academic challenge
• Frequency of working with instructors on activities other than coursework	• Active and collaborative learning
Support for learners	
• Amount of emphasis by college in providing the support to help students succeed at college	• Student–faculty interaction
• Amount of emphasis by college to	• Student–faculty interaction

CCSSE benchmark	Scale for international students
encourage contact among diverse students	
• Amount of emphasis by college to help students cope with nonacademic responsibilities	• Student–faculty interaction
• Amount of emphasis by college to provide financial support	• Student–faculty interaction
• Frequency of use of academic advising/planning	• Support for learners
• Frequency of use of career counseling	• Support for learners

Academic Challenge

Ten items were contained in the original CCSSE benchmark. For international students, only seven items loaded onto the academic challenge component. This newly established scale was renamed Cognitive Learning.

Student Effort

Six of the items originally included in the student effort benchmark did not load onto any factor for international students. This scale was renamed Academic Tasks to reflect the focus on time spent on a task for academic variables represented in this construct.

Support for Learners

For international students, the support for learners benchmarks mainly reflected frequent student use of support services, while the original benchmark combined items indicating use of support services and amount of college emphasis in providing student support. This scale also included items reflecting students' use of career counseling, academic advising, and tutoring services, and was renamed Academic Support.

Student–Faculty Interaction

None of the items under the original CCSSE benchmark were reflected in the student–faculty interaction benchmark for international students. While the original benchmark contained items reflecting the amount of interaction and feedback occurring between students and their instructors, the benchmark established through the data reduction process contained items showing college emphasis on student support in various aspects of their college experience. Accordingly, the title of the benchmark was changed to Environmental Support.

Active and Collaborative Learning

Four of the items originally under the student–faculty interaction benchmark loaded onto the active and collaborative learning scale for international students. Items under this scale reflect student collaboration with both peers and faculty on classwork, and was accordingly renamed Collaborative Learning.

We constructed subscales of the benchmarks for international students based on the organization of items loaded onto each newly established scale. All subscales demonstrated good internal consistency except for the academic tasks scale, which had a low Cronbach's alpha coefficient of .57. We conducted a second confirmatory factor analysis to confirm the model fit of the resulting structure. The values for NFI (Normed-Fit Index) (.776), TLI (Tucker Lewis Index) (.776), CFI (Comparative Fit Index)(.747), and SRMR (Standard Root Mean Square Residual) (.057) though indicated improved values from the original CCSSE benchmarks, still indicated an inadequate fit of the data.

DISCUSSION

The results confirm the inapplicability of the original five CCSSE benchmarks as valid constructs for international student populations. The analysis yielded the following conclusions: (a) Data reduction analysis derived items representing the latent construct of academic challenge (renamed Cognitive Learning) that were considerably different than those in the original CCSSE benchmark. (b) All items under the student–faculty interaction scale did not load onto a single factor. Rather, one loaded onto the cognitive learning scale and the remaining items loaded onto the collaborative learning scale. (c) While the original support for the learners benchmark included both environmental support and institutional support items, the factor analysis derived two separate constructs. (d) The model fit indices of the newly established constructs fell short of the guidelines for an adequate model fit.

Results support previous findings by Nora et al. (2011), who found differences in the way students characterized engagement items classically defined as student–faculty interactions as active and collaborative learning. Also, results of García et al.'s (2019) data reduction analysis yielded items in the socioacademic construct that matched those items included in the environmental support benchmark in the present study.

The items loaded onto the newly constructed academic challenge scale (renamed Cognitive Learning) included items originally correlated with the active and collaborative learning and student–faculty interaction benchmarks of the CCSSE structure. These findings highlight that what constitutes academic challenge for a domestic student may differ for an international student. For example, while using email to communicate with an instructor and contributing to class discussions were originally included in the student–faculty interaction benchmarks of the original CCSSE benchmarks, they were considered to be an academic challenge for international students. These results are confirmed by studies that demonstrate international students' difficulty in participating in class discussions and communicating with faculty due to language barriers, differences in teaching and learning styles, and acculturative stress (Mamiseishvili, 2012; Yu & Shen, 2012).

The lower than desired model fit indices for the newly constructed scales indicate that the 38 CCSSE survey items may not be an adequate representation of these underlying constructs for international students. These findings highlight the need to include culturally relevant variables in student engagement assessment tools, such as sense of belonging and cultural inclusivity (Museus & Quaye, 2009; Nuñez, 2009). While the objective of the CCSSE is to measure behaviors that are positively linked to engagement, research studies have documented the significant role of campus climate and sense of belonging on the engagement behaviors of international students (Banjong, 2015; Glass & Westmont, 2014; Glass et al., 2015). In their response to the criticisms posed by researchers regarding the lack of culturally relevant variables in student engagement surveys, McCormick and McClenney (2012) agreed with the concept that engagement surveys should better assess students from different racial backgrounds. They also suggested that the notion of intercultural effort posted by Dowd et al. (2011) should be expended to include students of different nationalities, social class, and abilities, not only ethnic minorities.

Figure 2 displays the International Student Engagement (ISE) model with the re- established CCSSE scales. Coherent with the premise of the non-cognitive domain of the ISE model, active and collaborating learning of international students is affected by their social and cultural values, particularly for students from collectivist cultures (Edgeworth & Eiseman, 2007). Students who are socialized in cultures where learning is more stringent and less focused on in class discussion may have a difficult time adapting to Western styles of teaching, which often contributes to a sense of isolation from faculty (Misra et al., 2003).

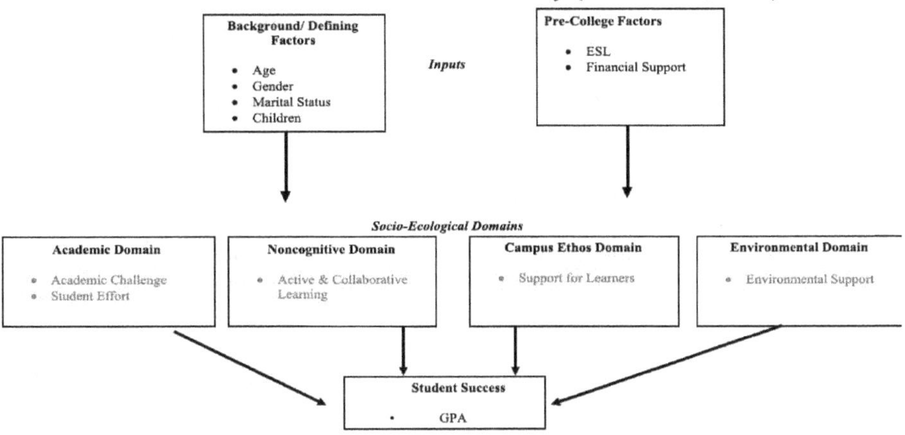

Figure 2: The International Student Engagement Model with Reestablished CCSSE Benchmarks

The ISE model proposes that international student engagement does not occur in a vacuum but is influenced by a variety of background and socioecological characteristics that influence students' perceptions and emotional responses to the different learning channels of their institution, which subsequently impacts their academic achievement. The model highlights the psychosocial aspect of engagement that includes attitudes, perceptions, and emotional responses, along with the behavioral aspect. This psychosocial aspect of student engagement, while included in some definitions of student engagement (e.g., Saloman & Globerson, 1987; Schuetz, 2008), is lacking in the way student engagement is currently defined through the CCSSE benchmarks.

Findings from this study confirm the need to reassess items contained in student engagement assessment tools in the community college context to include more culturally relevant items (Museus & Quaye, 2009; Nora et al.; 2011; Nuñez, 2009). Benchmarks of effective educational practice can support student learning yet simultaneously lack cultural relevance (Yosso et al., 2009). For this reason, relying solely on CCSSE benchmarks as indicators of ISE in community college is not recommended (Angell, 2009). A more holistic way of approaching research on this topic would be accompanying these assessment instruments with qualitative input from students (Quaye & Harper, 2014). Institutions wishing to better engage international students should establish regular methods to hear students' opinions about the nature of their experiences and challenges in order to uncover emerging patterns in their behaviors (ACPA & NASPA, 2004).

Limitations

There are limitations in this study that warrant discussion. The demographic section of the survey did not include any questions to identify students' country of origin, forcing the study to group all international students into a single population. This restricted the study's ability to account for differentiating characteristics of international students from different countries that could significantly influence their academic and social experiences in community colleges (Ghazzawi et al., 2020). Another limitation of this study is that students are not differentiated by the type of visa they hold. A single question on the CCSSE questionnaire simply asks students if they are international students (on F-1 or M-1 visas) or foreign nationals, and groups both categories as one. Distinguishing between international students holding different types of visas can yield valuable demographic information such as work and enrollment restrictions, which could in turn allow more in-depth research to be uncovered regarding the impact of such restrictions on student engagement and academic progress. Additionally, the self-reported nature of the survey responses limits the reliability of the CCSSE findings. Finally, the sample of international students examined in this study was limited to those in institutions that chose to and could afford to administer the CCSSE. Therefore, results of this study do not represent the wider population of international students present at community colleges not administering the CCSSE.

Recommendations for Policy and Practice

Given this study's findings that emphasize the importance of a holistic approach to student engagement tailored to international students, one of the most important ways that educational leaders can better support international students is by encouraging instructors, academic advisors, and student affairs professionals to learn more about international students, their cultures, backgrounds, and challenges through international student support training (Quaye & Harper, 2014). Also, given the significant role of faculty in creating diverse, comfortable classroom environments for international students, international student support training should include methods through which instructors can better engage international students in class through a variety of new approaches (Campbell, 2007; Lau et al., 2019; Korobova & Starobin, 2015). Instructors who demonstrate intercultural competence, exhibit genuine concern for the well-being and academic success of international students, and promote equitable and diverse classroom dialogue can significantly increase the sense of belonging and engagement of international students (Glass, 2012; Glass & Westmont, 2014; Lau et al., 2019; Urban & Palmer, 2014). Furthermore, it is important for faculty to encourage the social interaction of international students with domestic peers through in-class activities and discussions, as such interactions can reduce second language anxiety and, in turn, increase international student's sense of integration with their academic environment (Garcia et al., 2018).

CONCLUSION

Results suggest that using predefined items to measure international student engagement and success may be ill-conceived. Community college leaders are encouraged to use the recommendations provided by this study as a starting point to reassess their curricular and co-curricular components to provide more inclusive and welcoming campus climates for international students. International students are an extremely valuable asset to community colleges, as increasing enrollments enrich the diversity and global repertoire of these institutions. Given these benefits, it is paramount for community college leaders to provide greater support to allow these students to thrive both personally and academically.

REFERENCES

Anayah, B., & Kuk, L. (2015). The growth of international student enrollment at community colleges and implications. *Community College Journal of Research and Practice, 39*(12), 1099-1110.

Angell, L. (2009). Construct validity of the Community College Survey of Student Engagement. *Community College Journal of Research and Practice, 33*, 564–570.

Astin, A. W. (1993). *What matters in college: Four critical years revisited.* Jossey-Bass.

Banjong, D. N. (2015). International students' enhanced academic performance: Effects of campus resources. *Journal of International Students, 5*(2), 132–142.

Bevis, T. B., & Lucas, C. J. (2007). *International students in American colleges and universities: A history*. Palgrave Macmillan.

Bohman, E. (2010). Headed for the heartland: Decision making process of community college bound international students. *Community College Journal of Research and Practice, 34*, 64–77.

Carini, R. M., Kuh, G. D., & Klein, S. P. (2006). Student engagement and student learning: Testing the linkages. Research in higher education, 47(1), 1-32.

Chen, C. P. (1999). Professional issues: Common stressors among international college students: Research and counseling implications. Journal of college counseling, 2(1), 49-65.

Chickering, A. W., & Gamson, Z. F. (1987). Seven principles for good practice in undergraduate education. *AAHE Bulletin, 1987*, 3–7.

Cohen, A., Brawer, F., & Kisker, C. 2014. *The American community college* (6th ed.). Jossey-Bass.

Community College Survey of Student Engagement. (2007, October). CCSSE launches SENSE to improve entering student experiences and outcomes. *Talking SENSE Newsletter*, 2. https://www.ccsse.org/center/publications/newsletter/13.2/

Community College Survey of Student Engagement. (2016). *About the CCSSE survey*. http://www.ccsse.org/aboutsurvey/aboutsurvey.cfm

Dowd, A. C., Pak, J. H., & Bensimon, E. M. (2013). The role of institutional agents in promoting transfer access. *Education Policy Analysis Archives, 21*(15), 1–39.

Dowd, A. C., Sawatzky, M., & Korn, R. (2011). Theoretical foundations and a research agenda to validate measures of intercultural effort. *The Review of Higher Education, 35*(1), 17–44.

Edgeworth, K., & Eiseman, J. (2007). Going Bush: International student perspectives. *Journal of Research in Rural Education, 22*(9), 412–475.

Evelyn, J. (2005). Community colleges go globe-trotting. *The Chronicle of Higher Education, 51*(23), A11.

Furnham, A., & Alibhai, N. (1985). The friendship networks of foreign students: A replication and extension of the functional model. *International Journal of Psychology, 20*(6), 709–722.

Gallagher, H. C. (2013). Willingness to communicate and cross-cultural adaptation: L2 communication and acculturative stress as transaction. *Applied Linguistics*, *34*(1), 53–73.

García, H. A., Garza, T., & Yeaton, K. (2016). *Do we belong? A conceptual model for international students' sense of belonging in community colleges* [Paper presentation]. Annual Conference of the Association for the Study of Higher Education, Columbus, OH.

García, H. A., McNaughtan, J., Eicke, D., Li, X., Leong, M., & McClain, T. (2018). Engaging international students at community colleges:

Understanding the role of institutional support structures. *Journal of Applied Research in the Community College, 25*(1), 45–60.

Ghazzawi, D., McKinney, L., Horn, C., Carales, V., & Burridge, A. (2020). The road to the baccalaureate: Assessing the viability of community colleges as transfer pathways for international students. *Journal of International Students*, *10*(2), 420–442.

Glass, C. R., Kociolek, E., Wongtrirat, R., Lynch, R. J., & Cong, S. (2015). Uneven experiences: The impact of student-faculty interactions on international students' sense of belonging. *Journal of International Students, 5*(4), 353–367.

Glass, C., & Westmont, C. (2013). Comparative effects of belongingness on the academic success and cross-cultural interactions of domestic and international students. *International Journal of Intercultural Relations, 38*, 106–119.

Hagedorn, L. S., & Lee, M. (2005). *International community college students: The neglected minority?* (ED490516). ERIC. https://eric.ed.gov/?id=ED490516

Hagedorn, L. S., Maxwell, W., & Hampton, P. (2001). Correlates of retention for African-American males in community colleges. *Journal of College Student Retention: Research, Theory & Practice*, *3*(3), 243–263.

Harper, S. R., & Quaye, S. J. (2015). Making engagement equitable for students in U.S higher education. In S. J. Quaye & S. R. Harper (Eds.), *Student engagement in higher education: Theoretical perspectives and practical approaches for diverse populations* (2nd ed., pp. 1–14). Taylor & Francis.

Harris, F., III, & Luke Wood, J. (2016). Applying the socio-ecological outcomes model to the student experiences of men of color. *New Directions for Community Colleges, 2016*(174), 35–46.

Horn, L. J., & Nevil, S. (2006). *Profile of undergraduates in U.S. postsecondary education institutions: 2003– 04, with a special analysis of community college students* (NCES Publication No. 2006-184). U.S. Department of Education. Washington, DC: National Center for Education Statistics.

Institute of International Education. (2018). *Open Doors 2018: Fast facts.* https://www.iie.org/Research-and-Insights/Open-Doors/Fact-Sheets-and-Infographics/Fast-Facts

Institute of International Education. (2019). International student enrollments by institutional type, 1999/00-2018/19. *Open Doors Report.* https://opendoorsdata.org/data/international-students/enrollment-by-institutional-type/

Keeling, R. (Ed.). (2004). *Learning reconsidered: A campus-wide focus on the student experience.* American College Personnel Association & National Association of Student Personnel Administrators.

Korobova, N., & Starobin, S. (2015). A comparative study of student engagement, satisfaction, and academic success among international and American students. *Journal of International Students, 5*(1), 72–85.

Kuh, G. D. (2009). What student affairs professionals need to know about student engagement. *Journal of College Student Development, 50*(6), 683–706.

Lau, J., Garza, T., & Garcia, H. (2019). International students in community colleges: On-campus services used and its effect on sense of belonging. *Community College Journal of Research and Practice, 43*(2), 109–121.

Mamiseishvili, K. (2012). International student persistence in US postsecondary institutions. *Higher Education, 64*(1), 1–17.

Mandarino, C., & Mattern, M. Y. (2010). *Assessing the validity of CCSSE in an Ontario college.* Institute of Technology and Advanced Learning for the Higher Education Quality Council of Ontario.

Marti, C. (2009). Dimensions of student engagement in American community colleges: Using the Community College Student Report in research and practice. *Community College Journal of Research and Practice, 33*(1), 1–24.

McClenney, K. M. (2006). Benchmarking effective educational practice. *New Directions for Community Colleges, 2006*(134), 47–55.

McClenney, K., Marti, C., & Adkins, C. (2006). *Student engagement and student outcomes: Key findings from CCSSE validation research.* Community College Survey of Student Engagement.

McClenney, K., Marti, C., & Adkins, C. (2012). *Student engagement and student outcomes: Key findings from CCSSE validation research.* Community College Survey of Student Engagement.

Misra, R., Crist, M., & Burant, C. J. (2003). Relationships among life stress, social support, academic stressors, and reactions to stressors of international students in the United States. *International Journal of Stress Management, 10*(2), 137.

Montgomery, C., & McDowell, L. (2009). Social networks and the international student experience: An international community of practice? *Journal of Studies in International Education, 13*(4), 455–466.

Museus, S. D., & Quaye, S. J. (2009). Toward an intercultural perspective of racial and ethnic minority college student persistence. *The Review of Higher Education, 33*(1), 67–94.

NAFSA: Association of International Educators. (2018). *NAFSA international student economic value tool.* https://www.nafsa.org/policy-and-advocacy/policy-resources/nafsa-international-student-economic-value-tool-v2

Nora, A., Crisp, G., & Matthews, C. (2011). A reconceptualization of CCSSE's benchmarks of student engagement. *The Review of Higher Education, 35*(1), 105–130.

Nuñez, A. M. (2009). Latino students' transitions to college: A social and intercultural capital perspective. *Harvard Educational Review, 79*(1), 22–48.

Pascarella, E. T., & Terenzini, P. T. (2005). *How college affects students: A third decade of research* (Vol. 2). Jossey-Bass.

Price, D. V., & Tovar, E. (2014). Student engagement and institutional graduation rates: Identifying high-impact educational practices for community colleges. *Community College Journal of Research and Practice, 38*(9), 766–782.

Quaye, S. J., & Harper, S. R. (Eds.). (2014). *Student engagement in higher education: Theoretical perspectives and practical approaches for diverse populations*. Routledge.

Schuetz, P. (2008). Developing a theory-driven model of community college student engagement. *New Directions for Community Colleges, 2008*(144), 17–28.

Schmitt, M. T., Spears, R., & Branscombe, N. R. (2003). Constructing a minority group identity out of shared rejection: The case of international students. *European Journal of Social Psychology, 33*(1), 1–12.

Sherry, M., Thomas, P. & Chui, W.H. (2010). International students: A vulnerable population. *Higher Education, 60*, 33–46.

Smith, R. A., & Khawaja, N. G. (2011). A review of the acculturation experiences of international students. *International Journal of Intercultural Relations, 35*(6), 699–713.

Tinto, V. (1994). Constructing educational communities: Increasing retention in challenging circumstances. *Community College Journal, 64*(4), 26–29.

Urban, E., & Palmer, L.B. (2014). International students as a resource for internationalization of higher education. *Journal of Studies in International Education, 18*(4), 305–324.

U.S. Immigration and Customs Enforcement. (2015). *Student process steps: How to navigate the U.S. immigration system*. https://www.ice.gov/sevis/students

Wood, J. L., & Williams, R. C. (2013). Persistence factors for Black males in the community college: An examination of background, academic, social, and environmental variables. *Spectrum: A Journal on Black Men, 1*(2), 1–28.

Wu, H., Garza, E., & Guzman, N. (2015). International student's challenges and adjustment to college. *Education Research International, 2015*, 1–9.

Yeh, C., & Inose, M. (2003). Difficulties and coping strategies of Chinese, Japanese, and Korean immigrant students. *Adolescence, 37*(145), 69–82.

Yosso, T., Smith, W., Ceja, M., & Solórzano, D. (2009). Critical race theory, racial microaggressions, and campus racial climate for Latina/o undergraduates. *Harvard Educational Review, 79*(4), 659–691.

Zhang, Y. L. (2017). International students in transition: International community college transfer students in a Texas research university. *New Directions for Institutional Research, 170*, 35–48.

DINA GHAZZAWI, PhD, is a postdoctoral research fellow at the University of Houston's Department of Higher Education Leadership and Policy Studies. Her major research interests lie in the area of international student success, quantitative research methods, student engagement, and sense of belonging. Email: dalghazzawi@uh.edu

LYLE MCKINNEY, PhD, is an associate professor of higher education in the Higher Education Leadership and Policy Studies program at the University of Houston. His research interests focus on community colleges, improving educational outcomes for low-income students, and higher education policy. Email: llmckinney@uh.edu

CATHERINE HORN, PhD is a Moores Professor of Educational Leadership and Policy Studies and Director of the University of Houston's Education Research Center. She is also Executive Director of the Institute for Educational Policy Research and Evaluation at the University of Houston and Director for the Center for Research and Advancement of Teacher Education. Her major research interests focus on quantitative methods and systematic barriers to college access for traditionally underrepresented students. Email: clhorn2@uh.edu

ANDREA BACKSCHEIDER BURRIDGE, PhD, is the Associate Vice Chancellor, Research, Analytics, and Decision Support at Houston Community College. Her research focuses on student success and completion in community college. Email: andrea.burridge@hccs.edu

VINCENT D. CARALES, PhD is an assistant professor of higher education in the Educational Leadership and Policy Studies Program at the University of Houston. His research examines how institutional cultures, climates and structures influence Latinx and low-income students' experiences, opportunities, and outcomes in higher education. Email: vcarales@central.uh.edu

Peer-Reviewed Article

© *Journal of International Students*
Volume 11, Issue 2 (2021), pp. 459-483
ISSN: 2162-3104 (Print), 2166-3750 (Online)
doi: 10.32674/jis.v11i2.459-
ojed.org/jis

Understanding Country Differences: Predicting the Effect of Financial and Labor Market Conditions on International Doctoral Recipients' First Labor Market Destination

Osasohan Agbonlahor
University of Colorado - Colorado Springs, USA

Frim Ampaw
Central Michigan University, USA

ABSTRACT

This study used the Survey of Earned Doctorates, World Bank economic data of the doctoral students' home country, and hierarchical linear modeling analysis to examine the effects of financial factors and home-country macroeconomic indicators on international doctoral students' labor market destinations. We found that wealth disparities and economic opportunities in the home country affect international doctoral student outcomes. Higher gross national income per capita was associated with decreased likelihood of remaining in the United States, while higher unemployment rates in the home country significantly increased the likelihood of remaining in the United States. The study reveals a need to develop career services support for international doctoral students that are tailored to their needs as well as the need to internationalize the curriculum to support those who will eventually return to their home country.

Keywords: economic opportunities, international doctoral recipients, labor market outcome

---

INTRODUCTION

While experiences of international students in the United States have been discussed in the literature, research analyzing their transition into the labor market is relatively limited. However, the existing research suggests a low transition rate into the U.S. labor market, mainly due to the limited availability of work visas (Migration Policy Institute, 2018). There is some empirical evidence that shows the benefits of the immigration of high-skilled workers for the U.S. economy. Bound et al. (2017) constructed a general equilibrium model of the U.S. economy and calibrated it using data from 1994 to 2010. They found that in the absence of immigration, wages for U.S. computer scientists would have been 2.6% to 5.1% higher, and employment in computer science for U.S. workers would have been 6.1%–10.8% higher in 2010. However, complements in production benefited substantially from immigration, and immigration also lowered prices and raised the output of information technology goods by 1.9%– 2.5%, thus benefiting U.S. consumers.

Different studies have produced different results on who plans to transition into the U.S. job market, likely because they have been conducted at different periods when macroeconomic conditions of the home country might have significantly changed. In one of the earliest studies of student migration to the United States, Das (1969) found "a very small proportion of the African and Latin American students wish to remain here permanently. It is, students from the developed countries, who plan to stay in this country" (p. 130). However, later analysis identified those from less developed countries as more likely to stay (Finn, 2001; Glaser, 1978). Similarly, Finn (2001) found that 71% of international doctoral graduates in the science and engineering fields who received their degrees in 1999 were still in the United States in 2001. The research studies discussed above have limitations that may hinder our understanding of the factors impacting the labor market choices of international doctoral students. Most of these studies have not focused on the international doctoral student and the unique macroeconomic conditions in their home countries that could impact the outcome.

The studies on migratory decision making (e.g., Szelenyi, 2012) have used qualitative data to understand international student labor market decision making processes. However, the qualitative data is limited to very few countries and the experiences of very few individuals, which cannot be considered representative of the population. The studies that have used quantitative data (e.g., Das, 1969; Finn, 2001) are outdated and have relied on Immigration and Naturalization Service Data to reflect adjustment from nonimmigrant to immigrant status of international students. These data do not contain the rich attributes of Survey of Earned Doctorates, including the students' prior academic background and postgraduation plans. This study utilizes a conceptual model based on human capital theory and the push-pull model of international education flows, which presumes that the international doctoral student's labor market destination is a function of gender, country of citizenship, expected costs and benefits, and economic indicators in the home and host country.

Purpose of the Study

The purpose of this study is to examine the effects of financial aid and home-country macroeconomic indicators on international students' labor market destination choices. Hence, this study employed a nonexperimental research design using secondary data from the Survey of Earned Doctorates (SED) and economic data of the students' home country in addressing the following research questions:

1. What is the effect of demographic characteristics, financial aid packages, home-country economic factors, and institutional level variables on the location of the first job of international doctoral recipients?
2. Do international doctoral recipients differ in their labor market destination choices by region and classification of income of their home countries?

THEORETICAL FRAMEWORK

The conceptual framework for this research utilized the human capital theory and the push-pull model of international education flows. Human capital theory lends itself to the explanation of the decision-making process of international doctoral students. International doctoral students forgo wages and invest more in their foreign education with the hopes of gaining both intrinsic and extrinsic benefits. Extrinsic benefits from education include the higher expected future earnings as a result of their education and subsequent economic opportunities (Acemoglu et al., 2015; Becker, 1962). The extrinsic costs of foreign doctoral education include the tuition and fees paid to attain the education, plus the opportunity costs, which are the earnings the student forfeited upon undertaking full-time education. Financial aid subsidizes extrinsic costs, but the type and nature of funding could have an impact on the labor market destination outcomes for the student. For example, students receiving funding from their home country government or foreign fellowships or grants may be more likely to choose to return to their home countries upon graduation.

The conceptual model includes demographic characteristics, which can also be examined within the human capital theory opportunity cost framework. The opportunity cost includes the psychological costs of leaving friends and family, adjusting to the U.S. job market, and the time spent in efforts to attain H-1B employment rather than returning home. Societal norms place primary care responsibility on women, and thus, married women with dependents may choose to remain where their spouses are after graduation. Academic discipline is included in the model because their fields have research norms and standards that impact career choices. Also, with H-1B immigration laws, which favor those in the science, technology, engineering, and mathematics (STEM) fields to fill the demand for such skills in the United States' labor market, international students in those fields may be more likely to transition into the U.S. market than their non-STEM doctoral degree counterparts. Prior U.S. educational experience is also included in the framework because those who have spent a long time in the United States before beginning the doctorate will have invested more in their U.S. education, and may also have built more friendships and relationships, making them less likely to return home.

Human capital theory assumes opportunity costs affect student decisions that impact on their choices, but it does not explicitly consider macroeconomic conditions from the home country. The second part of the conceptual framework is based on the push-pull model of international education flows. Mazzarol and Soutar (2002) based the model on the decision process undertaken by an international student when choosing a study destination. In the first stage, the student decides to study abroad rather than in their home country. Several push factors influence this. Push factors refer to considerations within the home country such as the level of economic wealth, the degree of involvement of the developing country in the world economy, the priority placed on education by the government, and availability of educational opportunities in the home country that usually work together to push students to seek education internationally. These same factors will influence the student's decision to return home or remain in the host country. International doctoral students from low-income countries are more likely to be pushed out by harsher economic conditions in their country to search for greener pastures. In stage two, pull factors become crucial and determine why one country is preferred to another. Pull factors include the opportunities for employment during and after graduation, and the relative prosperity of the host country compared with the home country. Students from wealthier and more developed countries with lower unemployment rates and more opportunities for upward mobility are more likely to return home. The type of funding, the amount of time the student spends in the host country, and the relationships developed within the time spent studying in the United States will determine their labor market destination choices. For this study, we use this process to help understand the decision to exit or stay in a foreign country after the period of study.

The fundamental assumptions are that the more disadvantaged a country is, the more likely its citizens will seek opportunity outside its shores and that, given inequalities, there will be migration. That is, international students from countries with more economic, social, and political hardships are more likely to remain in the United States after graduation because of limited opportunities in the home country. For international students from poorer countries, these benefits will also include access to job opportunities in the host country and possibly higher earnings than what they would earn with the same degree at home because of international job market imperfections. Students from high-income countries and upper-middle income economies will gain higher intrinsic and extrinsic benefits from returning to their home countries.

While the push-pull model of education flows focuses more on the decision to embark on international doctoral studies rather than the decision to stay or return home after obtaining the doctoral degree, implicit in this model is that several negative or push factors in the country-of-origin cause people to move away, in combination with other positive or pull factors that attract migrants to a receiving country. The general criticism is that such models do not explain why within regions some people move and others stay, nor can they explain the direction of flows.

The neoclassical macroeconomic theory explains the development of labor migration within the process of economic development (Todaro, 1976). Wage differentials, caused by differences in the ratio of labor to capital, induce workers from low-wage countries to migrate to countries with high wages, thereby seeking to maximize individual incomes (Todaro, 1976). Migration causes wage differentials to decrease, ultimately leading to an equilibrium in which the remaining wage differential only reflects the costs of moving (Massey et al., 1993). In this type of model that focuses completely on labor markets, wage differentials measured in terms of observed wage rates at the origin and the destination are the main explanatory variables (Massey et al., 1993).

On the other hand, neoclassical microeconomic models assume that individuals make rational cost-benefit calculations. Assuming the benefits of expected higher wages are a function of wage differentials and employment rates, there are implied costs. Such costs include those related to travel, wages foregone while looking for work, efforts involved in adapting to another country, and the psychological costs of leaving friends and family (Todaro, 1976). Individual characteristics explain why individual cost-benefit calculations produce different outcomes concerning the decision to migrate. In general, the larger the difference between countries in terms of expected returns, the larger the size of the migration flow.

LITERATURE REVIEW

International graduate students' decisions regarding return to their home countries, remaining in the host society, or relocating to a third country are closely related to the literature on brain migration. The literature on international highly skilled migration has undergone significant changes since the 1960s. On one side of the argument is the notion of human capital transfers, with industrialized countries benefiting, while developing nations suffer significant losses in economic and educational development, as a result of the departure of their more educated citizens (Bhagwati & Dellalfar, 1973; Haque & Kim, 1995). There have been some studies on international students within the European Union given the open borders (Bryla, 2019; Sage et al., 2013). These studies have focused on all students and show that doctoral students were more likely to take jobs outside of their home country (Bryla, 2019).

In Johnson and Regets' (1998) study of foreign-born science and engineering graduate students earning doctoral degrees between 1988 and 1996, 63% of all students had plans to remain in the United States, while an additional 39% had firm plans to stay, indicating they had received firm offers to engage in postdoctoral research, gain employment, pursue teaching, or participate in other activities in the United States. (Johnson & Regets, 1998). In this study, while 47.9% of Chinese and 54.7% of Indian students indicated firm plans, only 22.6% of South Korean and 27.5% of Taiwanese students did so.

Desjardins (2012) sought to better understand the profile and labor market outcomes of recent doctoral graduates from Ontario universities who lived in Canada or the United States after 2 years of graduation. The results from the study revealed that at the time of graduation, 78% of the graduates had firm postgraduation plans, with 21% intending to leave Canada for the United States. Most who planned to move to the United States (62%) were young males with no dependents who studied life sciences, computer science, mathematics, or physical sciences, which reflects the demand and higher wages for such skills in the United States. Among the factors identified to attract Canadian doctoral graduates to the United States were: (a) the quality of the research facilities or the commitment to research of the organization; (b) better career advancement opportunities; (c) a greater availability of jobs in a particular field or industry; (d) a higher salary; (e) the quality of the research facilities or the commitment to research; and (f) the greater availability of jobs.

Szelenyi (2006) suggested that the less-developed a country is, the more elites of the country choose to pursue education and careers in other countries. According to Szelenyi (2006),

> This is not the case with nationals from the more highly developed countries, where mobility opportunities are more broadly shared and where people who move internationally have made much more marginal, risky, career decisions compared to those in nationalized careers from welfare-states with stable pay-offs at home. (p. 10)

Szelenyi (2006) used semi structured interviews and 26 international graduate students (Brazilian, Chinese, and Italian) who were enrolled in a U.S. Western institution in the 2003–2004 academic year to understand migratory decision-making. The author stated that:

> While the students presented a wide variety of experiences, intentions, and views, the transformational power of education abroad, within that diversity, was evident in redrawing students' conceptions of national boundaries and their own positions in relation to those boundaries. The students expressed a clear sense of national borders in their aspirations; the dilemma between returning to their home countries and staying within the geographical boundaries of the U.S., for example, was a major force shaping their plans for the future. (p. 84)

It is important to understand how economic conditions in the home country, in addition to individual and field variables, affect labor market choices of international doctoral students. This knowledge can guide career services on the U.S. campus, faculty advisors, and international advisors in better serving these students' career needs. In developing and implementing services to meet the needs of international doctoral students, Yang et al. (2002) identified the following ways that university career services can better meet the needs of international students: (a) Career services need to be responsive to the cultural contexts of the international students being served. (b) The services and interventions need to be provided through a cultural lens and not assumed that services designed for U.S.

students will necessarily meet the needs of international students. (c) More assessment tools and strategies that are culturally valid for diverse groups of international students need to be developed. (d) Having resources on career opportunities and employment-related information from other countries available is very important.

International graduate students are highly concerned about job placement because successful job placement may enable them to transition into the U.S. labor force and earn higher incomes than in their home countries (Hazen & Alberts, 2006). This may be particularly true for those from poorer countries. Advisors among the international student population are valued when they support conference attendance and co-authorship, refer job opportunities, and offer career advising. The findings in this study identify factors that affect the international doctoral recipients' choices across regions and field.

METHOD

Data Sources

We used the Survey of Earned Doctorates (SED) as the main source of data for our research. The SED is a nationally prepared, institutionally administered survey of all doctorate recipients in the United States. The survey is conducted annually for all doctorate recipients between the period July 1 and June 30 of the following year. We used an analytical sample of all international students who held a foreign visa during their time of study and who graduated between the period of 2011–2016. The institutional information (Carnegie classification) came from the National Center for Educational Statistics (NCES) Integrated Postsecondary Education Data System (IPEDS). We also used World Bank data, which provides the home country macroeconomic variables such as gross national income (GNI) per capita, wages, and unemployment rates of advanced degree holders. Data from the World Bank is for 2010–2015, which captures how macroeconomic conditions in the home countries of doctoral recipients impacted their labor market choices. Finally, this study uses data from the National Faculty Salary Survey, which provides information on the median U.S. assistant professor salary in different fields as a proxy for expected earnings.

Variables

The dependent variable reflects the students' labor market destination choice. In the SED, doctoral recipients are asked, "In what country or state do you intend to live after graduation? Please indicate the geographic location where you will work or study?" This variable reports the location (the United States or Non-United States) where the doctorate recipient will live, work, or study after graduation. In this study, the location of the first job (U.S. job) was coded as 0 (no) and 1 (yes). The independent variables that predicted these binary outcomes are categorized into five groups: student background characteristics, academic experiences, financial sources, external responsibilities, and economic conditions.

Student background characteristics include gender, nationality (with European students being the reference group for the first analysis and high-income countries being the reference in the second analysis), age, and parental education. Following the World Bank's (2017) categorization, we classified citizenship into six broad categories—North Africa, Sub-Saharan Africa, South East Asia, East Asia, Middle East, and Europe and Australia. We then conducted analyses by region and income classification. We determined first-generation status by using a combination of the mother's and father's levels of education. If neither parent attained a bachelor's degree, the student was considered a first-generation college student. If at least one of the parents attained a bachelor's degree or higher, we placed the student in the continuing generation category.

Prior educational experiences included whether the student received a bachelor's or master's degree from the United States. Doctoral students vary in the number of family responsibilities they hold during their pursuit of the degree. The predictor variables in this category included indicator variables of marital status and dependents. All three variables were dummy coded and included in the analysis. Employer type is a dichotomous variable representing the recipients either choosing or having obtained employment in a university/college or the industry/other type of employment (such as the military).

Financial aid variables include loans, assistantships, U.S. awarded grants and fellowships, and scholarships from the home country. Research, teaching assistantships, fellowships, and foreign sources were dummy coded. Loans for undergraduate and graduate education were combined and grouped into three categories based on frequency distribution—no debt, debt of $20,000 or less, and debt of $20,0001 or more.

The institutional level variable that is associated with labor market outcome is Carnegie classification. Carnegie classification is a dichotomous variable that refers to whether the institution is research extensive or research intensive. We also included the field of study to control for any unobserved effects. We coded the field of study into seven categories: biological sciences, engineering, physical sciences, social sciences, humanities, education, and business.

The push factors include macroeconomic variables in the home country, which work to push the student to obtain a foreign in less time while simultaneously impacting the labor market choices of the student. These include the real GNI per capita, unemployment rates, and wages of professionals in the home country. Pull factors refer to economic conditions in the United States (in comparison with the economic conditions of the home country of the students), that work to pull the student into the U.S. labor market. The U.S. assistant professor's salary in each field is a proxy for the living conditions in the United States.

Analytical Method

We used both logistic regression and then a hierarchical linear model (HLM) to determine the effects at two levels (individual and country). We used logistic regression to answer the first research question. Logistic regression is appropriate for binary dependent variables and allows researchers to determine the best combination of variables that predict an outcome by estimating the probability of the dependent variable occurring as the values of the independent variables change. The outcome variable, labor market destination outcome, was regressed on the independent variables. Separate regressions were conducted for the different economies to sharpen our focus on country differences, which is a major aim of the study. The effect sizes of the variables on the labor market destination are shown using odds ratios (Thomas & Heck, 2001).

Due to our interest in the effect of macroeconomic conditions of the home country, we conducted HLM to take advantage of the nesting structure of the data. We were able to then assess estimates of the effects of Level 2 variables (i.e., home country) more accurately on Level 1 outcome measures (Heck & Thomas, 2000). The Level 1 equation in HLM analysis is as follows:

$$Y_{ik} = \beta_{0jk} + \beta_{1k}(demographic\ variables)_{ik} + \beta_{2k}(finance\ variables)_{ijk} + \beta_{3k}(institutional\ variables)_{ik} + e_{ik} \quad (1)$$

where i = individual student, k = home country; Y_{ik} represents the dependent variable (labor market outcome) for an individual observation of student i from country k; β_{0k} is the intercept of the dependent variable and country-level predictor; β_{1k} is the slope of variable X_1 from country k; and e_i is the random error predicted for student i from country k.

An important assumption of HLM is that any Level 1 errors (r_{ijk}) follow a normal distribution with a mean of 0 and a variance of σ^2.

$$E(r_{ik}) = 0; var\ (r_{ik}) = \sigma^2 \quad (2)$$

$$\beta_{0k} = Y_{00} + Y_{01}w_k + \mu_{0k} \quad (3)$$

Y_{00} is the overall intercept; w_k is the country-level predictor; Y_{01} is the slope between the dependent variable, and the country-level predictor; and μ_{0k} is the random error component for the deviation of the intercept of a group from the overall intercept.

Treating missing data requires attention in HLM analysis (Wong & Mason, 1995). The HLM model assumes the data files are complete and does not allow for missing data; thus, we deleted any observations with missing data.

RESULTS

Table 1 presents the descriptive statistics of the categorical variables. For the sample, about 23% of international students who graduated between the period of 2011–2016 chose to return to their home country or a foreign country for employment while 77% chose to work in the United States. Sixty-two percent of the students obtained their doctorate degrees in STEM fields: biological sciences (18%), physical sciences (29%), and engineering (25%). Half of the students were from upper-middle income countries, followed by high-income countries (25%), lower-middle income countries (22%), and low-income countries (2.4%). Almost half of the students were from East Asia and the Pacific, followed by South Asia (17.96%), Europe and Central Asia (12.95%), Middle East and North Africa (8.79%), Latin America and the Caribbean (7.2%), Sub-Saharan Africa (3.25%), and North America (3.14%). Sixty percent of the sample had a previous degree from the United States. The majority of students were supported by a research assistantship (47%), and 83% of them indicated having secondary financial support in addition to their primary sources of funding.

Table 1: Descriptive Statistics for Categorical Variables

Variable	%
Postgraduation location	
Outside the United States	22.9
United States	77.1
Gender	
Male	62.7
Female	37.2
Parents' education	
First generation	38.2
Bachelor's degree	30.9
Graduate school	30.9
Region	
Europe and Central Asia	12.9
East Asia and Pacific	46.7
Latin America & the Caribbean	7.2
Middle East & North Africa	8.8
North America	3.1
South America	17.9
Sub-Saharan Africa	3.2
Economy	
High income	24.7
Upper-middle income	50.8
Lower-middle income	22.1
Low income	2.4
Prior academic experience	
U.S. bachelors	
No	91.2
Yes	8.8
U.S. masters	
No	40.2
Yes	59.0
Academic discipline	18.3
Biological sciences	29.3
Engineering	25.2

Variable	%
Physical sciences	11.2
Social sciences	4.6
Humanities	3.5
Education	3.7
Business management	4.0
Family/external responsibilities	
Single	
No	56.6
Yes	43.3
Dependents	
No	72.1
Yes	27.9
Program characteristics	
Prerequisite master's degree for doctoral program	
No	77.3
Yes	22.7
Financial resources	
Primary support	
Fellowships/grants/scholarships	20.8
Research assistantship	46.9
Teaching assistantship	22.8
Foreign government	4.3
Other (savings, loans, internships)	5.2
Full tuition remission	
No	31.1
Yes	68.9
Graduate level debt	
No loans	31.1
Loans <$20,000	68.9
Loans >$20,001	9.7
Secondary support	
No	16.1
Yes	83.9
Institutional variable	
Carnegie classification	
Research intensive	4.5
Research extensive	95.5

Table A1 presents the descriptive statistics of the continuous variables. The average age at which international doctoral students completed their degree was 32 years. Doctorate recipients from high income countries completed at an average of 34 years old, upper-middle income 31 years old, lower-middle income 32 years old, and low income 35 years old. The mean GNI per capita was $17,867, with high income having a mean of $38,416, and low income having a mean of only $2,003. This shows the level of wealth inequality among the countries of these students. The World Bank provided data for the wages of professionals in each country and employment rates among advanced degree holders for all economies except low-income countries. Hence, Table A2 only reports wages and unemployment rates for high income, upper-middle income, and lower-middle income economies. The table reveals that unemployment is the lowest in high income countries (5.36%) and highest in lower-middle income countries (14%). On the other hand, wages are highest in high income economies ($32,482) and lowest in lower-middle income countries ($2,388).

Using a conceptually grounded set of variables including the student characteristics, prior educational experience, financial support, and institutional characteristics, Table 2 presents the logistic results of labor market destination outcome with three separate models. The first model includes the four income classifications of the home country, the second includes the regions, and the third includes the economic variables from the home country. The logistic regression presents the odds ratio, which is the ratio of the probability that an event will occur to the probability that it will not happen. Factors with a greater value than 1 indicates the odds are increased, and those with odds less than 1 indicate the odds are decreased. The odds ratio can also be explained as the probability of the event occurring. The results of the first model show that the increased time to complete the doctorate significantly reduced the odds of choosing to work in the United States. The value for the odds of this variable indicates that every additional year reduced the odds of choosing to work in the United States by a factor of 0.95. Older recipients, single recipients, and recipients with dependents also had lower odds of choosing to work in the United States. Women, on the other hand, had higher odds of choosing to work in the United States. Having a U.S. bachelor's or master's degree and choosing to work in the academy rather than in the industry or other employment increased the odds of choosing to work and live in the United States by a factor of 1.64 for older recipients, 1.45 for single recipients, and 3.79 for recipients with dependents.

Table 2: Logistic Regression Results of Labor Market Outcomes

	By income		By region		Economic controls	
Variable	Odds ratio	*SE*	Odds ratio	*SE*	Odds ratio	*SE*
Student characteristics						
Female	1.09**	0.04	1.12***	0.04	0.97	0.08
Age	0.96***	0.04	0.96***	0.01	0.97***	0.01
Married	1.58***	0.07	1.57***	0.07	1.56***	0.13
Dependents	0.77***	0.04	0.77***	0.04	0.67***	0.07
First generation	1.03	0.04	0.99	0.04	1.11	0.09
Prior educational experience						
U.S. bachelor's degree	1.64***	0.13	1.59***	0.12	2.27***	0.29
U.S. master's degree	1.45***	0.06	1.49***	0.06	1.65***	0.14
Doctoral TTD completion	1.02	0.02	1.01	0.02	1.02	0.04
Year of doctorate completion	0.95***	0.02	0.95***	0.02	0.97	0.04

Variable	By income Odds ratio	By income *SE*	By region Odds ratio	By region *SE*	Economic controls Odds ratio	Economic controls *SE*
Employer type	3.79***	0.14	3.78***	0.14	5.29***	0.42
Academic discipline						
Biological sciences	1.89***	0.12	1.99***	0.13	1.59***	0.21
Engineering	2.61***	0.15	2.67***	0.16	1.83***	0.24
Physical sciences	2.18***	0.13	2.26***	0.13	1.87***	0.23
Humanities	1.19	0.10	1.17	0.10	1.06	0.17
Education	1.32***	0.13	1.35***	0.13	1.45	0.31
Business management	0.67**	0.12	0.66**	0.12	0.87	0.37
Financial support						
Secondary support	1.33***	0.07	1.37***	0.07	1.33**	0.17
Fellowship/grants/scholarships	0.71***	0.06	0.73***	0.06	0.55***	0.09
Research assistantship	1.39***	0.11	1.46***	0.12	0.92	0.17
Teaching assistantship	1.02	0.08	1.08	0.09	0.83	0.15
Foreign government	0.17***	0.02	0.17***	0.02	0.15***	0.03
Full tuition remission	1.38***	0.06	1.38***	0.06	1.36***	0.11
Graduate debt <$20,000	0.99	0.05	1.01	0.06	1.03	0.11
(Reference: No debt)						
Graduate debt >$20,001	0.91	0.05	0.91	0.05	0.89	0.11
Institutional characteristics						
Research extensive	0.88	0.08	0.87	0.079	1.242	0.232
Logged U.S. faculty salaries	4.79***	1.51	5.04***	1.59	4.42**	3.19
By income						
High income	0.61***	0.03	—	—	—	—
Low income	1.19	0.15	—	—	—	—
Lower-middle income	1.23***	0.06	—	—	—	—
By region						
East Asia and Pacific	—	—	1.18***	0.07	—	—
Latin America & the Caribbean	—	—	0.87	0.07	—	—
Middle East & North Africa	—	—	1.51***	0.12	—	—
North America	—	—	0.96	0.09	—	—
South Asia	—	—	2.01***	0.15	—	—
Sub-Saharan Africa	—	—	1.47***	0.16	—	—
Economic factors						
Logged GNI per capita	—	—	—	—	0.83**	0.13
Logged wages in home country	—	—	—	—	1.34***	0.13
Unemployment rates in home	—	—	—	—	1.05***	0.01
$p > \chi^2$	0.05		0.11		0.05	

Note. GNI = gross national income.

Compared with recipients in the social sciences, those in the biological sciences, engineering, physical sciences, and education were more likely to choose to work in the United States. Doctoral recipients from high income countries had lower odds than recipients of upper-middle income countries of choosing to work in the United States. On the other hand, recipients from lower-middle income countries were more likely to choose to remain in the United States. In the model controlling for region, we found all the same significance and direction for all variables except for the year of doctorate completion being statistically insignificant. Compared with recipients from Europe and Central Asia region, recipients from the Middle East and North Africa, South Asia, and Sub-Saharan Africa had greater odds of choosing to work in the United States.

With regards to sources of financial support, we found that holding a research assistantship during doctoral studies increased the odds of choosing to work in the United States. Also, having a secondary source of financial support also increased the odds of remaining in the United States. However, students who were supported by fellowships/grants and by their home country governments had significantly reduced odds of choosing to work in the United States. The final model controlled for economic factors from the home country but did not include students from low-income countries because data for wages and unemployment was unavailable. Just like in the first model, being an older student and having dependents decreased the likelihood of choosing to work and live in the United States. Married students had significantly higher odds of choosing to work in the United States. Across the board, higher U.S. faculty salaries significantly increased the odds of choosing to work in the United States. Among the economic indicators, we found that higher GNI per capita in the home country is associated with a decreased odd of choosing to work in the United States. Higher wages and higher unemployment rates increased the likelihood of choosing the U.S. labor market among students from higher income, upper-middle, and lower-middle income countries.

High Income Countries

Table 3 presents the logistic results of the predictors of labor market destination outcomes for each home country income classification. Those who were from high income countries who were older doctorate recipients or who had dependents were less likely to remain in the United States after graduation. Gender is not statistically significant with regard to the decision to stay or return home for recipients from high income countries. Recipients with longer time to doctoral degree completion and those with a U.S. bachelor's and master's degree were more likely to choose to work in the United States than their counterparts who obtained those degrees in foreign countries. Those who chose to work in the academy were also more likely to choose to remain in the United States. This is true for all economies. Among the academic disciplines, all the fields except for business are more likely than those in the social sciences to choose to work in the United States. The humanities discipline is not statistically significant. Among financial sources, recipients who were primarily funded through research assistantships and full tuition remissions were more likely to choose to work in the United States. The same is true for those who had secondary support to finance their degrees. On the other hand, recipients who received foreign government funds to finance their degree were less likely to remain in the United States after graduation. Attending a research extensive institution also increased the likelihood of choosing to work in the United States.

Table 3: Predictors of Labor Market Destination Outcomes Across Home Country Income Classifications (Logistic Regression)

	Full model		High income		Upper-middle income		Lower-middle income		Low income	
Variable	Odds ratio	*SE*	Odds ratio	*SE*	Odds ratio	*SE*	Odds ratio	*SE*	Odds ratio	*SE*
Student characteristics										
Female	1.09**	0.04	1.12	0.08	1.11	0.06	0.95	0.09	1.08	0.38
Age	0.96***	0.01	0.98**	0.01	0.97***	0.01	0.93***	0.01	0.95	0.03
Married	1.58***	0.06	1.49***	0.12	1.73***	0.10	1.35***	0.14	1.18	0.40
Dependents	0.79***	0.04	0.71***	0.06	0.87**	0.06	0.73***	0.08	0.62	0.20
First generation	1.04	0.04	0.99	0.07	1.07	0.06	1.05	0.11	1.16	0.36
Prior educational experience										
U.S. bachelor's degree	1.53***	0.11	2.17***	0.25	1.26***	0.16	1.38	0.28	1.84	0.98
U.S. master's degree	1.45***	0.05	1.30***	0.10	1.32***	0.07	1.99***	0.19	1.88	0.54
Doctoral time-to-degree completion	1.05***	0.01	1.05**	0.02	1.05**	0.02	1.05	0.03	0.98	0.09
Year of doctorate completion	1.09**	0.04	1.10	0.07	1.02	0.05	1.21**	0.11	1.20	0.33
Employer type	3.86***	0.14	6.76***	0.48	2.93***	0.16	2.86***	0.27	2.73***	0.87
Academic discipline										
Biological Sciences	2.23***	0.14	2.22***	0.28	1.69***	0.16	2.80***	0.41	0.77	0.32
Engineering	2.98***	0.17	2.08***	0.23	2.90***	0.24	2.55***	0.36	0.80	0.37
Physical Sciences	2.43***	0.14	1.76***	0.19	2.54***	0.22	2.02***	0.29	2.04	0.92
Humanities	1.06	0.09	1.12	0.15	1.02***	0.15	1.20	0.33	1.26	1.01
Education	1.32***	0.12	1.59***	0.25	1.22	0.18	1.23	0.30	0.25	0.17
Business Management	0.71	0.12	0.53	0.18	0.75	0.20	1.15	0.53	—	—
Financial support										
Secondary support	1.32***	0.07	1.45***	0.14	1.19**	0.09	1.53***	0.18	1.63	0.51
Fellowship/grants/ scholarships	0.76***	0.06	1.08	0.13	0.70**	0.10	0.32***	0.07	0.41	0.24
Research assistantship	1.53***	0.12	1.66***	0.22	1.49***	0.20	0.72	0.16	1.42	0.87
Teaching assistantship	1.15	0.09	1.23	0.16	1.04	0.14	0.61**	0.14	1.11	0.67
Foreign government	0.17***	0.02	0.24***	0.04	0.16***	0.02	0.14***	0.04	0.30***	0.78
Full tuition remission	1.38***	0.05	1.40***	0.10	1.38***	0.08	1.26**	0.12	1.55	0.43
Graduate debt <$20,000 (Ref: No debt)	1.04	0.06	1.08	0.11	0.88	0.07	0.99	0.11	2.52**	0.92
Graduate debt >$20,001	0.88**	0.05	0.87	0.09	0.86	0.08	0.98	0.16	2.52***	1.34
Institutional characteristics										
Research extensive	0.81**	0.07	1.23	0.20	0.78	0.12	0.89	0.15	0.49	0.27
U.S. faculty salaries	4.66***	1.42	6.12***	3.70	4.05***	1.79	3.15	2.38	0.86	2.67
$p > \chi^2$	0.05		0.17		0.00		0.06		0.00	

Upper-Middle Income Countries

For recipients from upper-middle income countries, age had a statistically significant effect. We found that older recipients, single recipients, and those with dependents are less likely to remain in the United States after graduation. Just like high income countries, having a U.S. bachelor's or master's degree and longer time to doctoral degree completion statistically increased the likelihood of remaining in the United States after graduation. Among the academic disciplines, only recipients from the STEM fields were more likely to choose to work in the United States after graduation. For upper-middle income recipients, funding through fellowships or scholarships and foreign governments sponsorship reduced the likelihood of remaining in the United States after graduation. On the other hand, research assistantships, secondary support, and full tuition remissions increased the likelihood of remaining in the United States postgraduation.

Lower-Middle Income Countries

We found that older recipients, single recipients, and recipients with dependents were less likely to choose to remain in the United States postgraduation. For this group of recipients, having a U.S. master's degree statistically increased the likelihood of choosing to stay in the United States for employment but having a U.S. bachelor's degree was not statistically significant. Similar to recipients from upper-middle income countries, we found that only STEM recipients were more likely to choose to work in the United States. For this group, having a research assistantship was not statistically significant in terms of labor market destination choices. We found that recipients who had secondary support and full tuition remission during their degree were more likely to remain in the United States. However, just like for other economies, recipients funded by a foreign government were less likely to remain in the United States.

Low Income Countries

For low-income countries, we found less statistical significance. There were very few statistical differences among students from low-income countries. Among the demographic and academic disciplines, the students did not statistically differ from one another in terms of the decision to stay in the United States or return to their home countries. This implies that the students in other academic disciplines were not statistically more or less likely to choose to work in the United States than those in the social sciences. The only sources of financial support that were statistically significant were foreign government and graduate debt. Just like their counterparts from richer economies, foreign government support reduced the odds of choosing to work in the United States after graduation while graduate debt significantly increased the odds of choosing to remain in the United States compared with others with no debt. The effect of debt over $20,000 had the largest magnitude among students from low-income countries.

HLM Analysis

To understand the effects at both levels—individual and country—we conducted the HLM analysis, and the results are presented in Table 4. The results of the HLM found that country of origin had a significant effect on the labor market choices for international doctorate recipients. After controlling for country of origin, we found that older recipients, single recipients, and those with dependents were less likely to choose to work in the United States. Having a U.S. bachelor's or master's degree increased the likelihood of choosing to work in the United States, and the magnitude was even larger for those who obtained their bachelor's degree in the United States. Those who chose to work in the academy (universities and colleges) rather than in the industry or other employment opportunities were more likely to choose to work in the United States. Recipients who received research assistantship and full tuition remission were more likely to choose to remain in the United States for work. The same is true for those who supplemented their primary sources of funding with secondary supports. However, doctoral recipients who were funded by foreign government or scholarships and grants were less likely to remain in the United States after graduation. We conducted separate analysis by academic field. In the STEM fields, we found that holding a U.S, master's degree, longer time to degree completion, and employer type significantly increased the odds of choosing to work in the United States. In engineering, research and teaching assistantships increased the odds of choosing to work in the United States, while foreign government sponsorship reduced the odds of remaining in the United States. Across all disciplines, foreign government support reduced the odds of the recipient choosing to work in the United States and choosing to work in a university/college increased the odds of remaining in the United States.

Table 4: Hierarchical Linear Modeling Results of International Doctoral Recipients Labor Market Destination Choices

Variable	Odds ratio	*SE*
Country-level variables		
Country intercept	0.41***	0.43
Logged gross national income per capita	0.03***	0.00
Student level variables		
Female	1.05	0.04
Age	0.97***	0.00
Married	1.43***	0.06
Dependents	0.83***	0.04
First generation	1.04	0.04
U.S. bachelor's degree	2.22***	0.17
U.S. master's degree	1.41***	0.05
Doctoral time-to-degree completion	1.04***	0.01
Year of doctorate completion	1.04	0.04
Employer type	3.08***	0.01
Secondary support	1.18***	0.06
Fellowship/grants/scholarships	0.83**	0.06
Research assistantship	1.75***	0.14
Teaching assistantship	1.09	0.09
Foreign government	0.30***	0.03
Full tuition remission	1.19***	0.05
Graduate debt <$20,000	0.98	0.05
Graduate debt >$20,001	0.97	0.06
Research extensive	1.04	0.09

DISCUSSION

The purpose of this study was to examine the effects of financial aid and home country macroeconomic indicators on international doctoral students' labor market destination choices. By conducting logistic regression analysis and HLM analysis, it was possible to compare the unique and common factors impacting international doctoral recipients in the United States across regions and economies of the home country. Previous studies on international doctoral recipients have not studied the relationship between individual characteristics, educational experiences, or financial aid sources and destination choices. Hence, this study was a novel attempt to investigate these relationships and offer possible explanations based on the results.

The results from this study yield interesting findings of how economic factors in the home country and financial aid sources are related to the labor market destination choices of international doctoral recipients in the United States. Furthermore, the results support previous research on brain migration and offer additional insights on what factors are important to consider for different home countries by region and level of development of the home country.

Single students and those with dependents are more likely to return to their home countries. Single recipients, particularly those from collectivists cultures, may feel that their chances of transitioning into marriage and family life are low if they remain in the United States, and recipients with dependents, born prior to their arrival in the United States, may face immigration challenges for their children, as well as adjustment and other psychological issues related to relocating dependents.

The human capital theory was supported. This study confirmed higher extrinsic costs will lead the recipient to seek higher benefits. We found that recipients who invested more in the U.S. system in form of tuition, fees, and general living expenses to obtain a U.S. bachelor's or master's degree were more likely to choose to work in the United States. Doctoral recipients who have spent a long time in the United States may seek to recoup some of their investment in the system. This is true across all economies and particularly true for low-income students who are 2 times more likely to choose to work in the United States compared with their counterparts with foreign education. It is also plausible that spending a long time in the United States implies that the recipients have more ties, relationships, and connections in the United States, making them less willing to return to their home countries. Employer type significantly increased the odds of choosing to work in the United States across all models. This is likely due to H-1B laws and regulations in the United States. American universities and colleges are not subject to the same H-1B lottery caps imposed on other labor market employers. Hence, doctoral recipients who have a desire to pursue academic careers are more likely to choose to work in the United States than their peers who desire to work in the industry or in nonacademic environments. It is possible that the odds are higher for university jobs because American universities have more sophisticated research facilities and offer higher standard of living and promotion opportunities than what is available in the home countries of many doctoral recipients. Many U.S. companies are located outside of the United States and can employ international students to work back home, but few U.S. universities have campuses abroad.

As expected, recipients from the STEM fields were more likely to choose to work in the United States and had greater odds than any other academic disciplines. This is true for all economies except for low-income countries, where only the physical sciences were significantly more likely than the social sciences to choose to work in the United States. H-1B visa immigration rules, which favor STEM recipients, may be largely responsible for this. In addition, students from upper-middle and lower-middle income countries (who make up the bulk of the STEM fields) may not have access to the same level of technological sophistication and scientific equipment in their home countries. For such recipients, returning to their home may imply that they would be unable to fully utilize the advanced knowledge and skills that they have acquired in the U.S. system.

The sources of financial support were also related to labor market destination choices for international doctoral recipients. Here, we found that U.S. sources of financial support, including research assistantships, teaching assistantships, and full tuition remissions, increase the likelihood of remaining in the United States to work after graduation. However, foreign sources, including foreign government aid, scholarships, and fellowships, reduced the likelihood of remaining in the United States to work. This is plausible for a couple of reasons. First, most foreign support is tied to commitments after graduation, including serving the home country government or sponsoring entity in an agreed capacity after obtaining the degree. In some countries, students are required to submit a proposed dissertation study and include how results from the study will be used in developing the country or advancing a foreign company. Secondly, most foreign sources of support typically cover all the student expenses while in the host country, and hence, the student may not feel the need to recoup their investment from the U.S. system after graduation. Finally, foreign aid, particularly from the government, may build or further foster a sense of patriotism in the recipient, causing them to be more likely to return to their home country. In the sub analysis, we found that foreign aid reduced the likelihood for remaining in the United States for all economies except low-income countries. Harsher economic conditions combined with unstable political climates that plague these countries may be responsible for this result. For low-income countries, we found that debt significantly increased the odds of remaining in the United States after graduation by more than 3 times for those who had debt over $20,000. Lower wages in these countries may imply that doctoral recipients may be unable to repay such loans if they return home.

The more interesting findings in this study involve the effects of the economic factors on labor market destination choices. The push-pull model was supported. Home country GNI per capita was found to be an important factor related to student choices, a finding that is consistent with Agbonlahor (2019) and the Szelenyi's (2006) study on migratory decision making. Szelenyi (2006) found that students from less developed countries were more likely to choose to transition into the U.S. labor force. This study found that higher GNI per capita was associated with decreased likelihood of remaining in the United States. It also found that higher unemployment rates in the home country significantly increased the likelihood of choosing to remain in the United States. A conflicting result is that higher wages in the home country were also related to increased likelihood of remaining in the United States. On the other hand, fields with higher U.S. faculty salaries significantly increase the likelihood of remaining in the United States. Compared with upper-middle income students, students from high income countries were less likely to remain in the United States after graduation, while recipients from low-middle- and low-income countries were more likely to remain in the United States after graduation. Compared with recipients from Europe and Central Asia, recipients from the Middle East and North Africa, South Asia, and Sub-Saharan Africa were more likely to choose to remain in the United States after graduation. This conclusively points to the economic conditions and opportunities for upward mobility available in those economies and regions. The results support the push-pull model, in that doctoral recipients in the United States make comparisons between economic conditions of their home countries and the United States, and the larger the difference, the larger the size of migration flow (Todaro, 1976).

Limitations of the Study

A limitation of this study is that it does not consider the role of mentoring in international doctoral students' labor market outcomes. Doctoral advisors play an important role because they are the primary socialization agent at the doctoral level and the principal connection between the student and the department (Girves & Wemmerus, 1988; Golde, 2005; Tinto, 1975; Weidman et al., 2001). International student literature has also examined the role of advisors in the socialization of students from foreign cultures. Jindal-Snape and Ingram (2013) discussed the importance of advisors on the adjustment of international doctoral students in developing supportive networks for student success. Thus, the relationship the advisor holds with the advisee may directly impact the students' socialization, the quality of their doctoral experiences, and their postgraduate options through the provision of opportunities to attend and present at conferences, participate in research projects, and co-author publications.

Secondly, because this study utilized existing data, perceptions of international students about the quality of their international education are not available. The dataset does not include other personal or institutional factors that could impact on the ability of the individual to access a U.S. position such as the quality of career services of the university, the number of publications or experience the student has, the faculty rank of the advisor, or marriage to a U.S. citizen. These factors could influence the ability of the student to secure a U.S. job more than some of the explanatory variables included in this study. It is also noteworthy that because the SED is collected when the students have just graduated, a number of the students may not have firm job plans and hence, the analysis is limited to those who know their job placement and location at the time of the survey.

Implications

The study reveals a need to develop career services support for international students that are tailored to their unique concerns and vocational challenges. Besides providing services such as resume and cover letter editing, university career services need to position international recipients to make a successful transition into the labor market. When international students seek to work in the United States, they need to go through rigorous immigration guidelines and bureaucratic procedures (Shih & Brown, 2000). Students who want to return to their home countries also need guidance as they return to a system that could have changed dramatically since they relocated to the United States. The results from the study found that international recipients from low-income countries with debt of more than $20,000 were more likely to choose to remain in the United States. Since it is not possible for all these students to transition into the U.S. labor market because of limited H-1B visas, university career services tailored to the global economy would be beneficial in assisting these students to transition to other high-income countries in need of their talent or skill. We recommend that university career services hire well-trained specialists tasked with the responsibility of understanding different countries' employment needs, immigration requirements, and opportunities by academic field and job roles. This could be posted on the university career services webpage and updated regularly. For example, career services could have a page where students could search for faculty positions in Europe and whether non-European Union citizens could apply for such positions. Similarly, positions in Sub-Saharan Africa, the Middle East and Africa, and all other regions could be included. This might ultimately yield to a more uniform distribution of talent and skill and reduce wage inequalities as a result of asymmetry of information.

The international student literature has also examined the role of advisors in the socialization of students from foreign cultures. International students have reported changing their faculty advisors because of lack of intercultural competence, reluctance to supervise a topic, racial discrimination, and language barriers (Wei et al., 2012). U.S. faculty members may be more reluctant to supervise a topic if the research is on a foreign country that they know little or nothing about. This has led many international students to choose topics within their advisors' expertise and interest. The problem with this is that most students will then be researching an issue important in the United States but may not have practical implications in their home country. If international students continue to develop thesis research that cannot be applied to local or national issues in their country, then the likelihood of returning home will remain low. On the other hand, recipients with foreign aid are supported by their government to research a particular issue and provide results or policy implications that can be applied to their national context.

Based on this finding and the extant literature on international doctoral students, we recommend that academic departments and the institutions work on internationalizing the curriculum so that international students can develop solutions to their home country's specific needs while training with more sophisticated technology and accessing more advanced knowledge in the United States. An internationalized curriculum and co-curriculum ensure that both domestic and international students are exposed to international perspectives and build global competence. An internationalized curriculum will address global issues, reinforce international elements of the curriculum, develop solutions to problems in countries outside the United States, facilitate discussion and interaction among students of different backgrounds, and support the integration and success of international students.

The study's framework was derived from the human capital theory and the push-pull model to explain international doctoral recipients' labor market destination choices. Prior to this study, international students have been examined along with domestic students, and thus, the unique factors in their countries of origin that impact their outcomes have not been considered. The new framework developed in this study explains how student characteristics, in addition to economic factors in the home country (push factors) and economic factors in the United States (pull factors), intersect to affect international doctoral students' choices and outcomes.

Finally, longitudinal data that tracks a sample of international doctoral recipients both in the United States and when they return home should be developed. A limitation of this study is that the international doctoral recipients' destination is for 1 year after graduation. While international students are legally authorized to work for any employer in the United States through the Optional Practical Training, most of them will eventually require their employers to sponsor their H-1B visas in order to remain in the United States. Hence, several of the students from this study who chose to remain in the United States will eventually have to leave the United States if they are unable to secure a position in which the employer is willing to file their H-1B visa and demonstrate that a United States citizen does not have the required skill for the job or the job search has been unable to fill the position domestically. Future studies need to use longitudinal data to study actual and long-term labor market destination outcomes of international doctoral recipients. This will provide a richer and deeper analysis of their transitions, career development, and life outcomes.

Note

Appendices for this article can be found on the JIS website at https://www.ojed.org/index.php/jis

REFERENCES

Acemoglu, D., Gallego, F. A., & Robinson, J. A. (2015). Institutions, human capital, and development. *Annual Review of Economics, 6*(1), 875–912.

Agbonlahor, O. (2019). *The impact of financial aid factors and home country economic conditions on international doctoral students' time-to-degree completion and labor market destination choices*. (Unpublished dissertation, Central Michigan University).

Becker, G. S. (1962). Investment in human capital: A theoretical analysis. *The Journal of Political Economy, 70*(5), 9–49.

Bhagwati, J., & Dellalfar, W. (1973). The brain drain and income taxation. *World Development, 1*(1–2), 94–101.

Bound, J., Khanna, G., & Morales, N. (2017). *Understanding the economic impact of the H1B visa on the U.S.* NBER Working Paper Series. https://www.nber.org/papers/w23153.pdf

Bryła, P. (2019). International student mobility and subsequent migration: the case of Poland. *Studies in Higher Education*, *44*(8), 1386–1399.

Das, M. S. (1969). *Effects of foreign students' attitudes towards returning to the country of origin on the national loss of professional skills.* Oklahoma University Press.

Desjardins, L. (2012, July). Profile and labor market outcomes of dcotoral graduates from Ontario universities. *Culture, Tourism, and Center for Education Statistics: Research Paper Series, 98*, 1–107.

Finn, G. (2001). *Stay rates of foreign doctorate recipients from U.S. institutions, 1999.* Oak Ridge Institute for Science and Education.

Girves, J. E., & Wemmerus, V. (1988). Developing models of graduate student degree progress. *The Journal of Higher Education, 59*(2), 163–189.

Glaser, W. (1978). *The brain drain: Emigration and return.* Pergamon.

Golde, C. M. (2005). The role of the department and discipline in doctoral student attrition: Lessons from four departments. *The Journal of Higher Education, 76*(6), 669–700.

Haque, N., & Kim, S.-J. (1995). Human capital flight: Impact of migration on income and growth. *IMF Staff Papers, 42*(3), 577–607.

Hazen, H. D., & Alberts, H. C. (2006). Visitors or immigrants? International students in the U.S. *Population, Space, and Place, 12*(1), 201–216.

Heck, R. H., & Thomas, S. L. (2000). *An introduction to multilevel modelling techniques.* Lawrence Erlbaum.

Jindal-Snape, D., & Ingram, R. (2013). Understanding and supporting triple transitions of international doctoral students: ELT and SuReCom Models. *Journal of Perspectives in Applied Academic Parctice*, *1*(1), 17–24.

Johnson, J., & Regets, M. C. (1998, June 22). *International mobility of scientists and engineers to the United States: Brain drain or brain circulation?* [SRS Issue Brief]. National Science Foundation.

Massey, D., Arango, J., Hugo, G., Kouaouci, A., Pellegrino, A., & Taylor, J. (1993). An evaluation of international migration theory: The North American Case. *Population and Development Review, 20*(4), 699–751.

Mazzarol, T., & Soutar, G. N. (2002). "Push-pull" factors influencing international student destination choice. *International Journal of Education Management, 16*(2), 82–90.

Migration Policy Institute. (2018, May 9). *International students in the United States.* https://www.migrationpolicy.org/article/international-students-united-states

Sage, J., Evandrou, M., & Falkingham, J. (2013). Onwards or homewards? Complex graduate migration pathways, well-being, and the 'parental safety net'. *Population, Space and Place, 19*(6), 738–755.

Shih, S.-F., & Brown, C. (2000). Taiwanese International students: Acculturation level and vocational identity. *Journal of Career Development, 27*, 35-47. doi:https://doi.org/10.1023/A:1007796509562

Szelenyi, K. (2006). Students without borders? Migratory decision-making among international graduate students in the U.S. *Knowledge, Technology, and Policy, 19*(3), 64–86.

Thomas, S., & Heck, R. (2001). Analysis of large sclae secondary data in higher education research: Potential perils associated with complex sampling designs. *Research in Higher Education, 142*(5), 517–540.

Tinto, V. (1975). Dropouts from higher education: A theoretical synthesis of recent literature. *Review of Educational Research, 45*, 89–125.

Todaro, M. (1976). A model of labor migration and urban unemployment in less developed countries. *The American Economic Review, 59*(1), 138–148.

Wei, M., Liao, K. Y.-H., Heppner, P. P., Chao, R. C.-L., & Ku, T.-Y. (2012). Forbearance coping, identification with heritage culture, acculturative stress, and psychological distress among Chinese international students. *Journal of Counseling Psychology, 59*(1), 97–106. https://doi.org/10.1037/a0025473

Weidman, J. C., Twale, D. J., & Stein, E. L. (2001). Socialization of graduate and professional students in higher education: A perilous passage? *ASHE-ERIC Higher Education Report, 28*(3).

Wong, G. Y., & Mason, W. (1995). The hierarchy logistic model for multilevel analysis. *Journal of the American Statistical Association, 80*(391), 513–524.

The World Bank. (2017). *World Bank country and lending groups*. https://datahelpdesk.worldbank.org/knowledgebase/articles/906519-world-bank-country-and-lending-groups

Yang, E., Wong, C., Hwang, M., & Heppner, M. J. (2002). Widening our global view: The development of career counselling services for international students. *Journal of Career Development, 28*(3), 203–213.

OSASOHAN AGBONLAHOR, PhD, is a postdoctoral research associate in the department of Leadership, Research, and Foundations at the University of Colorado - Colorado Springs. Her intellectual interests are in the fields of the economics of education, international education, and higher education policy. Her research focuses on labor market outcomes of higher education, the career trajectories of international doctoral recipients and the participation of underrepresented minorities in STEM fields. Email: oagbonla@uccs.edu

FRIM AMPAW, EdD, is Professor of Higher Education in the Department of Educational Leadership at Central Michigan University. Her research focuses on labor market implications of higher education, persistence of women and underrepresented minorities in STEM fields and the transition and persistence of students through the various levels of higher education. Email: ampaw1fd@cmich.edu

Peer-Reviewed Article

© *Journal of International Students*
Volume 11, Issue 2 (2021), pp. 484-504
ISSN: 2162-3104 (Print), 2166-3750 (Online)
doi: 10.32674/jis.v11i2.1548
ojed.org/jis

Chinese International Scholars' Work–Life Balance in the United States: Stress and Strategies

Chang Su-Russell
Illinois State University, USA

Anthony G. James
Miami University, USA

ABSTRACT

Acculturative stress and strategies have been investigated with undergraduate international students in the United States. However, not much is known about scholars who come to the United States for advanced educational or career opportunities. Guided by Berry's (2006) acculturative stress coping adaptation theory, the current study explored lived experiences of CISs through longitudinal interviews. Inductive analysis revealed themes about stressors that challenged work–life balance. Three types of coping strategies for these stressors were identified: (a) grandparents' and spousal support, (b) mental strengths, and (c) planning ahead for the future of their family. Practical implications are discussed for supporting CISs. Findings of the current study expand our knowledge about CISs' challenges and strategies for maintaining work–life balance.

Keywords: acculturation strategies, Chinese international scholars, work–life balance

International students' acculturation to the United States has gained more attention over the last decade, particularly with the increasing number of Chinese undergraduate and graduate students matriculating in U.S. institutions of higher learning. Approximately 363,341 Chinese students enrolled in U.S. institutions of higher education during the 2017–2018 academic year, which represents about 33% of the total number of international students studying in the United States

(Institute for International Students, 2018). Many of these students pursue educational and work experiences beyond undergraduate training. For this study, we focus on scholars of Chinese descent who are linked to U.S. institutions of higher learning and fit into one of the following categories: enrolled in doctoral training, pursuing a postdoctoral fellow or visiting scholar appointment, or obtaining permanent professoriate positions in the United States. Less is known about the acculturative stress and strategies of this group of Chinese international scholars (CISs), especially as they navigate in academia while simultaneously balancing their family life in a new culture.

The current study focuses on CISs and how they manage acculturation stressors to maintain a work–life balance in the United States. CISs deserve research attention for three reasons: (a) CISs are a collective group who are constantly influenced by the economic and political environment in the United States, such as the immigration policy; (b) CISs are transitioning to a new culture with new norms and expectations in the United States; and (c) CISs must balance pursuing an academic career while being caregivers. CISs in the current study shared these commonalities, even though they have different visa statuses. Importantly, CISs in the current study shared similar lived experiences with some within-group variations that enriched the data: different academic standings and various family structures.

THEORETICAL FRAMEWORK

Acculturation Theory

Stan Knapp (2009) noted that "theory performs vital descriptive, sensitizing, integrative, explanatory, and value functions in the generation of knowledge about families" (p. 133). Knapp conceptualized explanatory functions of theory as a process that allows scholars to develop ideas that help explain, understand, or interpret data. This study relies on Berry's (2006) theory that acculturation experiences occur on both the individual and group level, and these experiences lead to long-term adaptation. First, acculturation demands come from the conflict between an individual's culture of origin and the host culture, along with each set of norms and expectations. Second, in the process of navigating two cultures, individuals might encounter stressors due to the dissonance between these two cultures. When the high-level stressors sustain, they become acculturative stress, and individuals can address these stressors by developing coping strategies that promote adaptation.

Chinese International Scholars' Stress and Strategies Adjusting to Their Life in the United States

The acculturative stressors that CISs experience challenge work–life balance during their time in the United States. For many CISs, they acculturate as a family. The scholars' mental, physical, and academic wellbeing is influenced by their family life due to family and societal expectations (family systems theory; Cox &

Paley, 1997). The current study addresses the lack of literature investigating how this acculturation process occurs for CISs (i.e., stressors and coping strategies) as they strive for balancing work and life in the United States.

The few studies on Chinese international postgraduate students have identified acculturative stressors that derive from language barriers (Choi, 2006; Sato & Hodge, 2009; Yan & Berliner, 2013), which can result in low esteem and a sense of incompetence (Leki, 2001). Moreover, high levels of cultural distance between work and family can lead to great stress (Ward, 1996). For instance, CISs come from a collectivistic culture and must adjust to an individualistic culture that places a higher value on autonomy, individualism, and independence. How this manifests in U.S. classrooms (e.g., assertiveness) might put CISs at a disadvantage (Kim et al., 2001). Additionally, the acculturative stress arises from differences in education systems that result in new academic expectations, such as negotiating complex relationships with advisors while a part of U.S. institutions (Sato & Hodge, 2009; Yeh & Inose, 2003). These stressors can accumulate and influence CISs' psychological wellbeing, especially due to language barriers and becoming an ethnoracial minority (Lee & Rice, 2007).

Acculturative stress has been studied at length with Chinese international students, particularly with a heavy focus on Chinese undergraduates (e.g., Heng, 2017; Heng, 2018a; Heng, 2018b), or samples of both undergraduates and graduate students (Gautam et al., 2016; Li et al., 2018; Zhang, 2018). Postgraduate scholars from abroad are likely to experience stressors that are distinct from those of undergraduates, considering they are likely older and in a different phase of family life.

Work–Family Balance

The literature on work–life balance is broad and covers a wide range of topics. For the sake of parsimony, we focus only on the research relevant to the family life of the target population for this study.

Existing research reveals the stressors and management strategies of U.S.-born citizens balancing family and academic work. Sallee's (2015) study of 18 masters-level graduate students revealed a variety of strategies utilized to fulfill academic responsibilities (e.g., time management, prioritizing their parental role with academic roles, etc.). U.S. doctoral students utilized strategies such managing their time, clarifying responsibilities, and seeking social support across contexts to promote balance (Martinez et al., 2013). What remains unknown are the specific coping strategies of CISs with children when trying to balance family life and acculturating into their academic or career program. For CISs, work–family balance likely presents additional complexity in their acculturative adjustment compared with domestic parent students, because acculturative stress and strategies are not only encountered individually, but also within the context of complex family structures. CISs may have aging parents living with or near them in the United States while they work or study. Additionally, CISs may need to develop their own coping skills and then foster these skills in their children.

This study extends the work–life balance literature to the CIS population in the United States.

Research Questions

Guided by the integrated conceptual framework, the current study aims to investigate two research questions. First, in order to maintain work–life balance, what challenges have CISs experienced? Second, in order to maintain work–life balance, how have CIS coped with these challenges?

METHOD

Research Paradigm and Methodology

We used interpretivism to guide the current research. The core of interpretivism is to recognize the existence of the subjective meanings that are experienced by acting persons (Pizam & Mansfeld, 2009). Guided by this research paradigm, we aimed to search for the interpretations of culturally and historically situated social experiences of the participants, which are unique, qualitative, and in-depth (Crotty, 1998; Goldkuhl, 2017). Interpretivism is appropriate for this study because we believe the nature of CISs' reality and experience are situated in a culturally derived world where lived experiences have subjective meanings. Due to the nature of interpretations of social meanings as the guiding philosophy for the current study, we used hermeneutic phenomenology as our research methodology as it is the science of interpretations of social phenomenon through written or spoken texts with an emphasis on everyday conversations that reflect everyday lived experiences. According to hermeneutic phenomenology, meanings are expressed and can be interpreted through the way language is given. We aimed to identify and clarify the meanings of CISs' everyday life in the culturally and socially constructed world (van Manen, 1990). The goal of the current research is exploratory rather than explanatory, expanding our understanding of CIS's work–life balance in the United States. The current research sought to explore what problems CISs encountered and how they coped with them.

Data were collected over the course of three interviews with each participant, a data collection method commonly used in phenomenological studies (Seidman, 2006). The three interviews allowed the investigation of CISs' lived experiences at different points of time: (a) previous and present time; (b) detailed current academic and family life; and (c) future plans. This helped participants reconstruct their experiences as a CIS regarding their work–life balance.

The focus on finding varying perspectives (Lincoln & Guba, 2000; Olesen, 2000) guided researchers to conduct in-depth qualitative research using the purposeful sampling strategy to recruit a small group of participants ($N = 6$) who had similar lived experiences with various characteristics (Creswell, 2015; Gautam et al., 2016; Halic et al., 2009; Xing & Bolden, 2019). Purposeful sampling strategy helped us select participants with rich information related to work–life balance as a CIS in the United States. This sampling strategy is effective especially when there are limited resources and the research population is very specific and not commonly accessible (Patton, 2002). According to Morse (1991), this is an acceptable sample size for phenomenological research. Data saturation was evident when not much new information was generated from the interviews (Saunders et al., 2018).

Positionality Statement

The primary author led the data collection and analysis processes and is bilingual in English and Mandarin Chinese, which allowed for the study participants to feel comfortable sharing their lived experiences in a language they felt could best express their thoughts and feelings. The second author is an ethnic minority scholar in the United States and contributed to refining the theoretical framework. We both contributed to interpreting findings and the implications of the study. It is likely, however, our ethnoracial backgrounds influence our interpretations of the data. To avoid speaking for the data, we made efforts to bracket existing biases or assumptions. To avoid bias, we took notes on all preconceptions that arose about the study population in order to bracket these existing assumptions during data collection and analysis process (Lincoln & Guba, 1985).

Sites and Participants

This study was approved by the university Institutional Review Board of the first author. We recruited participants from a listserv that was used by students and scholars and by word of mouth in a Midwestern college town. We conducted a total of 18 face-to-face interviews with six CISs. All six participants shared similar lived experiences, which was being a postgraduate scholar who had a young child living in the United States. The within-group variations that enriched the sample and data were that these scholars were from different academic backgrounds and were in different academic standings. Their family structure while in the United States also varied (see Table 1).

We conducted interviews primarily in English, unless study participants felt they could not express themselves fully in English, at which point they used Mandarin Chinese. Each of the 18 interviews lasted 30–60 min. Interview protocol is presented in Appendix A.

All six CISs had similar lived experiences as international scholars from mainland China working in a U.S. institution with young children. They possessed different views regarding challenges and strategies in balancing these two roles in the United States. Those differences were rooted in varying characteristics (levels of training or status of scholarship, gender, and academic programs).

Table 1: Demographics of the Participants

Name	Years	Academic position	Gender	Child age	Child gender	Marital status	Spouse	Grandparents
Ling	6.5	Doctoral student	F	3.5	M	Married	Yes	Yes, on and off
Yan	5	Doctoral student	F	2.5	M	Married	Yes	Yes, on and off
Peng	10	Faculty	M	7	F	Married	Yes	No
Li	1	Postdoc fellow	F	1	F	Married	No	Yes
Ting	4	Postdoc fellow	F	3.5	M	Divorcing	No	Yes
Fang	1.5	Visiting scholar	F	5	M	Married	No	Yes

Note. Names are pseudonyms. Years = total number of years living in the United States at the time interviews occurred; spouse = whether participant's spouse was currently living in the United States; grandparents = whether at least one of child's grandparents had been living in the United States since child's birth or arrival.

Data Analysis Procedure

We used inductive analysis (Hatch, 2002) via an open-coding process in NVivo. The study goal was not to quantify experiences but rather to understand CIS stress and strategies to have a work–life balance. During interviews and after data transcription emerging themes and salient points were noted. Across the interviews, the themes and salient points reemerged during subsequent readings through the transcripts. We used open-coding by targeting the interactions that answered the research questions and highlighting the meaningful units to create codes line-by-line. Upon completion for one participant, we repeated this process for the next participant. We then coded the data and checked against and compared to themes and points found in the previous participant's coding (Corbin & Strauss, 2014).

Trustworthiness

Multiple tools can be employed to ensure trustworthiness (Lincoln & Guba, 1985). We used field journals to accumulate information and make sense of three interviews. We used personal logs to keep a record of personal biases, noting frustrations, post interview self-reflections, and methodological adjustments while transcribing interviews to note more in-depth probing opportunities. Secondly, one of the authors had prolonged engagement among the CIS community, building rapport with individuals, while being mindful of possible distortions of the research process. Third, we made initial contact through community engagement to assure the CISs' understanding of procedures of the research. Next, we used peer debriefing to get feedback on coding, outline a writing strategy, and make methodological adjustments. We used audio recordings and note-taking to maintain referential adequacy, along with multiple listening sessions and verifying the original data sources. We performed informal member checks with CISs who were parents but who were not in the current study. These nonparticipant members helped check analytic themes, interpretation of our results, and the conclusions for this study.

RESULTS

Bronfenbrenner's (1986) ecological system theory argued that individuals' lived experiences are influenced by their environments, which he split into five levels: the microsystem, mesosystem, exosystem, macrosystem, and the chronosystem. CISs struggled with balancing work and life (mesosystem), which is influenced by external (macro- and exosystem) factors. Family members (microsystem), especially spouses and their children's grandparents, helped CISs maintain work–life balance. Their future career decision (chronosystem) was determined by their family, mainly as a child-centered decision-making process when it came to their future career. Such a decision-making model demonstrated the interactions between person and environment and these interactions constantly evolved in proximal progress (Bronfenbrenner & Morris, 2006).

Challenges to Maintaining Work–Life Balance

CISs experienced psychological stress in trying to maintain a good work–life balance. Their stress came from being new to their academic program in a new education system, in conjunction with being a parent raising a young child in a new culture. In their second interview, all six participants discussed in length all the challenges they encountered in the United States. CISs' psychological stress and emotional turbulence was heightened when they strived to keep a balance of their work and their relationship with their young child. CISs also experienced frustrations when they aimed to maintain a balance of their work and their relationship with their spouse.

My Work and My Child

A consensus from their interviews emerged when CISs discussed their children. All CISs gave the highest priority to their children's wellbeing despite their stressful workload and pressure to succeed in their professional career. Their ways of attending to their children's wellbeing varied. Two CISs in the current study suffered intensely during the first few months of their staying in the United States since their ways of prioritizing children's wellbeing was to leave children behind in mainland China while they came to the United States to pave the way for their children's arrivals.

Both Li and Fang (pseudonyms) left their young children with their children's fathers and grandmothers back in China when they first arrived in the United States. They reasoned that by being here first without their children, not only could they smoothly transition to their academic career before their children's arrival, they could also settle down and make a new home out of their rental place for their children's transition to the United States. During the time being apart from their children, they struggled intensely emotionally because they missed their family, especially their children. They were also lonely because they had not established a social group in the community.

Sometimes the imbalance of work and life was because the CIS gave birth to children as they transitioned to a new academic program. Yan shared that she suffered from postpartum depression after giving birth to her son. "I couldn't focus very well on my study," she said. She had some emotional problems especially during the first 4 weeks postpartum. She expressed that

> My life was just messed up. I remember that when I first took class, it was very stressful. I feel like it was totally different life. In the first few months, he cried a lot. I need to feed him a lot. I cannot sleep very well, and in the meantime, I need to focus on my study. I'm from China, but the classroom is in English. I need to read a lot. The homework is about writing, not only several paragraphs, but 10 pages, for homework assignment. I need to talk a lot on the class.

She went on to discuss her struggles as a new parent still in the first few months of postpartum while battling her new role as a PhD student to survive, catch up, and succeed.

At the time of the interviews, all CISs were living with their young children. Similar to non-CISs, participants expressed that their work–life balance was well maintained in the aspect of their child's wellbeing. But when their children would get sick, it went off balance again. When asked what they thought about being in academia and simultaneously being a parent with a young child in the United States, Ling said, "Hard to handle … I have to miss some of the class sessions, if my son is sick, and [I need to] stay at home taking care of my son. I think it's not easy to handle parenting and being a student."

Other times, it was more about their children's mental and emotional wellbeing that CISs considered on top of their job responsibilities. Peng, Ting, and Fang shared their children's happiness was number one for them. In order to ensure that their children were happy, Peng "suffered a lot." He added, "I have to sacrifice myself to make both (my daughter and my boss) happy." This was because he was in academia and his boss believed that his time should be flexible when it came to research. As a H-1B1 visa holder at the time of the interviews, he had a lot of anxiety about job security while dealing with a harsh and demeaning boss. Both Ting and Fang had a preschool-aged child at the time of the interviews. Their children did not speak English growing up in China. When they first arrived in the United States and started school in a local daycare center, they did not know any English. Their preschoolers cried, struggled, and felt scared and confused. Fang's child said to her he did not want to go to school and threw tantrums in the mornings during the first few weeks of his time in the United States. Both Fang and Ting had very tight schedules, with the former as a visiting scholar with a more than 8-hr workday each day, and the latter recently having secured a postdoc position after working with a demeaning boss for a while in a different university.

My Work and My Spouse

Long distance relationships were also prevalent among CISs. Among six CISs, three (Li, Ting, and Fang) were living in separate countries from their spouses at the time of interviews. Their spouses had jobs in mainland China and did not see it possible to identify a promising opportunity to work in the United States.

In addition to these internal challenges to work–life balance, external factors at exo- and macrolevels further challenged work–life balance.

Becoming A Minority: External Challenges in Maintaining Work–Life Balance

International students, scholars, and families often find themselves as ethnoracial minorities as soon as they arrive in the United States. This is not only due to their physical appearance, but also to their English being a second language and their "alien" status.

"Secondary Citizens"

Challenges to CIS work–life balance came from local communities, such as when CISs tried enrolling their children at childcare or public schools. In explaining this, Fang (visiting scholar; mother of a 5-year-old child) shared that a local elementary school would not take her son's application for enrollment simply because he was Chinese. The administrators assumed that her son was not proficient in English and had to take the English language learner (ELL) classes, which were not offered at their school. In fact, Fang's son's English tested as proficient in reading, listening, verbal, and writing ability. A few weeks after the third interview was conducted, Fang shared that her child was able to attend that local elementary school after he proved his abilities on an ELL test, which he was able to take as a result of intense negotiations between Fang and the administrators. This was such a relief for Fang who could finally give undivided attention to her work during the day. Challenges like this that Fang and other CISs experienced may be a reflection of the local community's misconceptions of CISs and their families, and possibly an unwillingness to work together.

Immigration Policy

CISs in the current study faced work–life balance challenges at the macrolevel due to immigration policy: job insecurity for Peng (assistant research professor) and Ting (postdoc fellow); an uncertain future career trajectory for Ling and Yan (both doctoral students); and the limited period of parents or family legally being able to reside in the United States (6 month increments) on a B1/B2 visas. Although participants in the current study maintained slightly different immigration statuses (J-1 visa, F-1 visa, pursuing OPT, and H-1B1 visa), they all experienced job insecurity and an ambiguous career trajectory.

CISs were under high pressure to be productive, working long hours in order to maintain their visa status. Immigration policy also cast a constraint on their families, which were a significant source of support but who could only stay for 6 months per entry.

Ting, a postdoc and a mother of a 3.5-year-old child, shared in all three of her interviews that she was torn between asking their parents to help out (with childcare, mainly), and feeling guilty that her mother and father were not able to see each other for most of the year. She said:

> I cannot be dependent on my parents, it is bad for them to take turns. My mom goes back on the May 1st, my dad comes here on April 17th. One has to stay in China, one has to stay [in the] U.S. with me. … My whole family is separate. … I feel like it costs stress to me.

For Ting, her parent's presence helped her be productive at work and increased her confidence as a new parent. She relied on her parents as childcare support when she was occupied by her work. However, as Ting revealed during her interviews, she had a strong sense of guilt and frustration in the face of the dilemma between prioritizing her parents' marital relationship and the fact that one of the parents had to be here to take care of her son. Like Ting, Li, Ling, Yan, and Fang faced the same challenge.

Ethnic Identity

Some participants expressed concerns about their children's peer relationships in the U.S. schools (e.g., differential treatment of ethnic minorities). Ling, a doctoral student and a mother of a 3.5-year-old child, was concerned about her Asian identity, not only for herself, but for her young son, whom she believed was very shy and very possibly might become the target of peer bullies as he transitioned to a K–12 program. This concern was best expressed by the following quote:

> From what I know, children have ethnic identity since they are little. I'm not sure if this is correct or not. From what I know, since they are little, children like to hang out with people who look like them and have closer relationships with them (e.g., to play with them). Because of this, I hope my child can spend time with Chinese people, so that he is not an ethnic minority within a Chinese group, and he won't be impacted psychologically.

CISs also faced unique challenges due to their status in the United States. First, they had to manage long-distance relationships with their spouses who needed visas in order to visit. Second, CISs and their children were perceived as less competent in English and consequently faced stereotypes and systemic and personal racism. Third, in the context of current immigration policy, support was time limited. However, CISs weren't discouraged or destroyed. All CISs in the current study demonstrated successful adjustment to their life in the United States thanks to all the support they received from their spouses and their parents or in-laws. Their mental strengths also contributed to their transitions to being a parent and new to an academic program simultaneously.

Strong Family Support Helps Maintain Work–Life Balance

Actively Involved Grandparents

Grandparents played vital roles in helping CISs in this study maintain work–life balance among all but one family. The instrumental and emotional support CISs received from their children's grandparents helped alleviate pressure associated with balancing work and life. The presence of the children's grandparents allowed the CISs to focus more on their academic work. Fang expressed her appreciation to her mother-in-law: "Without my mother-in-law or other relatives, I cannot take care of [my child] by myself. My work schedule is quite quite tight." Grandparents contributed to a range of family tasks. For example, Li's mother-in-law "took care of her very carefully...Food wise, grandmother makes porridge, put in vegetables, balance nutrition at every meal." Their close family ties allowed CISs the opportunity to promote work and family life balance, while also adjusting to a new location.

Spousal Support

In addition, CISs also received support from their spouses. Ling expressed that "fortunately, his schedule is kind of flexible because he is a post-doctor researcher. So sometimes if I have to go to class, he can stay home taking care of my child." Yan also discussed at length the support from her spouse; they shared household choices, emotional support, and scaffolded study habits. The resources Yan received from her husband had microsystemic implications at home. Shortly after Yan gave birth to her son, she mentioned that her husband "did a lot to help me, so that I have time to take care of myself. Because I don't need to spend any time on housework." Yan also benefited from her husband regarding her academic program:

> Since he came to the U.S. before I got here, he had several years of experiences in American education system. He knows better than me and gave me so much support. For example, how to read the paper, how to finish homework, and so many other things.

This consequently helped Yan balance her role as a new mother and as a student in a new academic program. She also highlighted that "the most important thing for me is that I can take care of myself, in order to recover from giving birth to my son and focus on my study."

Mental Strengths

Not only were all the CISs adept at navigating resources in their surrounding environments over time, they were also motivated and demonstrated high levels of persistence in being both a scholar and a parent. For example, both Ting and

Yan emphasized their strategies of time management. Ting took advantage of the time, perhaps only 10 min in the car, when she was on her way to drop her son off and to pick her son up. She used this time to engage in teaching him English or other general knowledge. Similarly, Yan pointed out how she managed to balance her two roles:

> I need to balance my study and my family. I need to schedule the time very carefully. I do not do anything last minute. Once I have some homework, I need to finish it as soon as possible. Once I have any problems, I should solve them as soon as I can.

All CISs involved in the current study also had strong educational backgrounds and rich professional experiences prior to coming to the United States. They all were the top of the top students in their cohort growing up in China. Despite all the challenges to maintain a work–life balance, they all demonstrated a strong sense of incremental self (Dweck, 1996). The CISs reflected positive attitudes seeing being abroad as a very beneficial experience for their children. They perceived challenges as opportunities for self-enhancement in their career and as a parent, which ultimately helped them maintain and promote a work–life balance in the United States.

What About My Future? It Is *Our* Future.

When we asked CISs to think about themselves in the near future, some were uncertain and others were determined. What was similar across all six CISs was that their decision-making process was child-centered. Regardless of whether they decided to stay in the United States or wanted to return to mainland China, it was because they wanted to choose the most optimal environment for their children to grow up in. Yan and Li were uncertain about their future, specifically where their jobs or their spouses' jobs would take their families. Peng and Ting were determined to stay in the United States for their children. That was also why they fought hard to maintain job security. They believed that life in the United States would benefit their children' life in the long term. Ling and Fang were planning to return to China. Ling chose to go back to China to pursue her future career due to her concern that her son and her family became ethnoracial minorities in the United States. Fang was a visiting scholar and she knew that her family's staying in the United States would be temporary. They would eventually return to China. Her son's experience in the United States would help him learn English and provide him a valuable cultural experience. For both Fang and Ling, returning to China required efforts to rebalance work and family. However, social and family support back in China would ultimately promote their children's development.

Ling was concerned about her Asian identity. To cope with this stress, she was determined to return to China. She wanted her son to be in the majority group, not an ethnoracial minority. She was comforted by the fact that being in the United States was temporary and that her son would eventually identify himself as a majority as soon as he returned to China and was surrounded by his Chinese peers and family.

DISCUSSION

Guided by the stress coping adaptation model (Berry, 2006), we set out to investigate the research question regarding how CISs navigated challenges and developed coping strategies to maintain work–life balance in the context of different home and educational experiences. The current study was a response to Sharma's (2019) call to focus on further understanding international students and scholars who are in the United States for postgraduate study or work.

We examined the stressors and coping strategies used by CISs to promote work–life balance. Results revealed that CISs were actively engaged in proximal processes (Bronfenbrenner & Morris, 2006) as they were constantly negotiating their immediate and surrounding environments at meso, exo, and macro levels. CISs elicited support from their spouses, parents, and in-laws, as well as took full advantage of their mental strengths (perseverance and positive attitudes) as their coping strategies.

Challenges to Maintain Work–Life Balance

The "publish or perish" academic culture also applied to these international scholars, whose English was not fully developed and who may be in need of support from their mentors and their academic programs (Rockquemore & Laszloffy, 2008). Language barriers have been repeatedly evident in the existing literature as an acculturative stressor among international postgraduate students (Choi, 2006; Sato & Hodge, 2009; Yan & Berliner, 2013). Such a high personal level of constraint is potentially at the cost of CISs' future success. This constraint has a spillover effect on their other social roles—as a parent, a spouse, and an adult. It also takes time to alleviate such constraints.

CISs also experienced immense psychological stress as they strived to balance work and family as they constantly negotiated unfamiliar environments as a result of cultural distance (Ward, 1996) and differences in education systems for themselves (Sato & Hodge, 2009; Yeh & Inose, 2003) and for their children.

Becoming Ethnoracial Minorities in the United States

At times, these CISs were in situations that forced them to realize their ethnic minority status in the United States, which is similar to Sharma's (2019) argument that CISs can experience a sense of foreignness and also be perceived as outsiders due to nationalistic ideologies. CISs were concerned that their children may face neoracism, which refers to the discriminations and prejudices based on the rationales of cultural and national superiority among their peers. They were also concerned about their children getting admitted to public schools due to their cultural backgrounds, countries of origin, and English proficiency levels, as suggested from Lee and Rice (2007) who interviewed international students across several different countries. Both Fang's experiences and Ling's perspectives in this study extended our understanding that CISs do face racism due to personal characteristics— their Asian identity and English as a second language might concern them as parents raising young children as an ethnic minority. Thee children might encounter unfair treatment in micro (such as classrooms and families) and exosystems (local community and neighborhood).

Immigration policy (macrosystem constraint) is another level of strict regulations that encouraged feelings of helplessness. Not only was the concern that CISs could lose their visa statuses, which did not provide them a sense of job security, echoing a similar concern in a previous study (Yan & Berliner, 2013)—but also that their parents or parents-in-law could not remain in the United States for more than 6 months at a time. Despite the contributions of CISs' parents or parents-in-law, their support was usually time limited. Additionally, an older couple might not see each other for most of time during the year when taking turns to come to the United States to help their adult children.

Coping Responses to Maintain Work–Life Balance

In order to deal with challenges at multiple levels, CISs developed the following coping strategies: (a) relying on grandparents and spousal support; (b) drawing on mental strengths; and (c) thinking ahead to make a future career plan that is family-oriented (especially child-centered). Similar to U.S. domestic postgraduate student parents' coping strategies (Martinez et al., 2013), CISs in the current study also elicited social support to help them achieve work–life balance. What is different is that grandparents played an active and vital role to help CISs maintain and promote work–life balance due to Chinese cultural values. Chinese families value interdependence (Markus & Kitayama, 1991) and grandparents are expected to get heavily involved in their children's and grandchildren's life (Chen et al., 2011; Low & Goh, 2015), even when their adult children are abroad (Xie & Xia, 2011). These grandparents were present to assist with housework and child rearing, which is likely to enhance these scholars' cross-cultural adjustment (Chen & Lewis, 2015). The instrumental and emotional support from their children's grandparents helped CISs move through the challenging transitions to their new academic programs and their experience with being parents in a new culture (Chen & Lewis, 2015). This is different compared with the domestic U.S. postgraduate student parents, especially among the racial majority group of European American families who value independence and have lower expectations of grandparents' responsibilities.

Another important source of support came from their spouses. Cox and Paley (1997) argued that family subsystems are interdependent. A supportive spouse who performs as a coparenting figure or a mentor could provide CISs emotional and intellectual support that benefits CISs' academic success as well as alleviates parenting stress (Schoppe-Sullivan et al., 2016).

Mental strengths (e.g., perseverance, positive attitudes, and other practice strategies) also contributed to CISs' work–life balance, as it did for the U.S. domestic postgraduate student parents (Martinez et al., 2013; Salle, 2015). Dweck (1996) discussed that people with an incremental theory of self believe challenges can be dealt with and problems can be resolved. People with this mentality also believe that there is a promising future as long as they work hard and smart. CISs in the current study all had an incremental theory of self. Such a strong and positive mentality helped them cope with these challenges as they tried to balance work and family in the United States. This aligns with what Sallee and Hart (2015) found with international faculty fathers in U.S. research universities. The CISs in the current study, however, might have embraced more difficult times and obstacles due to lack of job security and less clear future with F- (student) or J- (postdocs and visiting scholars) visa statuses. Despite hurdles they faced in their everyday work and family life, they were able to rely on resources within contextual systems (e.g., family and their community). Additionally, intrinsic motivation, agency, and positive attitudes empowered and prepared them for new challenges and future uncertainty, which aligns with previous research on this topic (Pan et al., 2008; Ramburuth & McCormick, 2001; Sharma, 2019).

Another notable finding that helped CISs balance work and family in the long term is that when they made plans for their future career, CISs thought holistically with a heavy focus on their child. Chinese cultural values might influence CISs to prioritize their children over their marriage (Lynch & Hanson, 2011), and definitely above their work.

Findings of the present study extend the literature about CIS stress and strategies to maintain work–family balance. Though acculturation is a continuous, dynamic process, with possibilities for new stressors expectedly or unexpectedly, many of these CISs saw this process as a learning, growing, and thriving process as they adjusted to U.S. culture.

Limitations

The findings and implications are significant for educational institutions and local communities to understand CISs' stressors and coping strategies to maintain work–life balance. Despite the contribution of the present study, a few limitations are noted below.

One limitation is the small sample size found through one listserv of one university in the Midwest and a local church in the same college town, which limits the generalizability of the findings. To be sure, this is not the goal of qualitative research, nor was it the goal of this study; rather, we sought to develop a framework to allow a full description of the problem (Atieno, 2009) and some solutions. However, having a broader understanding of how these proximal processes influence CIS acculturative process has implications for how successful they are in U.S. institutions and what specific resources are needed to help support their education and career. For instance, the specific resource needs of these participants may vary from similar identified scholars with families working and/or studying at urban institutions in other geographical areas. We were essentially relying on the perspective of the family to provide us information about how they navigate home and education.

This study included multiple contact between researchers and participants, but much of the proximal processes being discussed were out of our purview. Thus, it may be that how the issue was articulated to or interpreted by the researchers does not fully represent the actual proximal processes experienced by the scholars. Although CISs shared similar lived experiences, especially as they strived to balance work and life in the U.S., participants in the current study cannot be viewed as a homogenous group (Shih et al., 2019). Future research can further delineate the intricate variations of CISs based on their academic positions.

Finally, our sample consisted primarily of mothers. How males and fathers experience similar proximal processes may be uniquely distinct from that of females and mothers. Further, some of these families included multiple generations and that perspective is missing from our analysis, which leaves a gap in the literature regarding how or whether multiple members of the same family unit experience these processes similarly or differently.

Implications

Findings from this study have several implications, particularly for universities that recruit Chinese international students or scholars with children. These CISs might encounter model minority stereotypes (Shih et al., 2019) when interacting with mentors, peers, or community members. A welcoming environment in higher education institutions and local communities could help the CISs with academic productivity and psychological adjustment. Potential workshops include the following topics: English speaking and writing skills in academia, active participation and collaboration in class, career opportunities and professional development, childcare and school enrollment for children, and support for families adjusting to local communities. The CISs played important roles in their academic programs as teaching assistants or research assistants, leading the lab experiments and lecturing for undergraduate level courses in their current institution, with several likely to become future faculty members. Providing early academic and social support can effectively conquer barriers in acculturation so that CISs can balance academia and parenting and also promote the success of diverse faculty (Rockquemore & Laszloffy, 2008; Turner et al., 2008). To be sure, institutions should use appropriate theoretical models to fully understand the challenges and needed support of CISs associated with their work inside the institution. In order to provide support that is the most needed and evidence-based, future research might also consider using Schlossberg's transition theory (Schlossberg et al., 1989) to guide studies that focus on the transitions that hinge on the situation, self, support, and strategies, as well as how higher education institutions may impact these transitions for CISs or international scholars in general.

As argued by both Collier and Hernandez (2016) and Sharma (2019), the host institutions need to provide out-of-class professional development that fosters CISs' agency via needs-based mentorship at international centers or through academic programs. Such programs need to be inclusive, easy to access, and encourage active engagement, with considerations of fostering CISs' academic skills, as well as supporting work and life balance. For example, advisors at international centers could potentially provide orientations to address practical issues in everyday life in the United States and provide these scholars additional support for academic achievements and professional development. The CISs and their spouses, who may also be in academic programs as well, voiced common challenges related to publication and strategies for searching for future careers. Perhaps joint support from international centers and academic programs might be useful resources, or networks with international student alumni who can offer support or advice in searching for jobs in the United States. Such implications might be applied to CISs who come to the United States by themselves without their families or children. Additional and unique support is needed for CISs with children and their families.

Support to CIS families and their mental wellbeing is still lacking (Collier & Hernandez, 2016). Effective collaborations between the host institutions and host communities are greatly needed. Local college town communities can keep updated with changing demographics of the university (e.g., increased international families). Further, other community institutions (e.g., childcare facilities and public schools) should also be aware of such changes. International centers at universities can serve as liaisons to connect the CISs and their families with the local community. It would also be beneficial for institutions to develop mechanisms for discussing challenges with potential students who intend to continue as scholars in the United States. Finally, and as shown in our model, given that acculturation is a process and CISs and their families are likely to continuously face new challenges as they come up with strategies to deal with existing challenges, academic and social support from host institutions and local communities should be provided to CISs and families continuously during their stay, not just limited to engagement during the recruitment process.

Note

An appendix for this article can be found on the JIS website at https://www.ojed.org/index.php/jis

REFERENCES

Atieno, O. P. (2009). An analysis of the strengths and limitation of qualitative and quantitative research paradigms. *Problems of Education in the 21st Century*, *13*, 13–38.

Berry, J. W. (2006). Stress perspectives on acculturation. In D. L. Sam & J. W. Berry (Eds.), *The Cambridge of acculturation psychology* (pp. 43–57). Cambridge University Press.

Berry, J. W., & Hou, F. (2017). Acculturation, discrimination and wellbeing among second generation of immigrants in Canada. *International Journal of Intercultural Relations, 61,* 29–39. http://doi.org/10.1016/j.ijintrel.2017.08.003

Bronfenbrenner, U. (1986). Ecology of the family as a context for human development: Research perspectives. *Developmental Psychology*, *22*(6), 723–742.

Bronfenbrenner, U., & Morris, P. A. (2006). The bioecological model of human development. In W. Damon (Series ed.) & R. M. Lerner (Vol. ed.), *Handbook of child psychology: Theoretical models of human development* (pp. 793–828). Wiley.

Chen, F., Liu, G., & Mair, C. A. (2011). Intergenerational ties in context: Grandparents caring for grandchildren in China. *Social Forces*, *90*(2), 571–594. https://doi.org/10.1093/sf/sor012

Chen, H.-M., & Lewis, D. C. (2015). Chinese grandparents' involvement in their adult children's parenting practices in the United States. *Contemporary Family Theory, 37*, 58–71. https://doi.org/10.1007/s10591-014-9321-7

Choi, T. (2006). Asian international students' academic adjustment in a U.S. graduate school and Stanton-Salazar's framework. *Pacific Asian Education, 18*, 51–68.

Collier, D. A., & Hernandez, X. J. (2016). Tatemae and honne: Interpreting the theory versus practice of international student development and outreach. *Journal of Diversity in Higher Education*, 9, 369–384.

Corbin, J., & Strauss, A. (2014). *Basics of qualitative research: Techniques and procedures for developing grounded theory.* SAGE.

Cox, M. J., & Paley, B. (1997). Families as systems. *Annual Review of Psychology*, *48*(1), 243–267. http://doi.org/ 10.1146/annurev.psych.48.1.243

Creswell, J. W. (2005). *Educational research: Planning, conducting, and evaluating quantitative.* Prentice Hall.

Crotty, M. (1998). *The foundations of social research: Meaning and perspective in the research process*. SAGE.

Dweck, C. S. (1996). Implicit theories as organizers of goals and behavior. In P. M. Gollwitzer & J. A. Bargh (Eds.), *The psychology of action: Linking cognition and motivation to behavior* (pp. 69–90). Guilford Press.

Gautam, C., Lowery, C. L., Mays, C., & Durant, D. (2016). Challenges for global learners: A qualitative study of the concerns and difficulties of international students. *Journal of International Students*, *6*, 501–526. https://www.ojed.org/index.php/jis/article/view/368/287

Goldkuhl, G. (2012). Pragmatism vs interpretivism in qualitative information systems research. *European Journal of Information Systems*, *21*(2), 135–146. https://doi.org/10.1057/ejis.2011.54

Halic, O., Greenberg, K., & Paulus, T. (2009). Language and academic identity: A study of the experiences of non-native English speaking international students. *International Education, 38*, 73–93.

Hatch, J. A. (2002). *Doing qualitative research in education settings*. State University of New York Press.

Heng, T. T. (2017). Voices of Chinese international students in USA colleges: 'I want to tell them that …' *Studies in Higher Education, 42*, 833–850. https://doi.org/10.1080/03075079.2017.1293873

Heng, T. T. (2018a). Coping strategies of international Chinese undergraduates in response to academic challenges in U.S. college. *Teachers College Record, 120*, 1–42.

Heng, T. T. (2018b). Different is not deficient: Contradicting stereotypes of Chinese international students in US higher education. *Studies in Higher Education, 43*, 22–36. https://doi.org/10.1080/03075079.2016.1152466

Institute for International Education. (2018). *Open Doors fact sheet: China.* Retrieved September 26, 2019 from https://www.iie.org/Research-and-Insights/Open-Doors/Data/International-Students

Kim, B. S. K., Atkinson, D. R., & Umemoto, D. (2001). Asian cultural values and the counseling process: Current knowledge and directions for future research. *The Counseling Psychologist, 29,* 570–603. https://doi.org/10.1177/0011000001294006

Knapp, S. J. (2009). Critical theorizing: Enhancing theoretical rigor in family research. *Journal of Family Theory & Review, 1,* 133–145. https://doi.org/10.1111/j.1756-2589.2009.00018.x

Lee, J. J., & Rice, C. (2007). Welcome to America? International student perceptions of discriminations. *Higher Education, 53,* 381–409. https://doi.org/10.1007/s10734-005-4508-3

Leki, I. (2001). "A narrow thinking system": Nonnative-English-speaking students in group projects across the curriculum. *TESOL Quarterly, 35*, 39–67.

Li, J., Wang, Y., Liu, X., Xu, Y., & Cui, T. (2018). Academic adaptation among international students from East Asian countries: A consensual qualitative research. *Journal of International Students*, *8*, 194–214. https://doi.org/10.5281/zenodo.1134289

Lincoln, Y. S., & Guba, E. G. (1985). *Naturalistic inquiry.* SAGE.

Lincoln, Y. S., & Guba, E. (2000). Paradigmatic controversies, contradictions, and emerging confluences. In N. K. Denzin & Y. S. Lincoln (Eds.), *Handbook of qualitative research* (2nd ed.; pp. 163–188). SAGE.

Low, S. S., & Goh, E. C. (2015). Granny as nanny: Positive outcomes for grandparents providing childcare for dual-income families. Fact or myth? *Journal of Intergenerational Relationships*, *13*(4), 302–319. https://doi.org/10.1080/15350770.2015.1111003

Lynch, E. W., & Hanson, M. J. (2011). *Developing cross-cultural competence: A guide for working with young children and their families* (4th ed.). Brookes Publishing.

Markus, H. R., & Kitayama, S. (1991). Culture and the self: Implications for cognition, emotion, and motivation. *Psychological Review*, *98*(2), 224–253.

Martinez, E., Ordu, C., Della Sala, M. R., & McFarlane, A. (2013). Striving to obtain a school-work-life balance: The full-time doctoral student. *International Journal of Doctoral Studies, 8*, 39–59.

Morse, J. M. (1991). Qualitative nursing research: A free-for-all? In J. M. Morse (Ed.), *Qualitative nursing research: A contemporary dialogue* (Revised ed.). SAGE.

Olesen, V. L. (2000). Feminisms and qualitative research at and into the millennium. In N. K. Denzin & Y. S. Lincoln (Eds.), *Handbook of qualitative research* (2nd ed.; pp. 215–256). SAGE.

Pan, J.-Y., Wong, D. F. K., Chan, C. L. W., & Joubert, L. (2008). Meaning of life as a protective factor of positive affect in acculturation: A resilience framework and a cross-cultural comparison. *International Journal of*

Intercultural Relations, *32*, 505–514. https://doi.org/10.1016/j.ijintrel.2008.08.002

Patton, M. Q. (2002). *Qualitative research and evaluation methods*. SAGE.

Pizam, A., & Mansfeld, Y. (2009). *Consumer behaviour in travel and tourism*. Howarth Hospitality Press.

Ramburuth, P., & McCormick, J. (2001). Learning diversity in higher education: A comparative study of Asian international and Australian students. *Higher Education, 42*, 333–350. https://doi.org/10.1023/A:1017982716482

Rockquemore, K. A., & Laszloffy, T. (2008). *The Black academic's guide to winning tenure without losing your soul*. Lynne Rienner Publishers.

Sallee, M. W. (2015). Adding academics to the work/family puzzle: Graduate student parents in higher education and student affairs. *Journal of Student Affairs Research and Practice, 52*, 401–413. https://doi.org/10.1080/19496591.2015.1083438

Sallee, M., & Hart, J. (2015). Cultural navigators: International faculty fathers in the U.S. research university. *Journal of Diversity in Higher Education, 8,* 192–211. https://doi.org/10.1037/a0039042

Sato, T., & Hodge, S. R. (2009). Asian international doctoral students' experiences at two American universities: Assimilation, accommodation, and resistance. *Journal of Diversity in Higher Education, 2,* 136–148. https://doi.org/10.1037/a0015912

Saunders, B., Sim, J., Kingstone, T., Baker, S., Waterfield, J., Bartlam, B., Burroughs, H., & Jinks, C. (2018). Saturation in qualitative research: Exploring its conceptualization and operationalization. *Quality & Quantity*, *52*(4), 1893–1907.

Schlossberg, N. K., Lynch, A. Q., & Chickering, A. W. (1989). *Improving higher education environments for adults. Responsive programs and services from entry to departure*. Jossey-Bass.

Schoppe-Sullivan, S. J., Settle, T., Lee, J. K., & Kamp Dush, C. M. (2016). Supportive coparenting relationships as a haven of psychological safety at the transition to parenthood. *Research in Human Development*, *13*(1), 32–48. https://doi.org/10.1080/15427609.2016.1141281

Seidman, I. (2006). *Interviewing as qualitative research: A guide for researchers in education and social sciences* (3rd ed.). Teachers College Press.

Sharma, S. (2019). Focusing on graduate international students. *Journal of International Students*, *9*(3), i–xi. https://doi.org/10.32674/jis.v9i3

Shih, K. Y., Chang, T.-F., & Chen, S.-Y. (2019). Impacts of the model minority myth on Asian American individuals and families: Social justice and critical race feminist perspectives. *Journal of Family Theory & Review, 11*, 412–428. https://doi.org/10.1111/jftr.12342

Turner, C. S. V., Gonzalez, J. C., & Wood, J. L. (2008). Faculty of color in academe: What 20 years of literature tells us. *Journal of Diversity in Higher Education, 1,* 139–168. https://doi.org/10.1037/a0012837

van Manen, M. (1990) *Researching lived experience: Human science for an action sensitive pedagogy*. The Althouse Press.

Ward, C. (1996). Acculturation. In D. Landis & R. Bhagat (Eds.), *Handbook of intercultural training* (2nd ed.). SAGE.

Xie, X., & Xia, Y. (2011). Grandparenting in Chinese immigrant families. *Marriage & Family Review, 47*(6), 383–396. https://digitalcommons.unl.edu/famconfacpub/82

Xing, D., & Bolden, B. (2019). Exploring oral English learning motivation in Chinese international students with low oral English proficiency. *Journal of International Students, 9*(3), 834–855. https://doi.org/10.32674/jis.v9i3.749

Yan, K., & Berliner, D. C. (2013). Chinese international students' personal and sociocultural stressors in the United States. *Journal of College Student Development, 54*, 62–84. https://doi.org/10.1353/csd.2013.0010

Yeh, C. J., & Inose, M. (2003). International students' reported English fluency, social support satisfaction, and social connectedness as predictors of acculturative stress. *Counseling Psychology Quarterly, 16*, 15–28. https://doi.org/10.1080/0951507031000114058

Zhang, Y. L. (2018). Using Bronfenbrenner's ecological approach to understand academic advising with international community college students. *Journal of International Students, 8*, 1764–1782. https://doi.org/10.5281/zenodo.1468084

CHANG SU-RUSSELL, PhD, is Assistant Professor in the Department of Family and Consumer Sciences at Illinois State University. Her research centers on the socioemotional wellbeing of the very young children with the considerations of social contexts during challenging times. Her two lines of research includes young children's wellbeing in the transition to siblinghood in urban mainland China, and how parents discuss challenging social issues with young children. Email: csuruss@ilstu.edu

ANTHONY G. JAMES, JR. holds a Ph.D. in human development and family studies from the University of Missouri. He is an associate professor, the director of the Family Science Program, and the interim vice president of institutional diversity and inclusion at Miami University in Oxford, Ohio. He is the editor-in-chief of Marriage and Family Review and previously served as the deputy editor of Journal of Family Theory & Review. Dr. James's research and thought leadership has appeared in Diverse Issue in Higher Education, TIME, and the Thrive Center for Human Development blog. He is the editor of Black Families: A Systems Approach and author of Diversity, Equity, and Inclusion: A Practical Guide. Email: jamesag2@MiamiOH.edu

Research-in-Brief

© *Journal of International Students*
Volume 11, Issue 2 (2021), pp. 505-513
ISSN: 2162-3104 (Print), 2166-3750 (Online)
doi: 10.32674/jis.v11i2.2065
ojed.org/jis

Understanding of International Doctoral Students' Challenges: A Literature Review Study

Yan Gao
University of Victoria, Canada

ABSTRACT

Studies pertaining to the challenges international doctoral students confront have been disseminated at various conferences and in journals. However, there is a need to synthesize recent research to assess and advance contemporary theories about international doctoral students. Using meta-synthesis, this article discusses the literature's main themes and the relationship between theory and the literature findings. A new tentative framework is proposed based on the results. Implications for international doctoral students' academic success are also discussed.

Keywords: academic success, international doctoral students, internationalization, students' experience

In the United States, higher education institutions enrolled 749,329 international graduate students, 34% of whom were doctoral students in the 2018 fall admission cycle (Okahana & Zhou, 2019). In the United Kingdom, 46% of students studying at the postgraduate level were international students in 2017–2018 (UK Council for International Student Affairs, 2019). However, not every international doctoral student completed their studies. The difficulties and challenges that could impact their degree completion have been receiving attention from scholars. Therefore, an updated synthesis of the research is needed to gain a basic overview of the recent research status. The present study sheds light on international doctoral students. Doctoral education is highly internationalized by nature. In this study, the focus is on students who do not speak English as their first language and who pursue a doctoral degree in an English-speaking country. This review aims to assess the scholarly literature on the challenges confronted by international doctoral students and propose a framework to view their experiences.

THEORETICAL FRAMEWORK

Tinto's integration model (1987, 1993) was chosen as a key theory to examine and assess the research examined in this study. Tinto's model focuses on students' experiences in higher education institutions holistically. It links students' experiences to degree completion, which is both the goal for institutions and students. Also, since the academic outcome of doctoral students is not measured by grade point average, degree completion is essential to indicate the academic success of this group of students. Therefore, the present study uses this framework to examine the literature and proposes a way to conceptualize international doctoral students' experiences based on this framework.

According to Tinto (1987), before entering higher education, individuals have different family and community backgrounds. They also have a variety of personal attributes, skills, value orientations, and varying types of pre-college educational experiences and achievements. Other than the personal characteristics of individuals, the subsequent experiences within the institution are centrally related to degree completion. Positive experiences intensify the goal of college completion and heighten the commitment between the individual and the institution; negative experiences weaken the intentions and commitments and lead to a higher chance of leaving without a degree. External forces (e.g., families, neighborhoods, peer groups, work settings, etc.) also influence the change of individuals' goals and commitments.

Due to the distinct nature of doctoral study versus undergraduate study, Tinto (1993) updated his model, in which he stated that doctoral students were more likely aligned with the norms of the specific field of study than with the broader university. Therefore, doctoral students' academic success, especially in the later stage of studies, would be more likely tied to a particular faculty member or a group of faculty members, such as one's supervisor or committee members.

METHOD

This study used qualitative metasynthesis as the method to investigate. Qualitative metasynthesis offers "a coherent description or explanation of a target event or experience, instead of a summary view of unlinked features of that event or experience" (Sandelowski & Barroso, 2007, p. 152). By synthesizing the findings between studies, it generated a more comprehensive integration to answer the research questions.

Data were extracted from two databases, *ERIC* and *Web of Science*, which are frequently used in literature reviews of a similar nature. Since negative experiences could lead to students' early departure, search terms included: "international doctora* students" or "international PhD students" combined with "experience," "difficult*," "challenge," "obstacle," "dilemma," "hardship," "pain," and "stress*," respectively.

After the initial search, only empirical qualitative studies within the scope of focus were selected. Studies, such as analyzing the writing texts from a linguistic perspective, were excluded. After applying inclusion and exclusion criteria and deleting duplications, 28 studies were left for analysis (see Table 1 for included studies).

Table 1: Studies Included

Campbell, T. A. (2015). A phenomenological study on international doctoral students' acculturation experiences at a U.S. university. *Journal of International Students, 5*(3), 285–299.
Chang, Y., & Kanno, Y. (2010). NNES doctoral students in English-speaking academe: The nexus between language and discipline. *Applied Linguistics (Oxford), 31*(5), 671–692.
Chatterjee-Padmanabhan, M., & Nielsen, W. (2018). Preparing to cross the research proposal threshold: A case study of two international doctoral students. *Innovations in Education and Teaching International, 55*(4), 417–424.
Cho, S. (2009). Disciplinary enculturation experiences of five East Asian doctoral students in US-based second language studies programmes. *Asia Pacific Journal of Education, 29*(3), 295–310.
Doyle, S., Manathunga, C., Prinsen, G., Tallon, R., & Cornforth, S. (2018). African international doctoral students in New Zealand: Englishes, doctoral writing and intercultural supervision. *Higher Education Research & Development, 37*(1), 1–14.
Fotovatian, S. (2012). Three constructs of institutional identity among international doctoral students in Australia. *Teaching in Higher Education, 17*(5), 577–588.
Gao, Y. (2019). Experiences of Chinese international doctoral students in Canada who withdrew: A narrative inquiry. *International Journal of Doctoral Studies, 14*, 259–276.
Goode, J. (2007). Empowering or disempowering the international Ph.D. student? Constructions of the dependent and independent learner. *British Journal of Sociology of Education, 28*(5), 589–603.
Holliday, A. (2017). PhD students, interculturality, reflexivity, community and internationalisation. *Journal of Multilingual and Multicultural Development, 38*(3), 206–218.
Jang, Y. J., Woo, H., & Henfield, M. S. (2014). A qualitative study of challenges faced by international doctoral students in counselor education supervision courses. *Asia Pacific Education Review, 15*(4), 561–572.

Khozaei, F., Naidu, S., Khozaei, Z., & Salleh, N. A. (2015). An exploratory study of factors that affect the research progress of international PhD students from the Middle East. *Education + Training, 57*(4), 448–460.

Ku, H. Y., Lahman, M. K. E., Yeh, H. T., & Cheng, Y. C. (2008). Into the academy: preparing and mentoring international doctoral students. *Educational Technology Research and Development, 56*(3), 365–377.

Le, T., & Gardner, S. K. (2010). Understanding the doctoral experience of Asian international students in the science, technology, engineering, and mathematics (STEM) fields: An exploration of one institutional context. *Journal of College Student Development, 51*(3), 252–264.

Lee, M. C. Y., McMahon, M., & Watson, M. (2018). Supporting the career decisions of Australian-based international Chinese doctoral students. *International Journal for Educational and Vocational Guidance, 18*(3), 257–277.

Lee, S. (2017). Peer support for international doctoral students in managing supervision relationships. *Journal of International Students, 7*(4), 1096–1103.

Li, M. (2016). Developing skills and disposition for lifelong learning: Acculturative issues surrounding supervising international doctoral students in New Zealand universities. *Journal of International Students, 6*(3), 740–761.

Mittal, M., & Wieling, E. (2006). Training experiences of international doctoral students in marriage and family therapy. *Journal of Marital and Family Therapy, 32*(3), 369–383.

Ours, J. C., & Ridder, G. (2003). Fast track or failure: A study of the graduation and dropout rates of Ph.D. students in economics. *Economics of Education Review, 22*(2), 157–166.

Russell-Pinson, L., & Harris, M. L. (2019). Anguish and anxiety, stress and strain: Attending to writers' stress in the dissertation process. *Journal of Second Language Writing, 43*, 63–71.

Sato, T. (2016). Doctoral sojourn experiences of adapted physical education students from Asian countries. *Journal of International Students, 6*(2), 339–366.

Son, J., & Park, S. (2015). Academic experiences of international PhD students in Australian higher education: From an EAP program to a PhD program. *International Journal of Pedagogies and Learning, 9*(1), 26–37.

Wang, T., & Li, L. Y. (2011). 'Tell me what to do' vs. 'guide me through it': Feedback experiences of international doctoral students. *Active Learning in Higher Education, 12*(2), 101–112.

Williams-Shakespeare, E. S., Bronteng, J. E., & Alahmari, A. (2018). Interpersonal hardiness as a critical contributing factor to persistence among international women in doctoral programs: A trioethnographic study. *The Qualitative Report, 23*(8), 1797–1822.

Winchester-Seeto, T., Homewood, J., Thogersen, J., Jacenyik-Trawoger, C., Manathunga, C., Reid, A., & Holbrook, A. (2014). Doctoral supervision in a cross-cultural context: Issues affecting supervisors and candidates. *Higher Education Research & Development, 33*(3), 610–626.

Xu, L., & Grant, B. (2017). International doctoral students' becoming: A dialogic perspective. *Innovations in Education and Teaching International, 54*(6), 570–579.

Ye, L., & Edwards, V. (2015). Chinese overseas doctoral student narratives of intercultural adaptation. *Journal of Research in International Education, 14*(3), 228–241. doi:10.1177/1475240915614934

Ye, L., & Edwards, V. (2017). A narrative inquiry into the identity formation of Chinese doctoral students in relation to study abroad. *Race Ethnicity and Education, 20*(6), 865–876.

Zhang, Y. (2016). International students in transition: Voices of Chinese doctoral students in a U.S. research university. *Journal of International Students, 6*(1), 175–194.

RESULTS

After extracting, editing, grouping and abstracting findings (Sandelowski & Barroso, 2007), I identifed seven themes.

The relationship with one's supervisor(s) and language barriers were the two most frequently mentioned challenges. Supervisors played a significant part in international doctoral students' academic lives (Goode, 2007; Lee et al., 2018; Russell-Pinson & Harris, 2019; Sato, 2016; Xu & Grant, 2017; Zhang, 2016). Some students experienced positive, equal, and collegial relationships with their supervisors; meanwhile, challenges could come from unequal power dynamics, tensions, and mismatches in research and expectations (Le & Gardner, 2010; Wang & Li, 2011). Language barriers, however, could bring misunderstanding and confusion, which worsened the problems for international doctoral students. Some studies have shown that students who were supervised by active researchers tend to have a lower attrition rate (Khozaei et al., 2015; Ours & Ridder, 2003). On the contrary, in other studies, inaccessibility of supervisors who were active researchers hindered the research progress of students (Gao, 2019; Ku et al., 2008).

Language barriers affected communication with supervisors and peers, undertaking academic tasks, social networking, and overall experiences in the host country for international doctoral students (Campbell, 2015; Li, 2016; Holliday, 2017; Winchester-Seeto et al., 2014; Son & Park, 2015; Ye & Edwards, 2017; Zhang, 2016). The fact that they were held to the same stringent standard as their domestic counterparts placed them at a severe disadvantage. However, English proficiency might not have the same value across different disciplines and might not always be critical to international doctoral students' academic success (Chang & Kanno, 2010). For instance, studies reported that humanities and social science fields placed stricter requirements of English proficiency than the STEM fields. (Chang & Kanno, 2010; Le & Gardner, 2010).

Studying abroad required international doctoral students to socialize, build networks, and make new friends in the new environment and the new culture. The cultural differences between the home country and the host country have been seen as the roots of adaptation (Doyle et al., 2018; Jang et al., 2014; Mittal & Wieling, 2006; Ye & Edwards, 2017). Baba and Hosoda (2014) specified that social disconnectedness, homesickness, discrimination, and culture shock negatively affected international students' sociocultural adaptation. Different home cultures also impacted them distinctively (Chatterjee-Padmanabhan & Nielsen, 2018; Cho, 2009; Holliday, 2017; Zhang, 2016). These differences also manifested in teaching and learning styles for some students (Jang et al., 2014; Son & Park, 2015; Wang & Li, 2011). Some students felt the learning material lacked cross-cultural content (Jang et al., 2014); some had a hard time adapting to discussion-based teaching styles (Goode, 2007; Wang & Li, 2011).

Separation from familiarities and the support system was another recorded challenge, which led to a need to reestablish new support systems. Peer support and faculty support from the academic setting and family/friend support from the social setting could have exercised an impact on the academic success of international doctoral students (Campbell, 2015; Le & Gardner, 2010; Lee, 2017; Son & Park, 2015; Williams-Shakespeare et al., 2018; Winchester-Seeto et al., 2014; Zhang, 2016). At a mature age, spousal/conjugal support was another source of support that could influence international doctoral students' experiences.

The transnational experiences caused identity issues as well; however, it functioned as a double-edged sword in international doctoral students' lives (Fotovatian, 2012; Mittal & Wieling, 2006; Ye & Edwards, 2015; Ye & Edwards, 2017; Zhang, 2016). When taken-for-granted or past habits can no longer reliably guide individual actions, some international doctoral students were reported to struggle with a new identity as an "outsider" and "invisible person" in the host country and apparent differences in self. Along with the adjustment and identity challenges, some students also expressed their emotions resulted from the transnational learning experiences, for instance, loneliness, anxiety, isolation, and frustration (Li, 2016; Mittal & Wieling, 2006; Russell-Pinson & Harris, 2019; Sato, 2016; Wang & Li, 2011). Yet, the study abroad experience facilitated the accumulation of international doctoral students' personal capital, providing opportunities for self-development. They became more attentive to cultural diversities, more tolerant with differences, and more responsible as adults and autonomous learners (Zhang, 2016).

Research challenges were another obstacle that came, on the one hand, from the very nature of conducting research, and, on the other hand, from the unfamiliarity of discipline-specific discourse such as adapting the writing style for academic purposes (Chatterjee-Padmanabhan & Nielsen, 2018; Sato, 2016; Son & Park, 2015). The implicit conventions of scholarly writing in a new educational context and understanding the tacit expectations can be especially overwhelming for international doctoral students who use English as a second language (Chatterjee-Padmanabhan & Nielsen, 2018). Lacking local connections could make it difficult for some students to access data sources, conduct interviews, and collect documents for their studies (Sato, 2016).

Last but not least is financial constraint. Financial burden impacts graduate students in general. Many students took on teaching assistant or research assistant roles while conducting their doctoral research to relieve financial pressure (Le & Gardner, 2010; Williams-Shakespeare et al., 2018). The working constraints of the student permit and the ineligibility to apply for local student loans and government grants placed international doctoral students in a more disadvantaged position. Students who brought family and children to the host country faced an even more harsh situation.

IMPLICATIONS FOR THEORY

Some identified themes correspond with Tinto's (1987, 1993) model, which emphasized that in the later stage of studies for doctoral students, persistence would link closely to a particular faculty member or a group of faculty members. In the findings, relationship with supervisors was the most frequently mentioned theme in the literature, which echoed Tinto's model. Support from peers and faculty members in the academic setting, and family and spouse from the social setting, also demonstrated influences on the academic success of international doctoral students.

Tinto's (1993) model explains some findings; however, some themes are left out of the model: language barriers, cultural assimilation, research challenges, identity issues, and financial constraints. In Tinto's (1987) model on domestic students, the transition from students' past forms of life, such as the family and neighborhood where they grew up, to the institutional environment was a challenge students needed to overcome. This transitional process for international doctoral students consists of the adjustment from one country to another country and from one culture to another culture. In other words, the transitional challenge is amplified, and the adjustment is not restricted to the institutional environment but a broader societal level in the host country.

Therefore, based on the findings and the structure of Tinto's model, I propose we view the challenges international doctoral students confront from five domains: academic, social, cultural, psychological, and economic, which form the experience of international doctoral students collectively. The academic domain includes the relationship with the supervisor(s), peer and faculty support, and research challenges; the social domain includes family/spousal support and social networking; the cultural domain includes language barriers and cultural adaptation; the psychological domain includes identity issue and emotions; and the economic domain includes financial constraints. But again, these domains work collaboratively and mutually affect each other in shaping the experiences of international doctoral students (see Figure 1).

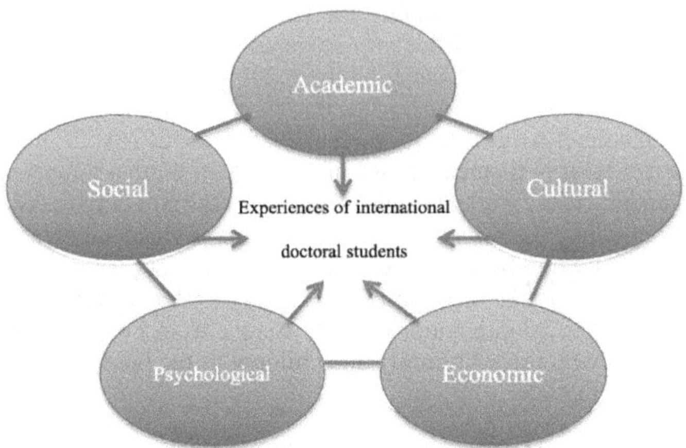

Figure 1: Five Domains of International Doctoral Students' Experience

In a nutshell, this synthesis provides educators and practitioners with a timely summary of the research status and a framework to better engage with international doctoral students. Institutions could consider providing orientation sessions and English preparation courses. International admission offices may facilitate the adaptation of students through organizing social family events and other activities. Professional development workshops could be held to raise professors' and supervisors' cultural awareness. A dialogic space needs to be created for respectful interactions and reciprocity. Faculties and departments could provide students with the opportunities that contribute to building the sense of community and belonging; encourage the integration of diverse teaching materials; and facilitate the formation of mentoring relationships where students can relate with supervisors on an individual basis. Overall, there is a need for all stakeholders to be culturally responsive for a successful international education.

REFERENCES

Baba, Y., & Hosoda, M. (2014). Home away home: Better understanding of the role of social support in predicting cross-cultural adjustment among international students. *College Student Journal, 48*(1), 1–16.

Okahana, H., & Zhou, E. (2019). *International graduate applications and enrollment: Fall 2018*. Council of Graduate Schools.

Sandelowski, M., & Barroso, J. (2007). *Handbook for synthesizing qualitative research*. Springer Pub. Co.

Tinto, V. (1987). *Leaving college: Rethinking the causes and cures of student attrition*. The University of Chicago Press.

Tinto, V. (1993). *Leaving college: Rethinking the causes and cures of student attrition* (2nd ed.). The University of Chicago Press.

UK Council for International Student Affairs. (2019). *International student statistics: UK higher education.* https://www.ukcisa.org.uk/Research--Policy/Statistics/International-student-statistics-UK-higher-education

Yan Gao, PhD, is a research associate in the Faculty of Education, University of Victoria in Canada. Her major research interests lie in the area of international students, academic success, cross-cultural education, and higher education research. Email: yangao@uvic.ca

Research-in-Brief

© *Journal of International Students*
Volume 11, Issue 2 (2021), pp. 514-518
ISSN: 2162-3104 (Print), 2166-3750 (Online)
doi: 10.32674/jis.v11i2.2741
ojed.org/jis

Understanding Black-African International Students' Experiences in United States Colleges and Universities Through Social Identity Theory

Diana Carole Awuor
Sam Houston State University, USA

ABSTRACT

In this Research in Brief, Tajfel's (1970) social identity theory is explained and examined as potentially useful for analyzing the experiences of Black-African international students in U. S. colleges and universities. Race has been and still is a major issue in the United States. Through a review of literature, I sought to find out how Black-African international students' race affected their experiences in the United States.

Keywords: Black-African international students, race, social identity theory

INTRODUCTION

In May 2020, George Floyd, a Black man, was killed by police officers in Minneapolis, Minnesota. Floyd died by asphyxiation after one police officer placed his knee on Mr. Floyd's neck for a prolonged period of 8 minutes and 46 seconds (Romo, 2020). George Floyd's death came on the heels of numerous other deaths of Black men and women at the hands of police. Black-African International students (BAISs) are caught up in the middle of these racial struggles when they never had any experiences as members of racial minority groups in their countries. For better understanding, I refer to international students as those students who have left their home countries and crossed borders to different countries with their main purpose being studies/studying.

In this article, I will discuss the relationship between the racial experiences of BAISs in U.S. colleges and the ingroups with which they identify. I seek to identify if the experiences of BAISs in the United States are connected with their relationships with ingroups, outgroups, or intergroups. Tajfel's (1970) social identity theory (SIT) serves as the theoretical orientation guiding this inquiry. Through the lens of SIT, I analyze evidence from current published empirical work about how BAISs relate with ingroup and outgroup members. Ingroups include BAIS from sub-Saharan African countries like Kenya, Nigeria, Ghana, Mali, Uganda, Tanzania, South Africa, Zimbabwe, Rwanda, and Benin, whereas the members of outgroups can include international students who are not BAISs, American students, faculty, and staff.

THEORETICAL FRAMEWORK

SIT was proposed by Tajfel (1970), who performed studies using boys who were divided into ingroups, outgroups, and intergroups. One of the experiments required that the boys choose who to give money rewards within the intergroup. Many chose to give more of the money to those members who were part of their ingroups. There was no fairness. According to Tajfel (1970), discrimination and prejudice is most probable where there are ingroups forming an intergroup (intergroup is the parent group that holds several ingroups within it). Most people will favor those people who are within their ingroup and become prejudicial and discriminatory toward those who are in outgroups. This finding forms the foundation of SIT.

Zhou et al. (2008) considered SIT as a higher education model for international students' adaptation and culture shock. SIT explains how people who move to new places relate with their host cultures, putting into consideration their own self-esteem, favor of own group members (ingroup), and the degrading that they undergo as nongroup members of the outgroups. Belonging to a social group comes with both pros and cons. A group member in an intergroup may be denied a service by members of different groups from theirs. A member of an ingroup also stands a chance of being a beneficiary of services offered only to members of their ingroup.

According to Zhou et al. (2008), SIT enables prediction of behaviors of individuals depending on how they relate with groups. BAISs, for instance, may perceive that people who do not belong to any of the BAIS racial or ethnic ingroups will be racially prejudicial toward BAISs as this is what international media propagates about the United States globally. This psychological grouping makes it possible to predict BAISs' interaction with African Americans, Caucasians, and members of other races. Disappointment may arise when the treatment BAISs receive from African Americans is the opposite of their expectations because of the perception that they belonged to the same ingroup as Africa Americans: the Black race ingroup. The expectation of favoritism within their ingroups could cause BAISs to perceive predominantly White institutions (PWIs) as institutions where they would receive poor treatment because they did not belong to the White majority ingroup, and historically Black colleges and universities (HBCUs) as institutions where BAISs expect better treatment because they blend in with the majority who are Black.

LITERATURE REVIEW

Number of BAISs in the United States

For the past 2 academic years, the number of BAISs in the United States has been on the increase according to the Institute of International Education (2019). In the 2018–2019 academic year, the number of BAISs from sub-Saharan Africa enrolled in U.S. colleges was 40,290, with Nigeria, Ghana, and Kenya ranking first, second, and third, respectively (see Table 1). The sub-Saharan region is mostly inhabited by Black-Africans.

Table 1: Enrollment Trends for Sub-Saharan Africa International Students (Top Five Exporters)

Countries of origin	2017–2018 academic year	2018–2019 academic year	% change
Nigeria	12,693	13,423	5.8
Kenya	3,322	3,451	3.9
Ghana	3,213	3,661	13.9
South Africa	2,040	2,042	0.1
Ethiopia	2,118	2,061	−2.7

Note. Nigeria's numbers are higher than all the other four countries combined. Adopted from the Institute for International Education *Open Doors* (2019) fact sheet.

BAISs' Racial Experiences in U.S. Colleges

BAISs work harder to prove they are intelligent because they are stereotyped as lacking in intelligence and intellectually inferior (Constantine et. al., 2005). Intelligence is often associated with White ingroups, and the Black ingroup members are often considered lacking in intelligence. BAISs at PWIs are not considered intelligent until they prove themselves and have reported being awarded grades they did not deserve and having academic advisors who were reluctant to offer them guidance (Inyama et al., 2016). In her study of 15 graduate students from sub-Saharan Africa, Beoku-Betts (2004) noted that BAISs perceived that their assigned mentors began to take their mentoring of BAISs seriously only when they found out that BAISs were as intelligent as their other students. Additionally, Beoku-Betts discovered BAISs' non-Black peers had the perception that BAISs could not complete their education. These perceptions from mentors and fellow students made BAISs feel isolated in a foreign country.

Constantine et al. (2005) investigated the cultural adjustment experiences of BAISs and indicated that White professors and White teaching assistants used racial slurs like "stupid nigger" to refer to BAISs (Constantine et al., 2005, p. 61). This indicates the conflict between two different racial groups within an intergroup; BAISs being in their ingroup and Whites in BAISs' outgroup. The researchers also reported that BAISs experienced racially prejudicial treatment from African Americans and fellow non-BAISs. Some of their respondents reported that African Americans would not date them because they thought that BAISs were "too Black" (Constantine et al., 2005, p. 61). Most BAISs perceive that African Americans belong to their ingroup (Black people's ingroup) only to find out that the Black race is an entire intergroup with several ethnic and cultural groups within it. In the Black race intergroup, BAISs belong to a different ingroup and African Americans belong to BAISs' outgroup. Additionally, other non-BAISs reported not wanting to relate to BAISs because they were "afraid" of BAISs due to the stereotypes they were exposed to about Africans in their countries (Constantine et al., 2005, p. 61). The situation with the non-BAISs presents the international students' population as an intergroup on its own.

Mitchell et al. (2017) conducted a qualitative study to explore how international students in the United States learned about and were impacted by race and racism. The researchers found that most international students learned about race and racism through the media like international media houses (e.g., George Floyd's killing was broadcasted globally and protests related to his killing were also organized globally) and education (e.g., African American studies, United States history, which includes civil rights movements, etc.). However, BAISs learned about racism through experience too. Mitchell et al. (2017) reported that some BAISs were victims of racial microaggressions by their professors and peers in U.S. higher education institutions. Racial microaggressions are offenses that are racially related, which Black people perceive as being directed to them through communication (Sue et al., 2007).

CONCLUSION

Society is a conglomeration. This means that higher education institutions are also conglomerations because they are formed by different groups coming together. These different groups are based on race, skin color, ethnicity, socioeconomic status, religion, gender, sexual orientations, etc. BAISs are part of the Black race, dark skinned, and African groups. Higher education practitioners should understand group dynamics through the lens of SIT in order to comprehend the experiences of BAISs and help improve BAISs' adjustment experience in the midst of a society riddled with racism.

Recommendations

More research focusing on the racial experiences of BAISs, especially with regard to their relationships with outgroups, is needed to aid future prospective BAISs in making informed decisions regarding studying in the United States. Findings from such studies can also create awareness among members of BAIS outgroups, especially those who are American citizens, to help them create a more conducive environment for BAISs' adjustment.

REFERENCES

Beoku-Betts, J. A. (2004). African women pursuing graduate studies in the sciences. Racism, gender bias, and third world marginality. *National Women's Studies Association Journal, 16*(1), 116–135.

Constantine, M. G., Anderson, G. M., Berkel, L. A., Caldwell, L. D., & Utsey, S. O. (2005). Examining the cultural adjustment experiences of African international college students: A qualitative analysis. *Journal of Counseling Psychology, 52*(1), 57–66.

Institute of International Education. (2019). *Open Doors 2019 fast facts.* Retrieved April 22, 2021, from https://opendoorsdata.org/wp-content/uploads/2020/11/Open-Doors-Fast-Facts-2010-2019.pdf

Inyama, D., Williams, A., & McCauley, K. (2016). Experiences of African students in predominantly White institutions: A literature overview. *Nursing Research and Practice, 2016,* Article 5703015. http://doi.org/10.1155/2016/5703015

Mitchell, D., Jr., Steele, T., Marie, J., & Timm, K. (2017). Learning race and racism while learning: Experiences of international students pursuing higher education in the midwestern United States. *American Educational Research Association Open, 3*(3), 1–15. https://doi.org/10.1177/2332858417720402

Romo, V. (2020, June 1). County officials rule George Flyod death was a homicide. NPR. https://www.npr.org/2020/06/01/867219130/george-floyd-independent-autopsy-homicide-by-asphyxia

Sue, D. W., Capodilupo, C. M., Torino, G. C., Bucceri, J. M., Holder, A. M. B., Nadal, K. L., & Esquilin, M. (2007). Racial microaggressions in everyday life: Implications for clinical practice. *American Psychologist, 62,* 271–286. http://dx.doi.org/10.1037/0003-066X.62.4.271

Tajfel, H. (1970). Experiments in intergroup discrimination. *Scientific American, 223*, 96–102.

Zhou, Y., Jinda-Snape, D., Topping, K., & Todman, J. (2008). Theoretical models of culture shock and adaptation in international students in higher education. *Studies in Higher Education, 33*(1), 63–75. https://doi.org/10.1080/03075070701794833

DIANA AWUOR, MA, is a doctoral candidate in the Department of Educational Leadership at Sam Houston State University. Her major research interests lie in the areas of international education, Black-African international students, diversity, multilingualism in education and multiculturalism.
Email: awuordiana2020@gmail.com

Research-in-Brief

© *Journal of International Students*
Volume 11, Issue 2 (2021), pp. 519-526
ISSN: 2162-3104 (Print), 2166-3750 (Online)
doi: 10.32674/jis.v11i2.2594
ojed.org/jis

The Internationalization of U.S. High Schools: Avenues for Future Research

Tara P. Nicola
Harvard Graduate School of Education, USA

ABSTRACT

Although the internationalization of the U.S. education sector is perhaps the most salient at the postsecondary level, U.S. secondary schools have increasingly experienced the effects of globalization. In recent years, these schools have witnessed a surge in their population of international students. However, there is relatively little scholarship focused on this student population. This Research in Brief article first highlights recent research on nonimmigrant, international high school students in the United States. Using Bronfenbrenner's (1977) ecological systems theory as a framework, the article then identifies areas where future research is needed to more fully explicate the unique experiences of these students and their effects on the U.S. secondary education sector.

Keywords: ecological system theory, high schools, international students, student experience

---

Historically, the effects of internationalization in the U.S. education sector have been most salient at the postsecondary level. Over the past decade, the population of international students, defined as those who are not U.S. citizens or permanent residents and who have entered the country on a nonimmigrant visa, has increased by 60% at U.S. colleges and universities, although the rate of growth has recently slowed (Institute of International Education [IIE], 2019). Yet, internationalization is not just limited to the postsecondary sector.

Albeit smaller, the population of foreign students on nonimmigrant visas enrolling in U.S. high schools has grown as more individuals consider pursuing educational opportunities outside of their home countries. Largely, families enroll their children in U.S. high schools in order to increase their chances of acceptance to top American colleges (Farrugia, 2017). In many ways, these international high school students experience the same challenges as their college-age counterparts. Homesickness and social isolation, struggles with English language proficiency, and difficulty adapting to American culture and its idiosyncrasies are just a few of the potential issues these students face. The population of international secondary school students, however, is distinct, as these pupils arrive in the United States during a stage of formative development—early adolescence.

Despite the recent surge in the number of international students attending U.S. high schools, little scholarship has focused on this student population. In this article, I first discuss recent studies that have focused on international high school students and highlight potential reasons why a relative paucity of research on this student population exists. Then, using Bronfenbrenner's (1977) ecological systems theory as a framework, I identify areas where future research can more fully explicate the unique experiences of these students.

LITERATURE REVIEW

International Students in U.S. High Schools

Although the United States hosts more foreign secondary school students than any other anglophone country, international students are an overlooked demographic within American high schools. Visa data from the U.S. Department of Homeland Security's Student and Exchange Visitor Information System indicated there were 22,589 exchange students and 59,392 diploma-seeking students attending U.S. high schools during the fall of 2016 (Farrugia, 2017).

This segment of the student population has experienced unprecedented growth, particularly with regard to the number of students pursuing full diploma studies on F-1 visas. Whereas participation in short-term exchange programs on J-1 visas grew only 5% between 2004 and 2016, the enrollment of overseas pupils in diploma programs increased by almost 300% during the same time period (Farrugia 2014, 2017).

Until recently, little was known about the composition of this particular high school population. Farrugia (2014) undertook the first detailed quantitative analysis of international student enrollment trends at the secondary level. Drawing upon Student and Exchange Visitor Information System and National Center for Education Statistics data, she found that China, South Korea, Germany, Mexico, and Brazil were the top five countries of origin for international high school students, with Chinese and Korean students alone representing 42% of all foreign pupils on J-1 and F-1 visas. Whereas Asian students overwhelmingly enrolled in diploma programs as a means of improving their chance of admission to U.S. colleges, European and Latin American students were more likely to participate in short-term exchanges that emphasized English language instruction and the development of cross-cultural relationships (Farrugia, 2014).

As Farrugia (2017) highlighted in a follow-up report, international high school students are now found in all 50 states plus the District of Columbia, although J-1 and F-1 enrollment patterns vary across the country. For example, the majority of F-1 students tend to study in California and Northeast states such as New York and Massachusetts; by contrast, exchange students typically attend schools in Michigan, Wisconsin, or Texas.

The Student Experience

Despite the growing presence of international pupils in high schools across the country, only a handful of published studies have investigated this population. For instance, Fontana (2015) and Shea (2019) undertook qualitative studies examining the experiences of Chinese students enrolled at American high schools. The findings from the two studies are largely in concordance, finding that pupils encountered a number of challenges including homesickness and low self-esteem, difficulty navigating classroom and social interactions, and institutional barriers stemming from homestay agencies that inhibited their smooth transition to the United States.

Other work has examined the sociocultural adjustment of international students. For example, in her study of 12 Chinese international high school students, Chan (2019) underscored how they perceive building friendships with American students as an important acculturative experience but that acculturative stressors like communicating in English as well as discrimination from American peers can leave international students feeling isolated.

Recently, research has examined other facets of the international high school student experience. For example, Cheng and Yang (2019) explored how studying in U.S. high schools facilitated development of global consciousness and competencies among Chinese pupils, while Yin (2013) examined the spiritual, as well as social and academic, development of youth attending an evangelical Christian school.

It is important to note that all of these studies have focused on Asian students holding F-1 visas. There is a significant gap in the literature related to understanding the experiences and outcomes of cultural exchange students on J-1 visas as well as foreign pupils from other regions including Europe, Africa, and South America.

Drivers of the Research Gap

Why is there such a paucity of research on international high school students, especially compared to the vast literature on their college-aged counterparts? The drastically different size of these populations is undoubtedly to blame, as the number of international secondary students pales in comparison to the 1.1 million international college students (Institute of International Education, 2019).

However, there are likely other drivers—including that these students enroll predominantly at small, private high schools. In fact, of the over 59,000 F-1 visa holders in 2016, 94% attended a private institution, the majority of which were small, rural, and religiously affiliated (Farrugia, 2017). This phenomenon stems from U.S. immigration policy, which limits international students' attendance at public high schools to only 1 year (Farrugia, 2017). The reality is that improving outcomes of students at private institutions, especially at small religious schools, is not a pressing priority among key education stakeholders. Due to the many issues plaguing the public education sector, federal and state governments as well as major funding bodies have historically poured—and continue to direct—money into improving public schools (Gross, 2018; Reckhow & Snyder, 2014).

Furthermore, not only is the population of international students at public schools too small to gain widespread recognition, but also these students tend to enroll in cash-strapped and geographically isolated school districts that may lack the resources to adequately support their own domestic students (e.g., Casto et al., 2012). Consequently, it makes sense that directing resources and research dollars toward supporting American students would be the priority.

By contrast, research on international college students is prized in part because they are major consumers of both private and public higher education. Their tuition dollars make up for steep tuition discount rates, changes in the demographics of the domestic high school population, and cuts in state and federal funding (Hegarty, 2014). American higher education needs international students to support its bottom line, but the same cannot be said of the K-12 public education system. This reliance on international students, coupled with the fact that international students are a highly accessible population to study on college campuses, likely contributes to the research gap.

In sum, the limited scope of research on international high school students likely stems from the combined effects of these structural factors—not because the topic is unworthy of rigorous study.

Avenues for Future Research

I offer Bronfenbrenner's (1977) ecological systems theory as one organizing framework for researchers interested in studying this population. This theory suggests many areas for future research, capturing the numerous interrelated systems that influence international students' experiences and outcomes.

THEORETICAL FRAMEWORK

Ecological systems theory posits that only through fully understanding the contextual factors that shape an individual's thoughts, values, and decision-making behaviors can their experiences be fully understood. It situates individuals within five nested environmental systems (see Figure 1). The first is the microsystem, which encompasses actors that most immediately impact an individual's development. Next is the mesosystem, which represents interactions among the various actors within the microsystem. The third system, the exosystem, includes environments that are external to an individual but nevertheless influential. Finally, the macrosystem encapsulates the cultural and societal norms within which an individual lives, while the chronosystem refers to the influence of time on the nested subsystems and the actors within them.

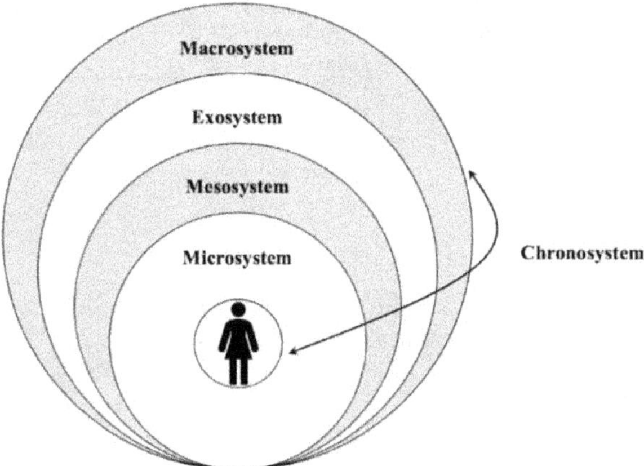

Figure 1: Bronfenbrenner's (1977) Ecological Systems Theory

With regard to the international high school student population, much of the research has been concentrated in the microsystem and mesosystem, with studies focused on foreign pupils and the actors—friends, family members, classmates, schools, and local communities—that shape their lived experiences. While these two subsystems are a critical lens for understanding the international high school student experience, they offer an incomplete picture. Studies that examine international students through the three other nested systems—the exosystem, macrosystem, and chronosystem—are just as important and yet are largely missing from the literature. In the following sections, I briefly highlight examples of future research on international secondary students that could fall within these three subsystems.

Exosystem

As an actor within a student's exosystem, the U.S. government indirectly affects international high school pupils through the policies it enacts as well as its communications. Given the nationalist rhetoric of the Trump administration, understanding how these policies and messages have impacted international students' conceptions of the United States and their likelihood of enrolling in American high schools is important. Because many small, religious schools are dependent on these students and the revenue they provide, major changes in how international families perceive the value of American education would have significant effects on the private education sector.

Macrosystem

Most extant studies on foreign high school students document how they navigate American culture and customs. Less well known, however, is how

American social mores shape the racial and ethnic identity development of these students. Given cultural differences in how race and ethnicity are conceptualized, studying how American notions of race inform students' own beliefs and understandings would be a major contribution to the literature and could join in conversation with the countless papers examining this issue among international college students.

Chronosystem

Research on international high school students has been cross-sectional, following students for a limited duration of time. Missing from the literature are robust longitudinal studies—both qualitative and quantitative—that track students throughout their journey in the American secondary education system and beyond. This time element is important because students' experiences and beliefs are likely to change as they become older as well as further habituated to American culture. Capturing these transformations would contribute immensely to our understanding of international student development.

DISCUSSION AND CONCLUSION

While the number of international secondary students in the United States has increased dramatically over the past decade, the number of studies investigating this unique student population has not. Although this student population often falls outside mainstream K–12 education research agendas, it is nevertheless important to study. Using Bronfenbrenner's (1977) ecological systems theory as a lens, this Research in Brief article highlights potential areas for research that can paint a more vivid portrait of the international high school student experience. It argues that more research is needed that extends beyond just a student's microsystem and mesosystem and that centers on less prevalent international student populations. Such research is needed to strengthen best practices that promote international high school students' success and ensure education stakeholders have the resources they need to serve these students effectively.

Acknowledgement

I would like to thank the National Association for College Admission Counseling (NACAC) for their support of the initial study which inspired this article. While portions of this article were highlighted in a policy report overseen and funded by NACAC while I was an employee of the organization, the opinions expressed here are my own and do not represent the views of NACAC.

REFERENCES

Bronfenbrenner, U. (1977). Toward an experimental ecology of human development. *American Psychologist, 32*(7), 513–531. https://doi.org/10.1037/0003-066X.32.7.513

Casto, H., Steinhauer, A., & Pollock, P. (2012). Potential synergy: Rural school districts and international student programs. *The Rural Educator, 34*(1), 12.

Chan, K. T. (2019). *Fostering friendships between Chinese international and American high school students* [Doctoral dissertation, University of Wisconsin-Milwaukee]. UWM Digital Commons. https://dc.uwm.edu/etd/2164

Cheng, B., & Yang, P. (2019). Chinese students studying in American high schools: International sojourning as a pathway to global citizenship. *Cambridge Journal of Education, 49*(5), 553–573. https://doi.org/10.1080/0305764X.2019.1571560

Farrugia, C. (2014). *Charting new pathways to higher education: International secondary students in the United States*. Institute of International Education. https://www.iie.org/Research-and-Insights/Publications/Charting-New-Pathways-To-Higher-Education-International-Secondary-Students-In-The-United-States

Farrugia, C. (2017). *Globally mobile youth: Trends in international secondary students in the United States, 2013–2016*. Institute of International Education. https://www.iie.org/Research-and-Insights/Publications/Globally-Mobile-Youth-2013-2016

Fontana, R. A. (2015). *Daughter's sighs: The social barriers female Chinese international students encounter when transitioning to private high school in the United States* (Publication No. 3701407) [Doctoral dissertation, California Lutheran University]. ProQuest Dissertations and Theses Global.

Gross, R. N. (2018). *Public vs. private: The early history of school choice in America*. Oxford University Press.

Hegarty, N. (2014). Where we are now—The presence and importance of international students to universities in the United States. *Journal of International Students, 4*(3), 223–235.

Institute of International Education. (2019). *Open doors: Report on international educational exchange.*

Reckhow, S., & Snyder, J. W. (2014). The expanding role of philanthropy in education politics. *Educational Researcher, 43*(4), 186–195. https://doi.org/10.3102/0013189x14536607

Shea, P. (2019). *Home away from home: Chinese, female, international students attending a high school in the United States* [Doctoral dissertation, University of Massachusetts-Amherst]. Scholarworks@UMassAmherst. https://scholarworks.umass.edu/dissertations_2/1582

Yin, L. (2013). Coming to America for spiritual or academic growth? Experiences of international students at one Christian school. *Journal of Research on Christian Education, 22*(2), 139–152. https://doi.org/10.1080/10656219.2013.808975

TARA P. NICOLA is a PhD candidate at the Harvard Graduate School of Education. Her research focuses on issues of access, choice, and equity in higher education, especially in relation to the college admission process. Email: tara_nicola@g.harvard.edu

Study Abroad Reflections

© *Journal of International Students*
Volume 11, Issue 2 (2021), pp. 527-535
ISSN: 2162-3104 (Print), 2166-3750 (Online)
doi: 10.32674/jis.v11i2.2115
ojed.org/jis

To Return or Not to Return: A Dilemma of Two Overseas Vietnamese Students in the Netherlands Amidst the Coronavirus Outbreak

Thai Quoc Cao
Center for Education Research and Development Edlab Asia, Vietnam
Radboud University, the Netherlands

Quynh Kim Chieu
Radboud University, the Netherlands

ABSTRACT

Amidst the worldwide outbreak of the coronavirus, many overseas Vietnamese students have decided to return to Vietnam to seek protection from illness. However, the decision to return in such a risky context requires intensive thinking about the outcomes of each possible choice. The aim of this reflection paper is to explore the personal considerations and dilemmas during the decision-making process of two Vietnamese students in the Netherlands using the expected utility framework. The experience of applying a systematic approach to assess risky situations not only informs decisions more comprehensively but also provides an opportunity to look deeply at one's values and interests.

Keywords: academic mobility, coronavirus, expected utility theory, the Netherlands, risky decision-making, Vietnam

In a developing country like Vietnam, studying abroad can be seen as a prestigious opportunity for many. After several years of preparation, thanks to our incredible luck, we were given this special privilege to receive a quality education in the Netherlands. Studying at Radboud University, Nijmegen has been a life-changing opportunity for us as we have had the chance to deeply immerse ourselves in the majors that we are passionate about. However, with the global upsurge of the

COVID-19 pandemic, a new type of coronavirus first reported in Hubei, China (World Health Organization [WHO], 2020d), the dream of studying abroad quickly turned into a distressing dilemma for many international students, including us.

Maneuvering Between Two Borders: The Coronavirus Outbreak in the Netherlands and Vietnam

Besides the differences between the perception of risks, diseases, and uncertainties between the Vietnamese and Dutch cultures, the discrepancy between the approaches that the two governments took in initially responding to the virus is clear. In late January 2020, the transmission of COVID-19 went beyond Chinese borders and reached the European region (Spiteri et al., 2020). Following that, on February 27, 2020, the first case of COVID-19 in the Netherlands was confirmed (RIVM, 2020). On March 16, in the first address to the nation in 46 years, the Dutch Prime Minister Mark Rutte, given the 1,413 positive cases in the Netherlands, announced that the maximum control strategy would be adopted and aimed at protecting vulnerable people as well as developing group immunity (Rutte, 2020). By March 22, 3,631 patients tested positive—an increase of 2,218 cases in 6 days (RIVM, 2020).

Meanwhile, having an adjacent border to China, Vietnam reported its first confirmed case on January 23, 2020 (Coleman, 2020). In order to contain the spread of the virus, the Vietnamese government immediately took serious precautions such as closing down the schooling system, locking down the borders, and tracking and quarantining thousands of people in contact with the confirmed patients. These actions succeeded in limiting the number of positive cases for a time (WHO, 2020b). Up until March 21, there were only a total of 91 confirmed cases in Vietnam (WHO, 2020c). To control the number of imported cases, the Vietnamese government took one step further and established a 14-day concentration quarantine program for anyone coming back from foreign countries (Phung, 2020). Given the outbreak in Europe and the drastic measures by the Vietnamese government, many overseas Vietnamese students and workers decided to return to Vietnam with the hope of guarding themselves against the virus. However, some of them also inadvertently became the carrier of the disease.

A Model for Risky Decision-making: Theoretical Reflection During Crisis

The trade-off between the consideration to return to Vietnam or to stay in the Netherlands emerged with a distinctive sense of urgency and risk for many Vietnamese abroad. As students who firmly believe in science, we decided to take a look into the literature of decision-making with the hope to consciously reach a more informed judgment. As proposed by prospect theory (Tversky & Kahneman, 1992), a prominent approach in describing people's preferences in risky situations, humans are generally risk-averse and more sensitive to loss than gain. Furthermore, Vietnamese are generally even more risk-averse when compared with the Dutch (Hofstede Insight, 2020). Indeed, we realized that our internal sensitivity to risk could cause us to make irrational decisions in the context of the pandemic. In order to overcome our subjective biases, we found the expected utility theory highly efficient in providing prescriptive rational decisions (for further details, see von Neumann et al., 1944). With personal decision-making, the model takes into account the beliefs about the probabilities of the outcomes that each possible decision might have and the personal utility assigned for each outcome. Figure 1 shows the expected utility model for a decision involving two choices, each with two outcomes.

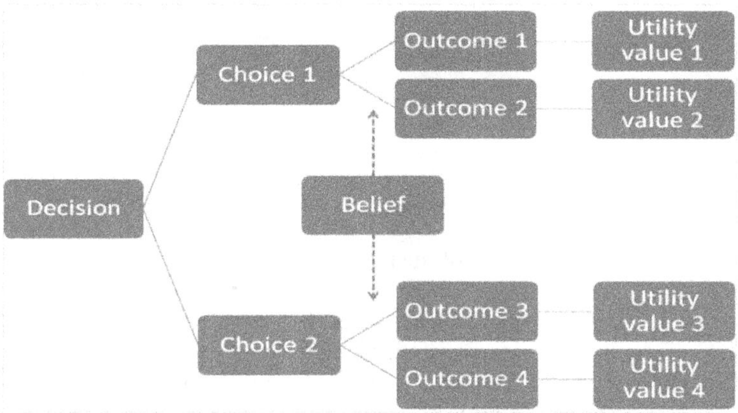

Figure 1: An Expected Utility Value Decision Tree

Beliefs about the chance of the outcomes are the foundation of the decision tree. The probability of each outcome is the weighting coefficient of the corresponding utility value. In this situation, the two possible outcomes for each of our choices were whether we would contract the disease or not. In order to form our own belief, we had to make an educated guess based on statistics of the number of patients and the rate of infection that we were aware of thus far. According to the Dutch Health Institute, around 60% of the country's residents must get COVID-19 for herd immunity (Pieters, 2020). Meanwhile, the risk of traveling back to Vietnam's airport and being quarantined for 14 days also heightened our risk of getting the disease despite the solutions that the government had taken. Admitting to our bounded rationality, we progressed by subjectively assigning the probability of getting the disease as 10% for returning to Vietnam and 30% for remaining in the Netherlands. Figure 2 shows a model of the choices with four outcomes and their respective probabilities.

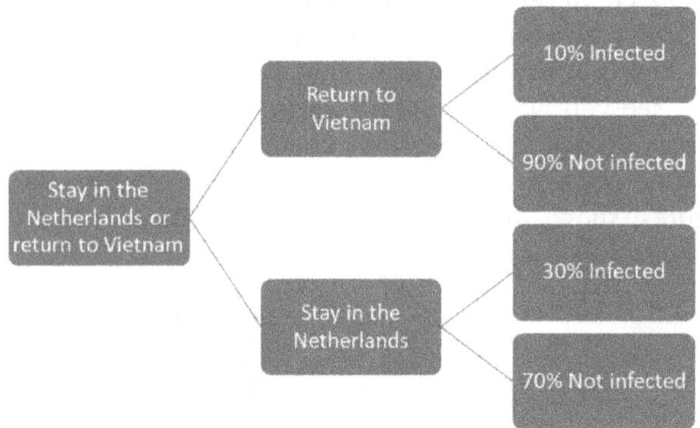

Figure 2: The Decision Tree Modeling Our Choices

The second component of the model is the expected utility that each outcome might have. Reflection was required in this step as we had to think deeply about what was really important to us and our decision. In order to validate the utility rating of each outcome, we defined four major personal values that greatly influenced our choice, including personal health, family, academic progress, and social responsibility. Table 1 provides a list of questions related to the four values that we asked ourselves. Each question was answered based on the parallel assessment between staying in the Netherlands or returning to Vietnam. By considering the questions with each outcome (i.e., getting infected or not) of the two choices, we asked ourselves each question four times. Subsequently, the total utility score for each outcome was calculated and multiplied with the respective probability coefficient. Thus, a total of 28 comparisons were completed in order to assess the utility of each outcome effectively. In the following sections, we will reflect on some of the dilemmas and considerations that we faced during the decision-making process. After providing our perspectives, we will present our models with utility values filled in to suggest how it could be used to inform decision-making.

Contemplation Amidst Chaos: Reflections on Personal Values

Personal Health

Amidst the coronavirus outbreak, we had to remain realistic since contracting the virus could considerably impact our physical and mental health. Even though the number of cases was increasing exponentially in the Netherlands, social distancing and frequent handwashing lessened the chance of infection (WHO, 2020a). On the other hand, the decision to return meant risking our physical health through exposure to public spaces such as airplanes or airports whose confined nature can provide an ideal environment for the virus to spread

Table 1: The Personal Value Questions and Ratings of Expected Utility for Each Decision

Outcomes	Personal Health		Family		Academic Progress	Social Responsibility		Total Utility Score	Expected Utility (EU)	Total EU of each decision
	How much impact does my decision have on my mental health?	How much impact does my decision have on my physical health?	How much impact does my decision have on my family's mental health?	How much impact does my decision have on my family's physical health?	How much impact does my decision have on my academic progress?	How much impact does my action have on Vietnamese society?	How much impact does my action have on Dutch society?			
Return to VN and get infected (10%)	3	2	2	1	1	1	2	12	12*0.10	23.7
Return to VN and not get infected (90%)	6	5	3	4	2	1	4	25	25*0.90	
Stay in the Netherlands and get infected (30%)	1	2	2	4	2	5	4	20	20*0.30	23.5
Stay in the Netherlands and not get infected (70%)	3	4	3	4	4	5	5	28	25*0.70	

Each question will be rated on a 7-point Likert scale, where 1 = Having a strong negative impact, 2= Having a moderate negative impact, 3 = Having a small negative impact, 4 = Having neutral impact, 5 = Having small positive impact, 6 = Having moderate positive impact and 7 = Having a strong positive impact. The total EU of the decision to return to Vietnam can be calculated as (Probability of getting infected) * (Total Utility infected) + (Probability of not getting infected) * (Total Utility not infected). The choice with higher utility will be the more rational choice.

The governmental plans of the two countries also played an important role in our consideration. While the Dutch government was reserving professional health care only for severe cases in the early stages of the pandemic, the Vietnamese government took a more circumspect approach, providing free testing and treatments for any suspected cases. Though the coronavirus had not shown any long-term effects or high mortality rate for young people like us when we were considering our decision, staying in the Netherlands constantly filled our anxious minds with the fear of uncertainty and longing for additional protective measures. In general, a long journey home would mean a short period of intense pressure of protecting ourselves from infection on the planes, yet receiving assurance afterwards. Meanwhile, the decision to stay would mean that the feeling of risks is spread out over a longer period of time.

Family

To us, the consideration for our family was another significant factor. Vietnamese people treat family values with great appreciation. The sense of intimacy in our families is expressed, not through words of love and kindness, but through actions. Home is where everyone is concerned closely with each other's problems. Our parents, like many others who have children abroad, were anxious to see us coming back to Vietnam, slightly due to the fear of the outbreak, yet mainly because of their feeling of helplessness. Our presence in Vietnam could offer them mental wellness since they could at least feel assured that they could physically be by our side. As the number of Vietnamese students who sought to return home began to accelerate dramatically, a sense of urgency grew within the people staying abroad as we witnessed our parents' apprehension intensifying with each and every passing day. Since both of our parents are approaching retirement age, to make them watch their child fighting the crisis alone would further put a lot of strain on their mental health. Ironically, just like our parents, taking action, making the dangerous trip home, was the only way for us to express our love to them and relieve their sorrow. Nonetheless, coming back would not do them much good, either. Upon our arrival, it would be inevitable that our family would visit us, either at the airport or the quarantine camp. This would put them in environments with a high infection rate, which might adversely affect their own health. In other words, the consideration for the physical and mental health of our family further complicated the decision of whether we should stay or leave.

Academic Progress

We also had to consider the influence of the outbreak on academic progress, as our sole intention in the Netherlands is to receive an education. Although the Netherlands had shut down most applied science and research universities, Radboud University began implementing various approaches to ensure the continuation of education via online learning and examination. Meanwhile, going back to Vietnam required a tremendous effort to adjust to the entirely new life at the quarantine camp as well as the weather of the tropical climate. Jet lag would inevitably leave us in a fatigued state, and as a result, we would have little energy to be productive. As examinations were still taking place, such obstacles would do great harm to our results. The 6-hour difference in the two countries' time zones would require us to wake up in the middle of the night in Vietnam to attend an online lecture or examination. In short, despite the fact that online learning allowed education to continue from afar, the adaptation process still posed plenty of formidable obstacles to our academic progress.

Social Responsibility

Having a Vietnamese nationality and a deep admiration for the Netherlands and how the Dutch were pressing ahead during this challenging time, we were aware that our decision could have effects on both countries. For the time being, the Vietnamese healthcare system was seriously strained as thousands of Vietnamese returnees underwent the 14-day quarantine period. Free testing and quarantine measures on a national scale was quickly exhausting facilities and resources on a daily basis. As the shortage of medical personnel became more and more problematic, Ho Chi Minh City, the economic capital of Vietnam, was considering the plan to employ retired doctors and medical students for additional aid (Dong, 2020). Therefore, our decision to return would add more pressure to the already fragile economy and healthcare system in Vietnam when aid was needed for people with more critical conditions. Given the lower chance of mortality for young people, the fear of becoming a "super-spreader" (Boseley & Belam, 2020), transmitting the coronavirus to many others, was more relevant to us. The decision to return required unwanted exposure and interactions in the public transport systems, which went against the social distancing precautions in both Vietnam and the Netherlands. If we stayed in the Netherlands, we could fully comply with both of the government's advice and protect other citizens as well as ourselves. In such an unprecedented crisis, a citizen should closely consider the safety of society alongside their own personal values.

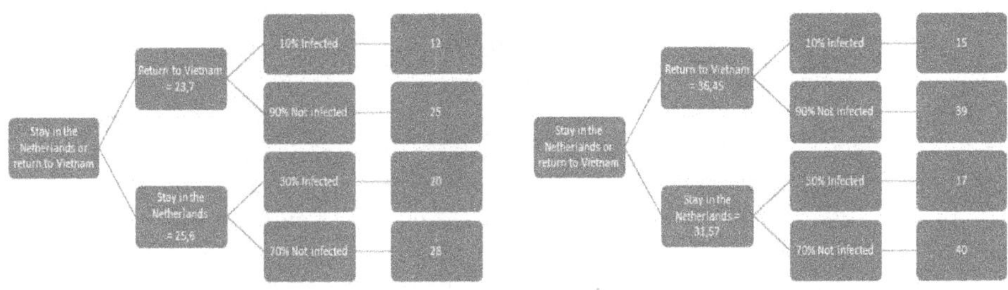

Figure 3: Our Decision Trees with Expected Utility

DISCUSSION AND CONCLUSION

In this paper, we illustrate the use of the model of expected utility to systematically convey our considerations on whether to return or not to return amidst the COVID-19 outbreak. As can be seen in Figure 3, which shows our decision trees, the model suggests that one of us should return to Vietnam. Since we were the only two remaining Vietnamese within our community, our decision has been strongly influenced by one another, which conclusively led one author to adjust their decision and stay. Indeed, in order to enact a risky decision, one must have more than just rationality and information (Soler et al., 2010). A sense of companionship has been also crucial for us to overcome the unexpected nature of this harsh time. Nevertheless, the expected utility model was still of great use by informing our decision-making in a systematic manner. However, this model also has two disadvantages. First, the model is fixed on the current inputs that we have. Therefore, updating our beliefs and values constantly is needed for future decision-making. For example, on March 20, 2020, President Mark Rutte renounced group immunity and decided to take on a more rigorous approach for the entire nation (DutchNews, 2020), which may have influenced many international students' decision to return or not. Secondly, as unpredictable as life and our own intuition are, this model is limited to our own bounded rationality and, therefore, is subjective. However, it has allowed us a chance to think deeply about our own values and intuition, which has provided a sense of rationality and agency in this current time. Furthermore, it is important that before everyone else, scientists should look into themselves to discover their biases and beliefs, and to counter them with a fierce attitude. Like a proverb that many Vietnamese mothers often say: "The battle between one and themselves is always the hardest."

REFERENCES

Boseley, S., & Belam, M. (2020). *Super-spreaders: What are they and how are they transmitting coronavirus?* The Guardian. https://www.theguardian.com/world/2020/feb/27/what-are-super-spreaders-and-how-are-they-transmitting-coronavirus

Coleman, J. (2020). *Vietnam reports first coronavirus cases.* Retrieved from https://web.archive.org/web/20200218074232/https:/thehill.com/policy/healthcare/public-global-health/479542-vietnam-reports-first-coronavirus-cases

Dong, S. (2020). *Ho Chi Minh City included a plan to mobilize retired doctors and medical students to join in against Covid-19.* Retrieved from https://thanhnien.vn/thoi-su/tphcm-tinh-ca-phuong-an-huy-dong-bac-si-ve-huu-sinh-vien-y-tham-gia-chong-covid-19-1198498.html

DutchNews. (2020). *MPs back ministers on coronavirus; herd immunity is not the aim, says Rutte.* https://www.dutchnews.nl/news/2020/03/mps-back-ministers-on-coronavirus-herd-immunity-is-not-the-aim-says-rutte/

Hofstede Insight. (2020). *Country comparison tool.* Retrieved March 21, 2020, from https://www.hofstede-insights.com/

Phung, T. (2020). *From 0h on 21-3, people who enter Vietnam must be isolated.* https://tuoitre.vn/tu-0h-ngay-21-3-nguoi-nhap-canh-vao-viet-nam-deu-phai-cach-ly-20200320171258515.htm

Pieters, J. (2020). *Around 60% of NL residents must get COVID-19 for herd immunity: Health Institute.* https://nltimes.nl/2020/03/17/around-60-nl-residents-must-get-covid-19-herd-immunity-health-institute

RIVM. (2020). *Patient with new coronavirus in the Netherlands.* https://www.rivm.nl/nieuws/patient-met-nieuw-coronavirus-in-nederland

Rutte, M. (2020). *Television address by Prime Minister Mark Rutte of the Netherlands.* Retrieved from https://www.government.nl/documents/speeches/2020/03/16/television-address-by-prime-minister-mark-rutte-of-the-netherlands

Soler, R. E., Leeks, K. D., Buchanan, L. R., Brownson, R. C., Heath, G. W., & Hopkins, D. H. (2010). Point-of-decision prompts to increase stair use. *American Journal of Preventive Medicine, 38*(2), S292–S300. https://doi.org/10.1016/j.amepre.2009.10.028

Spiteri, G., Fielding, J., Diercke, M., Campese, C., Enouf, V., Gaymard, A., Bella, A., Sognamiglio, P., Sierra Moros, M. J., Riutort, A. N., Demina, Y. V., Mahieu, R., Broas, M., Bengnér, M., Buda, S., Schilling, J., Filleul, L., Lepoutre, A., Saura, C., … Ciancio, B. C. (2020). First cases of coronavirus disease 2019 (COVID-19) in the WHO European Region, 24 January to 21

February 2020. Eurosurveillance, 25(9). https://doi.org/10.2807/1560-7917.ES.2020.25.9.2000178

Tversky, A., & Kahneman, D. (1992). Advances in prospect theory: Cumulative representation of uncertainty. *Journal of Risk and Uncertainty*, *5*(4), 297–323. https://doi.org/10.1007/BF00122574

von Neumann, J., Morgenstern, O., & Rubinstein, A. (1944). *Theory of games and economic behavior* (60th anniversary commemorative ed.). Princeton University Press. http://www.jstor.org/stable/j.ctt1r2gkx

World Health Organization. (2020a). *Coronavirus disease (COVID-19) advice for the public.* https://www.who.int/emergencies/diseases/novel-coronavirus-2019/advice-for-public

World Health Organization. (2020b). *Coronavirus disease 2019 (COVID-19): Situation Report – 46.* https://www.who.int/docs/default-source/coronaviruse/situation-reports/20200306-sitrep-46-covid-19.pdf?sfvrsn=96b04adf_4

World Health Organization. (2020c). *Coronavirus disease 2019 (COVID-19): Situation Report – 61.* https://www.who.int/docs/default-source/coronaviruse/situation-reports/20200321-sitrep-61-covid-19.pdf?sfvrsn=6aa18912_2

World Health Organization. (2020d). *Rolling updates on coronavirus disease (COVID-19).* https://www.who.int/emergencies/diseases/novel-coronavirus-2019/events-as-they-happen

THAI CAO, BS, is a master's student in behavioral science at Radbound University, The Netherlands. He also works as an educational investigator at Edlab Asia, Vietnam. His research interests include risky decision-making, education, and research policy. Email: thaicao@edlabasia.org

QUYNH CHIEU is an undergraduate student in the Faculty of Arts at Radboud University. Her major research interests lie in the area of second language acquisition and English linguistics. Email: quynh.chieukimquynh@student.ru.nl

Book Review

© *Journal of International Students*
Volume 11, Issue 2 (2021), pp. 536-539
ISSN: 2162-3104 (Print), 2166-3750 (Online)
doi: 10.32674/jis.v11i2.2333
ojed.org/jis

International Student Transitions: A Framework for Success

Maureen Snow Andrade & K. James Hartshorn, Newcastle, UK: Cambridge Scholars Publishing, 2019. 174pp. Paperback: £58.99. ISBN-13 978-1-5275-3034-8

Reviewed by Muhammad Sharif Uddin, *Morgan State University, USA*

International students from developing countries come to developed countries with a dream to achieve higher education. These students face many challenges (e.g., language barriers, cultural shock) in their transition to the higher educational institutions that may hinder their achievement. Andrade and Hartshorn's latest publication (2019) surrounds the transition that international students encounter when they attend universities in developed countries. The authors describe how some countries including Australia and the United Kingdom host more international students than the United States and provide some guidelines for U.S. higher education institutions to follow as they seek to host more international students.

The introductory chapter describes international student demographics in the United States, United Kingdom, Canada, and Australia. The data show that among these countries, the United States has the lowest percentage (5.2%) of international students (as a proportion of all enrolled students) due to poor policies and strategies in favor of international students, specifically in limited support for students' English language skill development. This chapter presents a framework for international student success that contains five steps: analyze, design, develop, implement, and evaluate. Across all five stages, vital components of the framework include the views and beliefs of administrators, support staff, and faculty who may guide curricular and co-curricular activities of those international students.

The second chapter discusses the views and beliefs of university personnel who work closely with international students at U.S. universities. This includes personnel who work in international student admissions, as there are common misconceptions regarding students' English language proficiency. Administrators and faculty may assume that the Test of English as a Foreign Language (TOEFL) is sufficient to measure students' English language proficiency. However, the authors argue that this test is not the only scale to assess students' language proficiency, though they do not provide any specific alternative suggestions. The authors also argue that by analyzing employee views and beliefs, a set of new and effective practices to guide future actions can be established. Furthermore, the assertion is made that current programs ought to be under ongoing evaluation by universities to determine their effectiveness and student-centeredness.

The third chapter is about the role of academic courses (degree programs) in developing the English language proficiency of international students enrolled at U.S. institutions. The authors mention that Australian higher educational institutions have useful practices and principles in designing and delivering courses improving international students' academic English. The authors then present a curricular model for the U.S. institutions that they argue will be supportive of international students' English language skill development along with their coursework. The model suggests four types of course design: "Adjunct Weak," which refers to stand-alone basic English courses presenting generic academic content; "Adjunct Strong," which refers to the English language support related to discipline-based courses for the specific needs of the students (e.g., presentation, paraphrasing); "Integrated," or English language support alongside specific discipline-based courses in the form of individual tutorials or workshops; and "Embedded," English language development within discipline-based courses based on extended collaboration with an English language expert (i.e., trained professional). However, the authors suggest that the model can be modified based on institutional context and the level of higher education.

"Cocurricular Consideration," the fourth chapter, addresses the advantage of reinforcing co-curricular and extracurricular components along with curricular components for cultural and language acquisition. For instance, there are examples of churches providing support to their student members in understanding local culture as well as language development. The authors argue that although these co-curricular and extracurricular components are less significant for international students than the formal curriculum, they nonetheless strengthen academic success. The authors also state that many international students may have a lack of understanding, experience, or skills to successfully engage in curricular activities based at U.S. higher education institutions due to the lack of cultural knowledge. These students need extra support, and the co-curricular and extracurricular activities help to enrich their knowledge and support curricular activities. These elements also boost their professional capabilities. However, there is not a clear model presented, and this seems to reflect an area for further research.

The title of the fifth chapter is "Evaluation." This chapter points to evaluation of university programs as essential, and shows the difference between assessment and evaluation. Assessment is the systematic process that gathers data to estimate students' knowledge, skills, attitude, and beliefs. The authors argue that assessment of students' learning is needed for their development in the field. On the contrary, evaluation is the process that judges the efficacy of a program, event, or product, necessary for institutions to evaluate their programs, academic curriculum, and extracurricular activities.

"Implementation," the sixth chapter, introduces the theory of constraints that focuses on the restrictions that limit an organization's ability to intervene. The theory consists of five steps: identify (identify obstacles that hinder goal achievement), exploit (implement existing resources immediately), subordinate (review other factors to enable maximum contribution), elevate (consider additional action), and repeat (continue the process). The authors also introduce the well-known Lean Six Sigma framework to improve current services and to offer new programs and services.

The last chapter of this book is "Institutional Change." The authors start this chapter with a rationale as to why organizational change is necessary given "cultural change" associated with international students enrolling at U.S. colleges and universities. However, the authors do not specify current areas of deficit thinking regarding international students' English proficiency. Instead, the authors say that many higher education institutions have been practicing the same policies for decades, which are not suitable for the international students in the present time. The authors then provide eight steps for creating change: increasing urgency, building the guiding team, getting the vision right, communicating for buy-in, enabling action, generating short-term wins, not letting up, and making change stick.

The book is a prescription for higher educational institutions of the United States to attract more international students like other developed countries (e.g., Australia, United Kingdom). The authors have provided guidelines on how to bring change in institutional policies to improve programs and culture impacting international students and facilitating their academic success. I support the authors' suggestions for taking a variety of practical measures to attract more international students. However, as a limitation, the authors do not provide any empirical study results indicating that their theories will increase the number of international students in the United States.

As an international graduate student, my understanding is that international students' academic success has an impact not only on them but also on their communities. Not only do students personally achieve better quality education but also they serve their community with new knowledge and experience. The community, in turn, gets a sophisticated workforce. These students are beneficial for the host countries, too. Referring to the U.S. Department of Commerce, the Institute of International Education (2020) reported that in 2019, international students contributed $44 billion to the U.S. economy. Besides contributing to the U.S. economy, international students enhance campus diversity (Hughes, 2019).

Thus, this book's suggestions for increasing international student numbers in U.S. universities through various initiatives are essential.

REFERENCES

Hughes, J. (2019). *Why international students are so important to their host countries.* Keystone Academic Courses. https://www.academiccourses.com/article/why-international-students-are-so-important-to-their-host-countries/

Institute of International Education. (2020). *United States hosts over 1 million international students for the fifth consecutive year.* https://www.iie.org/en/Why-IIE/Announcements/2020/11/2020-Open-Doors-Report

MUHAMMAD SHARIF UDDIN is a scholar in the Urban Educational Leadership Program at Morgan State University. He also works as a graduate research assistant and as an adjunct faculty in the Department of Teacher Education. He is a Fellow of International Leaders in Education Programs. His research interest is in critical pedagogy, teaching and learning, and curriculum and instruction. Email: muhammad.uddin@morgan.edu

Book Review

© *Journal of International Students*
Volume 11, Issue 2 (2021), pp. 540-542
ISSN: 2162-3104 (Print), 2166-3750 (Online)
doi: 10.32674/jis.v11i2.3638
ojed.org/jis

Multilingualism in the Classroom: Teaching and Learning in a Challenging Context

Margaret Funke Omidire (Ed.), Cape Town, South Africa: UCT Press, 2019. 256pp. Paperback. ISBN-13: 978-1775822691

Reviewed by Terra Gargano, *American University, USA*

Multilingualism in the Classroom: Teaching and Learning in a Challenging Context holistically explores the linguistic landscape in the educational context of South Africa. The authors ask the reader to rethink and reimagine what is possible for South African classrooms across nine provinces. Central to the book is the idea that existing policies and instructional practices do not reflect language realities and stand in stark contrast to research and literature in the field of multilingual education. The edited volume includes original qualitative and quantitative research that furthers an understanding of the importance of language in the co-construction of knowledge.

The book is divided into three sections. Section I focuses on language teaching and learning challenges in multilingual contexts, outlining the historical legacy and policy challenges in South Africa. Section II discusses proactive interventions and support for learning and learner development in multilingual settings, including a myriad of pedagogical approaches and resources to address articulated complexities in multilingual classrooms, mostly at the primary school level. Section III parses legislative and policy frameworks guiding multilingualism in education settings, examining South Africa's language identity in light of a historical context of colonialism and related Othering. Overall, the book both recognizes how language is a site of evolving contestation for many, while at the same time offering ways to advocate for change.

The contributors are professionally affiliated with or were educated at the University of Pretoria in South Africa. All but two of the authors, who hold appointments at Pennsylvania State University, are from African-based educational organizations, the University of Namibia or the University of Zambia, grounding the book in the lived realities of South Africans. The book includes a list of acronyms to help readers not familiar with the educational context on the African continent and a map to navigate the linguistic landscape of Africa.

The book grounds a contextualized analysis through a lens of colonialism and critiques national educational policies that do not acknowledge the lived realities of many students. There are 11 official languages in South Africa, which creates linguistically diverse classrooms. Yet, while English is widely used in education, under 10% of the South African population use English at home. Further compounding the diversity is the grouping of internationally mobile workers and immigrants who speak a language other than the one used for instruction.

Policies shape practice. The research and writing throughout *Multilingualism in the Classroom* delves into issues around the historical confluence of language, colonialism, and power relations to determine how policies shape practice. Situated in debates around the value of multilingualism and monolingual bias in classrooms, the authors advocate for challenging the deficit view of language variance in education and adopting a positive view—that the rich diversity of linguistic identities and language competencies construct an inclusive, creative, and collaborative space that recognizes expanded terrains of possibility through the social co-construction of knowledge, skills, and abilities.

Multilingualism in the Classroom overwhelmingly advocates for using multilingual skills as resources and explores the integration of translanguaging into a pedagogical framework aimed at inclusivity. However, the authors do not obscure the real obstacles that educators may face by affirming linguistic identities and adopting a multilingual perspective. Schools and educators face a variety of challenges, evidenced by the sheer number of languages spoken, literacy rates, the established role of English in South African society, a shortage of multilingual educators, students who are not proficient in either the home language or language of instruction, and limited resources in home languages. Yet, the contributors offer insights into ways of rethinking the role of language in education and in identity development, which in turn can reshape the possibilities and boundaries imposed on educators and students. The authors inherently recognize that students come from varying cultural, socioeconomic, and linguistic backgrounds that color an understanding of the world, and therefore, envision schooling as preparation for democratic citizenship, the development of realistic cultural empathy, and sustained open-mindedness for civic engagement.

Key topics tackled in this book include assessments, differential instruction, teacher education, school culture, parental support, and funding, all of which are related to linguistic diversity. It is important to acknowledge that the authors not only tackle multilingualism in the classroom, but also do so with a holistic approach to language learning, including chapters that address the range of language abilities of students, including students with dyslexia or special needs.

While most authors advocate for not just bilingualism but also multilingualism, the chapters in the text outline the ongoing debate about whether instruction should be in the mother tongue, English, or another language. While some advocate for the use of native languages and the idea that the "curriculum should be used as a storage facility for national heritage" (p. 178), others contend that English, due to its ability to situate students as global citizens and to create opportunities for social mobility, should be the dominant language of instruction throughout the country.

When Dr. Margaret Funke Omidire, the book's editor, was asked to share her vision for the book and why it was important to elaborate in such a multifaceted way on the issues that situate multilingualism in South African education, she responded by stating,

> The complexities of issues surrounding language in education across sub-Saharan Africa continuously generates debates...While not denying that more research is required, I believe stakeholders should approach the use of multilingual strategies with open-mindedness and see the languages as assets/resources that can be used to enhance learning, given that the pupils/students benefit from this many ways.

It is evident from the collection of perspectives throughout the book that the authors recognize the challenges and complexities of multilingual classrooms, but more importantly acknowledge the adoption and adaptation of teaching approaches, technologies, and resources that drive and support the need for crafting inclusive learning spaces where students thrive. There are lessons learned that can be extrapolated from the book to help inform the ways in which educators around the globe rethink what is possible in multilingual classrooms.

TERRA GARGANO, PhD, teaches undergraduate and graduate courses in intercultural communication, international education, and training program design. She spent time teaching English in Japan and was the Assistant Dean of Semester at Sea before serving as a faculty member at the University of Maryland and American University. Most recently she served as the Director of Online Programs in the School of International Service at American University. Her research interests reside at the intersection of culture, identity, and power in transcultural education and virtual spaces, examining the complex relationships between transnational mobility in higher education and the lived realities of academic nomads. Throughout her 20-year career in international higher education, she has managed dozens of institutional collaborations worldwide, conducted workshops for faculty at domestic and international organizations, and learned alongside her students about the ways culture impacts worldviews and resiliency. Email: terragargano@hotmail.com

---

Book Review

© *Journal of International Students*
Volume 11, Issue 2 (2021), pp. 543-546
ISSN: 2162-3104 (Print), 2166-3750 (Online)
doi: 10.32674/jis.v11i2.3740
ojed.org/jis

Higher Education Policy in the Philippines and ASEAN Integration: Demands and Challenges

Kolawole Samuel Adeyemo, Leiden, The Netherlands: Brill Sense, 2019. 142pp. Paperback: $54. ISBN-13 978-90-04-41130-2

Reviewed by Que N. Tran, *Montana State University, USA*

The Association of Southeast Asian Nations (ASEAN) includes 10 member nations (Brunei Darussalam, Cambodia, Indonesia, Laos, Malaysia, Myanmar, Philippines, Singapore, Thailand, and Vietnam) and is an integrated sociocultural, economic, and political community established in 1967. There are more than 6,500 higher education institutions (HEIs) and about 12 million students in ASEAN. One area of the association's vision for 2020 highlights economic development through education. This vision is meant to be operationalized through research cooperation, credit transfers, student mobility, and degree recognition.

Higher Education Policy in the Philippines and ASEAN Integration: Demands and Challenges by Adeyemo applies the lens of globalization to analyze ASEAN higher education integration policy. The publication evaluates the Philippines' higher education policies and policy implementation in the context of political symbolism that shows the distance between policy ideas and practical outcomes. The author provides an insightful and comprehensive understanding of the Philippines' higher education system. He also suggests approaches to improve the country's educational outcomes. Readers may extend their knowledge about educational policy implications and challenges the Philippines faces in balancing the nation's human resources needs and the region's integration policy.

The book consists of eight chapters. Chapter 1, "Philippines Higher Education in the Era of ASEAN Integration" provides a broad view of ASEAN education, evaluating student mobility in the region and education supply and demand in the Philippines. The author argues that the Philippines does not equally benefit from the ASEAN integration of higher education because regional policy formulation and implementation are based on the assumption of similarity and commonness, yet the Philippines has cultural and socioeconomic uniqueness.

Chapters 2 addresses "A Review of the Philippine Quality Assurance System." The author describes various definitions of quality in higher education and indicates the Philippines' issue of overproduction of skills-gap graduates. The Philippines focuses on three perspectives of quality including "fitness for purpose," being "exceptional," and "developing a culture of quality" (p. 31). Although there are quality regulations, quality compliance remains a challenge, especially the quality of teaching and learning as well as research capacity in the majority of the Philippines' HEIs. Only six out of 2,300 HEIs in the Philippines are in the QS Asia University Rankings. Moreover, the majority of private HEI owners have little or no relevant education background or experience in managing HEIs, while private HEIs account for 88% of all institutions. Private HEIs are voluntarily accredited and there is a disagreement of the role of the Philippines Commission on Higher Education (CHED) role in terms of quality assurance among HEIs. The author recommends a standardized framework to systemize the country's quality assurance.

Chapter 3 focuses on "Quality Improvement of Private Higher Education in the Philippines for ASEAN Integration." Along with the privatization of higher education trend globally, the for-profit HEIs have mushroomed in ASEAN. The private institutions have approximately 80% of college and university students in the Philippines, but only a few institutions have been accredited. These institutions have inadequate funding to hire full-time lecturers/professors or afford facilities suitable for learning. The CHED regulates private HEIs satisfying the minimum requirements for program and institution registration only. Adeyemo calls for proper regulatory measures to ensure and sustain high quality and standards of postsecondary education.

Chapter 4 explains "Predictors of the Use of Quality Management System (QMS) Processes for the ASEAN Agenda." ASEAN nation members determine integration strategies on their own, including whether to adopt QMS processes. The author details the QMS processes that the Philippines' higher education sector would need to undertake in order to achieve institutional improvement and align with ASEAN integration goals. The author also presents an empirical study of institutional administrators' readiness to use quality management tools, in which he found that higher education attainment and specialization in management fields among administrators predicted how QMS was implemented at their respective HEIs.

Chapter 5 describes "Total Quality Management (TQM) and the ASEAN Skills Development Agenda." The author introduces the history of TQM and its application in higher education. Adeyemo specifies the role of the CHED and the Technical Education and Skills Development Authority to develop indicators for quality delivery using TQM principles. These indicators aim to address skills development needs and institutional performance in a bid to increase the Philippines' competitive advantage. The author suggests a comparison between applied TQM versus non-TQM applied institutions in the Philippines to gain the benchmark of quality assessment. The author emphasizes the importance of leadership for TQM successful applications.

Chapter 6 concentrates on "Measuring Research Performance of ASEAN Higher Education." The author applies Parasuraman, Berry, and Zeithaml's Service Quality Model (SERVQUAL-1985) to discuss a method for improvement in the research performance of the Philippines' HEIs in contrast to other ASEAN state members. The author identifies research productivity issues in the Philippines as due to both (a) insufficient funding and training to develop and retain academics and researchers, and (b) researchers' low rate of publications in high-impact journals. Adeyemo indicates that SERVQUAL needs to be modified for the context of Philippines and suggests initiatives to enhance HEIs' research performance that meet the ASEAN's goals.

Chapter 7, "Cultural Barriers to ASEAN Integration Policy Implementation," highlights ASEAN policies on student mobility, credit transfer, and degree recognition. The CHED offers grants for institutions to develop the culture of quality in research and international cooperation between the Philippines' HEIs and other institutions in the region. The expected outcomes from these grants are increased international publications and collaboration within ASEAN. In terms of student mobility, strong institutional cultures in areas such as language of instruction affect the implementation of ASEAN policies. As English is not the instructional language in most institutions, international students are driven away. Also, restriction on student visas and credit transfer are major challenges in attracting international students to the Philippines. Only 26 institutions have joined the academic mobility and credit transfer system. The author critiques decentralized ASEAN policies for not guiding the implementation of academic exchange, like the Bologna process in Europe, which in turn affects the quality of ASEAN higher education integration.

Chapter 8, "Implications of ASEAN Integration for the Philippines Higher Education Policies," offers a synthesis of previous chapters. The challenges and demands of the Philippines' higher education sector include increasing domestic access to tertiary institutions, rising competition from other countries to recruit high-grade Filipino students, low international ranking of HEIs, and the need for overall quality improvement. Adeyemo recommends establishing a governmental priority reform of the higher education sector with an eye toward revamping funding and initiatives for HEIs to achieve the national goals, which would result in reaching regional needs.

This book compellingly argues that ASEAN higher education integration contributes to regional socioeconomic development, but that "concentrating on growing ASEAN countries and on smaller academic systems immediately raises the spectra of inequality" (p. 16), particularly for a developing country like the Philippines. Adeyemo provides a critical exploration of ways to improve the quality of the Philippines' higher education and suggestions for institutional improvement. The book may be useful for policy makers, administrators, researchers, and educational faculty to gain an overall understanding of ASEAN higher education integration and the postsecondary education of the Philippines in particular. There are, however, questions that the book does not address. These include: What professional development do faculty need to enhance their competence? Which industries do the Philippines prioritize for the country's economic development and regional competitiveness that require postsecondary education? Does the Philippines have policy or plan for developing English-taught programs at HEIs?

QUE N. TRAN is a doctoral candidate in the adult and higher education program at Montana State University. As an international student who has studied in Europe and USA beyond her home country of Vietnam, together with a school management certificate in the Philippines and more than a decade of higher education professionalism, her research interests are international education, college enrollment, socialization, college major choice, and diversity. Email: quetran@montana.edu

---

www.ingramcontent.com/pod-product-compliance
Lightning Source LLC
Chambersburg PA
CBHW070023100426
42740CB00013B/2582

* 9 7 8 1 7 3 6 4 6 9 9 4 1 *